Germany and the Black Diaspora

Studies in German History

Published in Association with the German Historical Institute, Washington, DC

General Editors:
Simone Lässig, *Director of the German Historical Institute, Washington, DC*
with the assistance of Patricia Sutcliffe, *Editor, German Historical Institute*

Volume 1
Nature in German History
Edited by Christof Mauch

Volume 2
Coping with the Nazi Past: West German Debates on Nazism and Generational Conflict, 1955–1975
Edited by Philipp Gassert and Alan E. Steinweis

Volume 3
Adolf Cluss, Architect: From Germany to America
Edited by Alan Lessoff and Christof Mauch

Volume 4
Two Lives in Uncertain Times: Facing the Challenges of the 20th Century as Scholars and Citizens
Wilma Iggers and Georg Iggers

Volume 5
Driving Germany: The Landscape of the German Autobahn, 1930–1970
Thomas Zeller

Volume 6
The Pleasure of a Surplus Income: Part-Time Work, Gender Politics, and Social Change in West Germany, 1955–1969
Christine von Oertzen

Volume 7
Between Mass Death and Individual Loss: The Place of the Dead in Twentieth-Century Germany
Edited by Paul Betts, Alon Confino, and Dirk Schumann

Volume 8
Nature of the Miracle Years: Conservation in West Germany, 1945–1975
Sandra Chaney

Volume 9
Biography between Structure and Agency: Central European Lives in International History
Edited by Volker R. Berghahn and Simone Lässig

Volume 10
Political Violence in the Weimar Republic, 1918–1933: Fight for the Streets and Fears of Civil War
Dirk Schumann

Volume 11
The East German State and the Catholic Church, 1945–1989
Bernd Schaefer

Volume 12
Raising Citizens in the "Century of the Child": The United States and German Central Europe in Comparative Perspective
Edited by Dirk Schumann

Volume 13
The Plans that Failed: An Economic History of the GDR
André Steiner

Volume 14
Max Lieberman and International Modernism: An Artist's Career from Empire to Third Reich
Edited by Marion Deshmukh, Françoise Forster-Hahn, and Barbara Gaehtgens

Volume 15
Germany and the Black Diaspora: Points of Contact, 1250–1914
Edited by Mischa Honeck, Martin Klimke, and Anne Kuhlmann

Volume 16
Crime and Criminal Justice in Modern Germany
Edited by Richard F. Wetzell

Volume 17
Encounters with Modernity: The Catholic Church in West Germany, 1945–1975
Benjamin Ziemann

Volume 18
The Respectable Career of Fritz K.: The Making and Remaking of a Provincial Nazi Leader
Hartmut Berghoff and Cornelia Rauh

Volume 19
Fellow Tribesman: The Image of Native Americans, National Identity, and Nazi Ideology in Germany
Frank Usbeck

Volume 20
The Second Generation: Émigrés from Nazi Germany as Historians
Edited by Andreas W. Daum, Hartmut Lehmann, and James J. Sheehan

Germany and the Black Diaspora

Points of Contact, 1250–1914

Edited by

Mischa Honeck, Martin Klimke, and Anne Kuhlmann

First published in 2013 by
Berghahn Books
www.berghahnbooks.com

©2013, 2016 Mischa Honeck, Martin Klimke, and Anne Kuhlmann
First paperback edition published in 2016

All rights reserved. Except for the quotation of short passages for the purposes of criticism and review, no part of this book may be reproduced in any form or by any means, electronic or mechanical, including photocopying, recording, or any information storage and retrieval system now known or to be invented, without written permission of the publisher.

Library of Congress Cataloging-in-Publication Data

Germany and the black diaspora : points of contact, 1250-1914 / edited by Mischa Honeck, Martin Klimke, and Anne Kuhlmann.
   p. cm. — (Studies in German history)
Includes bibliographical references and index.
ISBN 978-0-85745-953-4 (hardback) — ISBN 978-1-78533-333-0 (paperback) — ISBN 978-0-85745-954-1 (ebook)
 1. Blacks—Germany—History. 2. Blacks—Race identity—Germany—History. 3. African Americans—Germany—History. 4. African Americans—Relations with Germans—History. 5. Germany—Race relations—History. I. Honeck, Mischa, 1976– II. Klimke, Martin. III. Kuhlmann, Anne.
 DD78.B55G48 2013
 305.896'043—dc23

2012037867

British Library Cataloguing in Publication Data

A catalogue record for this book is available from the British Library

ISBN: 978-0-85745-953-4 (hardback)
ISBN: 978-1-78533-333-0 (paperback)
ISBN: 978-0-85745-954-1 (institutional ebook)

Contents

List of Illustrations   vii

Acknowledgments   x

Introduction   1
   Mischa Honeck, Martin Klimke, and Anne Kuhlmann

Part I. Saints and Slaves, Moors and Hessians

1. The Calenberg Altarpiece: Black African Christians in Renaissance Germany   21
   Paul H. D. Kaplan

2. The Black Diaspora in Europe in the Fifteenth and Sixteenth Centuries, with Special Reference to German-Speaking Areas   38
   Kate Lowe

3. Ambiguous Duty: Black Servants at German Ancien Régime Courts   57
   Anne Kuhlmann

4. Real and Imagined Africans in Baroque Court Divertissements   74
   Rashid-S. Pegah

5. From American Slaves to Hessian Subjects: Silenced Black Narratives of the American Revolution   92
   Maria I. Diedrich

Part II. From Enlightenment to Empire

6. The German Reception of African American Writers in the Long Nineteenth Century   115
   Heike Paul

7. "On the Brain of the Negro": Race, Abolitionism, and Friedrich Tiedemann's Scientific Discourse on the African Diaspora 134
Jeannette Eileen Jones

8. Liberating Sojourns? African American Travelers in Mid-Nineteenth-Century Germany 153
Mischa Honeck

9. Global Proletarians, Uncle Toms, and Native Savages: Popular German Race Science in the Emancipation Era 169
Bradley Naranch

10. We Shall Make Farmers of Them Yet: Tuskegee's Uplift Ideology in German Togoland 187
Kendahl L. Radcliffe

11. Education and Migration: Cameroonian Schoolchildren and Apprentices in Germany, 1884–1914 213
Robbie Aitken

Afterword. Africans in Europe: New Perspectives 231
Dirk Hoerder

Selected Bibliography 241

Notes on Contributors 249

Index 252

Illustrations

Figures

0.1. Gustav Sabac el Cher in a Prussian Military uniform, c. 1900, privately owned. — 2

1.1. Master of the Goslar Sibyls (attributed to), *Calenberg Altarpiece*, Boston, Museum of Fine Arts, c. 1515–20, detail of left panel *(St. Maurice and Companions)*. — 24

1.2. Master of the Goslar Sibyls (attributed to), *Calenberg Altarpiece*, Boston, Museum of Fine Arts, c. 1515–20, central panel *(Mystic Marriage of St. Catherine with Saints and Donors)*. — 26

1.3. Master of the Goslar Sibyls (attributed to), *Calenberg Altarpiece*, Boston, Museum of Fine Arts, c. 1515–20, detail of central panel *(Catherine of Saxony and Her Ladies-in-Waiting)*. — 27

1.4. Gerard Horenbout and others (?), *Solomon and the Queen of Sheba*, Grimani Breviary, Venice, Biblioteca Marciana, c. 1510–20. — 29

1.5. Barthel Beham, *Discovery of the True Cross*, Munich, Alte Pinakothek, 1530. — 31

1.6. Barthel Beham, *Discovery of the True Cross*, Munich, Alte Pinakothek, 1530, detail. — 32

1.7. Reliquary bust of St. Fidis, watercolor copy from the Halle *Heiltumsbuch*, Aschaffenburg, Hofbibliothek, 1525–27. — 33

2.1. *King Solomon and the Four Cardinal Virtues*, miniature in Remy Du Puys, *La tryumphante et solonelle entrée de Monsieur Charles en Bruges 1515*, Vienna, Österreichische Nationalbibliothek, Cod. Vind. 2591. — 40

2.2. Remys Du Puys, *King Solomon and the Four Cardinal Virtues*, 1515, detail of black courtier. — 41

2.3. South German Master, *St. Maurice and His Companions of the Theban Legion,* c. 1515–20, oil on panel, 68 x 70 cm, private collection of Marei von Saher, United States.   43

2.4. Tucher arms, stained glass medallion, 1500–99, London, Victoria and Albert Museum.   46

2.5. Detail, Christoph Jamnitzer, *Moor's Head,* Nürnberg, c. 1600 (silver, rock crystal), Munich, Bayerisches Nationalmuseum.   47

2.6. Jörg Breu the Younger, *A Duel with Two Sickles,* c. 1545, in Paulus Hector Mair's *Fechtbuch,* Munich, Bayerische Staatsbibliothek, Cod. icon. 393, fol. 227r.   50

5.1. Black tambour in a Hessian regiment in the 1780s (Source: G. C. T. Stiens, *Hochfürstliche Hessische Korps 1787,* Signatur 2° Ms. Hass. 267, Universitätsbibliothek Kassel Landesbibliothek and Murhardsche Bibliothek der Stadt Kassel).   97

5.2. Another black tambour in a Hessian regiment in the 1780s (Source: G. C. T. Stiens, *Hochfürstliche Hessische Korps 1787,* Signatur 2° Ms. Hass. 267, Universitätsbibliothek Kassel Landesbibliothek and Murhardsche Bibliothek der Stadt Kassel).   97

7.1. Table listing the physical features of different African male skulls from Friedrich Tiedemann's 1836 paper, "On the Brain of the Negro."   145

7.2. Anatomy plate of an African male brain used by Friedrich Tiedemann in "On the Brain of the Negro."   146

8.1. James W. C. Pennington's honorary doctorate from the University of Heidelberg, 1849 (University of Heidelberg).   155

9.1. Otto Ule, cover illustration from 1862 depicting exotic jungle wildlife and a savage-looking man/beast in a tree (upper right).   176

10.1. Members of the first expedition to German Togoland, left to right: Shepherd Lincoln Harris, John Winfrey Robinson, James Nathan Calloway, and Allen Lynn Burks (Source: Library of Congress).   197

11.1. Grave of Prince Equalla Deido in Mülheim, Germany (Source: Robbie Aitken).   213

11.2. Portrait of Prince Equalla Deido (Source: Unknown).   216

11.3. The window in the church at Bonamadourou that is said to depict Equalla and his sister (Source: Robbie Aitken).   226

Maps

9.1. Friedrich Ratzel, map of the spread of "colored races" in the United States, c. 1870.   171

10.1. Map of German Togoland (Source: Albert F. Calvert, *Togoland* [London: T.W. Laurie ltd., 1918], Plate I).   188

Acknowledgments

Since many hands were involved in the making of this volume, some words of appreciation are in order. The idea for this book was hatched in the spring of 2008, when our interests in the intersections of black and German history merged for the first time. We are grateful for the financial and institutional support we received from the German Historical Institute in Washington DC (GHI), and its director, Hartmut Berghoff, which allowed us to bring together some of the best scholars in the field to explore new directions in the study of Germany and the Black Diaspora. Without the GHI's generous funding, this project and the discussions that propelled it forward would never have materialized. At the GHI, Bärbel Thomas, Christa Brown, and Nicole Kruz deserve special praise for their professional handling of organizational and logistical matters. We would also like to acknowledge the cosponsorship of the Heidelberg Center for American Studies (HCA), which helped us cover some of the travel expenses. Dirk Hoerder's enthusiasm was equally crucial in getting the project off the ground. We owe the fact that so many scholars of Germany and the black diaspora working in different fields and time periods found their way to Washington to Dirk's encouraging words and skills as an academic networker.

As we were preparing the book for publication, we benefited from the talents of several close colleagues. Casey Sutcliffe, editor at the GHI, worked heroically on the manuscript, sharpening its prose and coordinating much of our correspondence with the individual authors. Words alone cannot express our indebtedness to Casey. We would also like to acknowledge the indispensable efforts of Laura Stapane, who assisted us in securing permissions for the illustrations included in this volume. Berghahn Books has been a professional and forthcoming partner all along the way. It is no small feat that Berghahn put its trust in us and accepted this book as part of its distinguished series on Studies in German History. Last but not least, we would like to thank our authors for their loyalty and patience. We hope that they are just as satisfied with the result they have helped generate as we are.

Mischa Honeck
Martin Klimke
Anne Kuhlmann

INTRODUCTION

Mischa Honeck, Martin Klimke, and Anne Kuhlmann

For more than ten years now, visitors to the German Historical Museum in Berlin have paused in amazement before a painting unlike any other in the museum's collection. It depicts a man in Prussian military uniform, impeccably dressed, his arm around a red-haired young woman resting happily in his embrace. This portrait of two lovers was created by the German artist Emil Doerstling in 1890 during the heyday of the Wilhelminean Empire. In the same year, the recently enthroned Wilhelm II drove Chancellor Otto von Bismarck from office, and the Germans yielded the island colony of Zanzibar to the British in exchange for the North Sea island of Helgoland. Much of Germany's newly gained imperial self-esteem was lodged in the country's military class, of whom the young officer captured in the painting is a proud representative.

One feature, however, stands out: the man in the picture is black. His name is Gustav Sabac el Cher. Gustav's father, August Albrecht Sabac el Cher, was brought to Germany in 1843 by a Prussian nobleman who received August as a "gift" from the Egyptian viceroy Mehmet Ali while traveling the Orient. The Sabacs fared well under the tutelage of the Prussian aristocrat. Gustav was educated by the best teachers, enjoyed close ties to the Hohenzollern court, served in the army, and rose to the position of imperial bandmaster. Well-respected and fully integrated into German society, Gustav performed in front of kings and emperors. When Gustav Sabac el Cher died, forlorn and almost forgotten after the Nazi takeover, Wilhelm II sent a letter of condolence to Gustav's family from his Dutch exile (see figure 0.1).[1]

Gustav Sabac el Cher's remarkable career is startling because it challenges widespread assumptions about Germany's historical relationship with people of black African descent. Although Germans joined the scramble for Africa in the late nineteenth century, subjugating and exploiting indigenous populations, the notion of black presences in German social and cultural life—that persons

---

Notes from this chapter begin on page 14.

Figure 0.1. Gustav Sabac el Cher in a Prussian Military uniform, c. 1900, privately owned.

of a darker hue had been actively involved in its making—have been all but expunged from national memory. Yet the footprints the Sabac family and other black Africans left in the country's history tell a different story. These footprints bear testimony to myriad black-white encounters in premodern and modern Germany from the Middle Ages to World War I. These encounters are the subject of this volume.

Persons of African descent have been present in central Europe throughout the past millennium. During the twelfth and thirteenth centuries, Africans crossed the Mediterranean to Spain, Sicily, and Italy or made their way to Europe via the Middle East and the Byzantine Empire. In later centuries, transatlantic networks of trade, slavery, and migration brought black people from the different regions of the Americas to the European continent, while the rising tides of white colonization of the New World created additional sites of black-German contact. African "court Moors," many of them shipped in from distant slave markets and subsequently baptized, became ever more visible in aristocratic Europe during the early modern period and were an integral part of courtly representation. By the eighteenth century, a growing number of black Europeans worked and lived in the bourgeois households of merchants, retired colonial officials, and plantation owners. Others made an independent living as seamen or guild members. Over time, however, as slavery, emancipation, and colonialism transformed perceptions of black people throughout the Atlantic world, the image of blacks deteriorated. The traditional term used to address black Africans, "Moors," which always bore a certain fascination and kindled visions of brave warriors, Christian saints, and the riches of Africa, was replaced by that of the "Negro," which alluded instead to a trading commodity; a childish, cheap, and unskilled hand.[2]

To map continuities and ruptures across eight centuries of perception and contact between blacks of diverse origins (the Americas, the Caribbean, Asia Minor, Africa, Europe) and people from the German-speaking parts of Europe, the present volume brings together scholars versed and trained in different eras and disciplines: history, art history, cultural studies, and literature. The essays collected in this book offer a correction to the view that black and German history rarely intersected before the twentieth century because of Germany's status as a latecomer to nation building and colonization. Focusing on earlier periods, they demonstrate that negative German perceptions of black people were largely formed in the nineteenth century, and that earlier constructions of "race" (a term that had yet to acquire its modern meaning) were far less rigid. Putting together a book with the ambition of bridging such a vast chronological span is no claim to modesty, but it is needed to illustrate the full scope of and diversity in the long history of interactions between Africa and Germany. Moreover, if retracing major developments over a broad period of time calls for a transepochal and interdisciplinary approach, it also requires adopting a transcultural and transnational outlook. In recent years, transnational historians have successfully challenged monolithic concepts of national identity by emphasizing the interconnectedness of various regional developments, no longer treating them as separate entities. Unlike traditional international historians, they look beyond the governmental sphere to include a wider range of nonstate actors, a perspective that will also be employed in this volume.[3]

Black Germany, the Black Atlantic, and Beyond

Germany did not exist as a political entity, with shifting borders, before the nineteenth century. Thus, studying encounters of white Germans and blacks across the centuries largely means studying interactions between blacks and Prussians, Hessians, Saxons, and so forth. The interactions themselves open up fresh opportunities for decentering and deprovincializing German history, but they also invite us to bring the burgeoning historiographies of empire, religion, race, ethnicity, nation, and transnational networks into fruitful conversation. Despite mounting scholarly fascination with these linkages, however, attempts to examine black presences in Germany's past with the aid of transimperial and transnational inquiry have been confined largely to the late nineteenth and twentieth centuries.[4] Too often, these studies revolve around socially constructed racial hierarchies and efforts to cement, challenge, or destabilize them without interrogating their long and multilayered prehistory.

This historiographical negligence toward earlier periods is striking, but it would be unfair to blame the scholars whose works have begun to sketch out ways to reconceptualize the German past along racial lines for this lopsidedness. The fault rather lies with the country's political and academic establishment and mainstream histories, in which black voices are either subdued or reduced to freak occurrences. Hence, it is no surprise that black Germans—who have rightly complained about their invisible status—were the ones to first draw attention to their presence in German history and contemporary affairs. Their search for and defense of a black German identity has added fuel to the project of challenging the master narrative of a lily-white nation, and Afro-German critical interventions have broken important ground by unearthing the broader significance that race possesses in the country's past.[5]

After the appearance of a series of scattered articles on black people in the German lands and Hans-Werner Debrunner's *Presence and Prestige*, a compilation of biographical fragments of black people in Europe, Peter Martin's *Schwarze Teufel, edle Mohren* was the pioneering work that charted the evolution of black-white dichotomies in German culture since the Middle Ages.[6] Although Martin deals primarily with changing images of blackness and perceptions of black people in German society and makes only brief forays into the realms of black agency because of the nature of his sources, his findings complicate static notions of racial difference and suggest a narrative of Germany's entanglement in the black diaspora that encompasses many competing strands of discourse vying for supremacy across time and space. The African image in the German mind, Martin argues, has been almost always of a "Janus-faced" nature: both promising and menacing, it has become a source of rejection and fear, but also of exotic fantasies and hidden desires.

This volume builds on the work of Afro-German intellectuals, Martin, Debrunner, and other black Germany scholars and expands them in various ways. First, while acknowledging the asymmetries and power imbalances that informed black-German relationships, most contributions move well beyond a brand of perception studies fixated on representations and reassert that cultural transfers are hardly ever monodirectional. Rather, they subscribe to a dialogical model of intercultural negotiation in which individuals from both groups actively engage in processes of mutual exchange and influence each other in significant, if often uneven, ways. Second, the book pays close attention to the dynamic, diverse, and historically contingent nature of the black-German encounter, to shifting discourses and practices with the potential for a variety of responses on both the local and the global level. Third, the volume connects the thriving scholarship on black Germany, black Europe, and the black Atlantic, thereby firmly placing the story of African-German encounters until World War I in a transregional and transatlantic framework.[7]

From the vantage point of such a broadened perspective, a couple of key concepts central to this endeavor come into view. The idea of diaspora has gained particular salience for scholars dedicated to "break[ing] the dogmatic focus on discrete *national* dynamics which has characterized so much of modern Euro-American thought," as Paul Gilroy put it, and salvaging the experiences of abduction, dispersion, exile, and uprootedness that lie at the heart of black modernity.[8] However, even as the term is now safely embedded in academic discourse, diaspora studies as a mode of countercultural analysis and promoter of pan-African identities has its critics. Some take issue with religious connotations coming out of the Judeo-Christian tradition, which allegedly make diaspora too inaccurate a term for probing the historically specific drama of black Africans enslaved and translocated to the Americas, Asia, the Caribbean, and Europe.[9] Others, like the literary scholar Sudesh Mishra, offer a more substantial critique of the concept by questioning the "tensional split between homeland and hostland" that supposedly plays a constitutive role for the diasporic subject. In privileging a set of territorial and cultural binaries, many black diaspora theorists, according to Mishra, focus solely on the implications of colonial domination at the expense of downplaying the plurality of options for self-expression and community building available at different historical moments.[10] For the purpose of this volume, therefore, it is fitting to adopt a more elastic conception of the black diaspora sensitive to black African dislocation and suffering, yet simultaneously capable of presenting a greater spectrum of black and German identity formation resulting from eight centuries of encounters between Africa and Germany.

Closely tied to locating Germany's place in the black diaspora is the question of geographical, social, and racial mobilities. Interactions between white Germans and people of African descent were neither confined to one particular territory nor limited to a socially exclusive set of actors, but instead constitute another thread in the grand, interwoven tapestry of globalization. This means that any investigation into the black roots of premodern and modern Germany should take into account that the history of the largely forced African diaspora coincided with a mainly voluntary scattering of people from the German-speaking regions of Europe throughout the Atlantic world and beyond.[11] These distinct yet interrelated mobilities linked the black and German experience to evolving transcultural webs of transportation, communication, and print, which in turn shaped and reshaped the terms of the black-German encounter. Regionally specific circumstances, as well as the politics of rank and religion, and later of class and race, mattered when an African-born court Moor made a conscious effort to forge new kin connections and social roles in a feudal society; when a German migrant to North America learned to distance himself from a black slave by emphasizing his whiteness and thus demanding inclusion in the dominant settler society; when a German scientist developed an antiracist perspective to critique and intervene in circulating Enlightenment discourses about racial inequality; and when African Americans joined an expedition to the German colony of Togo in west Africa to advance their vision of black uplift through education and self-help. Retrieving these and many other story lines—stories of blacks in Germany, of representations of black people, of African American travelers in Germany, of German responses to black literature—this volume excavates rich new veins of black presences in German history until 1914 and the spontaneous, systematic, individual, and collective responses that have emerged from these intercultural dealings. Germany's place in the black diaspora was anything but marginal. Situated at the nexus of premodern and modern ideas of culture, civilization, race, and belonging, it has been populated by people of different shades, origins, and status who were forced to adapt to changing power relations, but were never passive victims of the hybrid histories in which they partook.

Cultures in Motion

This book shares transnational history's interest in the movement, circulation, and interpenetration of individuals, ideas, and practices from diverse societies that transcend seemingly well-defined national boundaries. But it also exceeds that interest by going back long before the age of nation making and addressing interactions between blacks and Germans in a late medieval and early modern world dominated not by nations, but by city-states, principalities, and empires. Transculturality, rather than transnationality, therefore seems more capable of capturing both the local and global dimensions of this history up to the early twentieth century, and showing that these processes of exchange were highly interactive, complex, and contested, even as they were constrained by political, economic, and discursive power structures. Like transnationalism, the transcultural paradigm has been inspired by postcolonial studies and the concept of hybridity as well as by works on migrations and diasporas.[12] At its core, transculturality rejects the traditional notion of cultures as holistic, self-contained formations, embracing instead a definition of cultures that highlights their fluidity, permeability, and interdependency.[13] Revisiting questions of race, empire, mobility, diaspora, and nation making through a combined transnational and transcultural lens can shed new light on underexplored intersections and intermixtures of black and German history since the late Middle Ages and disrupt presumably fixed labels of identity and belonging.

"German" and "Germany" are geographically and politically defined concepts, but territorial borders in central Europe, and with them ideas of what it meant to be German or black, changed constantly over time. Seventeenth-century north German coastal cities and regions were intermittently governed by Danish, Swedish, and German rulers. The duchies of Schleswig and Holstein were constitutionally part of the Holy Roman Empire of the German Nation but were ruled by Danish kings. All of these regions were directly or indirectly involved in the slave trade, and some had their own overseas companies, trading colonial products, African art, and slaves. National frames of reference falsely limit German involvement in the transatlantic slave trade to the Brandenburg African Company, founded in 1682, which traded black slaves until the end of the 1710s, whereas transatlantic and global research has provided a more complex picture of German participation in the triangular trade, bringing to light a kaleidoscope of cultural flows and mobile actors:[14] Germans were present as slave traders in Seville and Santo Domingo, plantation owners and merchants in South America and the Caribbean, sailors on slave ships from the coastal regions of the North Sea, travelers in Africa and the Americas, employees of the transatlantic trade companies in Bordeaux and Cádiz with branch offices in Dutch, English, French, Spanish, and Portuguese cities, missionaries in the West Indies, west Africa, and North America, and soldiers and settlers in North and South America.[15]

As a growing number of black and white people migrated, traded, and interacted with one another and a rising interest in the diversity of the human species became manifest in art and print, influences on the perception of blackness and blacks from all these directions intermingled with earlier images. Analyzing this sort of phenomenon, Edward Saïd tied the evolution of modern hegemonic discourses and colonial ambitions to a certain "Western style for dominating, restructuring, and having authority over the Orient," which he termed Orientaism. He tended to minimize the German role in this development but saw German Orientalism as a "kind of intellectual authority over the Orient" that was largely in accord with French, British, and later American attitudes.[16] However, long before the evolution of modern colonial thought, from the twelfth century onward, academic as well as missionary interest in non-European cultures was central to European self-understanding, and shifting mental maps connected Africa to the classical Orient. The replication of Oriental life (or what it was held to be) in central European societies, as evident in images of converted Turks or baptized Moors, and "self-Orientalization" practices, as exemplified in the famous portrait of Madame de Pompadour as a Sultana, shed light on the premodern fascination with and the multifaceted roles of the nonwhite "other."[17] However, in order to assess why certain elements of "Africanness" were adopted and others were not, we need to take into account that regional cultures were diverse and internally divided between socially stratified groups, interests, and different forms of political organization. Paying attention to such fine points renders a more faithful representation of the historical arc of German perceptions of black Africans that over the centuries moved from less fixed views, with a correspondingly greater possibility of social mobility and inclusion, to a dichotomous, colonial perspective of blacks as servile and inferior.

Contacts across the Centuries

The paths of Germans and black Africans crossed as early as during the Crusades. Joining a military mission to regain the Holy Land for Roman Christianity, the crusaders encountered black Africans who were Muslims, "heathens" who influenced their perceptions of blackness just as the black or dark-skinned Christians who were allies in the war for religious supremacy did. Beginning in the twelfth and thirteenth centuries, sympathetic images of black Christians, among them the black magus and several black saints, evolved in art and literature all over Europe, and especially in the central and eastern parts of the German lands. The relatively high standing of blacks in medieval court culture becomes evident in the characters of Belacâne and Feirefiz in Wolfram von Eschenbach's Arthurian epic, *Parzival* (1197-1210). Belacâne is the Moorish Queen of Zanzamanc in Africa who gives birth to Feirefiz after being married to the Christian knight Gahmuret, who is also the father of Eschenbach's hero, Parzival. Significantly, Gahmuret's romance with Belacâne presents an interracial (and interreligious) relationship in a positive light, although Belacâne wishes to become Christian. Likewise, Feirefiz, who is described as having black-and-white-patched skin, is regarded as Parzival's equal. Parzival even claims that, together with their shared dead father, the three of them are in essence one because of their blood bond.

After renouncing his pagan faith, Feirefiz marries the white Grail bearer and is granted all the privileges of a Christian knight.[18]

At the time of the death of Holy Roman Emperor Frederick II in 1250, Christian universalism began to demonstratively include the black "other." His descendants, however, introduced more ambiguous images of blackness. These images were reinterpreted and transformed as black people continued to arrive from Africa, Asia, and later the Americas and as cultural influences from the south (especially Italy and the Iberian states), east (the powerful Ottoman Empire), and west (the evolving transatlantic slave trade) increasingly made themselves felt. The chapters in the first section of this volume, "Saints and Slaves, Moors and Hessians," examine these influences and show how processes of migration and cultural transfer interacted with one another in a European-wide and global context. Over the early centuries of contact, European perceptions of blacks tended to be far more open than the black-white dichotomy of later periods. The contributions of this section by and large trace a decline in the integration of African people in German culture as the notion of blacks as a racially subordinate group became hegemonic. At the same time, the chapters also reveal how African influences were "filtered" and adapted to the specific needs of the receiving cultures.

The opening chapter by Paul Kaplan addresses the relationship between the representation of black people in European and German art and their historical presence in these territories: Were these artistic representations an expression of European conceptions of and fascination with a still largely unknown "exotic"? Were the models white Europeans who masked themselves on certain occasions, or did they refer to a "real" presence of blacks? Mindful of these variants, Kaplan traces the complex patronage history of the Calenberg Altarpiece, acquired a few years ago by the Boston Museum of Fine Arts. Commissioned by Catherine of Saxony, a cousin of Archbishop Ernst of Magdeburg, who promoted the cult of the black Saint Maurice in Magdeburg, Halle, and farther east, the altarpiece, through its history, exemplifies the close connection between artistic representation and the likely physical presence of blacks in the patron's environment.

Kate Lowe's conceptually elaborate chapter then examines historical situations in which blackness is clearly portrayed as different from whiteness, pursuing fifteenth- and sixteenth-century traits of black presences among Germans. Starting off with the fascinating custom of a fictitious blackness in the context of carnivals, as well as pageants and plays on stage, she introduces the categories of "real," "notional," and "fictive" black presences in German lands. What were the intentions behind the creation of black masques, blacks in masquerades, or heraldic devices like the so-called Moor's head as a form of notional blackness? Also, what defined the roles of "real" blacks in the German-speaking territories in the context of fictive and notional blackness? As a scholar focusing primarily on black Africans in Renaissance Italy and Portugal, Lowe concludes that the presence of Africans in the German lands appears widely comparable to those on the Iberian and Italian peninsulas.

Such overlaps between visual representations and the actual presence of blacks in the German lands are equally central to the next chapter in this section. Anne Kuhlmann tackles the subject of black presences at early modern German courts. Analyzing the records of hundreds of attested blacks, she discusses the idiosyncrasies of black mobility in the world of German aristocratic elites within a circuit of related courts in central Europe. Kuhlmann elaborates on the positions of blacks, who undoubtedly depended on certain forms of princely patronage that limited or extended their agency, locating different forms of dependency of people of black African descent in a cultural environment that was itself largely structured by socially tiered, mutual dependencies. Although blacks adjusted to this social framework, their biographies indicate that many of them were in a position to successfully negotiate interests and to expand possibilities for social advancement.

Rashid-S. Pegah's chapter then turns to a specific professional niche of black people in the domain of the early modern nobility: the wide field of court entertainment, with its colorful pageants, plays, and masquerades. Apart from regular court service, some blacks became prominent actors in plays and operas, starring as black or even white characters side by side with members of the nobility. In the course of the seventeenth and eighteenth centuries, however, the specific roles and conceptions of a non-European "other" became more essentialized and were increasingly squeezed into hierarchical patterns. As Pegah shows, "civilized" European cultures were now clearly understood as being far more advanced than non-European ones, even if the distinguished rules of courtly representation required the nobility to ascribe at least a minimum of honor to non-Europeans in their midst.

Maria I. Diedrich's chapter, which concludes the first section, sheds light on the black Hessians during the American Revolution and dissects their collective and individual life stories. This group consisted of former slaves and their families who escaped from their owners or were kidnapped as war booty and subsequently served, as self-liberators and slaves, alongside pro-British Germans in their regiments during the Revolutionary War. Drawing on church, court, and military records, Diedrich reconstructs the circum-Atlantic worlds through which these "Kasseler *Mohren*" moved: from their African homelands via the slave fields of North America to the domain of Hesse's landgrave Wilhelm IX in 1783. Her pathbreaking analysis of these multiple passages and identities in transit stresses that black American–Hessian interactions in the New World, the blacks' integration into a local German community, and developing racial notions among white Hessians were largely the result of the active role the former American slaves played in this story.

While the relationships between black Africans and people from the German-speaking parts of Europe intensified through expanding networks of trade, migration, and communication, the eighteenth and nineteenth centuries also witnessed a growing interest in the diversity of the human species. The second section of this volume, "From Enlightenment to Empire," investigates major voices in this transnational discussion and highlights German intellectuals' influential, albeit contradictory, ideas about blackness and the value of black individuals. On another level, this section illustrates that, while white Germans were grappling with shifting images of blackness in an age of racial construction and nation making, persons of African origin were likewise contributing actively to this history. The latter did not stand idly by, but instead developed multiple strategies to cope with or counter white hegemonic claims. The chapters in this section explore changing notions of space and identity in conjunction with the proliferation of more rigid notions of racial and ethnic difference that informed black-German encounters from the late-eighteenth-century Atlantic revolutions to the imperialist rivalries on the eve of World War I.

A controversial term, the Enlightenment has come to signify many things: a revolutionary project of human liberation, secularization, bourgeois empowerment, and a quasi-totalitarian ideology of reason. At the heart of this movement, however, lay a new curiosity about the world, triggered by geographical discoveries and a mounting distrust in established authorities. Enlightenment philosophers, valuing rational thought and scientific empiricism, set out to probe, measure, and categorize their natural and social environments. Abstract generalizations about human nature were challenged by scholars compiling material from and about distant lands and cultures, and their publications prepared the ground for anthropological classifications of different human populations into biologically distinct races. Consequently, traditional images of blackness associated with Christian piety and courtly representation eroded and gave way to scientific discourses emphasizing racial difference and inequality, often with the effect of fortifying political hierarchies stemming from European colonialism and transatlantic chattel slavery. Late-eighteenth-century German philosophers like Immanuel Kant found blacks inherently inferior and were oblivious to the fact that individuals of African ancestry had made impressive careers in Europe as officers, scholars, merchants, and artists.[19] Apparently, the proliferation of Eurocentric notions of civilization and progress made it more difficult to accept nonwhite actors as equals even when they met Western standards of accomplishment.

Heike Paul speaks to this development in her survey covering the reception of black writing and authorship in late-eighteenth- and nineteenth-century Germany. With the tools of a literary historian, Paul dissects four texts written by Africans or African Americans—the autobiographies of Olaudah Equiano, Frederick Douglass, and Joshua Henson, and a novel by Frank Webb—and investigates the ways in which black voices became mutilated or partially erased in the process of translation. Her argument that black authorship was repeatedly contested by nineteenth-century Germans is particularly salient because it confirms that German representations of blackness partook in a larger effort to deny cultural literacy and political autonomy to nonwhite people.

Yet the same atmosphere of rational inquiry that led to the proliferation of racist ideologies also inspired dissent on the question of whether black subordination was hereditarily predetermined. In her chapter on the Heidelberg anatomist Friedrich Tiedemann, Jeannette Eileen Jones presents an intriguing case study of a German scientist rejecting notions of black inferiority with his empirical findings. Connecting liberal Enlightenment research to the abolitionist movement and the political revolutions in Europe, the Caribbean, and North America, Jones sensitizes us to the ways in which science and politics converged to produce knowledge about the social and intellectual status of black people. As scientific discourse, Tiedemann's writings illuminate an understudied egalitarian current in German theorizing about race; as antislavery propaganda, it shows that liberal Germans utilized their intellectual credentials to join the transatlantic battle against slavery.

Mischa Honeck follows an equally complex tale of transatlantic entanglements by revisiting the sojourns of African Americans in mid-nineteenth-century Germany. Tracing the European travels of abolitionist and churchman James W. C. Pennington and David F. Dorr, a slave accompanying his white master across Europe, North Africa, and the Middle East, Honeck contends that their idealized depiction of Germany grew out of their search for an egalitarian, nonracist society. Yet despite these misconceptions, both Pennington and Dorr returned to the United States empowered and imbued with a cosmopolitan nationalism that transcended the domestic confines of racial discrimination and strengthened their quest for freedom and equality. According to Honeck, these examples illustrate the need for a more balanced historiographical assessment of the legacies and pitfalls of African American travel and intercultural encounters during the nineteenth century.

Bradley Naranch picks up the German discussion concerning race and blackness in the turbulent years between the American Civil War and German unification. Concentrating on the two journalists Friedrich Ratzel and Karl Andree, Naranch reconstructs the popularization of race science in an age of heightened national sensibilities but also addresses the widespread concerns among white elites about how to mobilize a sufficient labor force to meet the demands of a global capitalist economy in a postemancipation world. Writers like Ratzel and Andree flooded the public sphere with a broad array of stories about the innate traits of the world's populations, shaping German perceptions of race before the onset of official colonialism. However, as Naranch states, contrasting images of the black diaspora, which alternately stressed primitivism, philanthropy, or savagery, did not lead to greater precision but only to more confusion.

Kendahl Radcliffe's analysis of the Tuskegee Institute's cotton production scheme in German Togoland between 1900 and 1909 offers another window onto the triangular transatlantic relationship between Germans and people of

African descent. Radcliffe situates this unique expedition at the invitation of the German government not only in the history of imperial expansion, but also contextualizes it in the debates between Booker T. Washington and W. E. B. Du Bois within the African American community. While capturing the rationale of Germans bent on developing methods of scientific agriculture in their colonies, she argues that the Tuskegeans in this endeavor intended, above all, to propagate their vision of raising the socioeconomic status of blacks, both in the United States and Africa, by means of education.

Robbie Aitken brings the discussion to the heart of the Hohenzollern Empire by charting the migration stream of young Cameroonians into German metropolises from 1884 to 1914. The migrants' experience, Aitken argues, was shaped by their status as colonial subjects, as well as by imperial policies that sought to restrict and control migrants' exposure to German society. He outlines how the colonial authorities monitored the effectiveness of this largely education-driven migration and eventually came to consider it counterproductive: the skills the migrants acquired did not offset their potentially subversive leanings upon returning to Cameroon, which were regarded as dangerous to the colonial project. Highlighting the racial discrimination and prejudices Cameroonians were exposed to in Germany, Aitken also stresses the linkage between education and a racially charged civilizing mission based on offering moral and religious guidance to the subjects of the protectorate.

The volume concludes with an afterword by Dirk Hoerder that assesses the presented findings in the light of recent scholarly discussions about the interrelatedness of black and European history. Even as the myth of Europe as a lily-white continent has begun to crumble, Hoerder emphasizes that the task of rediscovering African traces in Europe's past is ongoing and unfinished. In particular, he calls on researchers to take a closer look at how black Germans were connected to trans-European and transatlantic networks; how chattel slavery related to and unsettled other forms of bound relationships in European societies; and how the grids of meaning pertaining to terms such as "African," "black," and "German" diverged and were subject to change in different social and regional settings.

By binding together approaches from scholars of different disciplinary backgrounds, this book aims to break new ground in the complex, contested, and highly volatile history of the interaction of Africa and Germany prior to World War I. Rather than promulgate a linear narrative grounded in static notions of racial difference, it presents a differentiated picture of Germany's entanglement in the global black diaspora as one of many competing strands of discourse and social practice vying for dominance across time and space. Of course, nobody can expect all aspects of this history to be covered in one book. Much work remains to be done, as the volume only addresses Germany and the black diaspora in areas and time periods on which scholars are now working. Questions like the relationship of blacks to other nonwhite ethnicities in German history, German-black encounters in places outside central Europe, North America, and colonial Africa, and the circulation of racial ideologies among the white societies of Europe and North America, to name just a few, deserve greater attention. We hope that this book will spark further discussion along these lines and open up avenues for future inquiry.

Germany's place in the black Atlantic might have been peripheral in a geographical sense. Intellectually and discursively, however, it played an often underestimated and significant role in the formation of modern social, racial, and national identities. This is not to say that German nationhood would not have taken shape without the contributions of people of African descent. However, in light of the findings presented here, accounts of German nation making that conceal or ignore black agency are no longer acceptable. Even today, as Germans cautiously move toward accepting the reality of living in a multicultural society, antiblack racism remains a touchy and uncomfortable subject. Unaware of the racist legacy of American minstrel shows, a popular Berlin theater ensemble had a white actor play a role in blackface in January 2012. The directors were stunned that this move unleashed a torrent of criticism and passionate exchanges on various blogs and online forums.[20] Likewise, the decision of the investigative reporter Günter Wallraff to go undercover as a black man to expose racist behavior in contemporary Germany was probably well-intentioned but backfired when Afro-Germans faulted him for what they regarded as ill-informed and patronizing conduct.[21] No less disturbing is the survival of street names in Berlin such as "Togostraße" and "Lüderitzstraße," both allusions to German colonial rule and exploitation in Africa. To this day, city authorities have done nothing to change the names or at least furnish the street signs with explanatory captions.

These few examples should suffice to show that the tendency to treat blacks in German history and culture as perpetual strangers and as the immutable "other," in a very palpable sense, lasts into our time. True, historians of Germany and Germans themselves have started to confront the country's colonial and imperial legacies. Yet in light of recent neo-Nazi outrages and concerns about no-go areas for darker-skinned people cropping up all over Europe, many more steps are needed to arrive at a more tolerant and inclusive concept of community. We, therefore, hope with our volume to raise awareness about a long, though oftentimes still neglected, tradition of black presences in German society that has had and continues to have a place in the nation's sociopolitical fabric.

Notes

1. The story of August and Gustav Sabac el Cher is explored in Gorch Pieken and Cornelia Kruse, *Preußisches Liebesglück—Eine deutsche Familie aus Afrika* (Berlin: Propyläen, 2007).

2. Unlike "negro," the term "moor," as defined by an eighteenth-century German encyclopedia, was a much more ambiguous and unstable signifier for racial difference as it was applied to people of different religious affiliation, geographical origin, and with various degrees of blackness. See "Mohr, Aethiopier," in *Universal-Lexicon aller Wissenschafften und Künste*, ed. Johan Heinrich Zedler, vol. 21 (Leipzig, 1750), 864–66.

3. The literature on transnational history, both in the United States and Europe, is vast and growing. On the theoretical foundations of this blossoming field of research, see David Thelen, "The Nation and Beyond: Transnational Perspectives on United States History," *Journal of American History* 86 (1999): 965–75; Kiran Klaus Patel, "Überlegungen zu einer transnationalen Geschichte," *Zeitschrift für Geschichtswissenschaft* 52 (2004): 626–45; and C. A. Bayly, Sven Beckert, Matthew Connelly, Isabel Hofmeyr, Wendy Kozol, and Patricia Seed, "AHR Conversation: On Transnational History," *American Historical Review* 111 (2005): 1440–64. See also Oliver Janz, Sebastian Conrad, and Gunilla Budde, eds., *Transnationale Geschichte: Themen, Tendenzen, und Theorien* (Göttingen, Germany: Vandenhoeck & Ruprcht, 2006); and Akira Iriye and Pierre-Yves Saunier, eds., *The Palgrave Dictionary of Transnational History: From the Mid-19th Century to the Present Day* (Basingstoke, UK: Palgrave Macmillan, 2009). Critics of the transnational turn include Hans-Ulrich Wehler, "Transnationale Geschichte: Der neue Königsweg historischer Forschung?" in *Notizen zur deutschen Geschichte* (Munich: Beck, 2007), 63–77; and Konrad H. Jarausch, "Reflections on Transnational History," in *H-German*, 20 January 2006, http://h-net.msu.edu/cgi-bin/logbrowse.pl?trx=vx&list=h-german&month=0601&week=c&msg=LPkNHirCm1xgSZQKHOGRXQ&user=&pw=

4. German colonialism in Africa and its international and intercultural legacies have become a particularly productive field of inquiry. For examples, see Sara L. Friedrichsmeyer, Sara Lennox, and Susanne M. Zantop, eds., *The Imperialist Imagination: German Colonialism and Its Legacy* (Ann Arbor: University of Michigan Press, 1998); Stefanie Michels, *Schwarze deutsche Kolonialsoldaten: Mehrdeutige Repräsentationsräume und früher Kosmopolitismus in Afrika* (Bielefeld, Germany: Transkript, 2009); Volker Langbehn, ed., *German Colonialism, Visual Culture, and Modern Memory* (London: Routledge, 2010); Andrew Zimmermann, *Alabama in Africa: Booker T. Washington, the German Empire, and the Globalization of the New South* (Princeton, NJ: Princeton University Press, 2010); and David Ciarlo, *Advertising Empire: Race and Visual Culture in Imperial Germany* (Cambridge, MA: Harvard University Press, 2011). Important strides have also been made with regard to interactions between blacks and white Germans in later decades. See, for example, Sander Gilman, *On Blackness Without Blacks: Essays on the Image of the Black in Germany* (Boston: G. K. Hall, 1982); Carol Blackshire-Belay, ed., *The African-German Experience: Critical Essays* (Westport, CT: Praeger, 1996); David McBride, Leroy Hopkins, and Carol Blackshire-Belay, eds., *Crosscurrents: African Americans, Africa, and Germany in the Modern World* (Columbia, SC: Camden House, 1998); Michelle M. Wright and Tina M. Campt, eds., "Reading the Black German Experience," special issue, *Callaloo: A Journal of African Diaspora Arts and Letters* 26, no. 2 (2003); Clarence Lusane, *Hitler's Black Victims: The Historical Experiences of Afro-Germans, European Blacks, Africans, and African Americans in the Nazi Era* (New York: Routledge, 2003); Peter Martin and Christine Alonzo, *Zwischen Charleston und Stechschritt: Schwarze im Nationalsozialismus* (Hamburg, Germany: Dölling & Gallitz, 2004); Tina Campt, *Other Germans: Black Germans and the Politics of Race, Gender, and Memory in the Third Reich* (Ann Arbor: University of Michigan Press, 2004); Heide Fehrenbach, *Race after Hitler: Black Occupation Children in Postwar Germany and America* (Princeton, NJ: Princeton University Press, 2005); Maureen Maisha Eggers, Grada Kilomba, Peggy Piesche, and Susan Arndt, eds., *Mythen, Masken und Subjekte: Kritische Weissseinsforschung in Deutschland* (Münster, Germany: Unrast, 2005); Patricia Mazón and Reinhild Steingröver, eds., *Not so Plain as Black and White: Afro-German Culture and History, 1890–2000* (Rochester, NY: University of Rochester, 2005); Maria Diedrich and Jürgen

Heinrichs, eds., *From Black to Schwarz: Cultural Crossovers between African America and Germany* (Berlin: LIT, 2010); Maria Höhn and Martin Klimke, *A Breath of Freedom: The Civil Rights Struggle, African American GIs, and Germany* (New York: Palgrave Macmillan, 2010); Volker Langbehn and Mohammad Salama, eds., *German Colonialism: Race, the Holocaust, and Postwar Germany* (New York: Columbia University Press, 2011); and Larry Greene and Anke Ortlepp, eds., *African Americans and Germany: Two Centuries of Exchange* (Jackson: University Press of Mississippi, 2011). For perspectives on the presence and perception of blacks in other parts of Europe in the Renaissance, see Tom F. Earle and Kate J. P. Lowe, eds., *Black Africans in Renaissance Europe* (Oxford: Cambridge University Press, 2010). This was also the subject of an exhibition at Walters Museum in Baltimore, Maryland, from October 14, 2012–January 21, 2013 (for a review, see Holland Cotter, "A Spectrum from Slaves to Saints: 'African Presence in Renaissance Europe,' at Walters Museum," *New York Times,* November 8, 2012, available at http://nyti.ms/S1ge5m, accessed February 7, 2013. For the colonial era, see Jane Landers, *Atlantic Creoles in the Age of Revolutions* (Cambridge: Harvard University Press, 2011); Catherine Molineux, *Faces of Perfect Ebony: Encountering Atlantic Slavery in Imperial Britain,* Harvard Historical Studies 175 (Cambridge: Harvard University Press, 2012).

5. Three influential examples of this Afro-German scholarship are May Ayim, Katharina Oguntoye, and Dagmar Schultz, eds., *Showing Our Colors: Afro-German Women Speak Out* (Amherst: University of Massachusetts Press, 1992); Fatima El-Tayeb, *Schwarze Deutsche: Der Diskurs um "Rasse" und Nationale Identität 1890–1933* (Frankfurt: Campus Fachbuch, 2001); and Aija Poikane-Daumke, *African Diasporas: Afro-German Literature in the Context of the African American Experience* (Berlin: LIT, 2006).

6. Peter Martin, *Schwarze Teufel, edle Mohren: Afrikaner in Geschichte und Bewusstsein der Deutschen* (Hamburg, Germany: Hamburger Edition, 2001); and Hans Werner Debrunner, *Presence and Prestige: Africans in Europe* (Basel, Switzerland: Basler Africa Bibliographien, 1979). Among the eminent earlier, regionally framed studies are Ingeborg Kittel, "Mohren als Hofbediente und Soldaten im Herzogtum Braunschweig-Wolfenbüttel," *Braunschweigisches Jahrbuch* 46 (1965): 78–103; and Wolfram Schäfer, "Von 'Kammermohren,' 'Mohren'-Tambouren und 'Ost-Indianern,'" *Hessische Blätter für Volks- und Kulturforschung* 23 (1988): 35–79.

7. See Reinhold Grimm, ed., *Blacks and German Culture: Essays,* Monatshefte Occasional Papers (Madison: University of Wisconsin Press, 1986); Birgit Tautz, *Colors 1800, 1900, 2000: Signs of Ethnic Difference* (Amsterdam: Rodopi, 2004); Sara Eigen and Mark Larrimore, eds., *The German Invention of Race* (New York: SUNY Press, 2006); and Mazón and Steingröver, eds., *Not so Plain as Black and White.* Examples of recent scholarship on black Europe are Heike Raphael-Hernandez, ed., *Blackening Europe: The African American Presence* (New York: Routledge, 2004); Dominic Thomas, *Black France: Colonialism, Immigration, and Transnationalism* (Bloomington: Indiana University Press, 2006); Rita Chin, Heide Fehrenbach, Geoff Eley, and Atina Grossmann, eds., *After the Nazi Racial State: Difference and Democracy in Germany and Europe* (Ann Arbor: University of Michigan Press, 2009); Darlene Clark Hine, Trica Danielle Keaton, and Stephen Small, eds., *Black Europe and the African Diaspora* (Urbana: University of Illinois Press, 2009); and David Dabydeen, John Gilmore, and Cecily Jones, eds., *The Oxford Companion to Black British History* (New York: Oxford University Press, 2010); Eve Rosenhaft and Robbie Aitken, eds., *Africa in Europe: Studies in Transnational Practice in the Long Twentieth Century* (Liverpool: Liverpool University Press, 2013). On the black Atlantic, see Paul Gilroy, *The Black Atlantic: Modernity and Double Consciousness* (London: Harvard University Press, 1993); Hauke Dorsch, *Afrikanische Diaspora und Black Atlantic: Einführung in Geschichte und aktuelle Diskussion* (Münster, Germany: LIT, 2000); and Paul Tiyambe Zeleza, "Rewriting the African Diaspora: Beyond the Black Atlantic," *African Affairs* 104 (2005): 35–68.

8. Gilroy, *Black Atlantic,* 6. See also Brent Hayes Edwards, "The Uses of Diaspora," *Social Text* 66

(2001): 45–73; and Ruth Mayer, *Diaspora: Eine kritische Begriffsbestimmung*, Cultural Studies 14 (Bielefeld, Germany: Transkript, 2005), 73–122.
9. See Dorsch, *Afrikanische Diaspora*, 38–39; and Gwyn Campbell, "African Diaspora in Asia," Dieudonné Gnammankou, "African Diaspora in Europe," and Kevin A. Yelvington, "African Diaspora in the Americas," all in *Encyclopedia of Diasporas, Immigrant and Refugee Cultures around the World*, ed. Melvin Ember, Carol R. Ember, and Ian Skoggard (New York: Springer, 2004), 1:3–15, 15–24, 24–35, respectively.
10. Sudesh Mishra, *Diaspora Criticism* (Edinburgh, UK: Edinburgh University Press, 2006), 16. Other critical interventions are Neil Lazarus, "Is a Counterculture of Modernity a Theory of Modernity," *Diaspora* 4 (1995): 323–39; Patrick Manning, "Africa and the African Diaspora: New Directions of Study," *Journal of African History* 44 (2003): 487–506; and Ruth Mayer, "The Dangers of Diaspora: Some Thoughts about the Black Atlantic," in *Transcultural English Studies: Theories, Fictions, Realities*, ed. Frank Schulze-Engler and Sissy Helff (Amsterdam: Rodopi, 2009), 91–102.
11. For the exception to this rule, see the essays in this volume by Maria Diedrich and Dirk Hoerder, which emphasize the fact that the Hessian mercenaries were sent to fight in the American War of Independence against their will.
12. See Gayatri Chakravorty Spivak, "Can the Subaltern Speak?" in *Marxism and the Interpretation of Culture*, ed. Cary Nelson and Lawrence Grossberg (Chicago: University of Illinois Press, 1988), 271–313; Ania Loomba, Suvir Kaul, Matti Bunzl, Antoinette Burton, and Jed Esty, eds., *Postcolonial Studies and Beyond* (Durham, NC: Duke University Press, 2005); Nina Glick Schiller, Linda Basch, and Cristina Blanc-Szanton, eds., *Towards a Transnational Perspective on Migration: Race, Class, Ethnicity, and Nationalism Reconsidered* (New York: New York Academy of Sciences, 1998); James Clifford, "Diasporas," *Cultural Anthropology* 9, no. 3 (1994): 79–101; and Dirk Hoerder, *Cultures in Contact: World Migrations in the Second Millennium* (Durham, NC: Duke University Press, 2002).
13. Influential voices responsible for the rise of transcultural scholarship are Homi Bhaba, *The Location of Culture* (New York: Routledge, 1994); Wolfgang Welsch, "Transkulturalität: Zwischen Globalisierung und Partikularisierung," in *Interkulturalität: Grundprobleme der Kulturbegegnung*, ed. Paul Drechsel (Mainz, Germany: Universität Mainz, 1998), 45–72; and Seyla Benhabib, *The Claims of Culture: Equality and Diversity in the Global Era* (Princeton, NJ: Princeton University Press, 2002).
14. For a comprehensive research review, see Mark Häberlein, "'Mohren,' ständische Gesellschaft und atlantische Welt: Minderheiten und Kulturkontakte in der Frühen Neuzeit," in *Atlantic Understandings: Essays on European and American History in Honor of Hermann Wellenreuther*, ed. Claudia Schnurmann and Hartmut Lehmann (Hamburg, Germany: LIT, 2006), 77–102. On the history of the Brandenburg African Company, see Adam Jones, "Introduction," in *Brandenburg Sources for West African History, 1680–1700*, ed. Adam Jones, Studien zur Kulturkunde 77 (Wiesbaden, Germany: Franz Steiner, 1985), 6–16; Andrea Weindl, "Die Kurbrandenburger im 'Atlantischen System' 1650–1720," *Arbeitspapiere zur Lateinamerikaforschung* 2, no. 3 (2001); and David Eltis, Stephen Behrendt, David Richardson, and Herbert Klein, eds., *The Trans-Atlantic Slave Trade: A Database on CD-ROM* (Cambridge: Cambridge University Press, 1999).
15. Hermann Kellenbenz, "Deutsche Plantagenbesitzer und Kaufleute in Surinam vom Ende des 18. bis zur Mitte des 19. Jahrhunderts," *Jahrbuch für Geschichte Lateinamerikas* 3 (1966): 141–63; Christian Degn, *Die Schimmelmanns im atlantischen Dreieckshandel: Gewinn und Gewissen* (Neumünster, Germany: Wachholtz, 1974); Klaus Weber, *Deutsche Kaufleute im Atlantikhandel 1680–1830: Unternehmen und Familien in Hamburg, Cádiz und Bordeaux* (Munich: Beck, 2004); Catharina Lüden, *Sklavenfahrt mit Seeleuten aus Schleswig-Holstein*,

Hamburg und Lübeck im 18. Jahrhundert (Heide, Germany: Westholsteinsche Verlagsanstalt Boyen, 1983); Christian Georg Andreas Oldendorp, *History of the Evangelical Brethren on the Caribbean Islands of St. Thomas, St. Croix, and St. John,* ed. Johann Jakob Bossart, English edition ed. Vladimir Barac and trans. Arnold R. Highfield (Ann Arbor, MI: Karoma, 1987); and Debrunner, *Presence and Prestige.*

16. Edward Said, *Orientalism* (New York: Vintage, 2003), 19.
17. Urs App, *The Birth of Orientalism* (Philadelphia: University of Pennsylvania Press, 2010); Urs App, "William Jones's Ancient Theology," *Sino-Platonic Papers* 191 (September 2009); on the specifics of German Orientalism, see Suzanne L. Marchand, *German Orientalism in the Age of Empire: Religion, Race, and Scholaraship* (Cambridge, MA: Cambridge University Press, 2009); Andrea Polaschegg, *Der andere Orientalismus: Regeln deutsch-morgenländischer Imagination im 19. Jahrhundert* (Berlin: Walter de Gruyter, 2004); and Sabine Mangold, *Eine "weltbürgerliche Wissenschaft": Die deutsche Orientalistik im 19. Jahrhundert* (Stuttgart, Germany: Steiner, 2004).
18. See Werner Sollors, "Interracial Literature," in *The Harvard Sampler: Liberal Education for the Twenty-First Century,* ed. Jennifer M. Shephard, Stephen M. Kosslyn, and Evelynn M. Hammonds (Cambridge: Harvard University Press, 2011), 311-39.
19. On the Enlightenment production of racial stereotypes, see Eigen and Larrimore, *The German Invention of Race,* esp. section 2; and Wulf D. Hund, "'It Must Come from Europe': The Racisms of Immanuel Kant," in *Racisms Made in Germany,* ed. Wulf D. Hund, Christian Koller, and Moshe Zimmermann (Vienna: LIT, 2011), 69–98.
20. *The Local: Germany's News in English,* "Blackface in Berlin Play Just 'Tradition,'" 6 January 2012, http://www.thelocal.de/ national/20120106-39967.html (accessed 16 February 2012).
21. Henning Hoff, *Time World,* "Blackface Filmmaker Sparks a Race Debate in Germany," 18 November 2009, http://www.time.com/time/world/article/0,8599,1940290,00.html (accessed 16 February 2012).

Part I

SAINTS AND SLAVES, MOORS AND HESSIANS

Chapter One

THE CALENBERG ALTARPIECE
Black African Christians in Renaissance Germany

Paul H. D. Kaplan

Black Africans in Early German Art

During the reign of Emperor Frederick II of Hohenstaufen (1220–50), people of black African descent had begun to appear in German-speaking lands, and it did not take long for German artists—perhaps encouraged by Frederick's display of his black African retainers—to start creating images of people of color.[1] While Frederick's black subjects were evidently Muslims, drawn from an exiled colony of Sicilians established by the Holy Roman Emperor at Lucera in Apulia, and the most direct depiction of blacks showing fealty to Frederick—an extraordinary fresco from the 1230s in a tower adjoining the monastery of S. Zeno in Verona[2]—is entirely secular in tone, the first German visual responses to black African identity are in the context of sacred Christian art. The great Magdeburg statue of St. Maurice, from c. 1240 to 1250, is evidently the first instance of this prominent saint being shown with the features and complexion of an African black, and recent scholarship has emphasized Frederick II's important links to Magdeburg and even the imperial cast of monumental sculpture produced in that city during the second quarter of the thirteenth century.[3] In any case, by the fifteenth century the black St. Maurice had become a standard element around Magdeburg and in adjoining parts of northern and eastern Germany, where the saint's cult was strongly developed. There were also several lesser-known black saints of similar type, including St. Gregor Maurus of Cologne, whose likeness appeared in stained glass from the early 1300s onward.[4]

Notes from this chapter begin on page 34.

More than half a century earlier than the Magdeburg Maurice, Nicholas of Verdun's Klosterneuburg Altarpiece (1181) had already depicted another pious figure with dark skin, though without the secondary physiognomic features (hair, nose, and lips) normally associated with black African identity. Nicholas's figure is the Queen of Sheba, who acknowledges King Solomon's wisdom.[5] There are several other dark-skinned Queens of Sheba in late medieval German art, including a rather monumental example from the Baptistry of St. John in Brixen in South Tyrol.[6] The queen is, of course, not a Christian, but her veneration of Solomon as described in the Jewish bible was understood as a prefiguration of the veneration of Christ by the Gentiles—a theme most directly addressed in the visual arts through the depiction of the story of the Three Magi (also known as the Three Kings) who adored the infant Jesus. The Africanization of one of these three prescient Gentiles in texts and images took place in the course of the later 1300s and early 1400s, with the key developments unfolding almost entirely in German and adjacent Czech lands.[7] Though tales eventually emerged concerning the later baptism of the Three Magi, these figures were never quite treated as wholly Christian, but the African magus was soon associated with and said to be the ancestor of the contemporary Christian rulers of Ethiopia, collectively known to Europeans by the title of Prester John. By the late 1400s and early 1500s, the black African magus was everywhere in German art, and had become a relatively rare example of an iconographic motif that had spread from German painting and sculpture to nearly every other region of western Europe. Images of the black St. Maurice were also quite common in Germany around 1500, but were largely restricted to the provinces of Saxony, Brandenburg, and Pomerania. Very occasionally, an image of a black Maurice and a black magus would appear in the same work of art, as in Hans Baldung's 1507 altarpiece made for display in some sacred space in Halle at the order of Ernst von Wettin, archbishop of Magdeburg.[8] But this is an extremely rare case, since under normal circumstances the ecumenical point made by including a black saint was sufficiently articulated without this kind of doubling. The black magus, it is true, was often accompanied by African retainers of lesser status, and there are also a few images of Maurice appearing with his black "companions" (fellow soldiers of the imperial Roman army's Theban Legion who were martyred with him). Both these groupings were intended to suggest that the pious African was a representative of a larger nation of people with similar complexions. However, the immediate juxtaposition of two separate pious blacks was generally avoided, and even Baldung made sure to place St. Maurice on the right wing of his altarpiece, at a significant distance from the black magus, who stands at the left margin of the central panel.

Ruth Mellinkoff, in her exhaustive study of depictions of "outcasts" in late medieval northern European art, cites a number of examples of black Africans and figures with at least certain elements of stereotypically black African appearance among those who mock, torture, or execute Christ and the saints. Mellinkoff has claimed that "[a] white-skinned society could tolerate a black magus and a black St. Maurice because they represented an abstract piety, but more often white society viewed blacks as physically and morally ugly, and therefore inferior and despicable."[9] But the pejorative visual images on which Melinkoff's claim is based are themselves rather disconnected from the social reality of the era. Despite the numerous images of black Africans as executioners—including one in a drawing by Albrecht Dürer of *The Martyrdom of St. Catherine* from the early 1500s[10]—there is no real evidence that black Africans were employed in such capacities in Germany, and only one credible instance of this in Italy (from the 1460s).[11] Both the black saints and the black executioners found in German art of this period are projections rather than reflections.

We do not, however, as yet really know much about the dimensions and the character of the black African population of Germany in the early 1500s, and it will take one or more historians with the determination of Kate Lowe (who has undertaken an in-depth and already fruitful investigation of black Africans in Italy during this era) to begin to clarify this matter. Dürer's silverpoint *Katharina* of 1521 was created in Antwerp, and rendered an African servant to the Portuguese consul there; might Dürer's other fine drawing of an African man, which bears the date 1508, have been based on a black resident of Nuremberg?[12] It is impossible to say for sure, but an anonymous German altarpiece of c. 1515–20 (figures 1.1, 1.2, and 1.3), recently acquired by the Boston Museum of Fine Arts, provokes this kind of question and provides more contextual evidence to help answer it. This work, known as the Calenberg Altarpiece, displays one of the most unusual combinations of multiple black African figures of any European Renaissance image.[13]

The Calenberg Altarpiece

Attributed to the still-anonymous Master of the Goslar Sibyls, and probably the handiwork of several collaborating painters, the Calenberg Altarpiece measures 99 x 276 cm, including both the central panel and the two wings. The wings are also painted on their exterior, with figures of Gabriel and the Annunciate Mary. The central panel depicts the mystic marriage of St. Catherine, observed by the saints James, Lucy, Peter, and Paul, along with the local duke and duchess and their court attendants. The inner portion of the right wing features the saints Cyriacus, Nicholas, and Anthony Abbot. The inner surface of the left wing is occupied by St. Maurice and five martial companions.

The left panel (see figure 1.1) contains several noteworthy features. It belongs, first of all, to a relatively small group of German images of Maurice with his companions, made during the second and third decades of the 1500s. Perhaps the earliest of these is a 1511 panel by Georg Jhener von Orlamünde, which forms

Figure 1.1. Master of the Goslar Sibyls (attributed to), *Calenberg Altarpiece,* Boston, Museum of Fine Arts, c. 1515–20, detail of left panel *(St. Maurice and Companions).*

part of the high altar in the church of St. Maurice in Halle.[14] Halle had recently become one of the chief centers of the cult of Maurice thanks to Archbishop Ernst of Magdeburg (in office 1476–1513). The combination of sculptural and painted forms in the high altar was begun in the late 1400s. Maurice appears several times in sculpture and painting in the earlier phase of this project, but Jhener von Orlamünde's contribution was a group of three black African companions to the saint. Two other compositions of c. 1520, from Lüneburg and (perhaps) Münster (now in the Goudstikker Collection), include not only the companions but also Maurice himself, and are therefore more closely related to the group in the Calenberg Altarpiece.[15] This latter work (see figure 1.3), though it includes nearly three times as many companions as the Calenberg panel, was almost certainly inspired by it, and like the Calenberg panel it includes a range of complexions and physiognomies. The Goudstikker painting moves from very dark figures at the right to a medium-brown Maurice in the middle to comparatively light-skinned characters at the left, as if to acknowledge the variations of appearance among Africans. In the Calenberg panel, however, the companions all have emphatically dark skin, though only the soldier at the right, who wears no helmet and thus reveals all of his face, unquestionably displays each of the standard attributes of black African physiognomy as it was then understood by Europeans: dark complexion, full lips, wide nose, and tightly curled hair. By contrast, Maurice himself shows only a few of these traits: his skin is tawny and by far the lightest of the group, his nose is bony and projecting, his lips are hidden by a bushy moustache rarely worn by black Africans in European art, and his hair, though very curly, is much longer than the norm for European images of black Africans. Unlike the figure to the right, Maurice does not wear an earring, an embellishment that was one of the commonest ornamental attributes of black Africans in European artworks. There are in fact several images from this era of a black Maurice with *white* companions,[16] but it is most unusual to find what I would call a North African or Mediterranean Maurice with *black* companions.

Does this imagery reflect the artist's or the patrons' discomfort with the concept of a major black African saint? If so, it would have been an unusual response in German lands, where the black magus as well as the black Maurice (and the black Gregor Maurus) had been familiar for some time. Calenberg, however, is some distance from the German epicenter of the black Maurice cult in Magdeburg and Halle, as Gude Suckale-Redlefsen's mapping of black Maurice images makes clear.[17] Indeed, the more obvious question about the Maurice panel of the Calenberg Altarpiece is why it was commissioned at all, given that the saint was not the special object of cult veneration in this region, west of Cassel at the edge of Westphalia and Lower Saxony.

The answer to this question lies, not unexpectedly, in the work's patronage. The kneeling donor on the right side of the central panel (see figure 1.2) is Erich I (the Elder), Prince of Calenberg-Göttingen and Duke of Braunschweig-Lüneburg (ruled 1495–1540), a noted military commander belonging to a relatively minor branch of the Welf clan.[18] Erich's more major claim to artistic fame is that he may be the handsome knight in armor at the side of Emperor Maximilian in Dürer's *Feast of the Rose Garlands* of 1506; he was the emperor's most trusted general for many years.[19] In the Calenberg Altarpiece, however, he does not appear in martial dress. Neither he nor his blood relatives are especially connected to the cult of Maurice, but the situation is quite different with respect to his first wife, Catherine of Saxony, who kneels in what is actually a more honorific position—at the Virgin's favored right hand—on the left side of the central panel. Catherine (1468–1524) was the first cousin of Archbishop Ernst of Magdeburg, who, as we have already seen, promoted the cult of the black Maurice in Halle (as well as Magdeburg), and who commissioned both Hans Baldung's altarpiece with Maurice and Jhener von Orlamünde's panel with Maurice's black companions.[20] In 1521, Catherine's brother Duke Henry the Pious of Saxony named his

Figure 1.2. Master of the Goslar Sibyls (attributed to), *Calenberg Altarpiece,* Boston, Museum of Fine Arts, c. 1515–20, central panel *(Mystic Marriage of St. Catherine with Saints and Donors)*.

newborn son and eventual successor Maurice.²¹ Catherine and her entourage, rather than her husband Erich, occupy the zone that adjoins the St. Maurice panel at the left. A chronicler of 1584 informs us, in fact, that it was Catherine who had commissioned not only this altarpiece but also the Calenberg castle chapel on whose high altar it was installed.²² Oddly enough, Duke Erich seems to have had a taste for spouses whose relatives were devoted to Maurice; after Catherine's death in 1524, he immediately married Elizabeth of Brandenburg, the niece of Cardinal Albrecht of Brandenburg, who in 1513 had succeeded the above-mentioned Ernst as archbishop of Magdeburg. It was Albrecht, of course, who commissioned the most famous image of the black Maurice, by Grünewald, for display in Halle either just before or just after 1520, as well as a series of other images of Maurice, including reliquaries in precious metals.²³

The St. Maurice and companions panel of the Calenberg Altarpiece is certainly interesting, but the altarpiece's most remarkable representation of a black African figure is to be found elsewhere, on the central panel rather than on the left wing.

Figure 1.3. Master of the Goslar Sibyls (attributed to), *Calenberg Altarpiece,* Boston, Museum of Fine Arts, c. 1515–20, detail of central panel *(Catherine of Saxony and Her Ladies-in-Waiting).*

Among the handsome group of four ladies-in-waiting who kneel in prayerful posture behind Duchess Catherine in the central panel (see figure 1.3) is a person of color.[24] Her hair, like those of the other women, is hidden inside a tall, bulging container, but her dark complexion, upturned nose with a low bridge, and slightly fuller lips leave no doubt that she is intended as a person of black African descent. Her costume, like those of her three comrades, is less costly than that of the duchess but fundamentally similar, with a low neckline. Like the others, her hands have come together in prayer. No doubt responding to a finely drawn internal hierarchy among Catherine's ladies-in-waiting, the African woman is placed in the second pair at the extreme left, which also makes her function as something of a transition to the dark soldiers of the left wing. But it should be noted that she does not look toward them, and her contemporary rather than historical/sacred status is emphasized by her much smaller size as compared to Maurice and his companions.

In the above comments, I have assumed that this woman is a portrait of an actual lady-in-waiting to Duchess Catherine, though there is no published documentary evidence about such a person.[25] It need hardly be said that the presence of a black woman is extremely unusual in German and European donor portraits, even among the subsidiary figures flanking a principal donor. It is true that since the time of Frederick II European rulers and their relatives (in Italy, Catalonia, and France, for example) had at least intermittently adopted the practice of keeping black court servants, and this fashion was very much on the rise in the late 1400s and early 1500s, especially in northern Italy.[26] It is also true that artists had frequently depicted such African servants, both male and female, in attendance upon the masters and mistresses who owned or employed them. In most cases, the court servants appear either in secular works of art, like Mantegna's *camera picta* in Mantua of c. 1470, or in secular scenes in religious works of art for the laity, like the August calendar page in the Flemish Grimani Breviary of c. 1510–20.[27] There are also instances where a black court servant seems to have been inserted into a privately owned sacred subject as part of a deliberate "uploading" of particular court figures into the roles of biblical protagonists. This appears to be the case in Mantegna's 1492 drawing of *Judith and Her Maidservant with the Head of Holofernes*, which refers to Isabella d'Este, Marquise of Mantua, and one of her several black African retainers.[28]

Another miniature in the Grimani Breviary represents *The Queen of Sheba before Solomon* (figure 1.4), and if (as has been argued) the manuscript was commissioned by Margaret of Austria—daughter of Emperor Maximilian I, aunt of the future Emperor Charles V, and longtime governor of the Low Countries—there may be something of Margaret in the kneeling queen who venerates Solomon and his wisdom and offers him a gift.[29] In the early 1500s, the Queen of Sheba is hardly ever shown as a black African, but she frequently still has a black African figure in her entourage, as is the case here. We do not know if

Margaret employed a court servant of color, though there was a Christophle le More in her nephew Charles's entourage, and it has been suggested that he was the subject of a remarkable portrait (c. 1520–25) by Jan Mostaert of a black African man in European dress who wears a badge linked to a Christian pilgrimage site in the Low Countries on his fine hat.[30] We do know that Mostaert was employed by Margaret of Austria in the 1520s.[31]

The black woman behind the Queen of Sheba in the Grimani Breviary is part of a group of five ladies-in-waiting who indeed seem reminiscent of the four ladies behind Catherine of Saxony in the Calenberg Altarpiece. The woman with the dark complexion is pretty much in the same position as the African woman in the altarpiece, though of course all the women here are standing rather than kneeling. One difference is that the dark woman in the manuscript wears a turbanlike headgear—this may be a deliberately exoticizing touch—which would suit the Sheba and Solomon subject. A more important difference is that the manuscript's ladies-in-waiting are not donorlike, since they neither kneel nor put their hands together in prayer. Despite their similarities, the African figures in the Grimani illumination and the Calenberg Altarpiece represent two distinct approaches, and it is only in the Calenberg that we have a sense that the dark-skinned woman is engaged in the spiritual significance of the scene at which she is present.

Figure 1.4. Gerard Horenbout and others (?), *Solomon and the Queen of Sheba*, Grimani Breviary, Venice, Biblioteca Marciana, c. 1510–20.

Catherine of Saxony was, through her paternal grandmother, second cousin to Margaret of Austria,[32] but it is rather through Catherine's mother's family that we can build a reasonable circumstantial case that the black woman in the Calenberg Altarpiece denotes a particular person. Catherine's mother was Zedena of Bohemia, the daughter of the Bohemian king George Poděbrady and his wife Joanna of Rozmital. Catherine's great-uncle was the Bohemian noble Leo of Rozmital, who made a famous pilgrimage to Santiago de Compostella in 1465–1467, during which he also tried to advance the ambitious diplomatic interests of his brother-in-law King George.[33] After completing his pilgrimage, Leo continued on to Portugal, where he was warmly received. While visiting the city of Evora, he noted thousands of slaves (which the Portuguese had begun to obtain on their navigations down the west African coast starting in the 1440s), and in Braga, when King Afonso V asked Leo what gifts he would like, Leo requested two black slaves; Afonso's brother burst out laughing, since he saw such slaves as common possessions of little value.[34] Leo, however, was careful to bring the slaves home with him to Bohemia, where they were of course still rarities, and it seems likely that the woman depicted in the Calenberg Altarpiece was the daughter or more likely granddaughter of one or both of the slaves. (We have no explicit information about the gender of Leo's slaves, but we do know that in the 1490s the Duchess of Ferrara was "breeding" black court servants by hiring into her service a Venetian black gondolier and his pregnant wife.[35]) One of the other oddities of the Calenberg Altarpiece is that although Duchess Catherine kneels just behind her namesake St. Catherine of Alexandria, who symbolically receives a wedding ring from the infant Christ, she and her ladies-in-waiting are actually presented by St. James. James is dressed as a pilgrim and towers over the ladies as he gestures toward the head of the duchess. In light of Leo of Rozmital's famous pilgrimage to the shrine of St. James in Santiago de Compostella, the presence of St. James as well as the black lady-in-waiting below him may have been intended to allude to that part of the duchess's heritage.

But if the black woman in the Calenberg Altarpiece is a descendant of Leo's slaves, she had surely risen beyond her forebears in terms of social position. Her elaborate—but within her group unexceptional—costume and her pious posture and expression mark her as a courtier of some status. Her juxtaposition with the black companions of St. Maurice suggests that the ducal patrons believed it was appropriate for a black Christian to venerate pious Africans, but she is emphatically not marginalized by being shown as devoted only, or even particularly, to Maurice and his companions.

A slightly later Bavarian painting, by Barthel Beham, also includes two people of color of a contemporary type who demonstrate their Christian piety. This 1530 work depicts the discovery of the True Cross by St. Helena (figure 1.5), and once again a group of figures in distinctly contemporary dress and with the particularized features that suggest portraiture are included.[36] St. Helena herself is a portrait of the Bavarian Duchess Jacobäa of Baden. She is attended by a large group of elegantly dressed, kneeling ladies-in-waiting (figure 1.6), one of whom is a handsome black African woman; as in the Calenberg Altarpiece, this woman is in the second rank of female courtiers, and nearly but not quite at the farthest left of the panel.

A young black man is also present in the center of the composition. Though this work also includes a group of figures in Middle Eastern dress (especially at the far right), who are appropriate to the Holy Land setting of the narrative, the black lady-in-waiting shows no trace of the exotic in her costume. There may be a subtle reference to the iconography of the Queen of Sheba, since according to

Figure 1.5. Barthel Beham, *Discovery of the True Cross,* Munich, Alte Pinakothek, 1530.

medieval legend that queen had prophetically recognized a piece of wood later used for the True Cross and knelt before it, as St. Helena is doing in this image. But such an association with the Queen of Sheba story would not mean that the figure here is any less likely to denote an actual court servant, since the use of such court servants was, right from the start, deliberately meant to invoke the kind of cosmopolitan sovereignty embodied in historical/legendary figures like the Queen of Sheba.

I do not know if further archival research will be able to clarify the identity of the black German courtiers who, I have argued, are probably denoted by the African figures in the Calenberg Altarpiece and Beham's *Discovery of the True Cross*—though I certainly hope it will. Because so much of the history of the black presence in Europe has been deliberately or inadvertently effaced and forgotten, it is important to follow these leads. But, of course, not all of that history rests on the recuperation of individual lives; much of it rests on the construction of the meaning of black African identity by European writers and artists, which had long-term effects on intercontinental relations and the social roles that black Europeans and (later) black Americans were both forbidden and allowed. Individuals, however, could sometimes have an effect on the creation of new roles. In this context, it is useful to speculate whether the early presence of Christianized black African ladies-in-waiting at German Renaissance courts might have had something to do with the surprising (though short-lived) promotion of a sister saint to St. Maurice, St. Fidis.[37]

Fidis seems to have been the creation of Cardinal Albrecht of Brandenburg, for whom a reliquary bust of the saint was designed. The bust is gone, but a watercolor copy of c. 1525–27 survives (figure 1.7), which shows a young black woman in elaborate costume wearing the earrings that were then a marker of the exotic.[38] The cult of Fidis did not survive Albrecht, but it is worth noting that, as of 1525, he was the uncle of Erich I of Calenberg's new second wife, Elizabeth,

Figure 1.6. Barthel Beham, *Discovery of the True Cross,* Munich, Alte Pinakothek, 1530, detail.

and that a portrait of Albrecht (in the guise of the fourth-century Archbishop Macarios) appears next to Duchess Jacobäa of Baden (as St. Helena) and not far from her black lady-in-waiting in Beham's 1530 *Discovery of the True Cross* (see

Figure 1.7. Reliquary bust of St. Fidis, watercolor copy from the Halle *Heiltumsbuch*, Aschaffenburg, Hofbibliothek, 1525–27.

figure 1.6).[39] Perhaps Albrecht had begun to feel that there was a small but visible demographic constituency that needed a saint in its own likeness. Even in the Beham painting and the central panel of the Calenberg Altarpiece, with their more subordinated people of color, there is a chance that the visual presence of devout black Africans was intended not only to assert (to local elites and their subordinates) the increasing global authority of white European aristocratic and ecclesiastical hierarchies, but also to provide a recognizable reflection to contemporary black courtiers.[40]

Notes

1. Paul H. D. Kaplan, "Black Africans in Hohenstaufen Iconography," *Gesta* 26, no. 1 (1987): 29–36. Deep thanks to Shirin Fozi for bringing the key work in this essay to my attention.
2. Fulvio Zuliani, "Gli affreschi duecenteschi del palazzo abbaziale di San Zeno: un allestimento cerimoniale per Federico II," in *La Torre e il Palazzo Abbaziale di San Zeno,* ed. Anna Zangarini (Verona, Italy: Banca Popolare di Verona, 1992), 11–42, pl. 1, figs. 2, 6, 7; Fulvio Zuliani, "Gli affreschi del Palazzo Abbaziale di San Zeno a Verona," in *Federico II: Immagine e potere,* ed. Maria Stella Calò Mariani and Raffaella Cassano (Venice: Marsilio, 1995), 112–15; Paul H. D. Kaplan, "Introduction to the New Edition," in *The Image of the Black in Western Art,* new ed., ed. Henry Louis Gates Jr. and David Bindman (Cambridge, MA: Belknap Press of Harvard University Press, 2010), 2:1:1–30; hereafter referred to as IBWA 2:1.
3. IBWA 2:1:150–55; Gude Suckale-Redlefsen, *Mauritius: Der heilige Mohr/The Black Saint Maurice* (Houston: Menil Foundation, 1987), 14, 19–23, 36–47, 150, 158–61; Virginia Roehrig Kaufmann, "The Magdeburg Rider: An Aspect of the Reception of Frederick II's Roman Revival North of the Alps," in *Intellectual Life at the Court of Frederick II Hohenstaufen,* ed. William Tronzo, Studies in the History of Art 44 (Washington DC: National Gallery of Art, 1994), 62–88; Virginia Roehrig Kaufmann, "Magdeburg Rider and the Law," in *Kunst im Reich Kaiser Friedrichs II: von Hohenstaufen,* Akten des internationalen Kolloquiums (Rheinisches Landesmuseum Bonn, 2. bis 4. Dezember 1994), ed. Kai Kappel, Dorothee Kemper, and Alexander Knaak (Munich: Klinkhardt & Biermann, 1996), 127–36.
4. Cologne, St. Gereon, c. 1316; Suckale-Redlefsen, *Mauritius,* 152 (pl. 3), 274.
5. Klosterneuburg, Museum des Chorherrenstiftes; IBWA 2:1:120, 123, fig. 103.
6. Early 1400s; unpublished.
7. Paul H. D. Kaplan, *The Rise of the Black Magus in Western Art* (Ann Arbor, MI: UMI Research Press, 1985).
8. Berlin, Gemäldegalerie; IBWA 2:1:175, 179, fig. 147; IBWA 2:2:195–97, fig. 173; Suckale-Redlefsen, *Mauritius,* 84–85, 211–12. Another unusual combination of a black St. Maurice and a black magus is found in Hans Mülich's 1572 altarpiece in Dingolstadt (Liebfrauenmünster), 1572, where there are also black African servants and observers in the scenes of *Supper in the House of Simon* and *Christ Performing a Miracle.*
9. Ruth Mellinkoff, *Outcasts: Signs of Otherness in Northern European Art of the Late Middle Ages,* 2 vols. (Berkeley: University of California Press, 1993), 1:li; see also 1:126–27, 230, and 2:pl. 6.57.
10. Vienna, Fürstliche Liechtenstein'sche Kunstsammlung; Friedrich Winkler, *Die Zeichnungen Albrecht Dürers,* 4 vols. (Berlin: Deutscher Verein für Kunstwissenschaft, 1936–1939), 2:135, fig. 469.

11. Paolo Giovio, *Elogi degli uomini illustri*, ed. Franco Minonzio (Turin, Italy: G. Einaudi, 2006), 627.
12. Florence, Uffizi, and Vienna, Albertina; IBWA 2:2:278–79, fig. 264.
13. 2005.1951-4; http://www.mfa.org/collections/object/the-calenberg-altarpiece-469980; IBWA 2:1:187, fig. 159; Suckale-Redlefsen, *Mauritius*, 79–80, 240, cat. 138; Hans Georg Gmelin, *Spätgotische Tafelmalerei in Niedersachsen und Bremen* (Munich: Deutscher Kunstverlag, 1974), cat. 148, 442–48. Thanks to Ronni Baer and Frederick Ilchman for making it possible for me to study the altarpiece while it was in conservation.
14. IBWA 2:1:175, 184, fig. 153; Suckale-Redlefsen, *Mauritius*, 212–13, cat. 99.
15. Museum für das Fürstentum Lüneburg: Suckale-Redlefsen, *Mauritius*, 252–53, cat. 162; and IBWA 2:1:186–87, fig. 157. Goudstikker Collection: Suckale-Redlefsen, *Mauritius*, 103, 240–41; and Peter C. Sutton, *Reclaimed: Paintings from the Collection of Jacques Goudstikker* (New Haven, CT: Bruce Museum, 2008), 104–107, cat. 8.
16. See, for example, the 1524 watercolor by Nikolaus Glockendon (Aschaffenburg, Hofbibliothek), of c. 1525–27; IBWA 2:1:178, 180, fig. 149.
17. Suckale-Redlefsen, *Mauritius*, endpapers; see also IBWA 2:1:298.
18. Edgar Kalthoff and Alheidis von Rohr, with Heinrich Sievers, eds., *Calenberg: Von der Burg zum Fürstentum. Herrschaft und Kultur in Zentralniedersachsen zwischen 1300 und 1700* (Hanover, Germany: Historisches Museum am Hohen Ufer, 1979), 15, 17–20.
19. Prague, Narodni Galerie; Joseph Heller, *Das Leben und Werke Albrecht Dürers*, 2 vols. (Bamberg, Germany: Kunz, 1827), 2:254; Joseph Neuwirth, *Albrecht Dürers Rosenkranzfest* (Leipzig, Germany: G. Freytag, 1885), 54; Fedja Anzelewsky, *Albrecht Dürer, das malerische Werk* (Berlin: Deutscher Verlag für Kunstwissenschaft, 1971), 196, fig. 99; Isolde Lübbeke, "Dürer's Visualization of an Imagined Community," in *Albrecht Dürer: The Feast of the Rose Garlands*, ed. Olga Kotková (Prague: Národní galerie v Praze, 2006), 15–38, 17n9, 90. Some scholars have declined to put a name to this figure, and others have offered other names, but Erich's remains the most popular.
20. Catherine's father was Albrecht I, Duke of Saxony, whose brother, the Elector Ernst (1441–1486), was the father of Archbishop Ernst.
21. Duke Maurice, though he eventually became a Lutheran, commissioned an image of the black St. Maurice with his own features, in a curious, pious "blackface" fusion of elite portraiture and exoticism; Hans Krell, Leipzig, Rathaus, Museum für Geschichte der Stadt Leipzig, 1553; see Suckale-Redlefsen, *Mauritius*, 114, 265, cat. 183; Esther Schreuder, "'Blacks' in Court Culture in the Period 1300–1900: Propaganda and Consolation," in *Black Is Beautiful: Rubens to Dumas*, ed. Esther Schreuder and Elmer Kolfin (Zwolle, Netherlands: De Nieuwe Kerk, 2008), 25. Through his daughter Anna and her husband William the Silent, Duke Maurice was the grandfather of Maurice of Nassau.
22. Heinrich Bünting, *Braunschweig-Lüneburgische Chronik* (Magdeburg, Germany, 1584), part 2, 63v.
23. The Grünewald picture is in Munich, Alte Pinakothek; see IBWA 2:1:178, 182–83, 189–92, figs. 151–52, 162–67; Suckale-Redlefsen, *Mauritius*, 94–99, 214–20, cats. 102–103.
24. Cited but not illustrated in IBWA 2:1:284n301; and Suckale-Redlefsen, *Mauritius*, 240.
25. Gmelin, *Spätgotische Tafelmalerei*, 445, may have been the first to notice the dark-skinned figure, but he offers a strained interpretation, claiming that the woman depicts the deceased (and for that reason blackened) daughter (1492) of a different duke and duchess; this alternative identification of the principal patrons has been discarded.
26. Kaplan, *Black Magus*, 15; Schreuder, "'Blacks' in Court Culture," 20–21.
27. Mantegna: Mantua, Palazzo Ducale; IBWA 2:2:213, fig. 190. Grimani Breviary: Venice, Biblioteca Nazionale Marciana, f. 8v (attributed to Gerard Horenbout); Giorgio Ferrari, Mario Salmi, and Gian Lorenzo Mellini, *Breviario Grimani*, 2nd ed. (Milan: Electa, 1979), pl. 15.

28. Florence, Uffizi; Paul H. D. Kaplan, "Isabella d'Este and Black African Women," in *Black Africans in Renaissance Europe*, ed. T. F. Earle and K. J. P. Lowe (Cambridge: Cambridge University Press, 2005), 125–54.
29. F. 75r (artist uncertain); Ferrari, Salmi, and Mellini, *Breviario Grimani*, pl. 33.
30. Amsterdam, Rijksmuseum; Friso Lammertse and Jeroen Giltaij, *Vroege Hollanders: Schilderkunst van de late Middeleeuwen* (Rotterdam, Netherlands: Museum Boijmans Van Beuningen, 2008), 176–78, cat. 27; Jos Koldeweij, *Foi & bonne fortune: parure et devotion en Flandre médiévale* (Arnhem, Netherlands: Terra, 2006), 47, 54–57; Jan Piet Filedt Kok and Marieke de Winkel, "Een portret van een zwarte Afrikaanse man door Jan Mostaert," *Bulletin van het Rijksmuseum* 53 (2005): 381–412; Ernst van den Boogaart, "Christophle le More, lijfwacht van Karel V?, *Bulletin van het Rijksmuseum* 53 (2005): 413–34; Schreuder and Kolfin, eds., *Black Is Beautiful*, 255, 268–69, cat. 72; Kate Lowe, "The Stereotyping of Black Africans in Renaissance Europe," in *Black Africans*, ed. Earle and Lowe, 17–47, 44–47; Jean-Michel Massing in IBWA (2011), 3:2:216–17, fig. 138.
31. Koldeweij, *Foi & bonne fortune*, 54.
32. Her paternal grandmother, Duke Albrecht's mother, was another Habsburg Margaret, the sister of Emperor Frederick III, the grandfather of our Margaret of Austria.
33. Karel Hrdina, ed., *Commentarius brevis et iucundus itineris atque peregrinationis, pietatis et religionis causa susceptae ab Illustri et Magnifico Domino, Domino Leone, libero barone de Rosmital et Blatna* (Prague: In Officina Orbis, 1951); Malcolm Letts, *The Travels of Leo of Rozmital through Germany, Flanders, England, France, Spain, Portugal and Italy 1465–1467* (Cambridge: Cambridge University Press, 1957), with the two contemporary accounts of the voyage by Tetzel and Schaseck; John M. Klassen, *Warring Maidens, Captive Wives, and Hussite Queens: Women and Men at War and at Peace in Fifteenth-Century Bohemia* (New York: Columbia University Press, 1999), 242–59.
34. Letts, *Travels*, 106, 120; and Hrdina, *Commentarius brevis*, 69–70, 83.
35. Paul H. D. Kaplan, "Titian's Laura Dianti and the Origins of the Motif of the Black Page in Portraiture," part 1, "The Vogue for Black Servants in Renaissance Italy," *Antichità Viva* 21, no. 1 (1982): 11–18; Paul H. D. Kaplan, "Titian's Laura Dianti and the Origins of the Motif of the Black Page in Portraiture," part 2, "From Laura Dianti's Page to Othello and Van Dyck," *Antichità Viva* 21, no. 4 (1982): 10–18; Paul H. D. Kaplan, "Italy, 1490–1700," in IBWA (2010), 3:1:102, 107.
36. Munich, Alte Pinakothek; Gisela Goldberg, *Die Alexanderschlacht und die Historienbilder des bayerischen Herzogs Wilhelm IV. und seiner Gemahlin Jacobaea für die Münchner Residenz*, Bayerische Staatsgemäldesammlungen Kunstler und Werke 5 (Munich: Hirmer, 1983), 14–19; Volkmar Greiselmayer, *Kunst und Geschichte: Die Historienbilder Herzog Wilhelms IV. von Bayern und seiner Gemahlin Jacobäa: Versuch einer Interpretation* (Berlin: Gebr. Mann, 1996), 151–56; Kurt Löcher, *Barthel Beham: Ein Maler aus dem Dürerkreis* (Munich: Deutscher Kunstverlag, 1999), 95–100, 185, 186.
37. IBWA 2:1:192; Suckale-Redlefsen, *Mauritius*, 89, 91.
38. From the Halle *Heiltumsbuch*, Aschaffenburg, Hofbibliothek, f. 376v; IBWA 2:1:192–93, fig. 167 (and also a woodcut image of Fidis, fig. 164); Thomas Schauerte and Andreas Tacke, eds., *Der Kardinale Albrecht von Brandenburg: Renaissancefürst und Mäzen*, 2 vols. (Regensburg, Germany: Schnell + Steiner, 2006), 1:93, cat. 27. The Schaurte and Tacke volumes include many images of the black St. Maurice, but also some more unusual images, including a miniature of the reconsecration of a church after Easter, with a prominent black African woman (?) as an observer, 2:335, fig. 6; see also Josef Hofmann and Hans Thurn, *Die Handschriften der Hofbibliothek Aschaffenburg* (Aschaffenburg, Germany: Geschichts- und Kunstvereins Aschaffenburg e.V., 1978), 29–34, esp. 30 (Ms. 10, Missale Hallense, f. 162v). Another utterly remarkable German image of a person of color, commissioned by Albrecht's brother Johannes, Elector of

Brandenburg, and painted by Hans Hauser, appears in a Nuremberg manuscript of 1520–21, now in Krakow, Biblioteka Jagiellonska, Berol. Lat. 4o, 322, f. 1v. This volume consists of two astrological treatises, and the author portrait of the writer of one of the treatises, here called Zebel but best known today as Sahl ibn Bishr, depicts a scholarly black African busily penning the words of his text, with a pair of spectacles perched on his nose. Zebel/Sahl was a Jew writing in Arabic who flourished in the early ninth century under the patronage of several Muslim princes in the Middle East. I will consider this miniature—an extremely rare example of a European image depicting a person of black African descent engaged in writing—in more detail in a forthcoming essay: for now, see Ulrich Merkl, *Buchmalerei in Bayern in der ersten Hälfte des 16. Jahrhunderts; Spätblüte und Endzeit einer Gattung* (Regensburg, Germany: Schnell + Steiner, 1999), 476–79, cat. 133, pl. 468; Francis J. Carmody, *Arabic Astronomical and Astrological Sciences in Latin Translation: A Critical Bibliography* (Berkeley: University of California Press, 1956), 40–46.
39. Goldberg, *Die Alexanderschlacht,* 19; Löcher, *Barthel Beham,* 96.
40. A Tuscan painting of the Coronation of the Virgin (Esztergom, Kereszteny Museum) from the end of the 1400s with a single donor who is a black African man demonstrates that it was possible for such European pictures to be commissioned by and largely addressed to Afro-Europeans; see Kate Lowe, "Black Africans' Religious and Cultural Assimilation to, or Appropriation of, Catholicism in Italy, 1470–1520," *Renaissance and Reformation/Renaissance et Réforme* 31, no. 2 (2008): 67–86, esp. 74–79, figs. 1–2; IBWA 2:1:27–29, figs. I.12–13. For some interesting works of a related type from the late 1400s in Perugia, see Philine Helas, "Schwarz unter Weissen. Zur Repräsentation von Afrikanern in der italienischen Kunst des 15. Jahrhunderts," in *Fremde in der Stadt: Ordnungen, Repräsentationen und soziale Praktiken (13.–15. Jahrhundert),* ed. Peter Bell, Dirk Suckow, and Gerhard Wolf (Frankfurt: Peter Lang, 2010), 301–31, esp. 314–21.

Chapter Two

THE BLACK DIASPORA IN EUROPE IN THE FIFTEENTH AND SIXTEENTH CENTURIES, WITH SPECIAL REFERENCE TO GERMAN-SPEAKING AREAS

Kate Lowe

The topic of the black diaspora in Germany is timely and important, raising a whole host of questions that can as yet be formulated but not satisfactorily answered. This is particularly the case in the initial period of the diaspora in the fifteenth and sixteenth centuries, after black slaves were brought to southern Europe from the west coast of Africa in significant numbers from the 1440s onward. These include the most basic question of how the history of the black diaspora in German-speaking areas fits in with what is known of the trajectory of the black diaspora in southern Europe, and how it differs; and another very basic question of how slavery was practiced in countries where it was not supposed to exist. There has been pioneering and crucial scholarship in the field—from Hans Werner Debrunner, Peter Martin, Allison Blakely, and Paul Kaplan, for example—but only now is the topic's importance being universally recognized. This chapter will focus on three different categories of black Africans in German-speaking areas, fictive, notional, and "real," and these categories will be placed in a European context in order to illuminate their meaning.[1]

Before starting, a few comments on terminology are in order. First, the term "black African" is being used here as a construct, set in opposition to "white European." Its usage does not imply a belief in the label of "black," as "black" is a reductive signifier that often does not even signify skin color. Indeed, the full range of sub-Saharan skin colors was of interest to German speakers in the fifteenth and sixteenth centuries. Second, in most cases in this chapter where the term "black African" has been used, it could denote a first-, second-, or third-

---

Notes from this chapter begin on page 53.

generation person of African descent. Third, the word "Moor," which is frequently used in all western European languages, is a very imprecise descriptor originally relating to religion, and nothing about skin color can be deduced from its usage. Moors could be "white," "brown," "black," or anything in between.

The Performance of Fictive Blackness

Within the context of Renaissance Europe, the very complex theme of what was understood by blackness in relation to the human form requires attention. This chapter attempts to address this by looking at concrete examples of moments or occurrences when blackness can be seen most clearly to have been understood as different from whiteness. One of the most intriguing renditions of Renaissance blackness is to be found on those occasions when white Europeans decided to "black up" and depict themselves as fictive black Africans. There are myriad examples of this in Europe, both in pageants and in plays and masques on stage. Some of the best documented of these were in England, where stage paint or primitive makeup gave way in the early sixteenth century to more expensive transformative materials such as black lawn and velvet. The Draper's Company of London enacted a Midsummer pageant in 1521 that featured a King of the Moors and some "Moryans" ("Moryan/Murian" was the word used in parts of northern Europe as synonymous with "Moor"),[2] who appear to have worn blackened leather or cloth.[3] But the puzzle still remains—what did white Europeans think they were doing representing themselves as fictive black Africans in a period when black skin had so many negative connotations? Perhaps it was simply as a form of display that some journeymen from the guilds of Konstanz in southwest Germany at the ceremonial entry of King Maximilian I in 1492 thought of as "blacking up,"[4] thereby presenting a sort of "tableau vivant."[5] The chronicler Christoph Schulthaiss gives the setting: the journeymen had built a very large ship, placed a yew tree on it, and fastened a brushwood hut to the tree. Inside the hut there was a handsome Moorish "Rautz" [warrior?]. Everyone on the ship was naked and "blacked up." As no further information is available, one can only hypothesize as to its possible meaning. Maybe the representation was intended to be comic, maybe it was a projection of life in a "primitive" Africa, or perhaps there was a political or cultural catalyst—but it seems a bizarre choice of display, "disguise," or impersonation at that particular moment in that particular place.

The performance of fictive blackness appears to have remained attractive even in places and on occasions when real black Africans were to hand. Juana of Castile, later the mother of Charles V, was greeted by a series of pageants at her triumphal entry into Brussels in 1496. An illustration of one of these pageants showed an "Ethiopian" princess or queen surrounded by wild men with clubs.[6]

This would have been a much more "usual" representation of blackness. More interesting, because more open-ended, is the image of *King Solomon and the Four Cardinal Virtues,* which includes a black courtier, an illustration of part of the pageant put on by the resident Italian merchants for Charles V's entry into Bruges in 1515 (figure 2.1).

Figure 2.1. *King Solomon and the Four Cardinal Virtues,* miniature in Remy Du Puys, *La tryumphante et solonelle entrée de Monsieur Charles en Bruges 1515,* Vienna, Österreichische Nationalbibliothek, Cod. Vind. 2591.

This spectacular miniature appears in the manuscript of Remy Du Puys, "La tryumphante et solonelle entrée de Monsieur Charles en Bruges 1515," in the Österreichische Nationalbibliothek in Vienna.[7] The scene enacted by the Italian merchants has been interpreted as a flattering symbol of the young Charles. The presence of a black courtier, one of only six represented and the only one to be represented in profile, is unusual (figure 2.2).

The artist's skill appears to lie in decoration rather than in characterization or individualization—there are no portraits here—so the black courtier differs only in skin color and in hair type from his white peers, who are themselves presented in a uniform fashion. The African's hair is tightly curled and dark while theirs is straighter and longer, but he is not represented with other, standard "African" physiognomic features. How should he be interpreted? Was he a fictive black African, a white servant with short hair "blacked up" for the occasion, engaged in a performance of blackness? Had the Italian merchants included him for historical or intellectual reasons, because of Solomon's association with Sheba, who is often portrayed as black? Or was he imagined by the artist for aesthetic reasons? Alternatively, was he "real," a slave in the household of one of the Italian merchants, brought in to participate in the pageant because his obviously different skin color accentuated whiteness by contrast and enlivened the spectacle? The absence of African physiognomic traits could merely reflect the artist's ignorance or inability to paint them. Finally, is it possible that, fictive, notional, or "real," the black African was included in the tableau because Charles V had a "real" black courtier, and that the Italians were here making a topical allusion to him? This barrage of possibilities is reminiscent of those raised by the painting dated c. 1520–30 and attributed to Jan Mostaert, currently called *Portrait of an African Man* and previously known as *Portrait of a Moor*,[8] now in the Rijksmuseum in Amsterdam. But although both images probably represent black courtiers, the Mostaert painting is a genuine portrait, and there is no question whatsoever that the "sitter" was from sub-Saharan Africa. In terms of historical context for the black courtier in the Bruges entry pageant, there undoubtedly were black servants and slaves in the Low Countries

Figure 2.2. Remys Du Puys, *King Solomon and the Four Cardinal Virtues*, 1515, detail of black courtier.

at the end of the fifteenth and beginning of the sixteenth centuries,[9] especially in the households of merchants from southern Europe.[10] Thus, "real" Africans—and what "real" blackness looked like—were known. However, this knowledge may have been put to the side for this representation, and the black courtier may have been fictive. All through the Renaissance, and in all parts of Europe, representations of fictive black Africans continued to appear alongside realistic depictions (Paul Kaplan's work on the black king in depictions of the Three Magi attests to this); so that it must be acknowledged that fictive blackness in many instances was seen, not as a substitute, but as preferable to "real" blackness.[11]

Projecting Fictive Blackness

The line between supposedly benign fictive representations of blackness and projecting fictive blackness as a joke onto high-ranking individuals was one that was costly to cross, especially if the projection—correctly or not—was interpreted as an insult. In 1531, Maurice Ferber, the bishop of Warmia (then in Prussia and known as Ermland but now in Poland), interpreted the inclusion of a fictive black bishop in the Carnival masque or play performed in Elbing/Elbląg, a Hanseatic town, on 21 February as a direct insult against his person, on account of St. Maurice's association with the color black.[12] According to the narrative of his martyrdom (*passio*), Maurice was a third-century Roman who commanded a legion levied in the Thebaid, the province of the Roman Empire on the Upper Nile whose capital was Thebes. Maurice and his legionnaires were baptized Christians who either refused to persecute the Christians in what is now Switzerland (according to the fifth-century *passio*) or refused to sacrifice to the Roman gods before battle (according to a ninth-century interpolation), and were massacred for their disobedience.[13] The history of the depiction of St. Maurice as a black saint in German-speaking areas is long and convoluted, peaking in German art of the late fifteenth and early sixteenth centuries.[14] Yet few images address the issue of black skin color or performing human blackness in quite the same way as the unidentified "South German Master" (more likely north German) in his painting *St. Maurice and His Companions of the Theban Legion,* dated to c. 1515–20 (figure 2.3).[15]

Maurice stands at the center of the composition, dressed in a fur-lined outer garment over armor, and wearing a gold chain on his chest, from which a large gilt object hangs. Maurice's headgear is suggestive of his status as a Moor, but at the same time is interestingly different. Instead of the "normal" heraldic representation of a Moor's head, where a black man is represented with a white cloth headband bound around his forehead and tied at the back, Maurice is portrayed with a pale golden or yellow cloth tied under his chin, keeping in place a large red hat with a pale golden feather. The jut of his chin, too, seems exaggerated. Even

Figure 2.3. South German Master, *St. Maurice and His Companions of the Theban Legion*, c. 1515–20, oil on panel, 68 x 70 cm, private collection of Marei von Saher, United States.

in the German painting tradition, where exaggeration is the norm and people as a consequence often appear grotesque, Maurice and his companions seem marked by their ugliness. His surrounding legionnaires wear an assortment of very brightly colored clothes, often with multicolored stripes (stripes were often used to denote Africanness). In what is probably the most striking feature of this unusual painting, their complexions encompass the whole range of "nonwhite" skin, with Maurice's own skin color balanced in the middle between lighter shades on the left and darker shades on the right. The legionnaires to Maurice's left and right both wear armor—one carries a lance and the other a sword, symbols of Christian martyrdom; both also wear prominent gold earrings, another telltale signifier of Africanness.[16] Is it safe to assume that this artist was trying to convey a sense of the variety of skin color of Africans but also a sense of the homogeneity of facial features? Or was the artist trying to achieve something more by this representation of black people?

One point is certain: in this period, the name Maurice in German-speaking areas could be associated with blackness and black skin, and it was this certainty that led to Maurice Ferber's formal complaint. Ferber was born in the Hanseatic town of Danzig in 1471 and obtained a law degree from the University of Siena in 1515;[17] he was promoted to the bishopric in 1523 and died in 1537.[18] The story of his complaint unfolded in the spring and summer of 1531, both illuminating and complicating an analysis of the performance of blackness. On 31 March, Ferber wrote to the vicar of Elbing that he had been informed by Achacy Freundt, canon of Ermland and provost of Elbing, of "a certain comedy, performed by several Elbing citizens at the time of the last Carnival, during which the pope, the cardinals and especially the bishop were publicly ridiculed."[19] He demanded to be sent a list of the people involved. One of his difficulties may have been the fact that Ermland remained Catholic, in the midst of an area that had turned Protestant. On 8 May at the end of the deliberations of the General Diet of Royal Prussia, Ferber complained again, claiming that he had been depicted as a Moorish bishop and mocked during Carnival. The mayor of Elbing replied that the customary Carnival masque had been organized without the knowledge or permission of the town council, but assured Ferber that it was normal, as on a previous occasion another bishop had been impersonated.[20] On 9 July, Ferber wrote to Peter Tomicki, the bishop of Kraków, finally explaining why he was so incensed:

> What kind of disgraceful spectacle was exhibited at Elbing publicly and openly at the festival [Carnival] that has just passed, your most reverend Lordship will see from the enclosed sheet of paper. For although everyone was masked so that, [if] challenged, they could the more easily disavow, yet nonetheless, so that they might make me the more recognizable, since my name is Maurice and Maurice the Martyr is usually painted black or an Ethiopian color, they represented my person under the aspect of an Ethiopian bishop. Since this deed was done to dishonor the whole ecclesiastical establishment, though in the first instance, to disgrace my person, the deed would set a very bad example if it were to remain unpunished.[21]

Ferber maintained that he would take his complaint to Sigismund I, the King of Poland, if he did not receive satisfaction. Whether he managed to prosecute the Carnival participants remains unknown, but everyone except Freundt refused to cooperate with him.

Carnival, as is well known, was an occasion when the world was turned upside down and mockery of establishment figures was to be expected. It is known that many of the upper classes interpreted Carnival rituals as "subversive,"[22] and depicting a bishop as black was a step too far for Ferber, who was obviously enraged at the pun on his name. However, in the European context, it is striking that the first black Catholic bishop, formerly Ndoadidiki Ne-Kinu, baptized Henrique (a son of the ruler of the Congo, Nzinga Mbemba, baptized Afonso), had been appointed in 1518,[23] so a black bishop already existed. One way of reading this narrative, therefore, is that once again an encounter takes place between the real and the fictive, in which the fictive carries more weight than the real.

The offense must have been the criminal one of insult. According to Trevor Dean, insult across the Italian peninsula operated by overlaying allegations about sex, defecation, and rottenness onto the body, the devil, and animals.[24] In the case of Elbing, therefore, it seems likely that the insult lay in depicting Ferber's body as black; this was "an enactment of verbal insult, a translation into visual … form of the defilement that verbal insult sought to effect."[25] Ferber may have been particularly upset because the insult was pointed in a socially upward manner,[26] yet that would have been true of almost all Carnival escapades.

This story, in which a white person internalizes being represented as a fictive black person as a form of attack, focuses on a moment when blackness can be seen to be understood as different from whiteness. It might be objected that Ferber himself, even though he could articulate the connection between his name and blackness, did not accept it (and immediately labeled it as an insult), and there is a world of difference between comments that one can make about oneself and comments that it is acceptable for other people to make. But even if the difficulties of analysis appear to lie in the context of the representation, it is the combination of the external imposition and enactment of blackness with the context that made the behavior inflammatory.

Notional Blackness

A further important rendition of blackness in relation to the human form can be found by examining one category of notional blackness: the heraldic device of the so-called Moor's head. Many European families in the Middle Ages had incorporated Moors' heads into their coats of arms, and others in the fifteenth and sixteenth centuries had been allocated coats of arms that included Moors' heads as a reflection of their involvement in the slave trade. Two clear examples of this latter phenomenon were two early slave traders. The first was the Portuguese Fernão Gomes, ennobled in 1474, whose name was changed to Gomes da Mina and whose coat of arms contained three Moors' heads, all with gold necklaces, earrings, and nose rings.[27] The second was Sir John Hawkins, about whom a written blazon of 1565 explained that his new crest—a half-length bust of a bound Moor wearing gold earrings—had been chosen precisely on account of his victory against the Moors.[28]

The Tucher family of patricians from Nuremberg could serve as an example of a German family from the first category, whose coat of arms incorporated a

Moor's head as a heraldic device. What this signified for the family is unclear, although it is indisputable that many white families were clearly attached to their black devices and emblems. In their family book, the Tucherbuch, of 1592 is a series of miniatures of "portraits" of family members, including one of Anton II Tucher (1458–1524) and his wife Anna Reich, who were married in 1475;[29] a great many of them are represented with their coat of arms.[30] The Tucher Moor's head does not wear the headband that is characteristic of many heraldic Moors' heads. What is important here is that there is a standard depiction of the Tucher head across several centuries and many types of media. Heraldic designs depicted on glass were common in Renaissance Germany,[31] and in the Victoria and Albert Museum in London is a small, sixteenth-century stained glass medallion containing the distinctive Tucher arms (figure 2.4).[32]

The most striking aspect is the physiognomy of the Moor's head, with its exaggerated features. This exaggerated notional rendition of blackness, or notional

Figure 2.4. Tucher arms, stained glass medallion, 1500–99, London, Victoria and Albert Museum.

blackness, seems to be an essential element of the heraldic Moor's head in coats of arms where the families apparently have no connection to Africa or the slave trade.

This does not seem to be true of heraldic Moors' heads that have escaped the confines of their coats of arms, even if they are still being used to signal a family connection. A good example of this is Christoph Jamnitzer's gilt silver drinking vessel fashioned in the shape of a Moor's head, made in the same city of Nuremberg between 1594 and 1602 (figure 2.5).[33]

This beautiful object sports an extraordinary headband chased with eight letter Ts, perhaps proclaiming a connection to the Florentine family, the Pucci; the Pucci coat of arms was a Moor's head with a headband charged with three Ts,

Figure 2.5. Detail, Christoph Jamnitzer, *Moor's Head*, Nürnberg, c. 1600 (silver, rock crystal), Munich, Bayerisches Nationalmuseum.

which had originally been hammers, as the Pucci were in the carpenters' guild.[34] These commonplace renditions of notional blackness were not just representations but must also have had an impact on expectations of, and judgments about, sub-Saharan African appearance in the fifteenth and sixteenth centuries.

"Real" Black Africans in Europe

Given the cultural baggage associated with fictive and notional blackness, actual black Africans or people of sub-Saharan African descent caught up in the early diaspora in Europe who ended up in German-speaking areas during the fifteenth and sixteenth centuries cannot have had an easy time. They appear to have left traces especially in two distinct environments—the Hanseatic towns and princely or ducal courts—but these traces are often extremely fragmentary, partial survivals from baptismal, fiscal, or court records.

The difficulty in seeing a rounded picture when only one or two snippets of information from a life are known is clearly illustrated by the story of a female Murian who lived in the household of Henrik Lambert in the German parish of Stockholm at the end of the sixteenth century. Stockholm was a Hanseatic city with a substantial German population and an important German church. Swedish historians have interpreted the word "Murian" to indicate someone with black skin, but there is no certainty that this woman was black, because the term "Moor"/"Murian" is imprecise in all languages. In Sweden, as in other countries in northern Europe such as England, slavery was not legal, and yet "slaves" continued to be brought into the country and were treated in exactly the same manner as they had been when they were living with their "owners" in countries where slavery *was* legal. Slavery had been abolished in Sweden in the late thirteenth and early fourteenth century, nor was there real serfdom, so all Swedes were, in fact, personally free. It is not possible, therefore, to know the status of Henrik's Murian, although it is most likely that she was a slave. Records of 12 March 1598 of the Cathedral chapter merely note that Henrik Lambert had committed fornication with his Murian and she had given birth to a child, who had been baptized by Casparus, the parish priest of the German parish. Black female slaves across Europe must often have been subjected to forced sex, yet affective relationships could also develop. Nothing is known about this woman prior to this date, and the subsequent fates of the Murian and the child are also unknown. The tax records of 1613 reveal that Henrik was living with his wife, a son, and a maid (*pija*),[35] but there is no way of knowing whether this maid was the Murian. It is unlikely, as slaves who had become pregnant in southern Europe usually earned the disfavor of the wife and were sold, while the children of the slaves were left where possible at a nearby orphanage.[36] But it is clear from southern Europe that once a particular person or family had acquired a black slave, when that black slave died or was freed, a replacement black slave—as opposed to a white slave—was usually purchased.[37]

Hanseatic German merchants with black slaves could be the northern European equivalent of New Christians (Iberian Jews who were forced to convert to Christianity) with black slaves. Everywhere that New Christians are recorded, so too are their black slaves, and converted Jews must have taken their Iberian slave-owning mentality with them when they left Portugal. German Hanseatic merchants may have been another networked group with a similar interest in black slaves, both as domestic servants and as a trading commodity. The case of Caspar van Senden, a merchant from Lübeck, shows how black slaves could be used as a form of merchandise. An English privy council order of 1596 and a draft proclamation of 1601 name him in connection with a scheme to collect "Negroes and blackamoors" from across England and take them to Lisbon to offset eighty-nine English people he had brought to England after procuring their release from Spain.[38] The complex mercantile, financial, religious, and political contexts of this case made the project by van Senden less than successful, and, furthermore, van Senden may have had another agenda—"rescuing English prisoners in order to help Catholic spies."[39] But it is clear that the rounding up of numbers of black people in England would have allowed him to complete an exchange in human merchandise.

The second environment where black Africans were found in German-speaking areas was at princely and ducal courts, where the most obvious group of slave owners was the nobility. Black slaves must have been a fairly frequent sight at major and minor courts and in aristocratic households, as they were at such courts and in such households across Europe. For example, in 1596 a "blackmoore" on a camel was sent by the Landgrave of Hessen to meet Henry Clinton, the second Earl of Lincoln, who was Queen Elizabeth I's ambassador.[40] In another instance, the princeling Hans von Munster from Nuremberg brought two "Moors" to his hometown in 1589 with a great display of pomp.[41] Sometimes black slaves arrived at court in a shipment of exotica—as, for instance, the small black slave sent from Spain to Rudolf II in 1579, who featured in a list that also included seven parrots.[42]

Several of the black Africans in German-speaking areas—as in the rest of Europe—were not merely decorative domestic slaves but were employed in more specialized occupations. Three areas of specialization stand out. The first stems from the link between black Africans and animals, in particular horses, attested to across Europe. In 1509, a "Moor" is recorded as a stable boy at the court in Württemberg,[43] but this is too imprecise a term for us to be certain that he is black. Gregorio de Guinea, on the other hand, undoubtedly was, as the epithet "de Guinea" is one of very few cast-iron, sub-Saharan African identifiers. In 1562, Archduke Ferdinand II of Tyrol wrote to Philip II requesting safe conduct throughout Philip's territories for Gregorio, who was described as the emperor

Maximilian's *caballerizo* or master of horse in charge of a special type of small horse; Gregorio had been sent to Spain to buy horses for Maximilian's residence in Vienna.[44] It is interesting that he is described as a *caballerizo*, as this title signified a responsible position requiring specialist knowledge.

The second area of specialization is characterized by the link between Africans and physicality. In several European countries, some black Africans found an employment niche in the martial arts.[45] A licensing system for masters of arms was in operation in Europe, which meant masters of arms were referred to by their position and are clearly visible in the records. For instance, a "mulatto" fencing master, Jorge Fernandes from Setúbal, was routinely involved in brawls and was eventually exiled to Brazil in 1547 when he murdered an unarmed man.[46]

Although his identity is not yet known, the black sickle fighter illustrated by Jörg Breu the Younger in Paulus Hector Mair's *Fechtbuch*, datable to 1542–47,[47] entitled *De arte athletica*, now in the Bayerische Staatsbibliothek in Munich (figure 2.6),[48] is very likely to have been a real person. In the manuscript of 309 folios, he is the only nonwhite portrayed out of over 1,000 combatants, nearly all of whom have fair or reddish hair and conform to what could be described as a stereotype of Germanic appearance.[49] It would have been truly extraordinary if the artist had decided to include one black figure in the midst of this Germanic whiteness, if indeed the black sickle fighter had not existed.

Figure 2.6. Jörg Breu the Younger, *A Duel with Two Sickles*, c. 1545, in Paulus Hector Mair's *Fechtbuch*, Munich, Bayerische Staatsbibliothek, Cod. icon. 393, fol. 227r.

The third area of African specialization was music, which once again is well documented across Europe and throughout German-speaking areas, even if there is more evidence in German-speaking areas for the sixteenth than the fifteenth century. Black Africans usually sang or played one or more musical instruments, especially drums (Hörpagger, a black timpanist, is documented at the court of the later Duke William V of Bavaria in 1573)[50] or trumpets. Duke Christoph of Württemberg (ruled 1550–68) at Stuttgart even boasted a black musical theorist and composer called Vicente Lusitano. Vicente was probably born to a white father and black mother in the Alentejo in Portugal in c. 1522, gravitating to the patronage of Afonso de Lencastre, the Portuguese ambassador to Rome, and accompanying him to Rome by the early 1550s as a music teacher to his son. Although he is most famous for his high-profile debate over chromatic, enharmonic, and diatonic genera with Nicola Vicentino in 1551, his treatise on musical theory, the *Introdvttione facilissima,* published in Venice in 1561, was a more notable achievement. By this date, Vicente had converted to Protestantism and had arrived at Duke Christoph's court, but he is thereafter lost to view.[51] What is particularly interesting about Vicente's case is that he has become dissociated from his blackness; all musicologists know of him, but until recently, virtually none knew he was black.[52] He represents both great success and unusual failure. His successes (his book on musical theory and his compositions) are still admired today, but it is noticeable that, these notwithstanding, he failed to find a permanent position as chapel master at an Italian court or cathedral.

Actual sub-Saharan Africans in northern Europe had mixed fortunes. If they were domestic slaves or servants in courts or in merchants' households, they may have been in an anomalous legal position, but their day-to-day lives were unaffected by this, and they lived the same kinds of lives as their counterparts in similar positions in southern Europe. If they possessed recognized skills, on the other hand, they could prosper, although advancement was often limited to certain occupations and kept within certain bounds.

German Reactions to the Black Diaspora in Europe

This final section focuses on several German speakers who "captured" and transported back to their homelands written and/or visual descriptions of black Africans they had encountered elsewhere in Europe. A host of German diarists descended on southern Europe in the fifteenth and early sixteenth centuries and were quick to comment on the presence of black Africans; quite literally, they recorded what they found remarkable. One of the first Germans to visit Portugal after the arrival of enslaved blacks from west Africa and to leave a written record was Nicolaus Lankmann of Falkenstein, sent to Lisbon in 1451 in connection with the marriage between Emperor Frederick III and Leonor of Portugal. He noted a young black man (the word used is the generic "ethiops") referred to as "Pero Blanco" or Peter White, who had been given as a present by the Duke of Seville to the knight Christoffero Ungenad, both the nickname and the fact of giving a human present of this sort being worthy of record.[53]

The travels across Europe in the 1460s of Leo of Rozmital, a Bohemian count, were recorded by two separate diarists in his service: Schascko or Schaseck, who wrote in Czech, and Gabriel Tetzel from Nuremberg, who wrote in German.[54] Although Tetzel's description is judged the more interesting, it is Schaseck who gives the fuller account of the most relevant incident in terms of the black diaspora: Leo's request for two black African slaves as the present offered him by King Afonso V of Portugal. This request provoked guffaws from the king's brother, who stated that "[black Africans] are of no value," and that Leo "should ask for something greater and more worthy of your position than black Africans." An ape was added to the gift.

The most common reactions to the black diaspora in Renaissance Europe show a concern with appearance and number. The "Itinerarius" of the Nuremberg medical doctor Hieronymus Münzer, who toured Portugal and Spain in 1494–95, exemplifies this. As far as their numbers were concerned, Münzer several times marveled at the quantity of black Africans in Lisbon,[55] and he evidently found their presence one of the most extraordinary aspects of the city. Münzer's comments on appearance reveal a German interest in different skin tones, also apparent in a visual form in the German painting of *St. Maurice and His Companions of the Theban Legion* discussed above (see figure 2.3). According to Münzer, King João II of Portugal "had black Africans of various colors, reddish-brown, black, and paler black, speaking various languages,"[56] and "those from close to the Tropics of Cancer and Capricorn range from somewhat [or lighter] black tending to red in color, and those from the equatorial regions are extremely black."[57] The Latin word Münzer uses is *nigros,* so he is clearly referring to sub-Saharan Africans. What is interesting here is that Münzer is casting around trying to find words to describe the new skin colors he is encountering, and although he uses "black," he also uses "red" and tones of red. This is an excellent example of a writer who is making a genuine attempt to describe in a fresh and original fashion what he sees with his own eyes. He does not bracket together all black Africans, but acknowledges that they differ greatly in skin color and in language, according to their place of origin. This acknowledgment that not only are black Africans not all the same color, but that in any case that color might not be best described as black, is unusual in Renaissance Europe, and is the textual equivalent of the St. Maurice painting.

In this category of "capturing" images of black Africans must also be placed "souvenirs" of foreign travel taken back to Germany. An interesting image of two black gondoliers rowing a party of three couples, including a woman playing a lute, a man beating time, and another woman singing from a songbook, with the title *The Venetian Love of Display and Magnificence*,[58] was presented by David Brentel in 1585 to the *Bürgermeister* Anton Weihenmayer in Lauingen on the Danube, who put it in his *Stammbuch* or family album.[59] Although David Brentel was himself an etcher,[60] it is likely he bought this image as a souvenir when he went to Venice, because in the later sixteenth century these images were made for the Italian tourist market. The response of German speakers in general to encounters with actual sub-Saharan Africans elsewhere in Europe appears to have been one of heightened curiosity, and the choice of the image with two black gondoliers fits into this pattern.

Conclusion

Fictive and notional black Africans may almost independently have become an integral part of European culture, but "real" black Africans simultaneously caught the imagination of white Europeans, and caused white Europeans to consider issues about assimilation and integration, and about what blackness represented, that they may not have foreseen. Interaction between the categories further complicates an already complex set of representations. But although the numbers of black Africans in German-speaking areas may have been small in the fifteenth and sixteenth centuries, those fictive, notional, and "real" Africans discussed here appear comparable in many respects to their counterparts on the Iberian and Italian peninsulas. If that is correct, it should make research in Germany on the black diaspora in the fifteenth and sixteenth centuries easier and faster, and should also bolster arguments in favor of studying historical phenomena not only across disciplinary lines, but also across national and linguistic boundaries. But it is also likely that German-speaking areas had certain particularities in relation to the black diaspora, among which may be numbered a preoccupation with the typology of skin color and the unique status of the Hanseatic merchants, and these Germanic particularities also require scholarly attention.

Notes

1. I do not usually work on German-speaking areas, but I have been carrying out research for some years on black Africans in Renaissance Italy and, to a lesser extent, Renaissance Portugal.
2. Jean Robertson and D. J. Gordon, eds., *A Calendar of Dramatic Records in the Books of the Livery Companies of London, 1485–1640* (Oxford: Oxford University Press, 1954), 3:5–10; and Virginia Mason Vaughan, *Performing Blackness on English Stages, 1500–1800* (Cambridge: Cambridge University Press, 2005), 29–30.

3. John Forrest, *The History of Morris Dancing, 1458–1750* (Toronto: Toronto University Press, 1999), 100.
4. The phrase used by Christoph Schulthaiss in the chronicle is "schwartz geferbt": Konstanz, Stadtarchiv, A I 8/1, fol. 177r. Thanks are due to Gerrit Schenk for sending me a scanned image of this passage, Christof Rolker for transcribing the passage in the archives, and Cornelia Linde for providing the connection.
5. Gerrit Jasper Schenk, *Zeremoniell und Politik: Herrschereinzüge im spätmittelalterlichen Reich* (Cologne, Germany: Böhlau Verlag, 2003), 210–11.
6. Wim Blockmans, "The Emperor's Subjects," in *Charles V, 1500–1558, and His Time*, ed. Hugo Soly (Antwerp, Belgium: Mercatorfonds, 1999), 274–75, ill. on 276.
7. Fernando Checa Cremades, "The Image of Charles V," in *Charles V*, ed. Soly, 501, ill. on 500.
8. See Kate Lowe, "The Stereotyping of Black Africans in Renaissance Europe," in *Black Africans in Renaissance Europe*, ed. T.F. Earle and K.J.P. Lowe (Cambridge: Cambridge University Press, 2005), 44–47.
9. On this issue, see Kate Lowe, "The Lives of African Slaves and People of African Descent in Europe during the Renaissance," in *Revealing the African Presence in Renaissance Europe*, exh. cat., ed. Joaneath Spicer (Baltimore: Walters Art Museum, 2012), 14 and n10, 24 and n65.
10. See, e.g., Jan-Albert Goris, *Étude sur les colonies marchandes méridionales (Portugais, Espagnols, Italiens) à Anvers de 1488 à 1567* (Louvain, Belgium: Uystpruyst, 1925), 31–32.
11. Paul H. D. Kaplan, *The Rise of the Black Magus in Western Art* (Ann Arbor, MI: UMI Research Press, 1985), especially 103–12.
12. Marian Biskup, *Regesta copernicana (Calendar of Copernicus' Papers)*, Studia copernicana VIII (Wrocław: Polish Academy of Science Press, 1973), 143–45; and Heribert M. Nobis, Menso Folkerts, Stefan Kirschner, and Andreas Kühne, eds., *Nicolaus Copernicus Gesamtausgabe*, 9 vols. (Hildesheim, Germany: H. A. Gerstenberg [vols. 1–2], Berlin: Akademie Verlag [vols. 3–9], 1973–2002), 6.1 *Documenta Copernicana. Briefe: Texte und Übersetzungen*, ed. Andreas Kühne, 152–61.
13. *Bibliotheca sanctorum*, 13 vols. (Rome: Istituto Giovanni XXIII della Pontificia Università Lateranense, 1961–70), 9: cols. 193–205, 194.
14. For the history of representations of St. Maurice, see Gude Suckale-Redlefsen, *Mauritius: Der heilige Mohr/The Black Saint Maurice* (Houston: Menil Foundation; Munich: Verlag Schnell & Steiner, 1987).
15. Peter C. Sutton, *Reclaimed: Paintings from the Collection of Jacques Goudstikker* (New Haven, CT: Yale University Press, 2008), 104–107, ill. on 105; Suckale-Redlefsen, *Mauritius*, catalogue no. 139 and ill. on 103.
16. Lowe, "The Stereotyping of Black Africans," 23–24.
17. *Allgemeine deutsche Biographie*, 56 vols. (Leipzig, Germany: Duncker & Humblot, 1875–1912), 6:626–27; and *Neue deutsche Biographie*, 23 vols. (Berlin: Duncker & Humblot, 1953–2007), 5:80.
18. Conrad Eubel, Wilhelm Heinrich, Huberti Gulik, Stefan Ehses, Patrick Gauchat, Remigius Ritzler, and Pirmin Sefrin, *Hierarchia catholica medii aevi*, 8 vols., 2nd ed. (Padua, Italy: Il Messaggero di Sant'Antonio, 1913–78), 3:347.
19. Biskup, *Regesta copernicana*, 143; and *Nicolaus Copernicus Gesamtausgabe*, 6:1:153.
20. Biskup, *Regesta copernicana*, 143; and *Nicolaus Copernicus Gesamtausgabe*, 6:2:310–11.
21. For a résumé, see Biskup, *Regesta copernicana*, 144; and for the Latin text, see *Nicolaus Copernicus Gesamtausgabe*, 6:1:157: "Quid detestandi spectaculi Elbingi in bachanalibus proxime effluxis publice et palam exhibitum sit, Reverendissima d(ominatio) v(estra) ex scheda inedita cognoscet. Licet enim omnes vt tanto facilius deprehensi negare possent personati fuerint, Nichilominus tamen vt eo me redderent cognoscibiliorem, ex quo Mauricio mihi nomen est, et Mauricius martir nigro sive Ethiopico colore depingi consuevit, personam meam sub Ethiopici Episcopi specie, representauerunt. At cum hec res in tocius ecclesiastici ordinis depompatio-

nem, imprimis tamen persone mee traductionem facta, si impunita maneret, res esset pessimi exempli."
22. Peter Burke, *Popular Culture in Early Modern Europe*, 2nd rev. ed. (Aldershot, UK: Scolar Press, 1994), 189.
23. Hans Werner Debrunner, *Presence and Prestige: Africans in Europe: A History of Africans in Europe before 1918* (Basel, Switzerland: Basler Afrika Bibliographien, 1979), 44; and Nelson H. Minnich, "The Catholic Church and the Pastoral Care of Black Africans in Renaissance Italy," in *Black Africans in Renaissance Europe*, Earle and Lowe, 280n2 and 294–95.
24. Trevor Dean, *Crime and Justice in Late Medieval Italy* (Cambridge, UK: Cambridge University Press, 2007), 114.
25. Ibid., 123.
26. Ibid., 118.
27. A. Fontoura da Costa, "Fernão Gomes e o Monopólio do Resgate da Guiné," *Boletim da Sociedade de Geografia de Lisboa* 56 (1938): 193; and Mosteiro do Jerónimos, *Os Negros em Portugal—Séculos XV a XIX* (exh. cat.) (Lisbon: Comissão Nacional para as Comemorações dos Descobrimentos Portugueses, 1999), 187 (ill.).
28. London, College of Arms, MS ICB 101, fol. 109. See W. H. Smyth, "On Certain Passages in the Life of Sir John Hawkins, Temp. Elizabeth," *Archaeologia, or Miscellaneous Tracts Relating to Antiquity Published by the Society of Antiquaries* 33 (1849): 205–206.
29. Ludwig Grote, *Die Tucher: Bildnis einer Patrizierfamilie* (Munich: Prestel-Verlag, 1961), Table III and 90–92.
30. Ibid.; see, e.g., illustrations 47, 60, and 80.
31. Susan Foister, *Art of Light: German Renaissance Stained Glass* (London: National Gallery Company, 2007), 26.
32. Bernhard Rackham, *A Guide to the Collections of Stained Glass, Victoria and Albert Museum Department of Ceramics* (London: Board of Education, 1936), 85.
33. See Renate Eickelmann, ed., *Der Mohrenkopfpokal von Christoph Jamnitzer* (exh. cat.) (Munich: Bayerisches Nationalmuseum, 2002); and Lorenz Seelig, "Christoph Jamnitzer's 'Moor's Head': A Late Renaissance Drinking Vessel," in *Black Africans in Renaissance Europe*, Earle and Lowe, 181–209.
34. Seelig, "Christoph Jamnitzer," 184–85. For an alternative provenance of the Moor's head drinking vessel, see Jørgen Hein, "Der Mohrenkopfpokal von Christoph Jamnitzer—Provenienz, Deutung und Kontext," *Münchner Jahrbuch der bildenden Kunst*, 3rd ser., 53 (2002): 163–74.
35. Nils Staf, ed., *Stockholms stads tänkeböcker från år 1592* (Stockholm: Stockholms Stadsarkiv, 1964), 7:287.
36. Richard C. Trexler, "The Foundlings of Florence, 1395–1455," *History of Childhood Quarterly* 1, no. 1 (1973): 270; Philip Gavitt, *Charity and Children in Renaissance Florence: The Ospedale degli Innocenti, 1410–1536* (Ann Arbor: University of Michigan Press, 1990), 207; and Kate Lowe, "Black Africans' Religious and Cultural Assimilation to, or Appropriation of, Catholicism in Italy, 1470–1520," *Renaissance and Reformation/Renaissance et Réforme* 31, no. 2 (2008): 70–73.
37. See, e.g., Sergio Tognetti, "The Trade in Black African Slaves in Fifteenth-Century Florence," in *Black Africans in Renaissance Europe*, ed. Earle and Lowe, 217–18, and Florence, Archivio di stato, Catasto 923, fol. 635r.
38. P. L. Hughes and J. F. Larkin, eds., *Tudor Royal Proclamations*, 3 vols. (New Haven, CT: Yale University Press, 1964–69), 3:222.
39. Miranda Kaufmann, "Caspar Van Senden, Sir Thomas Sherley and the 'Blackamoor' Project," *Historical Research* 81 (2008): 366–71.
40. John Nichols, *The Progresses and Public Processions of Queen Elizabeth*, 3 vols. (London: John Nichols and Son, 1823), 3:384.

41. Peter Martin, "Un souffle venu de loin: Les 'Maures' Noirs au service des princes allemands de l'époque baroque," in *Les Africains et leurs descendants en Europe avant le XXe siècle,* ed. Dieudonné Gnammankou and Yao Modzinou (Toulouse, France: La Maison de l'Afrique à Toulouse, 2008), 116–17.
42. Almudena Pérez de Tudela and Annemarie Jordan Gschwend, "Luxury Goods for Royal Collectors: Exotica, Princely Gifts and Rare Animals Exchanged between the Iberian Courts and Central Europe in the Renaissance (1560–1612)," in *Exotica: Portugals Entdeckungen im Spiegel fürstlicher Kunst- und Wunderkammern der Renaissance,* ed. Helmut Trnek and Sabine Haag (Vienna: Kunsthistorisches Museum, 2001), 49.
43. Monika Firla, ed., *Exotisch-höfisch-bürgerlich: Afrikaner in Württemberg vom 15. bis 19. Jahrhundert: Katalog zur Ausstellung des Hauptstaatsarchivs Stuttgart* (Stuttgart, Germany: Hauptstaatsarchiv Stuttgart, 2001), 26.
44. Tudela and Gschwend, "Luxury Goods for Royal Collectors," 16 and 17.
45. Lowe, "The Stereotyping of Black Africans," 32–35.
46. Francisco Sousa Viterbo, *A Esgrima em Portugal: Subsídios para a sua História* (Lisbon: Manoel Gomes, 1899), 33–36, cited in Sydney Anglo, *The Martial Arts of Renaissance Europe* (New Haven, CT: Yale University Press, 2000), 9, 11.
47. Jane Turner, ed., *The Dictionary of Art,* 34 vols. (London: Macmillan, 1996), 4:760, entry by Gode Krämer.
48. Munich, Bayerische Staatsbibliothek, Cod. Icon. 393, fol. 227r, Jörg Breu the Younger, "A Duel with Two Sickles," Paulus Hector Mair, *Fechtbuch.*
49. Munich, Bayerische Staatsbibliothek, Cod. Icon. 393, fol. 177r.
50. Martin, "Un souffle," 119–20.
51. On his career, see Maria Augusta Alves Barbosa, *Vicentivs Lvsitanvs: Ein portugiesischer Komponist und Musiktheoretiker des 16. Jahrhunderts* (Lisbon: Estado da Cultura, 1977); Robert Stevenson, "The First Black Published Composer," *Inter-American Music Review* 5 (1982): 79–103; and Samuel A. Floyd Jr., *The International Dictionary of Black Composers,* 2 vols. (Chicago: Fitzroy Dearborn, 1996), 2:752–54.
52. Kate Lowe, "La place des Africains sub-sahariens dans l'histoire européenne, 1400–1600," in *Les Africains et leurs descendants,* ed. Gnammankou and Modzinou, 78–79.
53. Aires A. Nascimento, ed., with the collaboration of Maria João Branco and Maria de Lurdes Rosa, *Leonor de Portugal Imperatriz da Alemanha, Diário de Viagem do Embaixador Nicolau Lanckman de Valkenstein* (Lisbon: Cosmos, 1992), 40.
54. Munich, Bayerische Staatsbibliothek, Cod. Germ. 1279.
55. Basílio de Vasconcelos, ed., *Itinerário do Dr. Jerónimo Münzer (Extractos)* (Coimbra, Portugal: Imprensa da Universidade, 1931), 27, 52, 63.
56. Ibid., 54: "Habet item rex nigros varii coloris; rufos, nigros et aubnigros, de vario idiomate."
57. Ibid., 52: "Et qui sunt propinqui tropicis cancri et capricorni, sunt subnigri declinantes ad rubedinem, et sub æquinoctio sunt excellentes nigri."
58. Nürnberg, Germanisches Nationalmuseum, Sign. Hs. 123725, fol. 30.
59. See Walter Salmen, *Musikleben im 16. Jahrhundert* (Leipzig, Germany: Deutscher Verlag für Musik, 1976), 122 and 123 (ill.); Paul Kaplan, "Titian's *Laura Dianti* and the Origins of the Motif of the Black Page in Portraiture," part 1, "The Vogue for Black Servants in Renaissance Italy," *Antichità viva* 21, no. 1 (1982): 14 and 18n64; Peter Martin, *Schwarze Teufel, edle Mohren: Afrikaner in Bewußtsein und Geschichte der Deutschen* (Hamburg, Germany: Junius Verlag, 1993), 50; and Martin, "Un souffle," 115 and 116 (ill.).
60. Ulrich Thieme and Felix Becker, eds., *Allgemeines Lexikon der bildenden Künstler: von der Antike bis zur Gegenwart: unter Mitwirkung von 300 Fachgelehrten des In- und Auslandes,* 37 vols. (Leipzig, Germany: Engelman, 1907–50), 4:583–84.

Chapter Three

AMBIGUOUS DUTY
Black Servants at German Ancien Régime Courts

Anne Kuhlmann

From the very emergence of modern national historiography, European historical memory has excluded or marginalized peoples of different ethnocultural, religious, and other groupings in past European societies.[1] Black Africans were part of these societies, but only now have they become a topic of general interest. Owing to the work of pioneering black European studies authors like Hans Werner Debrunner, Allison Blakely, Peter Martin, and others,[2] black Africans and their descendants have now been attested in various, and not always marginal, positions in northern, central, and eastern Europe: as seamen, missionaries, musicians, servants, members of guilds, and in lower social positions, but also as priests, officers of honor, and higher-ranking noblemen. Some were displayed as curiosities at local markets; others rose to the rank of scholar, valet, princely tutor, or military officer.

Within this kaleidoscope of varied professions and social spaces, the premodern and ancien régime court keeps appearing as a place where black Africans were most visible over a period of centuries. Previous accounts have paid attention to the court as a social environment containing many people of African origin in the early modern German lands; among other things, they have noticed the nexus of sometimes highly successful blacks and the courtly world.[3] However, in black European studies the court does not generally figure as a peculiar social and political institution with its own rules and paradigms, as it does in early modern historical studies.[4] In black German history, the court is significant not only because it was the place where black stereotypes—which became fertile ground for modern European racism—were first carved out;[5] it was also a major social

---

Notes from this chapter begin on page 69.

environment, in purely numerical terms, for people of African origin, particularly in the central, eastern, and northern regions.

This chapter examines the encounters black Africans and their descendants had with central European courts from a sociocultural perspective. Black studies research has centered on the crucial question of the social and racial equalities and inequalities black people faced and reacted to in different societies. However, the issue of equality itself in the estate-based society is complex, since the culture was not based on equality but rather a fundamental inequality derived from rank, inherited social status, and religious denomination. Within this context, the chapter explores the issue of ethnic difference when black people at central European ancien régime courts acquired status. It argues that the "nation" as a paradigm of historical study in nineteenth- and early-twentieth-century historiography was an important, yet not the only, reason for their invisibility in traditional German historiography. For a long time, researchers have also been reluctant to approach the court as a field of research in its own right, because it was associated with notions of absolute power that left little space for human agency among courts' subjects. This strand of thought was in itself not concerned with the question of racial discrimination, but it influenced historical research on society and inhibited studies on blacks in this important social environment.

The roles of blacks appear in a different light against the background of newer approaches to social bonding and career building at the courts that have been applied to white court agents. Based on a sample of 380 persons of African descent living in parts of the Holy Roman Empire of the German Nation between 1600 and 1800, this chapter weighs the rather monolithic notion of dependent black court servants, who were subject to the arbitrary will of their "masters," against the actual diversity of roles black servants and courtiers played in the multifaceted social hierarchies of the court.

The first section introduces more recent historiographical approaches to the phenomenon of the court and their possible impact on black European studies: new insights into this complex social setting have generated the need to reevaluate the positions of blacks within it. The second section picks up the wider academic debate on the opportunities black agents had to integrate into German host societies, and the third section continues with an appraisal of blacks' professions and positions at court and outside of it. Religion was as central to early modern blacks' possibilities for integration and professional advancement in Europe as it was for their white contemporaries. The comparatively well-documented biography of a black chamber servant at the Wolfenbüttel court, exemplified in the fourth section, attests to this. Finally, the concluding section aims to place the diversity of black biographies at court into a comprehensive perspective on the paradigms of court service that applied to white as well as black agents, while weighing the opportunities and constraints of this social system for the latter.

The Ancien Régime Court: Changing Perspectives on White and Black Agents

Given the importance of the courts as political, social, cultural, and also religious centers of early modern Europe, one might assume that the black presence in them would have been allotted a comparatively prominent place in historical memory. Yet, what applies to court history in general applies equally to this black presence: "the study of the pre-French Revolution court has been, until recently, virtually an academic taboo,"[6] with the exception of the courts' artistic dimension—or, in our context, the meaning of blacks as icons.

One explanation for the neglect of historical research on the courts pertains to the two major intellectual schools of thought that dominated twentieth-century historiography: Marxism and liberalism. Both schools construe history as progressing toward modernity, with the early modern period dominated by the rise of the middle classes. Within this framework, the ancien régime court appeared to advocate and manifest monarchical "absolutism," which was considered a rather transitional phase in the evolution of the modern state, the phenomenon that was of primary interest. Of all the territories of the Old Empire, Prussia received special attention, as it most clearly anticipated modern structures of bureaucratic power. Prussia, however, was a monarchy in which the army, not the court, was central to the state.[7]

The work of historian and sociologist Norbert Elias in the first half of the twentieth century (but published later), in particular, established an image of the court as an instrument for "domesticating" the nobility and consolidating the absolutist state. Accordingly, the early modern court was widely seen as the "stage of absolutism," a link in an ongoing "process of civilization" between the feudal, decentralized, hierarchical world of medieval Europe and the democratic, centralized, egalitarian modern liberal state. In the past few decades, court historians have challenged this view, especially by pointing to the court's multilayered functions as the political and social center of society, the arena in which conflicting interests were negotiated between rulers and the nobility and between competing noble factions, as well as the site of court representation and hospitality, and the center of cultural patronage.[8]

Judging from the Elias model's perspective of absolute monarchical power, wherein even the nobility is seen as "tamed" by autocrats, blacks at court cannot but appear as extremely submissive and insignificant. Art, literature, and court representation, in which they took part, figure in this view as "a series of tricks intended to manipulate readers, listeners and viewers"—that is, as a line of coded symbols to be read as political messages and propaganda that aimed to convince a broader public of the reality of a central ruler's power.[9] Since the question of the legal status of black Africans in the empire is still unresolved, and since they clearly had representative functions at court—the typical portraits with black attendants come to mind—their role is seen as that of a largely passive tool of monarchical will.[10]

One undoubtedly passive role blacks in court circuits played was to be exchanged as "presents" between different rulers. There are several examples of both black children and adults fulfilling this function in German-speaking courts throughout the seventeenth and eighteenth centuries. In the 1660s, the Danish king sent two African children, a girl and a boy, to the Prince Elector of Saxony, a relative who, in turn, passed them to his daughter, the wife of the Margrave of Bayreuth.[11] After her death in 1670, the margrave remarried, taking a princess of Württemberg from Stuttgart as his bride and thereby expanding dynastic networks. When she arrived, or shortly thereafter, the black drummer Eberhard Christoph also came to the Bayreuth court—he is attested in court records in Stuttgart until at least 1667 and in Bayreuth from 1678. A few years later, in 1682, another black girl was sent to Bayreuth from the Aurich court of the princess's sister, the reigning widow of the prince of East Frisia.[12] Finally, in 1729, an eight-year-old boy, Anthon from the Danish Virgin Island of St. Thomas, was brought from Copenhagen to the Aurich court as a present from King Christian VI of Denmark and Norway to his sister-in-law, another princess of East Frisia.[13]

From these examples, it is apparent that Copenhagen, of central strategic importance in the Danish West Indian slave trade on the continent, had become a distributor of blacks in the network of European aristocracy. The courts of Copenhagen, Bayreuth, Stuttgart, and Aurich, as well as their dynastic networks, clearly appear to be determinants of black mobility. These courts were continuously connected through marriage policies and extensive exchange circuits. However, mobility was not limited to blacks, because royal children, members of the household, cooks, servants, and many others also moved between the courts. As none of them was asked for consent, one cannot attribute special oppression to the involuntary movement of blacks.

Also, these blacks as gifts did not remain mere passive gifts but often changed roles and status over time. The ceremonial of baptism was central to such changes, with conversion a precondition for any kind of social acknowledgment, marriage, and becoming a godparent, as well as being essential to acquiring a town's citizenship and entrance to the guilds and other institutions. Until well into the eighteenth century, conversion was seen as a matter of public concern, and the baptism of "heathens" remained an event of missionary significance, even prompting the sending of presents from faraway courts. In 1721, for example, an East Frisian princess being raised at the south German court of an aunt sent twelve guldens home on the occasion of the baptism of a black boy.[14]

The first years at court for Christian Ferdinand Mohr, one of the two children first sent as a gift from Copenhagen to Dresden and then to Bayreuth in the 1660s, can be regarded as typical of black servants in this environment, and it exemplifies the significance of conversion and baptism, which were carefully prepared for over many years: Christian Ferdinand attended primary school in Bayreuth, where he acquired reading and writing skills. With lessons in catechism as a compulsory part of the schedule, he passed an exam before the consistory in charge of the local church jurisdiction. On 18 December 1664, he was baptized at the Bayreuth parochial church, attended by fifty-five godparents, among them the reigning margrave Christian Ernst and his wife, followed by the margrave's uncle, who ranked second in state, the chancellor, and privy counselors, as well as the mayors of all five capitals of the margraviate.[15]

Christian Ferdinand later achieved a reputation as a professional drummer and became a member of the prestigious Guild of Trumpeters and Drummers. Married to a local woman, Susanna Clara Laickner, he had four children baptized in Bayreuth through 1675, but then he disappeared from the Bayreuth records. It remains uncertain whether he is "the drummer Christian Mohr" who appeared about thirty years later in the retinue of Albrecht Ernst II of Oettingen-Oettingen,[16] a nephew of the Bayreuth margrave. The close relationship between Oettingen and Bayreuth makes it quite possible that Christian Ferdinand moved between the two courts. In this context, another testimony to a drummer Mohr gains significance, a letter by the majordomo of the Bayreuth court to the Margrave of Bayreuth. In June 1692, the majordomo remarked that Princess Christine Charlotte of East Frisia, Albrecht Ernst's aunt and the Bayreuth margravine's sister, who often visited the Bayreuth court, had mentioned in a letter to her sister that she had met the drummer Mohr when she visited the regiment of the margrave and that he had bowed deeply to her to acknowledge their "old acquaintance."[17] Given the brisk exchange processes between the courts, it is likely that Christian Ferdinand may have constantly been on the move within the ramified networks of the Bayreuth and Oettingen courts.

This sort of movement might also explain some of the numerous disappearances of black servants from court registers. The frequency of similar names at certain courts—like everybody else, blacks were named after their godparents, whose political potency was correlated with the frequency of their names—makes it even more difficult to follow the biography of a particular individual. In any case, the rulers' self-conception as patrons and protectors of their subjects, especially in the case of highly visible blacks, suggests that such vanishing blacks are likely to be found somewhere within the circuits of related courts.

Integration vs. Exclusion: Recent Assessments

The records handed down to us on black Africans at court offer various interpretations concerning the possibilities they had to integrate into the societies of the Holy Roman Empire.[18] Some scholars, such as Peter Martin, have come to fairly negative appraisals, emphasizing the limits of integration. Martin points out the rather functional intentions behind black servants' roles in court representation, these servants' generally low life expectancy, their high degree of dependency on princely "masters," their great risk of poverty if they lost their post, as well as frequent renunciation in their host societies.[19] Since many came via the Mediterranean slave markets or the transatlantic and other slave trade routes, their legal status was located somehow in a "no man's land between free and unfree." However, Martin later grants that in everyday life, black servants' formal status as slaves did not have much meaning. Conversely, Uta Sadji assumes that blacks in eighteenth-century Germany were "legally speaking free, but still mostly lived like slaves" and that they were culturally not accepted by mainstream Germans.[20]

Renowned historian Bernd Roeck carries forth the image of black people as uprooted side figures in his survey *Outsiders, Marginal Groups, Minorities*. He states that "the history of blacks in the early modern Empire has never been one of integration.... Many had to face a sad existence, if not needed anymore as 'toy things' or if incessant financial hardship in the early modern states suggested a reduction of court staff."[21] From this perspective, the famous examples of successful Africans—including the philosopher Anton Wilhelm Amo, the Austrian courtier Angelo Soliman, the Russian general Abram Hanibal, and the Swedish court secretary Adolph Couschi Badin—appear to be rare exceptions.[22]

In contrast, several authors, particularly those of regional studies like Ingeborg Kittel, Wolfram Schäfer, Monika Firla, and Ute Küppers-Braun, insist that black integration into seventeenth- and eighteenth-century estate-based German society was possible and that it could extend further than the negative appraisals of their status might suggest. They highlight treatment and ranking of blacks at court that was basically equal, emphasizing also that they were regularly paid for their service and that many intermarried with locals. Some acquired property, including land or houses, and received regular pensions after retirement. According to Firla and Küppers-Braun, some even became favorites at court. For example, the black servant Ignatius Fortuna (before 1730–89) from Suriname died a respected and wealthy man at the court of the Essen Abbey. Similarly, Mustapha and Mahomet were two black Turkish favorites of the first Hanoverian to occupy the English throne, George I of England. Both had been taken prisoner by imperialists in Hungary and had entered King George I's service in return for having saved his life during the Siege of Vienna in 1685.[23] Other biographies refer to rather close relationships between members of the nobility and black servants, such as those of the African trumpeter Christian Gottlieb (before 1675–90) at the northern German courts of Ascheberg and Plön, Carl of Commani (c. 1694–1757) at the Stuttgart court, and Alzire from Suriname (c. 1729–51), a servant to the Margrave of Bayreuth.[24] Other examples include "chamber Moor" George Dominicus (before 1635–75), who enjoyed a high degree of social esteem at the court of Count Wilhelm of Schaumburg-Lippe at Bückeburg; Ferdinand Christian Coridon (c. 1748–after 1795), who became a court administrator in Berleburg; and Maria Viktoria Dolenta from the "coast of Congo in Africa," who was educated and treated almost like a family member by the landgraves of Cassel.[25]

As this chapter aims to show, the multitude of such exceptions suggests that integration was, if not the norm, achieved with some frequency. Above all, the records will illustrate the significant diversity in the kinds of positions and social advancements that blacks in ancien régime Europe obtained, indicating that generalizations about their status and life experience, such as those of Martin and Roeck, should be reconsidered.

Court Hierarchies and the Diversity of Black Positions

The reports of black Africans and their descendants in Europe upon which this chapter is based present a wide range of experiences, from extraordinary fame and mere representational functions in court culture to discrimination. Consequently, the status of these individuals can be interpreted across a broad scale. One indicator of social integration vs. exclusion that will be analyzed below is the access to social positions that particular individuals had. Methodologically, this chapter draws on the records of 380 persons variously referred to as "Moors," Ethiopians, Africans, blacks, or "Negroes" in seventeenth- and eighteenth-century German sources. The records encompass most of the data on black biographies currently available in varied primary and secondary sources, i.e., archival sources, scholarly surveys, and journal or newspaper reports. Certainly, the sample includes only a portion of persons of black African descent present in the seventeenth- and eighteenth-century German lands, who numbered some four to five thousand total in the nine hundred years up to the end of the nineteenth century, according to estimates by Peter Martin.[26] The information content, status, and reliability of both primary and secondary sources vary considerably; these sources are basically fragmentary and need further review. Geographically, the data were collected from an area confined to the territory of current Germany, not the entire Holy Roman Empire. Also, the identities of some individuals remain uncertain: in some cases, identical names refer to different persons; in others, a single individual is referred to by different names; and sixty-one persons remain anonymous. It is also possible that the same persons could be counted twice when analyzing their professions, since individuals changed their posts or combined professions, most commonly being both musicians and servants at court.

This chapter, like all research on blacks in premodern and early modern Europe, has to deal with terminological peculiarities.[27] Contemporary encyclopedia entries on "Africans," "Moors," and related terms discussed the question of skin color at length. However, religious notions still dominated the definitions: The inhabitants of various African regions whom eighteenth-century readers knew through travel reports and other sources were described as being "black" or "Arabian," while the term "Moor" was obscure. The Bible, still cited as an authoritative source, frequently mentioned "Moors" without specifying their skin color and/or places of residence. The term *"Neger"* ("Negro") rarely appeared in any of these sources, but when it did, it clearly denoted blackness. However, there was no separate entry for it, even in the most comprehensive eighteenth-century German encyclopedia, the *Grosses vollständiges Universal-Lexicon*, published between 1732 and 1754.[28] Up to the end of the eighteenth century, the term *"Mohr"* was understood rather generically as applying to persons of African as well as "Oriental" ancestry or of darker complexion. General terms for professions were, likewise, often imprecise, such as "servant" and "lackey."

Court service was as strictly hierarchical as the whole estate-based society. Individuals' opportunities to gain access to the ruler or other potent court agents largely determined their social esteem.[29] The entire system of court patronage was based on this principle and hierarchically scaled. The following analysis shows the range of positions and also attempts to estimate the number of blacks in different professional spaces.

Of the 380 men and women included in the sample, more than three-quarters were directly employed at court as servants, musicians, and in other professions, as well as in or near the army (308 persons, 27 women, 281 men). As soldiers, they were often employed in privileged army units like the Rotes Grenadierbataillon, an elite army unit of the Prussian kings.[30] Twenty persons (2 women, 18 men) lived in middle or lower social circumstances, in the private households of merchants and retired plantation owners or former plantation employees; some were referred to as private servants of army officers after the American War of Independence. Additionally, at least 7 persons (5 women, 2 men) came to court as missionaries and members of the Moravian Church, among them two famous black missionaries, Rebecca (widowed Freundlich) from St. Thomas and her later husband Christianus Jakob Protten from the region now known as Ghana.[31] A second rather coherent group is made up of 9 trade journeymen from the West Indies who were being trained at Ahrensburg, the northern German manor of Danish-German slave trader Heinrich Carl Schimmelmann.[32] Finally, at least 16 persons (13 women, 3 men) came to court as family members, 9 men occupied professions outside of the court and army, and 11 persons are mentioned in the sources without any further information.

Court musicians enjoyed an elevated social status, especially as members of the guilds, since being a citizen of a town and being legally free were basic requirements for membership.[33] Therefore, among the 380 persons of the present sample, 22 court musicians—7 trumpeters and 15 drummers—employed by different seventeenth- and eighteenth-century German sovereigns can be regarded not only as free, but, according to the eminent status of musicians at court and in the military, even as privileged. Another 7 blacks were mentioned as drummer journeymen and, thus, were evidently free, but nothing further is known about their fate. Their teachers may have been among the other black drummers, since 2 of the 15 were referred to as "masters" of the art, a title encompassing the right to teach. Nearly all of the skilled musicians seem to have been fairly well integrated into German society; many married local women, and their social standing was sufficiently independent for them to negotiate interests. However, 110 blacks employed as pipers and tambours in eighteenth-century Prussian, Hessian, and Brunswick troops were probably not members of the guilds or otherwise connected with that institutional framework.

Apart from the professions of court musician and servant, blacks occasionally appeared in professions of a different social standing, appearing as barbers, delivery boys or summoners, stable lads, burnishers, wardrobe maids, gardeners' journeymen, doormen, midwives, church musicians, fellows of the guild of carpenters, day workers, washing maids, one organist, and others. Generally, however, the court seems to have offered better options for social advancement than other social spaces, even when black people first arrived as "gifts." For example, Ferdinand Christian Coridon, who was born in Suriname or Berbice and was sent to the Count of Wittgenstein-Berleburg "as a present from Holland" later occupied primarily administrative positions at the court of Berleburg. There, he belonged to an income group second only to members of the cabinet.[34] Another example of extraordinary success is Carl of Commani, who was based at the Stuttgart court as an equerry of the guards, i.e., an officer of honor.[35] Still another attested profession of traditionally high standing was trainer of aristocrats' horses: two blacks in Stuttgart and Mecklenburg enjoyed this status.

Professional options were not static, however, as many blacks changed professions. Some deliberately turned away from army or court service and looked for better jobs elsewhere. The piper Johann Daniel Goldofsky left army duty and became an ordinary ploughboy. Similarly, lackey August Wilhelm Peter quit service at the Brunswick court to find a more favorable position. He eventually returned after nothing better turned up. Anton Wilhelm Amo, for his part, was a "chamber Moor" at the Wolfenbüttel court before he took up studies and later became the first black German university teacher of philosophy.[36] It is important to keep the possibility of shifting professions in mind when interpreting the records, since the same person may have been attested in different settings at various stages of his or her life.

Rank and Religion: A Chamber Servant at Wolfenbüttel

Among the 308 persons who were generally attached to the courts, 105 (14 women, 91 men) were in court service in a broader sense, i.e., they were mentioned as "servants," "lackeys," or "court Moors," whose concrete professional profiles were otherwise unspecified. Thirty-six persons (3 women, 33 men) were referred to as "chamber lackeys" or "chamber Moors," with positions more clearly situated in the princely household as the nucleus of the larger court.[37] However, 3 black chamber servants *(Kammerdiener)* in Wolfenbüttel and Mecklenburg stand out as comparatively high ranking in servants' hierarchies, as they served as principals to members of the ruler's (white and black) personal staff and occupied posts of absolute trust.[38]

One of them, whose biography will be detailed here, was Rudolph Mohr, who passed away on 21 March 1725 after almost fifty years of duty at the Wolfenbüttel court. His published obituary portrayed his life from the day he escaped his Jewish master, who had just bought him for fifty Reichstaler from a Portuguese merchant at the Leipzig Easter Fair of 1684:

> As from the beginning the odd direction of God made itself evident in him, it occurred that he left the Jew and retired behind the altar of the Leipzig main church, where he began a vast and piteous bawling so that the whole town awoke. As the rumor of this came to … Rudolph August, Duke of Brunswick and Lüneburg then present there … commiseration induced [him] to pay the Jew back the 50 Reichstaler … to most graciously receive him and to bring him to the Brunswick residence.[39]

From the central European aristocrat's perspective (the obituary was published by the ducal family), the initial circumstance, a customary deal, it would seem, was transformed into a generous act of rescue, with the duke's "graciousness" in "receiving" (not "buying") the slave directly opposing the former master's presumed commercial interests. Yet the obituary not only contrasted the merchant and duke—or Jewish "materialism" and Christian "commiseration"—but also, on a symbolic level, anticipated the slave's later conversion by emphasizing his peculiar choice of refuge. It later renewed this strand of his spiritual affinity with the Christian faith in relation to his profession when it stressed his initial intention to study theology. In the end, though, as the obituary stated, he decided to pursue a career at court, which was obviously considered to be a real alternative to a studied profession. That Anton Wilhelm Amo, who came to the same court just a few decades later, faced a similar choice and decided to enter university, attests that service was not always forced upon individuals. Like Amo and Mohr, at least some had options.

The obituary went on to provide details of Rudolph Mohr's family, including his wife and children. His widow, also of African descent, came to the Wolfenbüttel court in 1685 as a present of the Danish queen. She married Rudolph later, bearing him three sons and six daughters, only two of whom, however, survived their father. The necrology then elaborated on Rudolph Mohr's personal qualities and especially underscored the favor he found among the nobility, "because of his noble integrity." He was "loved by citizens and inhabitants of the duchy for his unblemished heart, his lively and cheerful character." Moreover, he was praised for his "adroitness in courtly life, agility without hurry, observance without defamation, eloquence without slander, courteousness without disguise," as well as for "passing on what the needy had told him," for being "solicitous towards his neighbors" without harming others, and for other moral qualities.[40] Generally, the description characterized him more in relation to the virtues of the court than to "nature" or "primitive" culture; it did not apply the concept of the "noble savage" nor further mention his initial slave status.[41] Furthermore, the indication that he transmitted "what the needy had told him" to the duke suggests that, to some extent, he controlled information flows directed toward the ruler. In other words, judging from the obituary, it seems that Rudolph Mohr was not just a faithful servant who responded to the demands of more powerful agents but was also one of those who controlled access to the duke.[42]

Rudolph Mohr's biography shows that positions encompassing power and control were possible for blacks at court. The courts could offer blacks exceptional opportunities for social advancement, often exceeding the possibilities for the middle classes. Hierarchies were trenchant, but there was no fixed, racially defined space. Rather, one's position and social esteem were defined by one's personal relationship with the ruler. Professional choices were not always and forever limited to service at court, as the example of Amo shows, though they were certainly influenced by the ruler's notions of responsibility toward his subjects—either black or white.

Dependencies and Reciprocities: The Structural Ambiguity of Black Court Service

The diversity of blacks' social positions within and outside court culture indicates that they were not exclusively defined by the color of their skin. Dark skin did not determine their social rank as a matter of course; both downward and upward social mobility were possible. At the same time, most of the attractive or available posts were located at the highly color-conscious courts scrambling to add the exotic glimmer and cosmopolitan cachet of people of black African heritage to their noble decorum. It has been stated that black servants at court had to rely, to an extraordinary degree, upon their ruler's personal support; that is, in historian Vera Lind's words, their status was one of "privileged dependency."[43] However, where multilayered dependencies and reciprocities are at the very core of societal structures, power and dependencies are always relational.[44] Relationships based on patronage—a social practice long regarded as random and largely corrupted—were the rule rather than the exception in European court contexts. Recent approaches to the politics of early modern princely patronage regard it as a major political and economic resource in prebureaucratic societies. Naturally, this applies to the careers of both white and black servants and courtiers, who maintained networks of influential patrons.⁴⁵ Like their white counterparts, people of African descent used their patrons to promote their social advancement, which meant that higher social positions were not, on principle, out of their reach.

To be sure, blacks' opportunity for social advancement did not arise out of a concept of social equality, the political countermodel to the estate-based society: at that time, there was no modern concept of individual civil rights and liberties, and inequality was taken as the basis of society as naturally as civil society now takes equality as its basis. The juridical attributes of residents as well as of in-migrants were not defined by citizenship, and grades of mutual dependency between the elites and their subordinates were hierarchically scaled across the entire society.⁴⁶ Even as enlightened concepts of social organization emerged in the eighteenth century, monarchs' ability to define social rank increased, with the courts becoming linchpins for the appreciation of status pretentions. Until the end of the century, the basic structure of the estate-based society was rarely called into question publicly. It remained a lived concept down to the basic unit of society, the family, where a father would—on a smaller scale—claim a position similar to that of the monarch on the state level.⁴⁷

Consequently, court service, in a symbolic sense, could be regarded as both an honor and a form of subordination. This ambiguity may help to explain the opposite decisions that Rudolph Mohr and Anton Wilhelm Amo made concerning their careers. For Rudolph Mohr, who chose to remain in service at the Wolfenbüttel princely court instead of studying, the social esteem of court service may well have surpassed that of an academic career. For Anton Wilhelm Amo, on the other hand, the sense of subordination at court may have prevailed when he decided to enter university. As an enlightened scholar, a pupil of the philosopher Christian Wolff, he followed different political strands and drew academic attention to the (formal) status of blacks in Europe, albeit casually.⁴⁸ Mohr, for his part, probably saw his status as deriving from that of the Wolfenbüttel princes, since the symbolic value of court service traditionally depended on the rank of the person served. The higher the rank, the higher the symbolic value of the duty being performed, but also vice versa: the higher the rank of the servant, the higher the symbolic value of his or her services to the receiver.⁴⁹

Beyond legal attributes in a strict sense, both this web of multilayered dependencies and the reciprocities of status acquisition should be taken into account when assessing the symbolic value and social status of people of African descent in ancien régime central Europe. Doubtlessly, the aesthetic value attributed to their physical appearance was part of court representation. Yet their status at court, their "prestige," to use Debrunner's term, was not restricted to such representation: it encompassed both a social dimension—learned professions, regular payment, at times elevated social positions, intermarriage with local women—and a religious one: baptism as an act of symbolic integration.

Notes

1. Eric J. Hobsbawm and Terence Ranger, eds., *The Invention of Tradition* (Cambridge: Cambridge University Press, 1983); Benedict Anderson, *Imagined Communities: Reflections on the Origin and Spread of Nationalism* (London: Knopf Doubleday, 1983); and Dirk Hoerder, "Europe's Many Worlds and Their Global Interconnections: Migration Movements in Historical Perspective," in *Enlarging European Memory: Migration Movements in Historical Perspective*, ed. Mareike König and Rainer Ohliger, Francia Beihefte Band 26 (Ostfildern: Jan Thorbecke, 2006), 21–32.
2. Hans Werner Debrunner, *Presence and Prestige: Africans in Europe: A History of Africans in Europe before 1918* (Basel, Switzerland: Basler Afrika Bibliographien, 1979); Peter Martin, *Schwarze Teufel, edle Mohren: Afrikaner in Geschichte und Bewußtsein der Deutschen* (Hamburg, Germany: Hamburger Edition, 2001); Allison Blakely, *Blacks in the Dutch World: The Evolution of Racial Imagery in a Modern Society* (Bloomington: Indiana University Press, 1993); Allison Blakely, "African Diaspora in the Netherlands," in *Encyclopedia of Diasporas: Immigrant and Refugee Cultures Around the World*, ed. Melvin Ember, Carol R. Ember, and Ian Skoggard (New York: Springer, 2005), 2:593–602; Allison Blakely, *Russia and the Negro: Blacks in Russian History and Thought* (Washington DC: Howard University Press, 1986); and Dieudonné Gnammankou, *Alexandre S. Pouchkine et le monde Noir* (Paris: Présence Africaine, 1999).
3. Ingeborg Kittel, "Mohren als Hofbediente und Soldaten im Herzogtum Braunschweig-Wolfenbüttel," *Braunschweigisches Jahrbuch* 46 (1965): 78–103; Wolfram Schäfer, "Von 'Kammermohren,' 'Mohren'-Tambouren und 'Ost-Indianern,'" *Hessische Blätter für Volks- und Kulturforschung* 23 (1988): 35–79; Ute Küppers-Braun, "Kammermohren: Ignatius Fortuna am Essener Hof und andere farbige Hofdiener," *Das Münster am Hellweg: Mitteilungsblatt des Vereins für die Erhaltung des Essener Münsters* 54 (2001): 17–50; Monika Firla, *Exotisch—höfisch—bürgerlich: Afrikaner in Württemberg vom 15. bis 19. Jahrhundert* (Stuttgart, Germany: Hauptstaatsarchiv, 2001); Monika Firla, "'Hof-' und andere 'Mohren' als früheste Schicht des Eintreffens von Afrikanern in Deutschland," in *Neue Heimat Deutschland: Aspekte der Zuwanderung, Akkulturation und emotionalen Bindung*, ed. Hartmut Heller (Erlangen, Germany: Universitätsbund Erlangen-Nürnberg, 2002), 157–76; and Weygo Comte Rudt de Collenberg, "Haus- und Hofmohren des 18. Jahrhunderts in Europa," in *Gesinde im 18. Jahrhundert*, ed. Gotthardt Frühsorge, Rainer Gruenter, and Beatrix Freifrau Wolff Metternich (Hamburg, Germany: Meiner, 1995), 265–80.
4. Court history has become a field of research in its own right since the 1970s. In the beginning, it was largely influenced by sociologist and historian Norbert Elias. See Elias, *The Civilizing Process*, 2 vols. (Oxford: Blackwell, 1982) (a first, German edition appeared in England in 1939, but only when it was reissued in 1969 was it more widely received in academia); and Elias, *The Court Society* (Oxford: Blackwell, 1983). Gerhardt Petrat provides a short introduction to the history of blacks at late medieval and early modern German courts from the perspective of court history; see Petrat, "Zwerge, Riesen, Mohren," in *Höfe und Residenzen im spätmittelalterlichen Reich*, ed. Werner Paravicini (Ostfildern, Germany: Jan Thorbecke, 2005), 2:1:69–74.
5. For the cultural transfer of black images in art history, see Paul H. D. Kaplan, "Black Africans in Hohenstaufen Iconography," *Gesta* 26, no. 1 (1987): 29–36; Paul H. D. Kaplan, "Isabella d'Este and Black African Women," in *Black Africans in Renaissance Europe*, ed. T. F. Earle and K. J. P. Lowe (Cambridge: Cambridge University Press, 2005), 125–54; and Gude Suckale-Redlefsen, *Mauritius: Der heilige Mohr/The Black Saint Maurice* (Houston: Menil Foundation, 1987).
6. The literature on the courts is vast and still expanding. For an overview of the most influential concepts, see John Adamson, "Introduction: The Making of the Ancien Régime Court,

1500–1700," in *The Princely Courts of Europe: Ritual, Politics and Culture Under the Ancien Régime, 1500–1750*, ed. John Adamson (London: Weidenfeld & Nicolson, 1999), 9; and Jeroen Duindam, *Vienna and Versailles: The Courts of Europe's Dynastic Rivals, 1550–1780* (Cambridge: Cambridge University Press, 2003).
7. Adamson, "Introduction," 40; and Ronald G. Asch, "Introduction: Court and Household from the Fifteenth to the Seventeenth Centuries," in *Princes, Patronage, and the Nobility: The Court at the Beginning of the Modern Age, c. 1450–1650*, ed. R. G. Asch and Adolf M. Birke, Studies of the German Historical Institute London (London: Oxford University Press, 1991), 1–4.
8. Elias, *Civilizing Process;* Elias, *Court Society.* For comprehensive critiques of Elias's influential model of the court, see Jeroen Duindam, *Myths of Power: Norbert Elias and the Early Modern European Court* (Amsterdam: Amsterdam University Press, 1994); Jeroen Duindam, *Vienna and Versailles;* and Asch, "Introduction," 3–4.
9. Peter Burke, *The Fabrication of Louis XIV* (New Haven, CT: Yale University Press, 1992), 11; and Adamson, "Introduction," 10, 40.
10. Petrat, "Zwerge, Riesen, Mohren," 72–73; Martin, *Schwarze Teufel, edle Mohren*, 41–66; and Debrunner, *Presence and Prestige*, 91–100. For blacks as "images of empire" at the Lisbon court, see Annemarie Jordan, "Images of Empire: Slaves in the Lisbon Household and Court of Catherine of Austria," in Earle and Lowe, *Black Africans in Renaissance Europe*, 155–80.
11. Rainer-Maria Kiel, "Das christgläubige Mohrenland oder Was Caspar von Lilien über Äthiopien predigte," *Archiv für Geschichte von Oberfranken* 65 (1985): 379–94; and Rainer-Maria Kiel, *Zwischen Integration und Sensation: Afrikaner im Bayreuth des 17. bis 19. Jahrhunderts* (unpublished paper, Bayreuth, 1998, 29 pp.), 3–10. I am deeply indebted to Dr. Kiel for sending me a copy of the manuscript based on his research in the Bayreuth archives.
12. Staatsarchiv Aurich (hereafter: StA Aurich), Rep. 4 A III b, 6 (22 or 23 November 1682). This transfer is not recorded at the Bayreuth court. However, the girl may have been Sophia Christiana Eleonora, who is recorded as having died at the age of about thirteen and buried in Bayreuth on 14 September 1683; Kiel, *Zwischen Integration und Sensation*, 11.
13. StA Aurich, Rep. 241 Msc A 43, fol. 123r-124v. From 1729, Anthon is listed in the register of the East Frisian state administration and court offices and their civil servants ("Verzeichnis der ostfriesischen Staatsbehörden und fürstlichen Hofämter sowie deren Beamte," StA Aurich, Rep. 4 B III a 20); see also Karl Herquet, *Miscellen zur Geschichte Ostfrieslands* (Vaduz, Liechtenstein: Sendig Reprint, 1985), 133–34.
14. Hessisches Hauptstaatsarchiv Wiesbaden (hereafter HHStAW), Abt. 131, R 97, Cammer Rechnung De Anno 1721, p. 141 (item 495); HHStAW, Abt. 131, R 291, no. 495 (hand-signed by Friderike Wilhelmine, Princess of East Frisia). I am greatly indebted to Rashid-S. Pegah for directing my attention to this and the two following sources from the Fürstlich Öttingen-Wallerstein'sches Archiv, Harburg, and the Geheimes Staatsarchiv Preußischer Kulturbesitz, Berlin.
15. Kiel, "Das christgläubige Mohrenland," 380–81; Kiel, *Zwischen Integration und Sensation*, 7–10, 24–25.
16. Fürstlich Öttingen-Wallerstein'sches Archiv, Schloss Harburg, Harburg (Schwab.), VII. 4. 1a, Fasz. 76; undated (c. 1702).
17. Geheimes Staatsarchiv Preußischer Kulturbesitz, Brandenburg-Preußisches Hausarchiv, Rep. 43 II J, no. 340.
18. Allison Blakely, "Problems in Studying the Role of Blacks in Europe," *Perspectives: American Historical Association Newsletter* 35, no. 5 (May–June 1997): 1–14. For a more detailed research review, see Mark Häberlein, "'Mohren,' ständische Gesellschaft und atlantische Welt: Minderheiten und Kulturkontakte in der Frühen Neuzeit," in *Atlantic Understandings: Essays on European and American History in Honor of Hermann Wellenreuther*, ed. Claudia Schnurmann and Hartmut Lehmann (Hamburg, Germany: LIT, 2006), 77–102.

19. Martin, *Schwarze Teufel, edle Mohren,* 129–32, 138, 144–50, 153–61, 178–81; Uta Sadji, "'Unverbesserlich ausschweifende' oder 'brauchbare Subjekte'? Mohren als 'befreite' Sklaven im Deutschland des 18. Jahrhunderts," *Komparatistische Hefte* 2 (1980): 42–52, 45–47, 50.
20. Martin, *Schwarze Teufel, edle Mohren,* 136; Sadji, "'Unverbesserlich ausschweifende,'" 357, translation A.K.
21. Bernd Roeck, *Außenseiter, Randgruppen, Minderheiten: Fremde im Deutschland der frühen Neuzeit* (Göttingen, Germany: Vandenhoeck & Ruprecht, 1993), 101–105, translation A.K. For the interpretation of blacks as "living 'toy things,'" see also Petrat, "Zwerge, Riesen, Mohren," 72.
22. Häberlein, "'Mohren,' ständische Gesellschaft und atlantische Welt," 85. The literature on Amo, Soliman, Hanibal, and Badin is abundant. For a bibliographic overview, see Dieudonné Gnammankou, "African Diaspora in Europe," in *Encyclopedia of Diasporas: Immigrant and Refugee Cultures around the World,* vol. 1, *Overviews and Topics,* ed. Melvin Ember, Carol R. Ember, and Ian Skoggard (New York: Kluwer Academic/Plenum Publishers, 2004), 15–24; and Jürgen Jensen, ed., *Afrikaner in Europa—Eine Bibliographie. Africans in Europe—A Bibliography. Africains en Europe—Une Bibliographie* (Münster, Germany: LIT, 2002).
23. On Ignatius Fortuna, see Küppers-Braun, "Kammermohren," 17–50; on Mustapha and Mahomet, see Eward Scobie, *Black Britannia: A History of Blacks in Britain* (Chicago: Johnson, 1972), 12.
24. For Christian Gottlieb, see Johannes Christian Kinder, *Aus der Chronik der Stadt Ploen,* vol. 1, *Christian Gottlieb der schwarze Feldtrompeter* (Plön, Germany: Hirt, 1887); and Martin, *Schwarze Teufel, edle Mohren,* 181–93. For Carl of Commani, see Firla, *Exotisch—höfisch—bürgerlich,* 57–65; and Monika Firla, "Quellen des Landeskirchlichen Archivs Stuttgart zur Erforschung der Afrikanischen Diaspora des 18. Jahrhunderts in Württemberg," *Blätter für württembergische Kirchengeschichte* 99 (1999): 92. On Alzire, see Kiel, *Zwischen Integration und Sensation,* 16–18.
25. On Dominicus, see Schäfer, "Von 'Kammermohren,'" 39; Silke Wagener-Fimpel, "Mohren in Schaumburg-Lippe im 18. Jahrhundert," in *Schaumburg und die Welt: Zu Schaumburgs auswärtigen Beziehungen in der Geschichte,* ed. Hubert Hoeing (Bielefeld, Germany: Verlag für Regionalgeschichte, 2002), 124–25; and Martin, *Schwarze Teufel, edle Mohren,* 141, 178. On Coridon, see Schäfer, "Von 'Kammermohren,'" 35–36. On Dolenta, see Schäfer, "Von 'Kammermohren,'" 42, 43–44, 66; Martin, *Schwarze Teufel, edle Mohren,* 427; and Wagener-Fimpel, "Mohren in Schaumburg-Lippe," 121–42.
26. Peter Martin, "Black Diaspora Studies in Germany: Some Remarks to the State of the Art at the Washington Conference" (paper presented at the conference Black Diaspora and Germany across the Centuries at the German Historical Institute, Washington DC, 20 March 2009).
27. Kate Lowe, "Notes on the Text," in Earle and Lowe, *Black Africans in Renaissance Europe,* xv–xvii; see also Kate Lowe's and Maria Diedrich's chapters in this book.
28. See the entries "Africaner," "Mauren," "Nubier"/"Nubien," "Chus," "Mohrenland," "Abißinien," and "Aethiopien," in *Grosses vollständiges Universal-Lexicon aller Wissenschafften und Künste, welche bisher durch menschlichen Verstand und Witz erfunden und verbessert worden ...,* ed. Johann Heinrich Zedler, 64 vols., 4 suppl. vols. (Halle, Germany: Zedler, 1732–1754; new ed., Graz, Austria: Akademische Druck- und Verlagsanstalt, 1993).
29. Asch, "Introduction," 1–38.
30. Peter Panoff, *Militärmusik in Geschichte und Gegenwart* (Berlin: Sigismund 1938), 73; Anonymous, "Schwarze Militärmusiker und Spielleute," *Deutscher Soldaten-Kalender* 7 (1959): 177; Jürgen Kloosterhuis, *Legendäre 'lange Kerls': Quellen zur Regimentskultur der Königsgrenadiere Friedrich Wilhelms I., 1713–1740,* ed. Geheimes Staatsarchiv Preußischer Kulturbesitz (Berlin: Geheimes Staatsarchiv, 2003), Q 251 (a-b), 252 (a-b), 253 (c), 255 (b). Thanks are due to Wiard Hinrichs of Göttingen, who generously provided this reference.

31. On Rebecca and her husband, see, especially, Jon F. Sensbach, *Rebecca's Revival: Creating Black Christianity in the Atlantic World* (Cambridge, MA: Harvard University Press, 2005).
32. Christian Degn, *Die Schimmelmanns im atlantischen Dreieckshandel: Gewinn und Gewissen* (Neumünster, Germany: K. Wachholtz, 1974), 114–15; and Martin, *Schwarze Teufel, edle Mohren,* 106, 162–68.
33. "Confirmatio/ vber 13. von Irer Matt. vnd der yezt alhie anweßenden Chur: vnd Fürsten Hoff: vnd Veldt Tromettern auch Horpaugger/ vbergebene Articul (27 February 1623)," in *Untersuchungen zur Geschichte der Trompete im Zeitalter der Clarinblaskunst,* ed. Detlef Altenburg, 2 vols. (Regensburg, Germany: G. Bosse, 1973), 2:47–55.
34. Schäfer, "Von 'Kammermohren,'" 35–36, 59.
35. Equerry *(Stallmeister):* a high noble official at a princely or royal court in medieval and early modern Germany, responsible for supervising the manorial stables with all stable servants being subordinate to him; see Rainer A. Müller, *Der Fürstenhof in der Frühen Neuzeit* (Munich: Oldenbourg, 2004), 22.
36. On Goldofsky, see Martin, *Schwarze Teufel, edle Mohren,* 148; on August Wilhelm Peter, see Kittel, "Mohren als Hofbediente und Soldaten," 87–88; on Amo, see, e.g., Debrunner, *Presence and Prestige,* 106–8; and Burchard Brentjes, *Anton Wilhelm Amo: Der schwarze Philosoph in Halle* (Leipzig, Germany: Koehler & Amelang, 1976).
37. Duindam, *Myths of Power,* 7–13.
38. Müller, *Fürstenhof,* 20.
39. "Beständiges Andenken der Redlichkeit des Weyland Hoch-Fürstl: Cammer-Dieners Rudolph Mohrens," Stadtarchiv Braunschweig, Handbibliothek, HIX: 256, translation A.K.
40. Ibid.
41. According to Urs Bitterli, French natural scientist Michel Adanson was the first to apply the concept of the "noble savage" to Africans after his travels to Senegal between 1749 and 1754; see Bitterli, *Die Entdeckung des schwarzen Afrikaners: Versuch einer Geistesgeschichte der europäisch-afrikanischen Beziehungen an der Guineaküste im 17. und 18. Jahrhundert* (Zurich: Atlantis, 1970), 44–46, 84.
42. Ronald G. Asch, "'The Politics of Access': Hofstruktur und Herrschaft in England unter den frühen Stuarts, 1603–1642," in *Alltag bei Hofe,* ed. Werner Paravicini, 3rd Symposium of the Residenzen-Kommission der Akademie der Wissenschaften in Göttingen (Sigmaringen, Germany: Thorbecke, 1995), 243–66.
43. Vera Lind, "Privileged Dependency on the Edge of the Atlantic World: Africans and Germans in the Eighteenth Century," in *Interpreting Colonialism,* ed. Byron R. Wells and Philip Stewart (Oxford: Voltaire Foundation, 2004), 369–91.
44. Richard White, *The Middle Ground: Indians, Empires, and Republics in the Great Lakes Region, 1650–1815* (Cambridge: Cambridge University Press, 1991); and Hartwig Isernhagen, "Dominance, Subdominance, Survival: The Middle Ground as Interpretive Paradigm," in *Berichten, Erzählen, Beherrschen: Wahrnehmung und Repräsentation in der frühen Kolonialgeschichte Europas,* ed. Susanna Burghartz, Maike Christadler, and Dorothea Nolde, Zeitsprünge, Forschungen zur Frühen Neuzeit 7, no. 2–3 (Frankfurt: Klostermann, 2003), 180.
45. On the politics of patronage as a subfield of research within early modern European court history that focuses on elite culture, see, especially, Asch, "Introduction," 1–38; and Ronald G. Asch, *Europäischer Adel in der Frühen Neuzeit* (Cologne, Germany: UTB, 2008), 112–23.
46. Gerhard Dilcher, "Der alteuropäische Adel—ein verfassungsgeschichtlicher Typus?" in *Europäischer Adel 1750–1950,* ed. Hans-Ulrich Wehler (Göttingen, Germany: Vandenhoeck & Ruprecht, 1990), 58.
47. John Miller, *Absolutism in Seventeenth Century Europe* (New York: Palgrave Macmillan, 1990); Nicholas Henshall, *The Myth of Absolutism: Change and Continuity in Early Modern European*

Monarchy (London: Longman, 1992); and Ronald G. Asch, "Absolutismus," in *Lexikon zum aufgeklärten Absolutismus in Europa,* ed. Helmut Reinalter (Vienna: UTB, 2005), 15–21.

48. Amo's 1729 dissertation at the University of Halle, *De iure Maurorum in Europa,* which might have offered deeper insights into the situation of black Africans in Europe, was probably never published but might have simply been an oral defense of his doctor's thesis.
49. Barbara Stollberg-Rilinger, "Ordnungsleistung und Konfliktträchtigkeit der höfischen Tafel," in *Zeichen und Raum: Ausstattung und höfisches Zeremoniell in den deutschen Schlössern der Frühen Neuzeit,* ed. Rudolstädter Arbeitskreis zur Residenzkultur (Munich: Deutscher Kunstverlag, 2006), 104.

Chapter Four

REAL AND IMAGINED AFRICANS IN BAROQUE COURT DIVERTISSEMENTS

Rashid-S. Pegah

For centuries black Africans were a distinctive part of European court culture. Early evidence of their presence can be found in the cosmopolitan court of Frederick II of Hohenstaufen (1194–1250), the German king, Roman emperor (from 1220), and successor of the Norman kings in Sicily. His court, a center of intellectual exchange in his time, shows black Africans in an array of positions that would later recur in Renaissance and Baroque court culture. Frederick, born of a Norman mother and a German father, was raised in Sicily and later founded the University of Naples and the medical school of Salerno. The Norman kings, bearing the title "Kings of Africa," received tribute from the ancient Roman province of Africa, roughly located in the territory of today's Tunisia. Frederick married Constanze of Aragon, who provided an additional cultural input with her retinue of Aragonese knights, court ladies, and troubadours.[1]

Examples of blacks in Frederick's court could be found among his military retinue. In Frederick's "Camere" at Melfi, Canossa, and Messina, black women manufactured precious textiles and weapons—but they were rumored to be the emperor's harem. In the 1220s, Frederick evacuated Muslims to the plains of Apulia, at the city of Lucera, where they formed a military colony with its own mosque and administration. From among these "Saracens" (as Christian Europeans used to call Islamic peoples, several of whom were black Africans), Frederick chose his bodyguard and some members of his permanent retinue. On his voyage to the northern parts of the empire in 1231, he was accompanied by black attendants gorgeously dressed in silk and linen who guarded the imperial treasury of

---

Notes from this chapter begin on page 88.

gold, silver, precious stones, textiles, and vessels. Frederick's court also included a band of young black musicians, mainly trumpeters, and as personal attendants he had *servitelli nigri,* African boys. With the chancery being bilingual, black boys received an education in reading and writing in Arabic and Latin. Johannes Morus (c. 1200–after 1250), a black and probably Muslim slave, became Guard of the Emperor's Personal Chamber, Prefect of the Chamber under Frederick's successor King Manfred, Commander of Lucera, and Vezir of the Sicilian Kingdom.[2]

Black Africans and Court Divertissement

At Frederick's court, the professional skills of blacks were mainly located in four fields: military and security service, domestic service, administration, and entertainment. Of these, this paper will focus on the last and particularly on the roles of blacks in the divertissements, an elaborate form of European court entertainment, concentrating on examples from the Baroque era. As in art history, the figure of the sponsor and his or her patronage policies are central to an understanding of these visual performances. These policies were influenced by the wider context of a German "court landscape" in which "[c]ities like Dresden, Stuttgart and Hanover were the showplaces of the Germany of the princes. In Weimar and Munich, a third of the inhabitants depended directly on the prince for their livelihood. In such places, the patterns of demand and spending established by princely patronage meant that most of the rest were in some measure dependent."[3] Princely patronage as outlined by Geoffrey Treasure was essential to the arts and culture and to the splendor of the early modern princely courts.[4] Most important in this respect were the royal French court from 1643 and the imperial court at Vienna. The standards they set with their lavish spectacles, for example, served as models throughout the Holy Roman Empire.

Other important influences came from beyond the Alps, where the courtly grandeur of nobility and clergy alike were ideals for the refinement of the arts in the empire. French and Italian artists, craftsmen, musicians, and other specialists traveling between the courts brought new incentives and genres to the German-speaking lands. Besides Vienna, princes like the archbishops of Salzburg, the electors of Bavaria in Munich, the electors of Saxony in Dresden, the dukes of Württemberg in Stuttgart, and the Palatine electors belonged to the first category of princely patrons, and their courts were important cultural centers of the Holy Roman Empire. After the Thirty Years' War (1618–48), the Electorate of Brandenburg-Prussia became another important power in the north of Germany, and soon a promoter of the arts, too. It was only during the last decade of the seventeenth century, however, that its capital, Berlin, began to flourish as a place where arts and craftsmanship were practiced on an even larger, broader, and more attractive scale than during the reign of Elector Frederick William "the Great"

(1620–88; ruled from 1640). His aim after the war had been to strengthen the economy rather than to reinforce his military and territorial power. Simultaneously, the dukedoms of the House of Brunswick-Lüneburg reached the peak of their power and patronage, and were temporarily seen as rivals to Brandenburg-Prussia in the northern territories. Yet, in the end, the dukes of Brunswick-Lüneburg were not able to raise their lands to the importance Prussia would gain in the eighteenth century. Only the duke of Brunswick-Lüneburg-Hanover achieved a relatively high status, becoming elector in 1692; his successors were kings of England.

On a comparable level of minor political relevance as the dukes of Brunswick-Lüneburg-Wolfenbüttel and Brunswick-Lüneburg-Celle were the margraves of Brandenburg-Ansbach and Brandenburg-Culmbach-Bayreuth,[5] whose territories were seen as Franconian dependencies of the electoral Berlin Hohenzollern.[6] Originating in southern Germany, the Hohenzollern were first burgraves of Nuremberg before coming to power in the margraviate and later electorate of Brandenburg.

Since the focus of this paper is the theatrical divertissements of the margraves of Bayreuth, it is necessary to take a brief look at the origins of Bayreuth and at its earlier developments as a town with a princely court. The town of Bayreuth became a princely residence after the death of Margrave George Frederick Sr. of Brandenburg-Culmbach (1539–1603; ruled from 1543/1557), when his estate was divided into Brandenburg-Culmbach-Bayreuth and Brandenburg-Ansbach. Christian (1581–1655; ruled from 1603), the son of a Brandenburg elector, became the first margrave of Brandenburg-Culmbach-Bayreuth. In light of recent research, he appears to have been a patron and promoter of the arts.[7] When his grandson Christian Ernst (1644–1712; ruled from 1662) came to power, the Bayreuth court rose to magnificence.

Real and Imagined Blacks in German Court Entertainment

Art patronage gave courts of limited political significance the means to counterbalance a lack of territorial or military power. The presence of black or Turkish servants also enabled the courts, politically significant or not, to broaden their scale of symbolic representation with an "exotic" note. During the two centuries between 1600 and 1800, black musicians, most of them initially bought at slave markets of the Mediterranean and in the west Atlantic world, played distinctive roles in the European courts. As a rule, they basically occupied a position as servants in the lower or medium ranks of court staff. Expensive and coveted as they were, the curiosity and exoticism that their traits excited at times helped them to gain a position within the rulers' immediate orbit, although they generally had to undergo religious conversion from pagan or Muslim beliefs to Christianity.

Besides their high visibility in works of both religious and profane art, real and imagined blacks were present in pageants, masquerades, and military parades as well as in festive celebrations of all the yearly and life occasions. Since the "state" in the German lands presented itself, much like the Ottoman Empire of the time,[8] as theater, black servants can even be regarded as "actors" on the everyday level of a "continuous theatre of courtly representation."[9] Moreover, Africa as a topic kept reemerging in art and on stage and in allegorical representations of the four continents then commonly known. In these allegories, the images of Africa and the other continents rose to the dimensions of a "world theater" in which the respective local sovereign would always claim the central role.

Ballets, too, often included entrées with "*Mohren*" ("Moors")—real or imagined—and they frequently appeared in operas, which accounted for the most expensive form of court entertainment. Operas also featured members of the higher nobility disguising themselves as "Moors" to deceive opponents. In the divertissements, this role, at times, ranked high among European rulers: for example, in a Racing of National Representatives,[10] carried out in 1662 during the splendid wedding festivities for the Saxon princess Erdmuth Sophia (1644–70) and Margrave Christian Ernst of Brandenburg-Culmbach-Bayreuth in Dresden, the bride and groom were cast "as a particular privilege [in] the prestigious roles of the black couple."[11] In some cases, African history also became a topic of musical drama.

In the following sections, a range of roles occupied either by blacks themselves or by white actors in disguise (often members of the nobility) will be introduced, offering various perspectives for a discussion on prevailing images of Africa and Africans: a burglar, a bird catcher, and a drummer, all represented by the same black African in Bayreuth ballets; figures from ancient African history in an opera performed in 1722 at the Bayreuth court; a lustful king disguised as a "Moor" to evade his heroic wife's wrath in another Bayreuth opera; and an example of Africa's treatment as part of an allegory of the four continents in the wedding festivities at the Prussian royal court in Berlin (1706). These examples, particularly thus juxtaposed, will highlight that there was no single, dominant view of blacks or Africans in court culture, but that they could stand on an equal footing or be regarded as inferior, less rational, or even more noble.

Timpanist Christian Ferdinand at the Bayreuth Court

The first example is Christian Ferdinand of the court of the margraves of Brandenburg-Culmbach-Bayreuth in south German Franconia. A politically minor court throughout the seventeenth and eighteenth centuries, it was closely connected through dynastic kinship with the court of the electors of Saxony at Dresden, which had the greatest cultural influence of all the courts. These electors included Johann Georg II, Johann Georg III, and Johann Georg IV, and their successor Friedrich Augustus I (1670–1733; ruled from 1694), who, as Augustus II "the Strong," also became King of Poland in 1697. The court of Brandenburg-Culmbach-Bayreuth also maintained close relationships with the Brandenburg electoral court at Berlin, where Margrave Christian Ernst spent part of his childhood, and with the kings of Denmark and Norway at Copenhagen.

Christian Ferdinand was probably the first of many blacks to serve the court in Bayreuth, having come there in the 1660s as a present of the Saxon elector to his daughter Erdmuth Sophia, who was married to the Bayreuth margrave Christian Ernst. His biography is thus related to the court of the Saxon elector at Dresden, as well as the Copenhagen court. Though Christian Ferdinand was originally "from Africa," his African name was not passed down. He attended a German school, learned to read and write, and underwent catechetical instruction. After passing religious exams, he was baptized Christian Ferdinand in December 1664 in the Bayreuth town church. Among his fifty-five godparents were the ruling couple, Christian Ernst and Erdmuth Sophia, Christian Ernst's uncle Margrave Georg Albrecht of Brandenburg-Culmbach (1619–66), the court chancellor and councilors, and the mayors of the capitals of the margraviate. Later, Christian Ferdinand received an education as a timpanist. As such, he earned forty Guldens in 1673/74, actually fifty-six less than the trumpeters, but ten more than the town's organist.[12]

Christian Ferdinand is portrayed as a timpanist in an illustration of the funeral procession of 1666 for Margrave Georg Albrecht, an uncle of Margrave Christian Ernst,[13] mounted on a horse and beating the kettledrums at his side. Two members of a small band of court trumpeters follow behind him. An illustration of another funeral procession for Christian Ernst's first wife four years later depicts Christian Ferdinand walking ahead of six trumpeters. Court trumpeters and timpanists belonged to a rather privileged and distinguished professional stratum in early modern Europe. Perhaps due to his social status, Christian Ferdinand was able to wed Susanna Clara Laickner on 21 February 1670. Rainer-Maria Kiel's research provides evidence of at least four children from this union, all of them born and baptized in Bayreuth between 1670 and 1675. Yet we do not know what became of Christian Ferdinand after 1675, as Kiel concluded in his study more than a decade ago. There is a 1692 letter by a Bayreuth court official that mentions a "timpanist Moor"[14]—although this might have been another black drummer or one of his sons.

In addition to his role as court timpanist, Christian Ferdinand also appeared in a number of stage productions in Bayreuth. The first one seems to have been a short, ballet-like composition, *Les Vaincus de L'Amour* (1668), a *boutade*[15] commissioned by Christian Ernst for the wedding of his chancellor Carl vom Stein (1626–75) to the widowed Baroness of Geyer on 7 June 1668. For many years, vom Stein had been a confidant of the young Christian Ernst, who appointed him as his chancellor after becoming the ruling margrave. The dancing master of the margravial family, François Maran (c. 1640/1641–97), had drafted a subject apt for the occasion. Philemon Fabri, professor of languages at the margravial Gymnasium Christian-Ernestinum, contributed the verses commenting on each of the entrées.[16]

As is typical for most Baroque ballets, *Les Vaincus de L'Amour* has no particular plot; it consists of five entrées that simply follow the general idea of showing different virile characters overcome by love. All the dancers were members of the margravial court, including François Maran and a Monsieur de Stein, probably a relative of the bridegroom. The third entrée, the *boutade*'s centerpiece, was danced by a "M[onsieu]r. de Kniesteedt & M[onsieu]r. Christian Ferdinand." Von Kniesteedt may be identified as a member of a family of Franconian nobility whose male descendants served in military ranks at the courts of Ansbach and Bayreuth, the two Brandenburg margraviates in Franconia. The introduction to this part of *Les Vaincus de L'Amour* reads as follows:

> What Cupid & the two Amours [of the first entrée] have said about their power is shown here by two burglars or porters, whose bodily strength, the quality that they represent, is overcome by these young children.[17]

Expressing the point of view of the two amorous porters, Fabri comments on the danced action in the following verses:

> Poor devils that we are;
> Scum and filth of mankind,
> We who bear on our body the weightiest burdens;
> We forget all our baseness,
> And Love alone, who wounds us
> With his sweet & powerful arrow,
> Shows that he, in his smallness,
> Has much more strength than we have.[18]

This 1668 libretto is—at least according to the present state of research—the earliest testimony to the participation of Christian Ferdinand in a divertissement at the court of Bayreuth. He served as a timpanist since 1666 at the latest, and, two years later, in 1670, he would also beat out the funeral march for the deceased margravine.

As he was addressed as "Monsieur," like his white counterpart, we may interpret Christian Ferdinand's participation in *Les Vaincus de L'Amour* as proof of his acceptance among the circle of higher-ranking court officials. He danced side by side with a member of a respected noble family, even if both were acting the parts of people of low social standing. The first cited portion of the text above may also hint at Christian Ferdinand's strong physical appearance.

The second stage production Christian Ferdinand appeared in took place in 1671, when Bayreuth witnessed the arrival of and festivities for the margrave's second wife, a Württemberg ducal princess. Again, the court's dancing master prepared a ballet—on a much more lavish scale than the one for the chancellor and his bride, of course—*Sudetische Frülings-Lust* (Sudetan Spring's Delight).[19] Like *Les Vaincus de L'Amour*, it has no particular plot. Presenting different deities and other persons, *Sudetische Frülings-Lust* gives an idea of the three "princely inclinations" of hunting, warfare, and love. Again, François Maran (this time together with other dancing masters) and members of the Bayreuth nobility took part as dancers, and Christian Ferdinand appeared in two entrées in the company of two courtiers. He is first mentioned as one of three bird catchers in the fifth entrée in the ballet's first part, which celebrates the margrave's fondness for the hunt. As a drummer, Christian Ferdinand also accompanied two fife players in the eleventh entrée in the second part of the ballet, which celebrates the margrave's taste for warfare. In this entrée, the actors were asked to express the public joy for the arrival of "the land's gods" (the margrave and the new margravine), although drums and pipes were ordinarily associated with military enterprises and wars.[20]

In the two ballets, Christian Ferdinand's participation as an African musician alongside members of Bayreuth court society, performing roles similar to their own, suggests that there was no clearly defined color line relegating people of different physical appearance to a strictly separated set of roles. This is even clearer when we consider the exclusivity of the *boutade Les Vaincus de L'Amour*, since the margravial chancellor's wedding was a more intimate occasion than the performance of *Sudetische Frülings-Lust*. The latter, part of the public entrées and festivities for the (second) marriage of the sovereign, was certainly addressed to a wider audience. These roles, together with his partaking in the official funeral processions for deceased members of the ruling family, even being depicted as something like a common part of the margravial retinue, shows that the perception of him merely as an exotic being had diminished.

Bayreuth 1722: African History in the Opera *Masinissa*

Whereas Christian Ferdinand's participation in parades and stage productions in Bayreuth suggests a seemingly full integration of a particular black individual into court society, the opera *Masinissa* performed there in 1722 gives an example of representation of ancient African royalty. When Margrave Christian Ernst died in 1712, his son Georg Wilhelm (1678–1726) succeeded him as the ruler of the margraviate Brandenburg-Culmbach. His wife, a princess of Saxe-Weißenfels remotely related to the Saxon electors, precipitated a shift in the language of the Bayreuth opera toward the German vernacular. Until then, Italian opera was most common at the residence. During their time as hereditary prince and princess, the margravial couple had already had at least one young black servant in their retinue.[21] Recent research shows that the Weißenfels court also developed a *goût* for the fashionable exoticism of black servants. And, as is well-known among music historians, the ducal residence of Saxe-Weißenfels also fostered German operas for over half a century. In Bayreuth (at least until 1714), the ultra-Baroque operatic genre was rendered in the language of its land of origin: Italian. In a musical drama entitled *L'Alfonso* (January 1693), an elder sister of Georg Wilhelm represented the goddess Minerva accompanied by two blacks as supernumeraries.

Of particular interest is an opera that the margravine commissioned for her husband's birthday in 1722. The opera is entitled *Masinissa* and was (most likely) written by Johann Wolfgang Kipping (1695–1747), the later court secretary and a well-educated son of the Bayreuth court bookbinder. It was set to music by Sigmund Martin Gajarek (1689–1723), the margravial court *Capellmeister*.[22] For his libretto, Kipping, who was obviously interested in ancient history, called upon the history of the Numidian king Masinissa, as represented in the tragedy *Sophonisbe* (1669) by Daniel Casper von Lohenstein, a Silesian poet.[23] Kipping focused on the relationships between the following characters: Sophonisbe (Sophoniba, d. 203 BCE);[24] her husband Syphax (fl. c. 220–c. 201 BCE), King of the Masaesylians (not to be confused—as in the libretto—with the Massylians); Masinissa (c. 241–148 BCE), King of Numidia; Vermina (fl. 204–200 BCE), one of Sophonisbe's sons; and Tullia, an alleged sister of Scipio Africanus (Publius Cornelius Scipio Africanus, 236–183 BCE), a Roman general who takes a prominent part in the libretto. Second in rank to Scipio Africanus is Laelius (Caius Laelius, fl. 209–c. 160 BCE), another Roman general.

The actual story follows a prologue in honor of Georg Wilhelm von Brandenburg-Culmbach and begins in the military camp of the King of Numidia. Masinissa had once been infatuated with Sophonisbe, but she is now married to his arch political rival, Syphax. Masinissa is torn between a desire for vengeance and his still smoldering passion for the former Carthaginian princess. Masinissa describes his opposing passions at the end of act 1, scene 3:

> How happy will I be
> To tie as captive who has formerly
> With her eyes tied me,
> And to my most heartfelt annoyance
> Has found in Syphax's arms a greater lust
> Than with Masinissa.
> I feel a desire for revenge already in my heart.
> Yet, besides there is a secret resistance
> As a trace of the old love-faith.
> I am spurred by revenge for disdained love,

Yet, remembrance of previous impulses
Entices me to mere kindness.
What once had moved us towards Love
That stays imprinted in the soul,
One still honors that always.[25]

    Throughout the opera, the behavior of the "African" (or rather, "Numidian") figures—Sophonisbe, Syphax, and Masinissa—is governed by their respective passions. While Masinissa evidences both a thirst for vengeance (he wants Syphax to be executed before his captains and officers) and a longing for the desired Sophonisbe, Syphax, too, seeks vengeance for the humiliation his rival Masinissa brought upon him and for the emotional power that the Numidian king still exercises over Sophonisbe. Sophonisbe displays sympathy toward her imprisoned husband Syphax, but cannot deny her enduring passion for King Masinissa when his soldiers take her and her husband Syphax prisoner. In contrast, the Romans figure as examples of rational conduct. Scene 9 of the second act, a dramatic climax following right after the priest Bogudes has married Sophonisbe and Masinissa in the temple, illustrates the differences between "Numidian" and Roman conduct. Laelius, the Roman second-in-command after Scipio Africanus, shows a lack of restraint only once: recognizing that his emphatic advice to Masinissa not to marry Sophonisbe is going to fail, he angrily predicts the Numidian king's death at Roman hands. Finally, Scipio Africanus, the personification of ratio status in this opera, untangles the political consequences of Masinissa's desire for Sophonisbe regarding his alliance with Rome. He stresses the danger Sophonisbe represents and insists that Masinissa marry Scipio Africanus's sister Tullia. Moreover, he prompts Masinissa to hand over Queen Sophonisbe to the Romans, who would present her as human war booty at the customary triumphal entry into Rome. Eventually, Masinissa complies and Tullia is sent to Sophonisbe with a poisoned beverage. Queen Sophonisbe and two of her sons fall victim; Tullia and Masinissa are united after Masinissa's last attempt to prevent his beloved from drinking the poison. The opera ends with a pageant celebrating the final triumph over Syphax.

    While the "Africans" Masinissa, Syphax, and Sophonisbe are dominated by emotions and passions, the two Roman generals comport themselves "rationally." Kipping—following von Lohenstein—emphasizes an "exotic" view of non-European cultures and people by setting a few scenes in temples and sacred ceremonies: scenes 5–9 of the first act are set in the temple of the deity Moloch. Having received the news of her husband's capture, Sophonisbe is seen in the temple with her entourage, aiming to placate the gods with human sacrifices. Following an initial sacrifice, only the return of Syphax prevents the queen from giving one of her own sons to the sacred fire. The second half of act 2 (scenes 7–13) is set in another temple, where Masinissa and Sophonisbe are about to marry. During the ceremony, the priest foresees misfortune when examining the intestines of doves—birds traditionally and allegorically associated with love.

Ancient authors had already reported on sacred acts like these carried out by Numidians. Von Lohenstein's representation of them, adapted by Kipping for the Bayreuth opera stage, echoes Christians' continuing attitudes toward the paganism and, thus, the inferiority of non-Christian societies and cultures. Descriptions of "pagan" practices, such as human sacrifices or slaughtering family members, especially children, were available in ancient Roman reports on Africa, which anticipated later European attitudes toward non-Europeans: in these ancient reports, depictions of the ancient Numidian royalties as governed by passions contrast with a representation of Romans as European prototypes of ideal restrained behavior. Published travel reports of European travelers added to the image, which remained alive in notions of non-Europeans. In seventeenth-century Germany, the reports on some regions of Africa (especially Congo, Gabon, Mozambique, the Cape of Good Hope, and the "Gold-Coast"), published between 1590 and 1630 in the "East-Indian" and "West-Indian" travel reports by Johann Theodor de Bry and his brother Johann Israel, were the most influential.[26] The Bayreuth opera *Masinissa* of 1722 clearly renders classical images of "Africa" as completely—rather than gradually—different from Europeans' "own" alleged culture, which regarded itself as heir to the Roman and Christian world.

Dressed Up as a "Moor": *The Generous Queen of Sarmatia, Amage*

While the foregoing part gave an example of representation of historically real blacks, the following deals with one example of how the then popular disguise as a black was treated in opera. Disguises were popular elements in spoken and sung drama, ways of deceiving enemies and friends alike, of helping someone to escape from prison, and so on. A disguise favored by inventors and/or adapters of opera was that of a "Moor." For example, Elvira, the heroine in a musical drama entitled *La fede ne' tradimenti* (Siena, 1689), dresses as a "Moorish" wizard when attempting to rescue her brother from prison; Flavius Bertaridus, King of the Longobards, and protagonist of the eponymous opera (*Flavius Bertaridus, König der Longobarden,* Hamburg, 1729), likewise disguises himself as a "Moor" in an attempt to regain his kingdom, which is in the hands of a usurper.

In the opera *Amage, regina de' Sarmati* by Giulio Cesare Corradi (c. 1650?–1702) and Carlo Francesco Polaroli (c. 1653–1723), we encounter another "false Moor." This musical drama premiered in Venice during Carnival 1693/1694 and was subsequently staged in other Italian cities. In 1699, there were two productions in Bayreuth. Two decades later, Georg Wilhelm ordered a German version of the libretto from Johann Wolfgang Kipping for another production to be set to new music. Titled *Die | Großmüthige Königin von Sarmatien | AMAGE* (The Generous Queen of Sarmatia, Amage), it was staged during Carnival in 1718. Scenes 5–8 of the first act are set on a battlefield, introducing the audience to the military actions of the Amazon-like heroine, Amage. "Moorish guards" accompany her in her military endeavors, and from the second act onward, this special military detachment plays a crucial part as a kind of hiding place for a "false Moor."

Yet in order to understand the action better, we have to look back to the very beginning of the drama: while the heroic queen leads her forces on the battlefield, her husband King Ulderico of Sarmatia (so christened by the Venetian librettist, although, according to ancient sources, his real name was Medosach),[27] disguised as the god of wine, Bacchus, revels in the company of his favorite, Orontéa, in decadent debauchery. His counselor Ergisto raises the critical question of whether the king should not fight rather than indulge in pleasure, but Amage returns before Ulderico has a chance to consider leaving his residence and his favorite to join the battle. Soon after having greeted her disloyal husband, she uncovers his cavortings with Orontéa. Ulderico feigns flight from his residence, while the queen orders the imprisonment of Orontéa. However, the king immediately joins the "Moorish guards" to be near Orontéa. His darkened skin protects him from being recognized and seized.

At the beginning of act 2, Ulderico, standing in front of the dungeons, overhears a conversation between Queen Amage and the court counselor Ergisto. The queen announces that she will punish her husband's favorite, and Ergisto receives an order to search for the vanished king. When Ergisto asks the guards for information on the king's whereabouts, he addresses the disguised Ulderico, who stutters due to his astonishment. But when threatened with arrest, Ulderico tells Ergisto that the king is probably at the royal *maison de plaisance,* where Orontéa used to live, at some distance from the royal palace. While the others search for their missing king, Ulderico, with the help of a servant, frees Orontéa. All three flee. Despite their caution, the guards capture Orontéa again, and Ulderico and the servant, too, have to return to the palace. The second act concludes with a "ballet of Moors." In scenes 2 and 3 of the third and final act, the disguised king, still undetected, faces his judgment by Queen Amage. She accuses him of having freed Orontéa, and of deliberately misdirecting the court counselor and guards. In his defense, the disguised king merely attributes his misdemeanor to "love's delight" (*Liebes = Lust*). It smacks more of high Baroque century than of antiquity when court counselor Ergisto exclaims: "O was vor ein *galanter* Mensch ist er" (O, what a gallant person he is). Soon after Amage has left the stage, Ulderico turns the situation in his favor: the counselor provokes his opposition when addressing the disguised man as "Du Schwartzer!" (You black one!), and the *galant homme* reveals himself to be the king.

In the spirit of an absolute sovereign who would never tolerate disobedience, he orders the court counselor to give Queen Amage the news of her banishment from the realm; Orontéa, instead, is to become the queen. However, it is discovered that Orontéa herself had an affair with one of Amage's kinsman, and Ulderico expels her from the throne and eventually welcomes back Queen Amage.

The opera shows a king using a disguise that clearly connotes lower social rank, that of an ordinary black guard with no power over the socially higher-ranking counselor. He regains power only by leaving his black skin color behind and unmasking himself as the king. In contrast to the biography of Christian Ferdinand and to the depiction of the ancient African royals in *Masinissa,* the disguise in *Amage, regina de' Sarmati* could be a hint of a backward-looking attitude toward the "exotic other."

An Allegory of the Four Continents: A Royal Masquerade at the Berlin Court

This final example of the depiction of blacks in Baroque divertissements turns again toward the presentation of black exoticism: the personification of the "black continent" Africa as part of an allegorical masquerade. At the beginning of December 1706, King Frederick I of Prussia (1657–1713; ruled from 1688/1701) celebrated the wedding of his son, the future "roy-sergeant" Frederick Wilhelm (I) (1688–1740; ruled from 1713), to Princess Sophie Dorothée von Brunswick-Lüneburg-Hanover (1687–1757). In addition to a magnificently sung ballet, comedies, and other divertissements, the king ordered a masquerade on a favorite subject of festivities at Baroque European courts, an allegory of the four continents then commonly known. Imagined visions of the continents permitted a sovereign the illusion not only of being at the core of the world, but also in a realm above the planet's other realms and regions, since these also paid homage to the sovereign.[28] The Berlin masquerade consisted of four quadrilles, each of which featured members of the royal family as the leading couple and a dozen female and male courtiers of their retinue as representatives of Europe, Asia, Africa, and America. Each quadrille started its march in a different room of the palace, with the whole company coming together in one of the great halls for a banquet and a ball.

During the evening, singers and court musicians performed a vocal *musique de table,*[29] whose verses of the allegories were written by Benjamin Neukirch (1665–1729), a noted Silesian poet; the identity of the composer remains uncertain. It opens with the singer representing Europe alluding to the War of the Spanish Succession (1701–13/14) and the military successes achieved with the essential support of Prussian contingents. Next, the singer representing Asia flatters the royal family with similar allusions, noting how happy the provinces of Asia might be under Prussian rule. Then a singer representing Africa joins in:

The praise of half the world is much too little.
I know thee, o great king, too!
I know thee and thy power, too.
Rome, which earlier had despised everyone,
Was by Hannibal,
By my Hannibal defeated.
He would have been foolish to take on Prussia:
But Hannibal, who weakened Rome,
Would, had he lived,
Would, had he wished to fight,
Have this very hour been Prussia's slave.

Aria
All that the valiant world,
All that so many heroes
Have ever done to establish their fame
Can here be seen united,
Can here most truly be discerned
in Prussia's Hero,
Can be seen in you, Frederick,
Can be seen in you, great son,
Can here be seen,
Can here be seen united.[30]

As in the Bayreuth opera *Masinissa,* the poet here resorts to ancient African history, this time alluding to Hannibal Barkas (c. 246–183 BCE), the famous Carthaginian general who was the main cause of the First and Second Punic Wars.[31] And, as in the cases of Europe and Asia, Africa admits that even Hannibal would have to cede to the Prussian heroes, the sovereign and his heir, uniting the virtues and powers of the ancient heroes. The "Africa" depicted here with her (male) heroes differs from the picture drawn in Caesar Ripa's (c. 1555–1622) influential *Iconologia* (Iconology), conceived as a guide to the symbolism in emblem books. In that work, among the moral emblems, "Africa" is described as:

> A Blackmoor Woman, almost naked; frizl'd Hair; an Elephant's Head for her Crest; a Necklace of Coral, and Pendants of the same, at her Ears; a Scorpion in her right hand, and a Cornucopia with Ears of Corn, in her left; a fierce Lion by her, on one Side and a Viper and Serpent on the other. Naked, because it does not abound with Riches. The Elephant is only in Africa. The animals show that it abounds with them.[32]

By contrast, the "Africa" alluded to in the Prussian allegory is neither naked nor weak, neither mature nor immature, and not poor. She is part of the ancient Roman world and of Western history, not a mere geographical or natural place "abounding with animals," lacking history.[33] However, the allegory casts all achievements of African history and all merits of her mighty heroes, of course, as culminating in the superior virtues of Prussia and especially the king in Prussia, just as those from Europe, Asia, and America do. However, following the praises of Prussia's latest military achievements, the singer of America changes the subject from war to Crown Princess Sophie Dorothée, praising her for her beauty, but also for having replaced the late queen, who was likewise a descendant of the House of Brunswick-Lüneburg-Hanover. The singer representing Africa then joins in a general homage to the bride, enumerating her attributes:

> Happy Prince! What many strive for in vain
> is today visibly granted to you.
> Heaven has inclined to you in preference to many.
> You discover youth,
> You discover virtue,
> You discover beauty, you discover wit.[34]

The fact that representatives of Africa and America single out the virtues of the young crown princess in this allegory makes Sophie Dorothée unique. Her youth, virtue, beauty, and wit might well have been discovered in any number of marriageable princesses in the Holy Roman Empire, yet in this context she rises above the rest. The homage of the four parts of the world thus serves its purpose: Asia, America, Africa, and also Europe all become humble, but honorable, witnesses to the supreme authority of Brandenburg-Prussia at the world's core.

Conclusion

While on that night in December 1706 the Berlin royal court received the (imagined) homage of virtually the whole world, including Europe, some fifteen years earlier, at the court of the Elector Palatine at Düsseldorf, Amor searched the world's four continents for his lost quiver. Finally, Europa (the personification of the eponymous continent) found it in the hands of a Florentine princess (from the House of Medici), who happened to just recently have married the elector. And while a Carnival opera in Venice (*Amage, regina de'Sarmati,* Venice, 1693/1694), and later in Bayreuth, presented the vicissitudes of a decadent king disguised as a "Moor," another opera (*Moro per amore,* Genoa, 1681) showed a young prince—in the same disguise—seeking the love of a future queen, as well as a conciliatory solution to a warlike conflict between his father and the object of his desires. Whether these disguises had any deeper implications concerning the values attributed to blacks in general is difficult to determine. Viewed superficially, they were practical expedients: disguised individuals could not be recognized; their darkened skin masked their traits well. Aside from that, the operas gained an exotic dimension and aesthetic attraction.

In any case, the conjured representations of Africans in Baroque opera presented here generate curious contrasts. They fall between rather savage black figures set in opposition to Western civilization and Christian belief and superiorly noble, if subordinate, blacks who serve the state and court of their sovereigns. In 1668 and 1670, a black African danced on an equal footing with other courtiers in ballets. However, as blacks gradually gained omnipresence in the divertissements and artifacts of European higher society throughout the Baroque era, they were increasingly represented as inferior.

An intriguing pair of representations concerns the ancient Africans as compared to the ancient Romans. While ancient Numidian royalties functioned, with their passionate behavior, as inferior counterparts to "civilized" Romans in works as early as 1722, personalized Africa helped to glorify the Prussian royal family in an allegory of the four continents in 1706. Africa's strength and power was represented by Hannibal Barkas subduing even almighty Rome: in the allegory, ("civilized") Rome was inferior to the military forces of Africa, even though Prussia, strong and glamorous, was presented as still superior to these forces. Thus, powerful Africa, if paying homage to the Prussian king, played a humble part, but only in relation to an imagined, omnipotent Prussia, and unanimously with Asia, America, and Europe.

Notes

1. During the thirteenth century, Sicilian culture achieved a fusion of Islamic, Latin Christian, and Jewish as well as Byzantine Christian elements. Christianization was not imposed on Muslims but was partially achieved through the immigration of settlers. Ernst Kantorowicz, *Kaiser Friedrich der Zweite,* main vol., 7th rev. ed. (Stuttgart, Germany: Klett-Cotta, 1994), 242–43; suppl. vol., 4th ed. (Stuttgart, Germany: Klett-Cotta, 1994), 140; Dirk Hoerder, *Cultures in Contact: World Migrations in the Second Millennium* (Durham, NC: Duke University Press, 2002), 45; and Jean Devisse, *The Image of the Black in Western Art,* pt. 2, *From the Early Christian Era to the "Age of Discovery,"* vol. 1, *From the Demonic Threat to the Incarnation of Sainthood* (New York: Harvard University Press, 1979), 81–141.
2. Nicolò di Jamsilla, "Historia antea edita sub inscriptione Anonymi de rebus gestis Frederici II: Imperatoris," in *Rerum Italicarum Scriptores,* vol. 8, ed. Ludovico Antonio Muratori (Milan, 1726); Kantorowicz, *Kaiser Friedrich,* main vol., 242–43; Hans Werner Debrunner, *Presence and Prestige: Africans in Europe: A History of Africans in Europe before 1918* (Basel, Switzerland: Basler Afrika Bibliographien, 1979), 19–20; and Peter Martin, *Schwarze Teufel, edle Mohren: Afrikaner in Geschichte und Bewußtsein der Deutschen* (Hamburg, Germany: Hamburger Edition, 2001), 37, 379–80.
3. Geoffrey Treasure, *The Making of Modern Europe, 1648–1780* (London: Routledge, 2003), 377, 379.
4. See, for example, T.C.W. Blanning, *The Culture of Power and the Power of Culture: Old Regime Europe 1660–1789* (Oxford: Oxford University Press, 2002), 53–77; and Helen Watanabe-

O'Kelly, "Early Modern European Festivals—Politics and Performances, Event and Record," in *Court Festivals of the European Renaissance: Art Politics and Performance,* ed. J. R. Mulryne and Elizabeth Goldring (Aldershot, UK: Ashgate, 2002), 15–25.
5. For the following, see Anita Gutmann, *Hofkultur in Bayreuth zur Markgrafenzeit 1603–1726* (Bayreuth, Germany: Rabenstein, 2008), 51–59.
6. Since 1806, Franconia has been a part of Bavaria, which is one of Germany's federal states today.
7. Dianne M. McMullen, "Venuskräntzlein: Late-Renaissance Courtly Poetry and Music for a Goddess," *Daphnis* 32 (2003): 231–48, esp. 231–32 and 242; Gutmann, *Hofkultur,* 74–82, 101–8, 118–20; and Irene Hegen, *Neue Materialien zur Bayreuther Hofmusik. Katalog zur Ausstellung 1998 im Steingraeber-Haus Bayreuth* (Bayreuth, private print, 1998), 15.
8. Jürgen Osterhammel, "Die mentale Abschließung Europas (ca. 1770–1830)," in *Europa und das Fremde: Die Entwicklung von Wahrnehmungsmustern, Einstellungen und Reaktionsweisen in der Geschichte unserer Kultur,* ed. Jörg Calließ (Loccum, Germany: Rehburg-Loccum, 1998), 173–74.
9. Ronald G. Asch, "Introduction: Court and Household from the Fifteenth to the Seventeenth Centuries," in *Princes, Patronage, and the Nobility: The Court at the Beginning of the Modern Age, c. 1450–1650,* ed. R. G. Asch and Adolf M. Birke, Studies of the German Historical Institute London (London: Oxford University Press, 1991), 3.
10. *Ringrennen der Nationen* in German.
11. Uta Deppe, *Die Festkultur am Dresdner Hofe Johann Georgs II. von Sachsen (1660–1679)* (Kiel, Germany: Ludwig, 2006), 88.
12. On Christian Ferdinand and other blacks at the Bayreuth court, see Rainer-Maria Kiel, *Zwischen Integration und Sensation: Afrikaner im Bayreuth des 17. bis 19. Jahrhunderts* (unpublished manuscript, Bayreuth, 1998). I gratefully acknowledge Dr. Rainer-Maria Kiel's generous help with this chapter.
13. For an illustration of the procession, see Caspar von Lilien, *Höchst-betrauerlicher Kronen-Fall/ Bey dem Hoch-Fürstlichem Leich-Begängnuß der Durchleuchtigsten Princessin und Frauen/Frauen Erdmuth Sophien …* (Bayreuth, 1670). On blacks as trumpeters and timpanists, see also Monika Firla, "Afrikanische Pauker und Trompeter am württembergischen Herzogshof im 17. und 18. Jahrhundert," *Musik in Baden-Württemberg,* Jahrbuch 3 (1996): 11–41.
14. "Paucker Mohr," in W. v. Forstner to Margrave Christian Ernst zu Brandenburg-Culmbach-Bayreuth, Esslingen, 30 June 1692 (*Geheimes Staatsarchiv SPK* Berlin-Dahlem [hereafter GStA SPK], BPH Brandenburg-Preußisches Hausarchiv, Rep. 43 II Markgraf Christian Ernst, J. no. 340).
15. *Boutade:* a ballet in a whimsical style.
16. Two copies of the printed libretto are extant: Landesbibliothek Coburg (hereafter LBC), Sche 989:13; Ratsschulbibliothek Zwickau, 49.6.3.(139). On *Les Vaincus de L'Amour,* see Rashid-Sascha Pegah, "Divertissements am Bayreuther Hofe unter Markgraf Christian Ernst zu Brandenburg-Culmbach," *Archiv für Geschichte von Oberfranken* 79 (1999): 161, 167, 184–85; and Thomas Betzwieser, "Musiktheatrale Geschmacksbildung im 17. Jahrhundert: Ansbach und Bayreuth," in *Barock in Franken,* ed. Dieter J. Weiß (Dettelbach, Germany: J.H. Röll, 2004), 104n79.
17. "Ce que Cupidon & les deux jeunes Amours ont dit de Leur puissance, se fait icy remarquer par deux Crocheteurs ou portefaix, dont la force corporelle qu'ils representent, est surmontée par ces jeunes enfans." If not otherwise indicated, all translations are my own.
18. "Pauures Diables que nous sommes / La lie & rebut des homes / Qui portons sur le corps les plus pesants fardeaux[;] / Nous oublions tous nous [recte: nos] maux, / Et l'Amour seul qui nous blesse / De son trait puissant & dous [recte: doux] / Montre qu'en sa petitesse / Il est bien plus fort que nous."

19. Extant copies of the printed libretto are available in Berlin-Brandenburgische Akademie der Wissenschaften Berlin, Akademiebibliothek, B4/556: Aa 14902; LBC, Sche 989:12; Stadtbibliothek Nürnberg, 6 an Will. IV. 79. 2°; Anna Amalia Bibliothek SWK Weimar, 19 B 5451; Herzog August Bibliothek Wolfenbüttel (hereafter HAB), Textb. 4° 14; for a description of *Sudetische Frülings-Lust,* see Pegah, "Divertissements," 163, 168.
20. "Die wir sonst / zum marchiren / zum strengen scharmütziren / das Spiel im Felde rühren: / iezt keinen Feind wir spüren. / Die LandesGötter kommen. / Nun sol das Kalbfell brommen / sol brummen / nicht verstummen. / Nun muß man den Quärpfeifen / auch in die Augen greifen. / Die treuen Untern stehen / in Gollern und Livreen, / der Freud entgegen gehen."
21. Bayerisches Staatsarchiv Bamberg, Markgraftum Brandenburg-Culmbach-Bayreuth, Hofkammer, Nr. 491 [1707]; GStA SPK, BPH, Rep. 43 II Markgraf Christian Ernst, B. no. 3, fol. 11r. [1707].
22. A copy of the printed libretto is extant: Universitätsbibliothek Bayreuth, Bibliothek des Historischen Vereins für Oberfranken 47 / LR 53500 B361.
23. Elfriede Storm, *Massinissa: Numidien im Aufbruch,* Schriften der Wissenschaftlichen Gesellschaft an der Johann Wolfgang Goethe-Universität Frankfurt am Main 16 (Stuttgart, Germany: Steiner, 2001).
24. On Sophoniba, see Barbara Kowaleswski, *Frauengestalten im Geschichtswerk des T. Livius,* Beiträge zur Altertumskunde 170 (Leipzig, Germany: Saur, 2002), 219–39.
25. "Welch eine Freude werd ich nicht empfinden / Die als Gefangene zu binden / Die mich zuvor mit Augen band / Und nur zum innigsten Verdruß / In Syphax Armen größere Lust / Als bey dem Masinissa fand. / Die Rache kochet schon in meiner Brust. / Doch äussert sich dabey gleich ein geheimer Widerstand / Als eine Spuhr der alten Liebes = Treu. / Mich spornet die Rache verschmäheter Liebe / Doch das Gedächtnuß vorger Triebe / Reitzt mich zu lauter Gütigkeit. / Was uns einmahl zur Lieb beweget / Das bleibt der Seelen eingepräget / Das ehret man noch allezeit."
26. For an analysis of the image of "Africa" in these accounts, see Ernst van den Boogaart, "De Brys' Africa," in *Inszenierte Welten—Staging New Worlds: Die west- und ostindischen Reisen der Verleger de Bry, 1590–1630 = De Brys' Illustrated Travel Reports, 1590–1630,* ed. Susanna Burghartz (Basel, Switzerland: Schwabe, 2004), 95–155.
27. For the original story of Amage, see Elisabetta Bianco, *Gli stratagemmi di Polieno: Introduzione, traduzione e note critiche,* Fonti e studi di Storia Antica 3 (Alessandria, Italy: dell'Orso, 1997), 272–73.
28. For further examples of the world's four parts as allegorical means, see Monika Firla, "Das Ballet 'Atlas Oder Die vier Theil der Welt' (Durlach, 1681): Ein seltenes Libretto in der Württembergischen Landesbibliothek Stuttgart," *Musik in Baden-Württemberg* 4 (1997): 133–48.
29. Extant copies of the printed libretto are located in the Staatsbibliothek zu Berlin SPK, Yq 9321; Sächsische Landesbibliothek—Staats- und Universitätsbibliothek Dresden, Hist. Boruss. 258,23 & Hist. Boruss. 259,25.m; Deutsches Theatermuseum München, Bibliothek, R 390; HAB, M: Gm 1257 (1).
30. "Africa: Das Lob der halben Welt ist viel zu wenig. / Jch kenne Dich auch o grosser König! / Jch kenne Dich auch und Deine Macht. / Rom/ das vor Jeden hat veracht / Ward doch vom Annibal / Von meinem Annibal geschlagen / Der dürfft es nicht mit Preussen wagen: / Doch Annibal / der Rom geschwächt / Der würde / wenn er leben solte / Der würde / wenn er fechten wolte / Noch diese Stunde Preussens Knecht. / Aria/ Alles / was die tapffre Welt / Alles/ was so mancher Held / Je gethan / sein Lob zu bauen / Kan man hier in Einem schauen; / Kan man hier von Preussens Helden / Mit der größten Wahrheit melden. / Kan man Friderich / in Dir / Kan man Grosser Sohn in Dir / Kan man hier / Kan man hier in einem schauen. / Alles was die tapfre Welt / Alles was so mancher Held / Je gethan / sein Lob zu bauen / Kan man hier in Einem schauen."

31. Livy, *Titi Livi Ab urbe condita,* recognovit et adnotatione critica instruxit Robertus Maxwell Ogilvie, Oxford classical texts [without vol. no.] (Oxford: Oxford University Press, 1974), 22–24, (on Syphax: 24/48.1–49.8), 25 (on Massinissa: 25/34.1–36.16), 26.
32. Caesar Ripa, *Iconologia: Or Moral Emblems* (London, 1709), 53, as cited in Allison Blakely, *Blacks in the Dutch World: The Evolution of Racial Imagery in a Modern Society* (Bloomington: Indiana University Press, 1993), 82.
33. Some three centuries after the first Italian edition of Ripa's *Iconologia* in 1596, German philosopher Georg W.F. Hegel (1770–1831), in his *Lectures on the Philosophy of World History,* saw Africa as "the Unhistorical, Undeveloped Spirit, still involved in the conditions of mere nature … on the threshold of the World's History"; Georg W.F. Hegel, *The Philosophy of History,* trans. J. Jibree (New York: Dover, 1956), 99.
34. "Africa: Glücksel'ger Printz! was viel umsonst begehren / Das sieht man heute Dir gewehren. / Das hat der Him[m]el Dir vor vielen zu gewandt. / Du findest Jugend / Du findest Tugend / Du findest Schönheit / Du findest Verstand."

Chapter Five

From American Slaves to Hessian Subjects
Silenced Black Narratives of the American Revolution

Maria I. Diedrich

29 February 1788 was a day of jubilation for Kassel's[1] garrison: Landgrave Wilhelm IX was visiting his troops. As an expression of his special bond with his soldiers, he deigned to serve as godfather at a twenty-four-year-old tambour's baptism—a rare mark of favor, indeed. The garrison church book records the tambour's original name as Moritz Moses. He was renamed Wilhelm, after his powerful godfather, in whose prestigious *Regiment du Corps* he served.[2]

Only one day before this spectacular adult baptism, the garrison church book registers yet another baptism: this time for a more typical candidate, a baby girl christened Anna Elisabeth, after her godmother and maternal aunt Anna Elisabeth Ernst. As proud and grateful parents the register identifies Marie Elisabeth (née Ernst) and Johannes Sabadon, who like Wilhelm Moses was a tambour in the landgrave's *Regiment du Corps*.[3] Expressions of joy at their baby's christening must have mingled with a more solemn mood on the parents' faces. For how could they forget that only nine months previously, almost to the day, their daughter Anna Christina—one year, ten months, and three days young—had passed away?[4]

What connects these baptisms and renders them special is the fact that both Wilhelm Moses and Anna Elisabeth were black. What also renders Landgrave Wilhelm's visit special, indeed, is the fact that more than thirty of the soldiers parading before him in splendid uniforms were black, and among the crowds cheering their sovereign were the faces of their numerous black and mixed-race family members.[5]

Notes from this chapter begin on page 108.

Starting in 1776, Landgrave Wilhelm's father and predecessor to the throne, Friedrich II, had sent Hessian soldiers across the Atlantic to fight the American Revolution as British mercenaries—had sold them like slaves, his German and American critics would charge. Of these 16,992 men,[6] approximately two-thirds returned to Kassel after the war; almost six thousand were killed in combat, died during their American sojourn, deserted, or opted to stay in the New World when the defeated Hessian forces were finally transported back to Europe. Friedrich II no doubt knew that a considerable number of the men he had sent across the Atlantic would never return to Hesse. But could he have anticipated how dramatically the physical composition of his forces would be changed by the American expedition? Could he have envisioned a Hessian *Regiment du Corps* in black and white? Could he have imagined regular black soldiers, formally enlisted in the Hessian regiments, and their dependents—not just three or four black faces adding exotic splendor to the Hessian troops, but a sizeable group of black Americans-turned-Hessians who had come to Kassel to stay?

Sources and Methodological Considerations

Between 1782 and 1783, more than one hundred black American women, men, and children boarded the ships returning the defeated Hessian troops to Germany after the Paris Peace Treaty,[7] and they settled in Kassel, then one of Germany's most dynamic and attractive royal seats, with a population of approximately twenty thousand people.[8] The documentation available on this African diasporic move is scarce, scattered, and was never identified or collected systematically. It exists in fragmented form only, for valuable material—especially community and church records—were destroyed during the bombing of Kassel in World War II. Even more importantly, the documentation available represents this black diasporic experience exclusively through the white Hessian perspective and narrative voice: Hessian journals and letters, army and court records, church books. Hessian soldiers and administrative staff responsible for the military records often spoke little or no English, but they were the men equipped with the authority to assign—and more often than not that meant misassign[9]—a name and personal data to black American volunteers joining the troops, thus inventing and imposing an official identity upon individuals whose personal identity was in flux. Also, the military records identify only those formally enlisted men; they do not include the numerous dependents that accompanied these soldiers, just as they do not mention the Hessian women and children traveling with the white Hessian officers and men; also, they failed to identify the black women, men, and children who came as personal servants or as slaves to Hessian officers.

At the center of this black American-Hessian encounter are people of African descent who joined the Hessian troops on the North American continent between 1776 and 1783. They were a highly diversified group, considering their legal status: Hessian and British military papers, as well as documents held by state or local archives in Virginia, Georgia, the Carolinas, New Jersey, New York, Connecticut, Rhode Island, and Nova Scotia, Canada,[10] show that the majority consisted of young men in their teens and twenties who had run away from their masters to enlist with the Hessians—proud self-liberators. Some had been kidnapped as war booty by Hessian foraging parties and opted to stay with these troops, improving their situation and transforming themselves from slaves into common soldiers. Contemporary records also show that during the Revolutionary War many slaves-turned-soldiers did not run alone; encouraged and empowered by British liberation proclamations, they brought family and friends. At times, the entire population of a plantation sought freedom, shelter, and income among the British and Hessians.[11] Yet not all blacks eventually transported to Germany were volunteers: Adjutant General Major Carl Leopold von Baurmeister's letters and journals, Captain Johann Ewald's diary, and the personal data of black refugees listed in Graham R. Hodges's *The Black Loyalist Directory* reveal that many children and adolescents surfacing in the records had simply been confiscated as war booty[12] without their consent and shipped back to Hesse as gifts to the nobility, like crates of exotic fruit. Many Hessian officers, i.e., members of the lesser nobility and gentry, who were accustomed to an authoritarian system of lifelong serfdom back home, felt no compunction whatsoever about purchasing slaves at local auctions or stealing them from rebel plantations or households.[13] So black self-liberators and slaves lived side by side in the Hessian army camps during the American campaigns, and they traveled to Kassel together, into a future that for them could have no tangible definers as they boarded the British ships in New York Harbor in the summer and fall of 1783.

All blacks aboard the British vessels heading for Europe had lived on the North American continent, and most had opted to leave this territory. But for the eighteenth century, with the transatlantic slave trade still in full swing, this broadly defined locale "North America" does not necessarily imply that these individuals originated from the same place, or experienced the same national context; it is most likely that they did not even speak the same language.[14] The negotiation of individual and communal identity in which they were involved was most definitely one between worlds, of people in transit in more ways than one.

The places of birth or origin the fugitives identified for themselves upon enlisting with the Hessian forces[15] show that the majority were blacks whose ancestors had been kidnapped and transported to the Americas in the seventeenth and eighteenth centuries. Consequently, their families had been enslaved for generations. These enlistees had been part of that complex communal venture of enslaved blacks reinventing themselves as African Americans, creating an African American language, identity, history, memory, and culture. Others came from the Caribbean or South America; most of these were multilingual, and spoke

Spanish, Portuguese, Dutch, and/or French. Some of the fugitives, however, were first-generation slaves: Johannes Sabadon escaped from his carpenter master for the Hessian camps in Philadelphia in 1777 or 1778 and claimed to be born in "Hautgerva, Africa"; other examples include tambour July/Juley, tambour London, and tambour Wilhelm, all of whom stated that they had been stolen from Africa.[16] These were men for whom the Middle Passage was raw memory, people traumatized and uprooted. These individuals were not yet African Americans, nor were they Africans. Not long before, they had been Hausa and Fulani, Asante and Yoruba, Igbo and Fon, people who defined themselves as members of a local community rather than a nation. They had never heard of "Africa," this invention of European colonialism and the slave trade.[17] The New World reinvented them as African, as Negro, as slave, determined to transform them from human beings into chattel and, in the act, delete them from the human species, from culture and history.

The definers of the women, children, and men that eventually traveled to Kassel thus are diaspora and difference—personifications of what the transnational African diaspora and black Atlantic paradigms evoke as in-between identities and their in-between or plurilocations; fractured and variously connected disparate identities, geographies, and temporalities. These people in flux then interacted with Hessian soldiers, staff, and their dependents, who were also people in a transmigratory situation: many Hessians had been transported across the Atlantic against their will, in a state of semibondage—a transnational in-betweenness these Hessians, in turn, were struggling to negotiate for themselves. Together, they migrated or returned to a particularist Germany where, the chapters in this volume contend, under the impact of the Enlightenment, scholars of all disciplines were beginning to write systematic and complex natural histories of the human species, determined to "scientifically" classify humanity and redefine nation in racial terms—Kant, Blumenbach, Herder, and, of utmost importance for Kassel, the anatomist Samuel Thomas Sömmerring.[18] The white soldiers and their families returned to Germany with conflicting, often incompatible images of blackness and slavery firmly implanted in their minds—on the one hand, the degrading racial American identification of blackness, African, Negro, and slavery; on the other, their abhorrence at the reality of American chattel slavery, combined with their admiration for the black self-liberators now transformed into fellow Hessians. In the decades that followed, the British controversies over the transatlantic slave trade, news of the Haitian Revolution, and the abolitionist campaigns in the United States were widely reported and debated in Germany. In the German debates, in turn, the privileged and exotic *Mohr* would gradually lose out to the *Neger*, and the *Neger* would become identical with the degraded slave, the essentialized racial inferior.

Any attempt to reconstruct this African diasporic experience and black American-Hessian interaction faces an overwhelming challenge: how can we return a voice, how can we represent the agency and subjecthood of black women, men, and children who, as a rule, left no written documentation whatsoever and who are beyond the reach of oral history? In her pathbreaking biography of the illiterate abolitionist Sojourner Truth, Nell Irving Painter contends that the biographies of individuals who left no "caches of personal papers" can be written, provided we develop "means of knowing our subjects' way(s) of making themselves known beyond the written word."[19] One way of identifying these "ways of making themselves known," I argue in what follows, is to make use of the analytical tools provided by African diaspora, black Atlantic, and transmigration paradigms, as well as postcolonial theory, critical whiteness studies, and discourse analysis, to revisit the existing white German texts, to identify, negotiate, and reconstruct at least fragments of the silenced black voice in the white Hessian narrative.

Blackness and the White Hessian Experience

The white Hessian interaction with black Americans on the North American continent and in Kassel can only be deciphered if we keep in mind that many Hessians had, indeed, encountered black people before they crossed the Atlantic in 1776. Peter Martin's *Schwarze Teufel, edle Mohren* (2001), Sander L. Gilman's *On Blackness without Blacks* (1982), and Wolfram Schäfer's "Von 'Kammermohren,' 'Mohren'-Tambouren und 'Ost-Indianern'" (1988), as well as this volume, offer ample documentation of the presence of blacks in Germany ever since the Middle Ages. They were there as slaves; as sailors; as so-called *Kammer-Mohren* (chamber moors), proudly displayed as tokens of wealth and power by the courts, the gentry, and rich merchants; and, finally, of increasing importance during the eighteenth century, as army musicians. European aristocrats and the bourgeoisie competed for *Mohren,* a competition that resulted in skyrocketing prices for Africans on European slave markets and even kidnappings of precious black staff. This competition increased when a reformatting in military tactics, i.e., marching in formation, required that each regiment have its own musical staff, and black musicians became the fashion of the day.

Wolfram Schäfer's sophisticated article on Kassel contends that the landgraves of Hesse-Kassel, never to be outdone when it came to displaying their wealth and power, had eagerly participated in this rush for exotic *Mohren.* Court records at the Hessian State Archive in Marburg reveal that the various landgraves, since the mid-seventeenth century, had invested enormous sums to have their power reflected in gloriously dressed and usually financially and socially privileged chamber moors. In fact, long before the American venture, Friedrich II's personal *Regiment du Corps* boasted at least ten black musicians. Contemporary images of this Corps, held by the Murhardsche Library in Kassel and reprinted below (figures 5.1. and 5.2.), show these black tambours dressed in fancy uniforms and

Figure 5.1. Black tambour in a Hessian regiment in the 1780s (Source: G. C. T. Stiens, *Hochfürstliche Hessische Korps 1787,* Signatur 2° Ms. Hass. 267, Universitätsbibliothek Kassel Landesbibliothek and Murhardsche Bibliothek der Stadt Kassel).

Figure 5.2. Another black tambour in a Hessian regiment in the 1780s (Source: G. C. T. Stiens, *Hochfürstliche Hessische Korps 1787,* Signatur 2° Ms. Hass. 267, Universitätsbibliothek Kassel Landesbibliothek and Murhardsche Bibliothek der Stadt Kassel).

wearing white turbans with red feathers to emphasize the exoticism of this black corps.[20]

This means that the Hessian officers and many commoners had interacted with privileged blacks before their departure for the North American continent. Furthermore, from Baurmeister's, Ewald's, and other Hessians' journals and letters, we can see that the Hessian officers were aware of the landgrave's predisposition to increase their numbers. Friedrich II could very well imagine a retinue in black and white. Colonel von Donop's last will reveals[21] that his officers, in turn, knew of this craving and were eager to please their sovereign or other influential courtiers by making gifts of slaves—as a means of furthering their own careers.

In deciphering the Hessians' conduct toward the black Americans with whom they would live side by side in the years that followed, it is essential to understand that their images of blacks differed dramatically from the images they would encounter in revolutionary America. As the terminology they originally used—*Mohren*—illustrates, the Africans who came to live in Europe, though almost as a rule purchased as slaves, were associated not primarily with slavery or savagery but with the black Magi; with black saints and madonnas in German churches; with memories of the medieval Crusades and the exotic black women and men the returning crusaders brought to Germany; with the Turks and their spectacular black soldiers before Vienna; with Oriental splendor that the German nobility and bourgeoisie emulated. Most court or chamber moors had been purchased as slaves, their legal status was precarious, and their situation was one of dependence. However, the officers and commoners who went to the American war were members of a society that affirmed social inequality and dependence as natural. As subjects to a state in which status came with proximity to power, they perceived the moors as privileged, even pampered, individuals. These Hessian images of black sainthood or of aristocratic and Oriental splendor clashed fiercely with the misery of the American slaves—exploited, degraded, denied their humanity in their legal definition as chattel. These Hessians brought images of the *Mohr* to America, and there they began to add "Negro" and *Neger*, with implications of bondage and degradation, to their vocabulary, a transformational process of racialization that can be traced in Ewald's, Baurmeister's, and other white Hessians' narratives.

From monthly journals of the various regiments, held by the Hessian State Archive in Marburg, we know that the Hessians began recruiting black Americans as soldiers, personal servants, and nonmilitary staff almost immediately upon their arrival in 1776 in New York, then one of the hubs of slavery in North America.[22] Losses in manpower and vacancies the army faced in the first two years, especially during the New York and Philadelphia campaigns—from epidemics, as well as soldiers being killed, wounded, taken prisoner, or deserting—were often made up by enlisting black Americans as soldiers or hiring them as laborers. The HETRINA[23] papers document at least 150 such formal enlistments in military units, with most enlistees serving as musicians, but some also as fusiliers, grenadiers, musketeers, and privates. In addition, there were the camp followers of no official status—day laborers, personal servants, midwives, cooks, maids, laundresses, grooms, nurses, wagoners, prostitutes—who far outnumbered the regulars from the very start. Reports often mention foraging parties in which blacks became war booty. Recruiting or employing fugitive slaves in the Hessian army thus was an act of military expediency as well as a strategy to economically harm and subvert the authority of their rebel masters. For the majority of Hessians, who, after all, had come from a highly stratified, authoritarian context, these practices did not result from humanitarian considerations, antislavery sentiments, or moral or political convictions—at least during the early encounters, i.e., before black agency taught them to listen to a different narrative, the black narrative, to see blackness with new eyes.

That the Hessians still harbored the image of the prestigious and precious chamber moor became clear when officers ordered Hessian army chaplains to educate and train black children they had bought or confiscated. These children were then sent back to Kassel as soon as the officers felt they were "ready" for court display. For instance, Adjutant General Major von Baurmeister, who served as first adjutant to all three Hessian commanders and wrote regular reports to the Hessian Minister of State and War Friedrich Christian von Jungkenn-Müntzer, mentions in a letter of 1 December 1777 a "negro boy about thirteen years old" whom Colonel von Donop, killed in action during the Philadelphia campaign, "bequeathed to your Lordship"—the act of transfer expressive of the boy's status as property. After months of "instructions in the German language and also in the Christian religion" by Army Chaplain Georg C. Köster, he would be shipped to Hesse "at the first opportunity,"[24] von Baurmeister announced. Similarly, Hessian officers had two black American children of unidentified background—a girl of twelve and an adolescent boy—shipped to Landgravine Philippine. They received religious instruction and served as her personal servants, and in 1780, she had them baptized and confirmed in her court chapel. The confirmation questioning was conducted in German, and both "answered in a lively manner, loudly and without hesitating."[25] These American slaves and Negroes were thus reinstalled as orientalized *Mohren,* though their legal status is not recorded. These examples illustrate that it did not take long for some members of the Hessian lower nobility to conveniently embrace America's "peculiar institution": when stealing and dealing in slaves, after all, they behaved in accordance with the feudal or absolutist state's strictly hierarchical understanding of the human species and the prescriptions of the social and political discourses of the day, in accordance also with their specific Hessian context.[26]

However, even more important than Hessians "foraging for Negroes" was the interaction between the Hessians and black Americans that the slaves themselves initiated, an interaction, this chapter insists, that had a powerful transformational impact on the Hessian attitude toward blackness and slavery. American slaves, recent scholarship contends, were neither passive victims nor mere observers of a Revolutionary War fought by (and for) whites only; they redefined this war as their war of self-liberation. Many supported the patriots, hoping their service would be rewarded with personal emancipation at the end of the struggle for national independence. But tens of thousands also ran from their masters and struggled to cross the lines into British-occupied territory after Lord Dunmore's famous proclamation of November 1775, which promised freedom to any slave joining the British forces—Jefferson later spoke of more than thirty thousand black refugees in Virginia only. Succeeding British commanders would regularly confirm and expand this proclamation, which slaves all over the colonies eagerly embraced as liberation news and promise.[27] Associating the Hessians with the British and, thus, with the British proclamation, these slaves offered their service as their ticket to freedom and protection, to an independent income, to agency and ultimate subjecthood. There was relatively little need and incentive for the Hessians to compel blacks to enlist. In fact, they quickly learned that bondspeople kidnapped or foraged into service usually deserted at first opportunity, as Baurmeister attested.[28] It was the slaves themselves who made the decision to serve—certainly a powerful way of "making themselves known."

During their seven years on the North American continent, the Hessians thus encountered black women and men not primarily as brutalized victims of American racism and chattel slavery, but as trustworthy, valiant soldiers, competent midwives and nurses, skilled cooks and carpenters. They could not help respecting them for their personal courage, their stamina, their integrity. For the Hessian commoners and their dependents in the camps, fugitive slaves became fellow soldiers and laborers, buddies whose right to freedom they affirmed and, if required, defended.

This transformational process, army documents reveal, impacted not only the lower ranks but also the Hessian officers and their conduct toward blacks. Interacting with black soldiers and service personnel, these officers learned to acknowledge that the black fugitives in their regiments and in their camps, in their daily conduct as freedpeople, refuted the core assumptions of American and German racisms. Even the most conservative officers, coming from a society that affirmed inequality and strict hierarchies, found American chattel slavery to be simply incompatible with their notion of responsible patriarchy. Also, a considerable number of Hessian officers, as well as Landgrave Friedrich II, were Masons,[29] who were fascinated with an Enlightenment creed that, brought up against both American racism and black agency, tended to translate into antislavery, liberation activities. Reformatted from the perspective of the transformational impact of black and white interaction, the inhuman act of stealing or purchasing a black child could and occasionally did acquire a new, emancipating quality: Quartermaster Hunter, boarding the *Polly*, bound for Bremerlehe, in New York Harbor in August 1783, was accompanied by fifteen-year-old John, whom he "bought ... of Benjamin Carpenter of Jamaica, Long Island." However, the entry "(Formerly the property) of the Quartermaster"[30] in *The Black Loyalist Directory* clearly attests that John had become a free man, and was traveling as the officer's personal servant.

Under the impact of American racial slavery and black self-liberation, Hessian officers, commoners, and their dependents thus not only added *Neger*/Negro, with its implications of brutalization and essential inferiority, to their vocabulary. A careful scrutiny of the army records, diaries, and war correspondence also confirms the transformational power of black agency and its influence on white perceptions: racial assignments became rarer as the war progressed, and interaction became routine. The Negro/slave resurfaced as refugee, laborer, groom, forager, and guide, all assignations focusing on military rank, social class, and performance rather than race.

General Leopold von Heister, first commander of the Hessian troops in North America, as well as his successor, General Wilhelm von Knyphausen, encouraged their officers to enlist black runaways as soldiers and to hire them as personal servants and grooms, as wagoners and laborers. In a letter to the landgrave, written near Germantown, Pennsylvania, in October 1777, von Knyphausen, complaining of the disconcerting sickness rate among his soldiers, reported that the solution to this problem was the enlistment of black soldiers. He had first accepted white American volunteers to the Hessian ranks, but the result had been desultory, "for neither can they march in line, and they are likely to return to the rebels. Also, they are not well suited as soldiers, on account of their cowardice and their undisciplined notions of freedom." Fortunately, there was an alternative: "But we have recruited several Negroes as tambours for the infantry and grenadier battalions, and several have been performing well for the entire year." He was especially pleased to report that "several have already decided to return to Hesse with us."[31] Von Knyphausen claimed that the decision to migrate to Kassel lay exclusively with these free black men. He was pleased to welcome them as assets to the Hessian troops and state—testimony to von Knyphausen's awareness of how eager Frederick II was to increase his prestige by adding black musicians to his personal corps, and expression also of the nobleman's belief in the superiority of his Hessian culture to which the refugees would and could adapt. But, above all, this letter was a tribute to the men's performance as soldiers and potential Hessian subjects.

In the years that followed, increasing numbers of black adolescents considered too young for armed service were recruited as musicians, as tambours, trumpeters, and fifers, freeing mature white Hessian soldiers for service as musketeers or grenadiers. Also, officers were urged not to use white Hessian soldiers as personal servants but to replace them with black refugees. Yet black Americans served not only as regulars and personal staff; their familiarity with the local territory and structures, combined with their determination to be free, made them indispensable as spies, informers, foragers, and laborers.

During the Southern campaigns, especially into the Carolinas, Georgia, and Virginia between 1780 and 1781, the numbers of black Americans who enlisted as regulars—or at least accompanied and supported the troops—increased dramatically, to the point that they far outnumbered the actual troops, as Captain Johann Ewald of the Jaeger Corps reported in June 1781 from the Virginia campaign. Ewald, a fiercely disciplined, self-controlled, and authoritarian officer, was exasperated at "a cavalcade" in black and white, which he compared in disgust to "a wandering Arabian or Tartar horde":

> Lord Cornwallis had permitted each subaltern to keep two horses and one Negro, each captain, four horses and two Negroes, and so on, according to rank. But since this order was not strictly carried out, the greatest abuse arose from this arrangement … Every officer had four to six horses and three to four Negroes, as well as one or two Negresses for cook and maid. Every soldier's woman was mounted and also had a Negro and Negress for her servants. Each squad had one or two horses and Negroes, and every non-commissioned officer had two horses and one Negro.
>
> Yes, indeed, I can testify that every soldier had a Negro, who carried his provisions and bundles. This multitude always hunted at a gallop, and behind the baggage followed well over four thousand Negroes of both sexes and all ages.[32]

Captain Ewald explicitly blamed Lord Cornwallis and his aristocratic decadence for what he castigated as multiracial Carnivalesque excess, which undermined the discipline, hierarchy, and order he proudly associated with European military conduct and code of honor.

With Lord Cornwallis's capitulation at Yorktown, Virginia, in October 1781, the dream of self-liberation through military service, which many ex-slaves dreamed of, collapsed, although the British evacuated hundreds of enlisted blacks, and sometimes even their families. They were first removed to New York, then, with the British recognition of American independence in November 1782, thousands were resettled in the Caribbean, Nova Scotia, or England; many would later join the Sierra Leone project.[33] However, the majority were left behind, to a fate that spelled punishment and reenslavement. The black Hessians who ended up in Kassel were among the fortunate self-liberators who were able to maintain their freedom by making the decision as free women and men to leave behind their in-between American home and embrace an equally precarious new diasporic fate in Hesse.

Captain Johann Ewald's Narrative and the Black Voice

The Hessians were bureaucrats; they kept records of every man who enlisted with them. Similar to the famous British *Black Loyalist Directory,* they entered a name, place of birth/origin, approximate age, army status, regiment, salary, benefits, equipment, and any career moves, reassignments, military misconduct, or punishments. In addition, local church books and the landgrave's budget records provide information about income, benefits, housing arrangements, births, marriages, deaths, baptisms, and confirmations. But there is no authentic black narrative, no documented black voice. Still, it is possible to identify at least traces of the black voice and reconstruct black agency by critically revisiting the white Hessian gaze and narrative.

As a test case for this critical revisiting and its applicability to my further research and writing, I will turn to Captain Johann Ewald's *Diary of the American*

War. Ewald,³⁴ orphaned son of a lower-middle-class family, was born in Kassel in 1744, joined the military service (Infantry Regiment Gilsa) as a cadet at age sixteen, and studied military science with the famous Jakob von Mauvillon at the Collegium Carolinum at Kassel. As captain of the elite Jaeger Corps, he left for North America in May 1776 and returned to Kassel in May 1784, after eight years of service in which he had participated in most of the major campaigns. He kept a diary, a curious medley of private and public narratives, a copy of which he sent to his superior in Hesse-Kassel, Minister of State and War von Jungkenn-Müntzer, at regular intervals. Despite its semipublic quality, it is of high value because it represents the experience and perspective not of an administrator but a man of active service, with a focus always on military activities. In it, Ewald displays no interest whatsoever in the racial composition of the colonies or in the institution of slavery; in fact, he usually speaks of servants or *Neger* rather than slaves. All the same, black Americans are a continuous presence in his narrative, at first surfacing only in the representational stasis of the formulaic reports on successful military expeditions "to collect Negroes and livestock," or "to collect Negroes, forage, and cattle."³⁵ There is stasis also in the fact that throughout the American campaigns the black women and men he encounters remain the anonymous "Negro," "Negroes," or "Refugees." It is a stasis that must be qualified, however: the common Hessian soldier in his text, as in all Hessian order books, regimental journals, letters, diaries, or memoirs of the day, is never identified by name, either. Class rather than race thus defines the relationship between the white Hessian captain and the black Americans he meets.

And yet a close reading of the first interaction Ewald reports on 26 November 1776, only three weeks after his arrival in New York, reveals that this static "othering" of the black as an object of white agency is challenged from the very start by a discourse of black semi-individual agency that forces its way into the text and reformats the nondifferentiating white voice and gaze. This early encounter is representative of dozens of similar interactions narrated in this journal: a Hessian patrol captures "a Negro" who informs them "that an enemy corps stood in the vicinity of Newark, and also that there was a plantation situated an hour away which was not deserted by its occupants and had a stock of wine and beer." Not only are the Jaegers able to successfully raid the plantation of its precious stock after "the Negro led us along the footpath through the woods";³⁶ the information he provides on patriot troops under General Henry Lee in the Newark area also proves reliable and enabling for the Hessian and British forces.

In this brief, tightly constructed episode, a pattern emerges that will be confirmed and strengthened in later years. The "Negro" as war booty and tool transforms himself into a valuable informer and guide, thoroughly familiar with the local setting and situation, on whom the Hessians rapidly learn to rely as knowledgeable and trustworthy. He is not identified by name, there is no description of his physical appearance or status, no reference to his blackness aside from the all-inclusive identification as "Negro," and, most importantly, his motivation for turning informer is never investigated. The narratives do not explicitly evoke slavery; still, Ewald establishes a firm link between Negro and slave status. However, and this is of utmost importance, from that "Negro equals slave" identification, he implicitly extrapolates not exclusively and reductively black victimization and degradation but the Negro as potential and actual Hessian ally and partner against the patriot as slave master: black American intelligence and agency claim the right to speak in the Hessian text and reformat the encounter as a partnership ultimately controlled by black individual agency.

The impact of this black agency and voice in this journal becomes even more powerful and complex once we turn to the Southern campaigns of 1780, during which Ewald and his men, for the first time in their lives, enter a territory where people of African descent, as slaves, form a numerical majority. In the initial encounter with his first black Southerner, which Ewald records on 14 February, we can identify two competing narratives: a white "master" narrative of black deprivation and degradation, a model of racialized "othering"; and parallel, or perhaps even clashing with it, the black narrative of self-empowerment and agency—two seemingly conflicting, even incompatible, narratives. And yet, within a few pages, they merge.

Ewald's memories of the event are structured by the Hessian's shock at not being able to communicate with "these people."[37] Cultural "othering" becomes a self-protective move to retain his authority as a white European and officer; race and class intersect. The Hessians are totally disoriented because they disembarked without maps or guides on Simmons (now Seabrook) Island off the South Carolina coast. All white inhabitants had fled from the island upon the approach of the British fleet. Fortunately, the Jaegers get hold of "a Negro boy of eleven or twelve years who knew the way there." Ewald's text focuses entirely on the black child's "poor dialect," his Gullah—which the white officer who depends absolutely on the boy's knowledge calls simply "his gibberish."[38] And yet, the youngster reduced to and defined by "gibberish" enters the text as a calm and circumspect scout who guides the Hessians safely through "an impenetrable morass." The Jaegers know they can and have to depend on him, and Ewald expresses his sense of mutuality, while yet struggling to affirm the strict military hierarchy he has internalized through the man-above-child opposition, through the endearing yet emasculating formula of "our boy."[39] Six days into the march through unknown, swampy territory, Ewald admits that now "[e]ach party had its own guide," runaway slaves who take them expertly through the Cox Swamp. And yet, despite their expertise, Ewald again complains that "none of us could manage to talk with these people because of their bad dialect, even had we spoken with the tongues of angels."[40] The inability to communicate is located exclusively with the black "other." The black agency permeating the text clashes with the writer's Eurocentric reading and evaluation. In a situation in which black expertise and power determine every move of the lost and desperate Hessian officer, he imposes a reading of cultural hegemony upon them that defines the black experts' language as deficient "gibberish"—rather than admitting to the Hessians' deficient English. And yet the black guides "make themselves known" as experts in the narrative, triumphing over the white racial reading. They transform the white Hessian monologue into a dialogue.

The multidimensionality and complexity of this episode is revealed in the formula of "these people" that Ewald employs: on the one hand, "these" is a gesture of racialized and hierarchical distancing; on the other hand, Ewald's usage of "people" illustrates that even after four years of exposure to the American slaveholding context that reduced the slave to chattel, the black protagonists in his narrative defy this denial of their humanity. In fact, the longer Ewald remains in the South, the more he speaks of refugee, worker, laborer, sailor, usually without racial assignment, focusing on class rather than race. Also, after only one month in South Carolina, the communication issue simply disappears from his journal, to be replaced by Ewald's expressions of sincere gratitude for the black support, both voluntary and enforced, upon which the European troops depend and which they receive from black Americans: gratitude for valuable information and precious work; for the enormous workloads they (are made to) shoulder during the difficult approach of Charleston through treacherous swamplands, when they, together with unidentified sailors and soldiers, carry cannons through endless marshes; for the information that the swamps can be crossed and drained; for hundreds of black workers who strengthen the redoubts and dig ditches around Charleston during the long and bloody siege.[41]

The precarious alliance between black and white that the Hessian narrative constructs is strictly hierarchical up to this point. Ewald never mentions blacks as soldiers. They enter the text only as informers, spies, and workers who excel in whatever they do, but he leaves intact the hierarchy he as officer constructs between the value of military and nonmilitary action, between a white European performance of the superior military task and the supportive, essential, yet inferior service work performed by the army's black allies. However, he also maintains this differentiation when elaborating on the labor performed by equally anonymous British sailors and laborers. When the European forces finally take Charleston in May 1780, the social hierarchy he has internalized reveals the essentializing, racialized dimension that defines it to its very core: Ewald writes that Charleston boasts a population of "six thousand whites and mulattoes ..., without counting the Negroes."[42] His white gaze continues to battle the black agency that permeates his narrative. At the same time, the cultural hegemony Ewald evokes is constantly being challenged and undermined by a discourse of mutuality, dependence, and respect that is forced upon him by black agency.

The battle between the black and the white voice pervades the entire narrative, revealing the power of both European discourses of class and race and of black determination to penetrate and subvert these structures.

The balance is tipped from hierarchy toward mutuality during the second Southern military involvement of Ewald's Jaegers in 1781,[43] which takes Ewald to Richmond, Portsmouth, and Norfolk, into North Carolina, and ultimately to Gloucester and Yorktown, Virginia, where he witnesses Lord Cornwallis's defeat in October. In May 1781, as commanding officer in Norfolk, he trains twelve fugitive slaves as cavalry and even has them "mounted and armed." This decision is based on a scarcity of European personnel as a result of malaria and a long, bloody campaign. Yet the Hessian officer also leaves no doubt that, despite their extremely brief training period, the refugees provide him with "thoroughly good service." Given the chance to excel in the military realm, the black recruits perform as any good soldier should, without racial qualification. The explanation Ewald offers at first smacks of patriarchal condescension: "I sought to win them by good treatment, to which they were not accustomed."[44] Yet Ewald's journal is full of similar references to the white Hessian commoners under his command, wherein he affirms his sense of paternal responsibility as an officer, as well as the loyal service he receives in return. Again the Hessian notion of class stratification is more important to the narrative than race.

The degree to which black Southerners acquire voice and control in Ewald's diary is revealed during the catastrophic British defeat by patriot and French troops in Virginia in the summer and fall of 1781. Only two days before Lord Cornwallis capitulates at Yorktown on 17 October, the British, facing shortages and military defeat, drive thousands of black camp followers from their camps. Although he is fully aware of the seriousness of the British situation, Ewald is appalled at this "cruel happening" he "would just as soon forget to record." But he does record it. For him, these black Americans have transformed themselves into more than mere tools the army had "taken along to despoil the countryside," more than mere laborers they had used "to good advantage and set ... free." He embraces "these unhappy people," "these unfortunates," as "our black friends," and he cannot bear to give them up to the mercy of "their cruel masters." While, as a rule, the British act would be justified as self-defense, Ewald affirms his personal responsibility as well as the blacks' right to freedom, arguing that "we should have thought more about their deliverance at this time."[45] The anonymous black war "booty" of the early journal—people treated as things who had to struggle for voice each time they performed in the white narrative—have reformatted themselves as women and men with the right to human respect, deliverance, and freedom.

Ewald's diary constructs, marks, and mediates race and class difference and otherness. In this, it is representative of the autobiographical Hessian texts produced during and after the war. Yet the black presence—two hundred years later

Toni Morrison would diagnose an "Africanist Presence"—in the white narrative succeeds in renegotiating these static constructions of racial, social, and cultural alterity in diverse and complex ways. It thus initiates the intriguing dynamic of these narratives and powerfully challenges the exclusive authority of the white Hessian monologue.

On 3 November 1781, the defeated British and Hessian officers boarded the vessels at Yorktown that would take them back to New York. Despite American protests, Ewald records that, thanks to Cornwallis's intervention, more than two hundred black and white servants and camp followers "of both sexes" and races were on board the *Andrew* alone (the same holds true for other ships of the fleet), hiding their faces; "probably," he states, they "were contraband."[46] Ewald seems relieved that at least some of "our black friends" could be saved. The black soldiers in Hessian service, as well as their dependents, would have to wait two more years in New York before they could be shipped to Hesse. The memoirs of a fugitive black minister in the British forces, Boston King, published in 1798, recall that these New York years of waiting und uncertainty were marked by "inexpressible anguish and terror,"[47] caused especially by the refugees' dread that their former masters would track them down and reclaim the self-liberators as "property."

Concluding Remarks

The slaves' decision to run from their American masters and enlist with the Hessians was an act of self-liberation. That they continued to move and decide as free individuals—expressed, as we saw, in von Knyphausen's statement that "some have already decided to return to Hesse with us"—was confirmed as the time approached for the Hessians to depart from the North American continent. Like their white Hessian comrades, they chose between three options, which the HETRINA records document: large numbers simply deserted and opted for an American future, perhaps hoping against hope that the young republic would abandon the pernicious and inhuman system of chattel slavery. Others, perhaps connected through family ties, asked for regular dismissal, which was granted. A third group of approximately seventy regulars chose migration to Germany, and were supported in this by their white Hessian superiors—tangible proof that they had served to satisfaction and were acknowledged as fellow Hessian soldiers and subjects. Also, we have to add to our list an unidentified number of dependents as well as officers' personal servants and purchased or foraged slaves. These dependents and slaves certainly had little choice and limited agency.

The last Hessian troops, among them Ewald and his Jaegers, arrived in Kassel on 18 May 1784. They were inspected by the landgrave and, the profitable British subsidies having expired, dramatically reduced in numbers on the spot. Now considered military failures and financial liabilities, many Hessian common soldiers, all so-called strangers from other states, and especially all elderly and wounded servicemen, were dismissed from service, finally free(d) to return to their families and homes. "All services performed were forgotten and we poor 'Americans,' who had flattered ourselves with the best reception, were deceived in our expectations in the most undeserved way,"[48] an embittered Ewald concludes. However, the landgrave chose to confirm all black American regulars, for they would enhance his glory among the German and European nobility and royalty. In his official proclamation for the returning troops, Friedrich II decreed on 31 October 1783: "No Negroes are to be dismissed; but they shall all be retained, and until they can be transferred to my First Batallion Garde they shall receive a monthly bonus payment from the accumulated peace budget from my royal chatoul."[49] Within months, all black Hessian soldiers were integrated into the landgrave's personal elite corps and served in and around Kassel. American Negroes/*Neger* and fugitive slaves were thus redefined as privileged *Mohren* of an enormous representational value for their white sovereign and patron. They and their family members were transformed from American slaves into the landgrave's subjects,[50] with both the utter dependence on his goodwill and the powerful protection and respect their new position in court entailed in this strictly hierarchical society where, as Anne Kuhlmann's chapter in this volume illustrates, status came with proximity to power. They had freed themselves from the terrors of American chattel slavery, hoping, perhaps against hope and their deeper knowledge of human nature, that by relocating to Hesse-Kassel, they would move toward a freedom beyond race, toward a freedom without racism. In a Germany that was in the process of developing "scientific" theories of race, racial difference, and racialized nationhood, race—though in the new and unexpected local German expressions this volume traces across time—would continue to be their and their descendants' daily companion. But in Kassel they were free, their human status uncontested and affirmed.

Notes

1. Kassel was spelled Cassell until 1928. For consistency, however, it will be spelled Kassel throughout this text.
2. Kirchenbuch reformierte Gemeinde Kassel (KGK), Landeskirchliches Archiv Kassel (LKA), 78.
3. KGK, LKA, 78.
4. KGK, LKA, 995.
5. Inge Auerbach, *Die Hessen in Amerika, 1776–1783* (Darmstadt, Germany: Selbstverlag der Hessischen Historischen Kommission Darmstadt und der Historischen Kommission für Hessen, 1996), 357–86; Inge Auerbach, F.G. Franz, and O. Fröhlich, *Hessische Truppen im*

Amerikanischen Unabhängigkeitskrieg (HETRINA), 6 vols. (Marburg, Germany: Archivschule Marburg–Institut für Archivwissenschaft, 1972-87); Graham R. Hodges, *The Black Loyalist Directory: African Americans in Exile after the American Revolution* (New York: Garland Publishing, 1996); George F. Jones, "The Black Hessians: Negroes Recruited by the Hessians in South Carolina and Other Colonies," *South Carolina Historical Magazine* 83 (1982): 287-302; and Wolfram Schäfer, "Von 'Kammermohren,' 'Mohren'-Tambouren und 'Ost-Indianern': Anmerkungen zu Existenzbedingungen und Lebensformen einer Minderheit im 18. Jahrhundert unter besonderer Berücksichtigung der Residenzstadt Kassel," in *Fremdsein: Minderheiten und Gruppen in Hessen*, ed. Andreas C. Bimmer and Heinrich J. Dingeldein (Marburg, Germany: Jonas, 1988), 35-80.

6. Joseph P. Tustin, "Introduction," in Johann Ewald, *Diary of the American War: A Hessian Journal: Captain Johann Ewald, Field Jäger Corps*, ed. and trans. Joseph P. Tustin (New Haven, CT: Yale University Press, 1979), xix.
7. Hodges, *Black Loyalist Directory*, 119ff.
8. Heide Wunder, Christina Vanja, and Karl-Hermann Wegner, eds., *Kassel im 18. Jahrhundert: Residenz und Stadt* (Kassel, Germany: Euregio Verlag, 2000).
9. Jones, "The Black Hessians"; Schäfer, "Von 'Kammermohren,'" 41ff.; Auerbach, *Die Hessen*, 357ff.
10. For a detailed list of archives in Great Britain, Canada, and the United States, see Sylvia R. Frey, *Water from the Rock: Black Resistance in a Revolutionary Age* (Princeton, NJ: Princeton University Press, 1991), 333-40.
11. See, e.g., Hodges, *Black Loyalist Directory*, 120-21; Ira Berlin, "The Revolution in Black Life," in *The American Revolution: Explorations in the History of American Radicalism*, ed. Alfred F. Young (DeKalb: Northern Illinois University Press, 1976), 351-82; Douglas R. Egerton, *Death or Liberty: African Americans and Revolutionary America* (New York: Oxford University Press, 2009); Frey, *Water from the Rock*; Cassandra Pybus, *Epic Journeys of Freedom: Runaway Slaves of the American Revolution and Their Global Quest for Liberty* (Boston: Beacon Press, 2005); Benjamin Quarles, *The Negro in the American Revolution* (Chapel Hill: University of North Carolina Press, [1961] 1996); Simon Schama, *Rough Crossings: Britain, the Slaves and the American Revolution* (New York: HarperCollins, 2006); James W. St. G. Walker, *The Black Loyalists: The Search for a Promised Land in Nova Scotia and Sierra Leone, 1783-1870* (Toronto: University of Toronto Press, 1992); and Ellen Gibson Wilson, *The Loyal Blacks* (New York: Putnam, 1976).
12. Examples will be discussed below.
13. See the example of ten-year-old David, a "likely boy" purchased by the Hessian Major General von Kospoth in Philadelphia and transported to Germany aboard the *Hind*: Hodges, *Black Loyalist Directory*, 119.
14. Ira Berlin, *Many Thousands Gone: The First Two Centuries of Slavery in North America* (Cambridge, MA: Harvard University Press, 2003), esp. chap. 1.
15. For a detailed list of these enlistments, see Auerbach, *Die Hessen*, 357-86.
16. Hessisches Staatsarchiv Marburg (StAM) Best. 10c, SR 68, f. 14 v. See also Auerbach, *Die Hessen*, 371-72, 385.
17. James Sidbury, *Becoming African in America: Race and Nation in the Early Black Atlantic* (New York: Oxford University Press, 2007).
18. Peter Martin, *Schwarze Teufel, edle Mohren: Afrikaner in Geschichte und Bewusstsein der Deutschen* (Hamburg, Germany: Hamburger Edition, 2001), esp. chap. 4; Sander L. Gilman, *On Blackness without Blacks: Essays on the Image of the Black in Germany* (Boston: G.K. Hall, 1982), chap. 4; and Nell Irvin Painter, *The History of White People* (New York: W.W. Norton, 2009), chaps. 5-6.
19. Nell Irvin Painter, "Representing Truth: Sojourner Truth's Knowing and Becoming Known,"

Journal of American History 81 (1984): 462. See also Nell Irvin Painter, *Sojourner Truth: A Life, a Symbol* (New York: W.W. Norton, 1996).
20. Schäfer, "Von 'Kammermohren,'" 38ff.; Uwe Peter Böhm, "Farbige in Hessischen Diensten," *Zeitschrift für Heereskunde* 47 (1983): 81–84; and M. Rischmann, "Mohren als Spielleute und Musiker in der preussischen Armee," *Zeitschrift für Heeres- und Uniformkunde* 91/93 (1936): 82-84.
21. Carl Leopold Baurmeister, *Revolution in America: Confidential Letters and Journals 1776-1784 of Adjutant General Major Baurmeister of the Hessian Forces*, ed. and trans. Bernard A. Uhlendorf (New Brunswick, NJ: Rutgers University Press, 1957).
22. Graham R. Hodges, *Root and Branch: African Americans in New York and East Jersey, 1613-1863* (Chapel Hill: University of North Carolina Press, 1999), esp. chap. 5; and Graham R. Hodges, "Liberty and Constraint: The Limits of Revolution," in *Slaves in New York*, ed. Ira Berlin and Leslie M. Harris (New York: The New Press, 2005), 91–109.
23. HETRINA is short for *Hessische Truppen im amerikanischen Unabhängigkeitskrieg*, a six-volume index that lists all individuals enlisted as Hessian soldiers and officers during the American War of Independence. The index was assembled by the Archivschule (archival school) Marburg in the 1970s.
24. Baurmeister, *Revolution in America*, 131.
25. Friedrich J. von Günderode, *Briefe eines Reisenden über den gegenwärtigen Zustand von Cassel* (Frankfurt: Fleischer, 1781), 85. All translations are my own unless otherwise indicated.
26. For a theoretical conceptualization of the importance of context, see Demetrius L. Eudell, *The Political Language of Emancipation in the British Caribbean and the U.S. South* (Chapel Hill: University of North Carolina Press, 2002), 37.
27. Schama, *Rough Crossings*, 67–68.
28. Baurmeister, *Revolution in America*, 89.
29. See Ortrud Wörner-Heil, "'Extreme Formalität und Gleichheit': Freimaurerlogen in Kassel von 1766–1794," in Wunder, Vanja, and Wegner, eds., *Kassel im 18. Jahrhundert*, 229–61.
30. Hodges, *Black Loyalist Directory*, 120.
31. "Bericht des Generalleutnants v. Knyphausen an den Landgrafen," vol. 1, 17 October 1777, StAM 10c,I/Ia, 18-19.
32. Ewald, *Diary of the American War*, 305.
33. Schama, *Rough Crossings;* and Walker, *The Black Loyalists*. In 1792, almost 1,200 black refugees living in Nova Scotia and New Brunswick, as well as a large number of "black poor" refugees living in England, migrated to Sierra Leone. This exodus was organized and funded by the British abolitionist Sierra Leone Company.
34. For biographical information on Johann Ewald, see Tustin, "Introduction," xix–xxxi.
35. Ewald, *Diary of the American War*, 120, 214.
36. Ibid., 20.
37. Ibid., 199.
38. Ibid., 197.
39. Ibid.
40. Ibid., 199.
41. Frey, *Water from the Rock*, 108–10; Schama, *Rough Crossings*, 100–20. For contemporary Hessian renderings of the siege, see Bernhard A. Uhlendorf, ed. and trans., *The Siege of Charleston: With an Account of the Province of South Carolina: Diaries and Letters of Hessian Officers* (Cranbury, NJ: The Scholar's Bookshelf, [1938] 2007).
42. Ewald, *Diary of the American War*, 240.
43. After Charleston had been taken by the British and Hessian forces in March 1780, Ewald and his Jaegers were ordered back to New York. See Ewald, *Diary of the American War*, chap. 2.
44. Ewald, *Diary of the American War*, 298.

45. Ibid., 335–36.
46. Ibid., 343.
47. Boston King, "Memoirs of the Life of Boston King, a Black Preacher: Written by Himself, during his Residence at Kingswood-School," in *Unchained Voices: An Anthology of Black Authors in the English-Speaking World of the 18th Century*, ed. Vincent Carretta (Lexington: University Press of Kentucky, 2004), 356. King's memoir was originally published in London in 1798.
48. Ewald, *Diary of the American War*, 361.
49. "Journal von dem hochfürstlichen Hessischen, des General Major von Knoblauch aus dem Amerikanischen Krieg, von anno 1776 bis anno 1783," StAM 10e, I 12, 618–19.
50. For a sophisticated analysis of the concept of subjecthood, focusing on Britain but also in many aspects applicable to the Hessian context, see Christopher Leslie Brown, "Empire without Slaves: British Concepts of Emancipation in the Age of the American Revolution," *William and Mary Quarterly* 56 (1999): 273–306: "In the eighteenth century, the meaning of subjectship retained the quasi-medieval connotations of a personal bond between individual and lord. Subjectship could be natural or acquired.... In either case, subjectship was understood as natural, perpetual, and immutable, a civic analogue to the relation between parent and child. The relationship entailed obligations: the monarch owed the subject protection, and the subject owed allegiance" (282).

Part II

FROM ENLIGHTENMENT TO EMPIRE

Chapter Six

THE GERMAN RECEPTION OF AFRICAN AMERICAN WRITERS IN THE LONG NINETEENTH CENTURY

Heike Paul

Introduction

Currently, there is a wide range of publications addressing the transatlantic dimension of American slavery and abolitionism as well as the African/African American diaspora in Europe. Although "transatlantic" in many of these Anglo-American–based projects still almost exclusively refers to contacts between the Americas and Britain, and rarely to those with the European mainland or Germany,[1] there is also a more sustained effort these days to include Germany in the scholarship of the black Atlantic.[2] These studies trace evidence of black life in Germany, engage with representations or omissions of black "alterity," and scrutinize concepts of American and European "whiteness" and modernity as co-constructed with those of black otherness and black "primitivism."

This chapter does not deal with the physical presence of black people in the German states or the circulation of black images in a German imaginary, but rather reconstructs and investigates the presence of black voices in German literature in the eighteenth and nineteenth century. By "black voices," I mean self-representation(s)—of black identity, experience, and life in autobiographical and fictional texts, which is to say in published (usually translated) documents—as opposed to the presence of blackness as representation(s) of alterity.[3] More specifically, I argue that German readers encountered black writing and authorship through texts by African Americans, that is, black individuals who resided in North America. The circulation of black-authored texts concurred with an inter-

---

Notes from this chapter begin on page 129.

est in slavery and abolitionism. In white-authored German-language literature throughout the eighteenth and nineteenth centuries, black people appeared in exotic settings, as moors or slaves to be pitied (in representations that infantilized and/or feminized black figures) or to be despised (in representations that demonized them). Most of these works operated at least partially in a sentimental mode, often concocting sensationalist plots. All of them seemed to avoid acknowledging "black" difference on its own terms.[4]

In the course of quite comprehensive research, I have found only four texts by African Americans that appeared in German-language editions in the eighteenth and nineteenth centuries, and it is on these that I base my analyses: Olaudah Equiano's slave narrative *Olaudah Equiano's oder Gustav Wasa's, des Afrikaners merkwürdige Lebensgeschichte von ihm selbst geschrieben,* (The Interesting Narrative of the Life of Olaudah Equiano, or, Gustavus Vassa, the African, Written by Himself) published in 1789 (London) and 1792 (Göttingen); Frederick Douglass's autobiography *Sklaverei und Freiheit* (My Bondage and My Freedom), published in 1855 (New York) and 1860 (Stuttgart); Frank Webb's novel *Die Garies und ihre Freunde* (The Garies and Their Friends), published in 1857 (London) and 1859 (Leipzig); and Josiah Henson's slave narrative, *Truth Stranger than Fiction: Father Henson's Story of His Own Life,* published in 1858 (Boston) and 1878 (Bremen). To investigate them in their respective cultural contexts, I will look more closely at three different historical moments: (1) the late eighteenth century circumstances of the publication of Equiano's slave narrative; (2) the negotiations of slavery, blackness, and emancipation in the 1850s and 1860s that coincided with the publication of Douglass's and Webb's texts; and (3) the discussions surrounding Henson's narrative when it appeared in German somewhat belatedly in the late 1870s. I argue that in each of these four instances of a black-authored text being published in Germany, this authorship was contested. In each case, an introduction or preface—sometimes rather lengthy—sought to authenticate the black voice and thereby, ironically, undermined its authority; all of the prefaces anticipated articulations of distrust and disbelief toward the fact of black authorship and practiced strategies of "midwifery," to use Mary Dearborn's phrase, and containment.[5] In one of these case studies, the reception of the work completely eradicated the black author, giving credit instead to the translator of the book. Overall, each of these instances concern a black voice "under erasure," in the Derridean sense.

Olaudah Equiano and the "Discovery" of Black Humanity

To contextualize the publication of Olaudah Equiano's narrative in Germany, let me begin by sketching contemporary discourses of the new world in the old. In his seminal work *Germany and the American Revolution,* the German historian Horst Dippel diagnoses a widespread ignorance about America in the German states prior to the American War of Independence, even among the elite: "About the political and geographical structure of the continent, which must be the basis for any further and detailed understanding, the German bourgeoisie had very little information."[6] Yet with the onset of the Revolutionary War, the first "experts on America" could be found in Germany, among them Matthias Christian Sprengel, who "had succeeded in gaining a reputation as an authority on America among both academicians and the educated bourgeoisie."[7] Sprengel was born in Rostock in 1745, educated in Göttingen, and appointed professor there in 1778. At the University of Göttingen, then the center of geographical scholarship in Germany, Sprengel lectured on "the history and the present state of the British colonies in America." In 1779, he moved on to another appointment in Halle. In his inaugural lecture, delivered and published that same year and titled "About the Origin of the Slave Trade" (Vom Ursprung des Negerhandels), he took a mildly abolitionist position. From the beginning, Sprengel's interest in North America was linked to an interest in the institution of slavery and the slave trade, which was not uncharacteristic at that time. By the late eighteenth century, according to Dippel, "important libraries such as those in Göttingen and Dresden began ... to acquire many books about North America and on the events taking place there."[8]

It was also in Göttingen, in the midst of this first small-scale "America boom," that the first text by an African American author was made available to a German audience: *Equiano's, oder Gustav Wasa's, des Afrikaners merkwürdige Lebensgeschichte von ihm selbst geschrieben* appeared in Göttingen in 1792, published by Johann Christian Dieterich. Equiano's slave narrative was the first minor best seller by a black author in Europe: it was published in England, the Netherlands, Denmark, Germany, and several other European countries. Equiano's text is an extraordinary tale of suffering and emancipation, of bondage and mobility, of false promises and new hopes. The protagonist grows up in Africa, where he is kidnapped and enslaved and brought to the West Indies. From Barbados, he is carried to Virginia, then to England, where he is employed on a warship. Eventually, he converts to Christianity and is baptized; numerous expeditions and journeys follow: to Turkey, Portugal, Spain, Grenada, and Jamaica, toward the North Pole, to the United States, and to England. Time and again, the protagonist moves between new and old worlds and around the world mostly as a slave, and later as a free black. Equiano closes with an explicitly abolitionist statement: "I hope the slave trade will be abolished. I pray it may be an event at hand."[9] He then affirms that his Christian faith and moral integrity inform his autobiographical account: "My life and fortune have been extremely chequered, and my adventures various.... I early accustomed myself to look for the hand of God in the minutest occurrence, and to learn from it a lesson of morality and religion; and in this light every circumstance I have related was to me of importance."[10]

German readers of the time would most likely have recognized Equiano's manifold references to the Bible and other religious writings as well as to works such as *Robinson Crusoe* (1719) and *Gulliver's Travels* (1726). The publisher announced the book as an "exotic travel narrative," omitting any explicit reference to Enlightenment abolitionism while the author himself dwelled on the urgency of abolishing the slave trade and slavery. Equiano's narrative clearly placed his critique of slavery in a context of processes of global mobility and the evolution of a new transatlantic economic system that was generating novel and cruel forms and practices of exchange and exploitation. An African author, a former slave who had traveled widely, must indeed have struck a German reader as "exotic" at a time when the generic textual ascription of the "slave narrative" did not yet exist.

Modern interpreters have focused on literary qualities in interpreting the reception of Equiano's text. Rather than its ethnographic value, Werner Sollors, editor of the Norton critical edition, emphasizes Equiano's literariness in the positive reception of the book. Sollors notes:

> Equiano's literary language made his book much more than a generic abolitionist tract or conversion narrative; for at a peak period of the culture of the printed book, here was one written by an African writer and reader whose image, holding the Bible, must have appealed to an audience that he impressed by his self-conscious employment of literary devices and allusions.[11]

And Henry Louis Gates stresses the role of Equiano's text as a foundational text for American and diasporic black writing in general:

> It was Equiano whose text served to create a model that the ex-slaves would imitate.... Equiano's strategies of self-presentation and rhetorical representation heavily informed, if not determined, the shape of black narrative before 1865.[12]

Whereas Sprengel's *Antrittsprogramm* marked an academic interest in the institution of slavery in North America, the publication of Equiano's narrative evidenced an interest in African American slaves as human beings in Germany. As the historian Volker Depkat has observed: "The way in which black people were referred to in [German] newspapers [of that time] mainly served the purpose of bringing them to the attention of the German readers as *human beings*."[13] Reminding the audience of the fact that a black man *is* a human being was also the main didactic intention the German philologist and translator George Friedrich Benecke expressed in his preface to Equiano's narrative:

> Three editions in one year and one translation clearly justify also the German translation, in case someone should ask for a justification. It is hopefully not importunate hawking when the translator declares that he is of the non-authoritative opinion that

from a book in which a lot of things appear with which we in Germany for the most part have no direct experience, we can learn as much from it as from a story of love or marriage whose heroes and heroines we meet all the time also in natura.[14]

In his view, the success of the book manifested a general, universalist interest that transcended national boundaries; in scope and dissemination, the publication of Equiano's narrative was an international phenomenon. Benecke went on to elaborate the particular position of the German audience, who came to the story as "strangers to slavery" and might have expected the common love plot. Perhaps he had the popular novels by Sophie von La Roche or August Lafontaine in mind—stories of pursued innocence and the suspension of feudal hierarchies and class boundaries that were widely read mostly by a female audience.[15] Such stories, one has to note, were also concerned with (intracultural) social borders and relationships of (domestic) exploitation. Still, Benecke contrasted them with the intercultural dimensions in Equiano's text, which exposed its readers to otherness and difference of another kind, even though Equiano himself tried to tone them down. Benecke's preface clearly emphasizes Equiano's cultural status as an outsider and as a representative of "Africanness": "I only beg the reader not to forget that the author of this book is nothing more than a poor negro whose hand for the most part of his life was busy with other things than the pen."[16]

With this topos of modesty regarding African American authorship, Benecke picked up on Equiano's own self-effacement and modesty as a writer, yet blatantly misunderstood the author's elaborate literariness. Thus, the German "discovery" of black humanity is linked to the black man's *literacy*—not *literariness*. In retrospect, Equiano's narrative, in its diasporic range and its transcendence of national boundaries, in many ways anticipated what Goethe in 1827 would refer to as *Weltliteratur*, although it has not been acknowledged as such. Benecke was employed at the university library in Göttingen and later had quite a career as a professor of German and English. Between 1789 and 1795, he translated four English books into German, among them Equiano's text.[17] Yet, as his introduction signals, Equiano was not recognized *as an author*. Indeed, in spite of sustained efforts, I was unable to discover a single review of Equiano's narrative. In the words of Peter Martin, Equiano figured as an "object of demonstration" in the context of the Enlightenment notion of a great chain of being *(große Seinskette; lex continui)*, which conceived of humanity as a great and varied yet coherent kind of mosaic.[18] As a black man, Equiano served as an exemplar of edification, illustrating an individual effort at self-refinement when writing and literacy still figured, in the words of Henry Louis Gates Jr., as nothing less than a "signature of humanity."[19] Equiano was consistently referred to as a "Negro" and "African"—at no point did the preface explicitly describe him as affiliated with America or Europe. Thus, somewhat paradoxically, Equiano was reclaimed as a member of the family of mankind on the basis of Enlightenment universalism with the same gesture that "localized" him as an "other" belonging to some "other" place—not to the "West" but to "the rest," to pick up a distinction by Stuart Hall.[20]

Equiano's German publisher was Johann Christian Dieterich, a publisher and printer of the Age of Enlightenment as well as a close friend of Georg Christoph Lichtenberg. The philosophical faculty at the university in Göttingen had added many new disciplines to its curriculum (such as history, ethnology, geography, and psychology) in the last decades of the eighteenth century, and Dieterich's publishing program documented this development.[21] Although Equiano's narrative was not part of Dieterich's scholarly publications for the university, its topic echoed the discussions going on in many disciplinary fields at the time. Yet, the Göttingen- (and Halle)-centered interest in slavery and its subjects provided a singular opening for German publishing of black-authored texts.[22] After the publication of Equiano's narrative at the end of the eighteenth century, it would take more than half a century for the next text by a person of African descent to appear in Germany.

Frederick Douglass's Autobiography and the Thwarted Reception of Black Authorship

The project of a German edition of Frederick Douglass's second autobiography paradigmatically reveals the erratic twists and turns in the German reception of black-authored texts. Frederick Douglass, one of the best-known nineteenth-century African American authors and intellectuals (and a fugitive slave), had published his first slave narrative in 1845; in 1855, he followed this up with an updated and expanded second autobiography titled *My Bondage and My Freedom*. In the second work, Douglass described the circumstances under which he had written the first book and chronicled his abolitionist work and his travels in the United States and England. Scholars usually perceive the narrative persona of the second autobiography as much more self-confident than the first, and as the construction of a black public figure.[23] Douglass negotiated the conventions of the slave narrative, which demanded a certain representativeness as well as modesty of its narrative subject; at the same time, he moved beyond these conventions by asserting himself as an internationally known intellectual, highlighting his roles as the editor of a newspaper and as a well-established figure in the abolitionist movement. By that time, he had separated from his former white abolitionist mentor, William Garrison, and stood on his own as perhaps the first African American public intellectual of his time. Douglass firmly believed in the non-emigrationist fight against slavery. He considered himself to be an American who worked to abolish slavery in the United States rather than to propose the relocation of blacks to Africa, Canada, or South America, as some of his black contemporaries did. In order to successfully pursue his abolitionist agenda, Douglass forged a number of international, mainly transatlantic alliances and also agreed to a German-language edition of his second autobiography.

The translator of his book into German was Ottilie Assing, a journalist and the first German (half-Jewish), full-time America correspondent employed by Johann Friedrich Cotta's *Morgenblatt für gebildete Leser*. Assing moved to the United States in the early 1850s and became an abolitionist soon after her arrival. She was a close friend of Douglass's and worked with him on many projects, such as translating articles and statements for the German press.[24] Assing translated the autobiography in 1858 and 1859 while staying with Douglass and his family in Rochester, New York;[25] the book was published in 1860. Incensed by the phenomenal success of Harriet Beecher Stowe's (merely fictional) sentimental reform novel *Uncle Tom's Cabin,* which struck her as unbearably evangelical, Assing at the same time was fascinated with Douglass's personality and his life story, as her preface to her German translation of his autobiography attests:

> If this life story were a work of the imagination, an artistic creation, we would have to regret that it was not published several years earlier, before the interest in such stories was exhausted by the almost countless narratives of slave life which constitute—ever since the publication of the famous "Uncle Tom"—their own literary genre. Yet, the present work is not such a creation, rather it is a true story, the stringing together of naked, unadorned, horrible facts which, as it is a matter of reality with all its consequences, must affect those who can bear to hear the truth in an ever more striking, moving, and convincing way than all works of fiction.[26]

Tapping into contemporary German discourses on the harmfulness of fiction rooted in Enlightenment discourses, Assing here contrasted fictional slave narratives such as Stowe's with the authentic slave narrative by Douglass and advocated taking the latter more seriously than the former. Assing had to insist on the meaningfulness of this contrast to attract an audience that had already been "exhausted" by fictional stories about slavery; Douglass's "true" story, Assing suggested, far surpassed all of the fictional slave stories in truthfulness, as well as in "human interest."

A number of scholars have speculated about the role Assing's own Jewish background played in her interest in abolitionism and the African American politics of emancipation. Certainly, Assing had faced "anti-Semitic prejudices and social isolation" growing up in Hamburg as the daughter of a Gentile and a Jew.[27] For her, the marginalization of Jewish people in Europe and black people in the United States seemed to have a common basis in long-standing pre-Enlightenment prejudices, "false" religion and superstition, and economic interests that were often camouflaged. Maria Diedrich suggests that Assing's interest may also have been more profane and that she may have aimed to carve out her own economic niche as a transatlantic communicator:

In the slave narrative she had discovered a literary genre that had been neglected by her competitors. She could enhance her reputation as a translator and, even more desirable, would present herself as the authority on slavery and African-American life, as Germany's Negro expert.[28]

Whereas Assing's preface cleared space for Douglass's story and advertised it, her attempt to bolster Douglass's authorship and authority backfired. Assing affirmed the identity of "her" black author in much the same way that white abolitionists and philanthropists would—by composing prefaces and afterwords as authentication and legitimation devices (both William Garrison and Wendell Phillips did so for the American publication of Douglass's first slave narrative). Quite conventionally, she referred to meeting him in person and being convinced of his extraordinary personality and abilities. Like Equiano's voice, Douglass's did not stand on its own. Yet, unlike Benecke's rather short and reserved note, Assing fervently and enthusiastically extolled Douglass's merits at some length (six pages):

> Douglass is a rather pale mulatto of unusually tall, slim, and strong build. His features are marked, and a strongly domed forehead with a curiously deep incision at the root of the nose, his curved nose, and his slim, beautifully drawn lips betray more of his white than his black ancestry. His thick hair, already peppered with streaks of grey, is curly and erect, but not woolly. In his whole appearance, which tells of past storms and battles, there is an expression of great energy and strong will, which does not shy away from any obstacle, and, indeed, by virtue of which alone—against all odds—he has been able to work himself up into his present situation.... Everything about him is fresh, genuine, true, and characterful. He has an unusual talent for conversation, he knows how to stimulate the other and to lift him up, and in conversations he is cheerful, lively, witty, and very knowledgable. Filled with passion for the cause to which he has dedicated his life, he is far too wide-ranging in his interests not to engage in any other worthy cause with energy. We touched upon a variety of things—large and small, general and personal—in the course of our conversation, and everywhere I encountered understanding and sympathy—Douglass's wife is totally black, and his five children thus bear more of the Negro type in them than does he.[29]

Assing's preface was, perhaps, a little too enthusiastic. As Maria Diedrich and others have pointed out, Assing turned Douglass into a "noble savage" and a heroic, larger-than-life figure. She then undermined her abolitionist intent with her comparison of Douglass to his wife and children, which echoed common racist stereotypes ("totally black," "Negro type").

But whatever the merits and pitfalls of Assing's preface, the book was well received, although it did not go beyond a first edition. The reception was much more limited than Assing had hoped for and certainly much more limited in scope than that of *Uncle Tom's Cabin*, yet reviews were favorable. For example, one reviewer in *Unterhaltungen am häuslichen Herd* commented: "The simple, plain representation of this authentic slave life conveys a no less moving and—with the omission of all romantic dramatization—still much sharper picture of American slavery than the previous accounts in Beecher-Stowe's *Onkel Tom's Hütte*."[30]

Nonetheless, when one traces the book in subsequent bibliographies, it is apparent that there was some confusion about its status. From the date of its initial publication, critics have tended to record it as Ottilie Assing's biography of Frederick Douglass's life, not as Douglass's own text—perhaps due to misconceiving the rhetorical strategies of Assing's preface, or perhaps due to the precariousness of black authorship. For instance, in her otherwise impeccable study and annotated bibliography, the American German studies scholar Grace Edith MacLean wrote about *Sklaverei und Freiheit*:

> This is the work of a German woman in New York, who tried to write a second *Uncle Tom's Cabin*. She had read the *North Star*, a paper of which the former slave, Frederick Douglas [sic], was editor, and conceived the idea of writing the story of his life to help the anti-slavery cause as *Uncle Tom* had done.[31]

The skepticism toward black authorship and authority may have had an impact on the misperceptions by MacLean and others. Following the bibliographic "career" of the book, I was again surprised when I read in Leroy Woodson's study on *American Negro Slavery in the Works of Friedrich Strubberg, Friedrich Gerstäcker and Otto Ruppius* that "Ottilie Ossing" [sic] was a defender of the institution of slavery, that she published her work *Freiheit und Sklaverei* in "1856," and that she considered "the problem [of slavery] from the point of view of the slaveholder":[32] name of author, book title, year of publication, and political agenda—all wrong. In the same ignorant manner, Peter Brenner seems to have copied from Woodson when he considered Assing and Friedrich A. Arming to be two proslavery authors.[33] Arming's *Weiß und Schwarz: Historische Erzählung aus der ersten Zeit des Sonderbundkrieges in Amerika* (1865) was indeed a defense of slavery. Although the title page of *Sklaverei und Freiheit* clearly credited Douglass as the author and Assing as the translator, it is hard to come by a correct reference to or even a bibliographic entry on the text. Frederick Douglass's second book certainly had a strange German career, going the long way from being the autobiography of a former African American slave and leading abolitionist to the text of a female German proslavery author! Of the two names on the title page, only Assing's was remembered.

The Enigma of the Publication of Frank Webb's Novel in Germany

The German publishing history of Frank Webb's novel *The Garies and Their Friends* is even more mysterious than the twisted remembrance of Frederick

Douglass's translated autobiography. Webb's novel was only the second novel by an African American ever to be published—the first being William Wells Brown's *Clotel* (1853). Like Brown's book, Webb's was first published in London. The German edition of Webb's book, titled *Die Garies und ihre Freunde,* was listed as part of an American literature series published by Kollmann—bookseller and publisher in Leipzig—in the mid-nineteenth century. Kollmann's *Amerikanische Bibliothek* was quite comprehensive and offered readers a popular mix of contemporary American literature. Harriet Beecher Stowe's *Uncle Tom's Cabin* was published as volumes 9–12 of the series (*Onkel Toms Hütte*); Richard Hildreth's narrative *The White Slave* appeared as volumes 17–19 (*Der weiße Sklave*). Other authors included James Fenimore Cooper, Susan Warner, and E.D.E.N. Southworth, who was immensely popular in her day, though she has since been forgotten. Frank Webb's novel is listed as volumes 369–71 of the series. Very little is known about the author except that Webb was a free black Philadelphian born in the late 1820s who was apparently well educated and, in addition to writing the novel, later wrote for abolitionist journals such as the *New Era*.[34]

As Webb's narrative was quite marginal for a long time even in the American context, it may seem surprising that it was published in a German translation in the nineteenth century.[35] Contrary to other black nineteenth-century authors, Webb did not primarily deal with slavery in the American South but was the first to address in a novel the racism free African Americans in the Northern United States faced.[36] In the story, the Garie family, including a Southern plantation owner and his light-skinned "wife" (actually his slave) and their two children, relocate to the North, to Philadelphia. The couple wish to be legally married, to ensure the future of their children as free Americans, and to protect the family from the Southern institution of slavery. However, life in the North is full of obstacles for the racially mixed family: the streets of Philadelphia are marked by mob violence instigated by Irish immigrants hunting down African Americans, and Mr. and Mrs. Garie ultimately meet their tragic deaths there. Webb's novel is different from all other black writings of that time in its thematic "shift from slavery to color discrimination,"[37] which countered the conventional North-South dichotomy that operated in most antislavery writings. Thus, Webb's text was not all that useful for the antislavery cause but rather focused on attacking racial discrimination—in the South and the North; it clearly could not be enlisted to support abolition. Webb's narrative even maneuvered dangerous territory by allowing for a line of interpretation that misread it as an apology for slavery:

> [I]n setting up a contrast between the bucolic pastoral life on the Garie plantation and the brutal racism awaiting the couple in Philadelphia, Webb takes the sentimentalist's view of the South. ... This treatment of slavery may have suited the structural needs of his plot; but, like Stowe before him, Webb thereby stumbles into the trap of indirectly justifying the existence of slavery.[38]

Although we do not know whether this ambiguity played a role in Kollmann's decision to publish Webb's novel in German translation, the German career of this text was, in any case, highly enigmatic. The title appears in the *Gesamtverzeichnis des deutschsprachigen Schrifttums (GV) 1700–1910,* yet I have been unable to find a single extant copy in any library—in Germany or outside of it. No bibliography of American literature or African American literature in Germany lists this title, nor has any review, to my knowledge, ever been published. I did trace one copy in a used book auction in Germany in 2003, where it sold for one hundred euros. We may speculate that the novel was originally scheduled for publication because it had a connection with the most famous white American writer about American slavery, Harriet Beecher Stowe, whose novel, as the annoyed Ottilie Assing pointed out in her preface to Douglass's autobiography, was enormously successful in Germany. Stowe, who was a friend of Webb's wife Mary, had agreed to write a preface for Webb's novel—a gesture that was tremendously helpful in promoting the book. In the preface, Stowe said little about the text or the author, but she gave her name to support Webb's narrative. In terms of content, Webb's novel was a far cry from the abolitionist mainstream of the time, yet, on the stylistic and structural level, Webb, like Stowe, drew on the sentimental mode, focused on the domestic sphere, and thus met contemporary readers' expectations. As Reid-Pharr points out, "Webb was clearly in conversation with a score of authors, mostly female, of the mid-nineteenth century whose sentimentalism and emphasis on the domestic helped shape the ideological structures of the antebellum American writing world."[39]

That Kollmann's catalogue explicitly listed Stowe's preface lends credence to the idea that her association with the text motivated the publisher to include the novel in his American literature series. However, the narrative of a free black-and-white family living in the racist urban North did not appeal to the German readership. On the whole, the titles in the series indicate that the publisher preferred to stick to white-authored narratives about black life, such as Stowe's and Hildreth's; at least this was true of the mass-circulated titles that dealt with slavery and saw several editions. Thus, in the end, Kollmann's listing of Frank Webb's novel in German translation today reads as an obscure presence of a black voice never fully heard.

Josiah Henson's Narrative and the Colonization of Africa

Josiah Henson's slave narrative is a classic: it is the story of a fugitive slave who later claimed to be the model for Stowe's Uncle Tom figure. A first version of Henson's narrative was published in 1849, prior to the publication of *Uncle Tom's Cabin;* a second—and best-selling—version that referred to Stowe's novel and

Henson's role as her model was published in 1858. Henson's work relates how he grew up as a slave in New Orleans, escaped slavery, and became "Father Henson," the leader of a free African American community in Dawn, Canada.[40] Today, this settlement is one of the historical sites and museums documenting slavery and the Underground Railroad in Canada. Even if there is no explicit identification on Stowe's part of Tom with Henson, there is also no rejection of that assumption—and there are obvious parallels between Henson's life story and Tom's literary fate. There is contradictory evidence as to whether Stowe and Henson ever met personally or whether Stowe had simply read Henson's text before writing her novel. Winks recounts the relationship between the two people and texts in detail:

> The books of Mrs. Stowe and Henson did morally reinforce each other ... and she wrote an introduction to the second or 1858 edition of his book, in which he carried his story to 1852. But at this date—when association with Mrs. Stowe would bring a cachet to his account—he made no mention of any meeting, nor did she in her introduction, which was bland and noncommittal. Moreover, the introduction was retained unaltered in Henson's 1878 edition, in which he claimed to have met her in Andover, but either she met Henson there after nearly all of *Uncle Tom's Cabin* was written or both unaccountably had forgotten their venue.[41]

Henson's second narrative was reprinted in America in 1878; the first German edition appeared in that same year. Titled *Wirkliche Lebensgeschichte des Onkel Toms in Frau Beecher-Stowe's "Onkel Tom's Hütte,"* this edition clearly maintained that there was a strong connection between the text and Stowe's enormous success. By then, Josiah Henson's tale had been translated into twelve languages. This German translation of the narrative obviously has to be seen in conjunction with Stowe's foregoing literary success—the original title *(An Autobiography of the Rev. Josiah Henson)* was altered for this purpose, quite dramatically promising the "true story" behind Stowe's fiction.

This marketing strategy echoed that of Assing in her introduction to Douglass's autobiography. In the preface written by Henson's translator, Marie Schweikher, Henson's story was tied much more intimately to Stowe's novel than the scholarly evidence now corroborates.[42] Describing the text as authored by a "black man," Schweikher insisted that Stowe's "original idea" for her book had come from Henson's story and that he was her main source of inspiration, even if she eventually drew on "other sources" as well. Comparing the two works, Schweikher was quick to remark that the story of the black preacher Josiah Henson fortunately did have a "happy ending," whereas Stowe "from an artistic-literary standpoint had to allow 'Uncle Tom' to die."[43]

In addition to selling Henson's story as the inspiration for Harriet Beecher Stowe, Schweikher also aimed in her preface to further a Christian missionary agenda. She noted that reading Henson's life story would not only provide a

German reader with a pleasant read for hours on end but that it would be a blessing.[44] This showed her terminology, along with her agenda, to be religious rather than political. Translating Henson's narrative after slavery had been abolished, Schweikher saw it as an evident model and as an instrument for the complete "evangelization of the African tribes,"[45] particularly since a united Germany at that time intended to participate in the "scramble for Africa." At the same time, in the United States the spirit of reconstruction was dimming and a racial backlash was underway. If, as Henson's story indicated, an illiterate African American slave could be converted and become a rhetorically skilled black preacher, then, with God's help, Schweikher hoped, many more black souls would be saved. Her preface thus connected Henson's narrative of the conversion of an African American to the Christian mission and to the colonization of Africa, thus silencing the black voice and crossing out its political message.

It is bitterly ironic that the victim of slavery in this case was ideologically instrumentalized to foster and legitimize another form of "enslavement" in the future colonies in Africa. Schweikher's Christian discourse and colonialist logic of "the white man's burden" seemed to anticipate and camouflage Germany's brutal and violent colonization of parts of Africa. Schweikher's recounting of Henson's conversion thus made him into a new kind of African Christian but did not portray him as an African American, equal to whites, living in North America.

At the same time, Schweikher's argument is also reminiscent of the ending that Stowe chose for her novel, wherein the light-skinned slaves who managed to escape to the North found fulfillment in a mission to Africa rather than remain in the United States. It is perhaps not coincidental that Schweikher's German translation of Henson's book was not published in Leipzig, Stuttgart, or Frankfurt but in Bremen, a city close to the North Sea that would soon become heavily involved in the German colonial enterprise.

Conclusion

Investigating the presence of black voices in eighteenth- and nineteenth-century Germany, I have discussed four texts by African Americans in German translation representing four black voices that labored to convey a critique of slavery and racism. Three of them took the form of autobiography (Equiano, Douglass, Henson), and one of them was a novel (Webb). As my analyses of these texts' contextualization and reception has shown, all of these voices were cracked or muted in their German translations.

In the eighteenth century, Olaudah Equiano was a singular phenomenon; his narrative today is part of the Anglo-American literary canon of the early black Atlantic. It its historical context, the text was received primarily as an "exotic travel account" rather than as a contribution to the discussion of slavery.[46] The nineteenth-century texts by Frederick Douglass, Frank Webb, and Josiah Henson all have to be viewed in relation and proximity to Stowe's best seller, from whose popularity they profited. To this day, Stowe's spectacular success remains somewhat enigmatic—many explanations have been offered, yet no single explanation can wholly account for the enthusiastic worldwide response to the novel.[47] Douglass published his second autobiography in the wake of Stowe's success; Webb could boast a preface by the world-famous author; and Henson's tale was most strongly associated with Stowe's novel, as his life story was seen as her source. Due to the boost that the enormous popularity of Stowe's novel in Germany brought these texts, all of them were listed in the catalogues of German publishing houses. Yet none of these black-authored texts ever went beyond the first edition, whereas Stowe's novel saw hundreds of editions that sold in the thousands. Although Stowe's reform novel may have paved the way for these half-hearted attempts to publish black authors in Germany, the German audience did not "recognize" their voices as black voices connoting black agency. Apart from a small "transatlantic intellectual network … nourished by personal contact, travel, intellectual exchange of letters, books, and journals"[48] to which Ottilie Assing and a number of the so-called German Forty-Eighters belonged, there was no interest whatsoever in black human beings and black subjectivity in Germany.

As the nineteenth century drew to a close, Germans' sympathetic investment in African American suffering (even if in somewhat sanitized and sentimentalized versions) came to a rather abrupt end, not only because the institution of slavery had been abolished in the United States, but also because the German audience at that point was flocking to new romances of colonialism. These colonial narratives glaringly contradicted earlier tales of black emancipation and solidified German white self-fashioning as the "master race" that stood apart from nonwhites.[49] By then, the adult readership had largely discarded Harriet Beecher Stowe's reform novel, which had mutated, by and large, into a children's book focusing on little Eva's evangelical altruism rather than on the suffering of the slave Tom.

Nonetheless, because of the earlier success of the novel, "[f]or better or worse, it was Mrs. Stowe who invented American blacks for the imagination of the whole world."[50] Nineteenth-century Germans seem to have appreciated Stowe's black slaves as a projection screen for many of their anxieties,[51] but they were apparently far less interested in being confronted with black voices that controlled their own narratives. Ironically, the most concentrated form of nonfictional black discursivity Germans were to read about in their own language was probably Harriet Beecher Stowe's companion piece to her novel, *A Key to Uncle Tom's Cabin,* which she published in 1853 to counter criticisms that her representation of slavery was exaggerated and unfounded. Five verifiable German editions can be traced between 1853 and 1855. In this book, Stowe revealed many of her sources, referred to eyewitness accounts, and reprinted fugitive posters and court records, conversations with slaves and fugitives, and newspaper excerpts. This valuable sourcebook and unique documentation of American slavery (which also drew on Theodore Weld's *Slavery As It Is: Testimony of a Thousand Witnesses* [1839], which was never published in Germany) was presented to a German audience as fact—much in the same way the slave narratives were. Yet, in the mid-nineteenth century the voice of a white woman (although ridiculed as a cranky spinster and as a religious fanatic by some German reviewers) still carried more weight than the voice of a black man. Applying Gayatri Spivak's famous question of whether the subaltern can speak to the historical context in which these African American voices tried to communicate to the German readership across the Atlantic, we must answer in the negative.

Notes

1. Examples of "transatlantic" scholarship focusing mainly on Britain include Denise Kohn, Sarah Meer, and Emily B. Todd, *Transatlantic Stowe: Harriet Beecher Stowe and European Culture* (Iowa City: University of Iowa Press, 2006), which includes many case studies, none of them dealing with Germany; Audrey A. Fisch, *American Slaves in Victorian England* (Cambridge: Cambridge University Press, 2000); Helen Thomas, *Romanticism and Slave Narratives* (Cambridge: Cambridge University Press, 2000); Sarah Meer, *Uncle Tom Mania: Slavery, Minstrelsy, and Transatlantic Culture in the 1850s* (Athens: University of Georgia Press, 2005); and Cindy Weinstein, ed., *The Cambridge Companion to Harriet Beecher Stowe* (Cambridge: Cambridge University Press, 2004), particularly the chapter by Fisch. Concerning transatlantic black-German interactions, W.E.B. Dubois's stay in Germany has recently been researched quite intensively by Werner Sollors, e.g., Werner Sollors, "W. E. B. Du Bois in Nazi Germany, 1936," *Amerikastudien/American Studies* 44, no. 2 (1999): 207–22; and Sieglinde Lemke, e.g., Sieglinde Lemke, "Transatlantic Relations: The German Du Bois," in *German? American? Literature?* New Directions in German–American Studies, ed. Winfried Fluck and Werner Sollors (New York: Peter Lang, 2002), 207–16.
2. On the broader public attention being drawn to issues of the black Atlantic in Germany, the exhibitions and events that took place at the Haus der Kulturen der Welt in Berlin in 2004 were of eminent importance. See the volume *Der Black Atlantic*, ed. Haus der Kulturen der Welt with Tina Campt and Paul Gilroy (Berlin: Haus der Kulturen der Welt, 2004). Recent scholarly contributions include Mischa Honeck's *We Are the Revolutionists: German-speaking Immigrants and American Abolitionists after 1848* (Athens: University of Georgia Press, 2011); and my own *Kulturkontakt und Racial Presences: Afro-Amerikaner und die deutsche Amerika-Literatur, 1815–1914* (Heidelberg, Germany: Winter, 2005).
3. By using the terms "black authorship" and "black writing," I do not intend to affirm any kind of racial essentialism; still, such terms refer to social and cultural practices and their discursive effects.
4. Hans Werner Debrunner, *Presence and Prestige: Africans in Europe* (Basel, Switzerland: Basler Afrika Bibliographien, 1979), 29–30, 60, 283–84, 293–300, 367, provides a summary of these representations. Gottfried Herder's "African Idyllic Scenes" (Neger-Idyllen) and Heinrich von Kleist's *Verlobung von Santo Domingo* are among the more ambivalent representations of Africanness in Debrunner's collection. Herder acknowledges a common humanity of mankind

and even extols some of the cultural specificities of African peoples. His poem "Neger-Idyllen," for instance, contrasts the figure of the indigenous noble African savage with the figure of the white devilish colonizer. Kleist also ambiguously questions prevailing discourses of racial and cultural superiority in his novella. For scholarship on these texts, see Susanne Zantop, *Colonial Fantasies: Conquest, Family, and Nation in Precolonial Germany, 1770–1870* (Durham, NC: Duke University Press, 1997); Ingeborg Solbrig, "Herder and the 'Harlem Renaissance' of Black Culture in America: The Case of the 'Neger-Idyllen,'" in *Herder Today: Contributions from the International Herder Conference, November 5–8, 1987, Stanford, California*, ed. Kurt Mueller-Vollmer (Berlin: Walter de Gruyter, 1990), 402–14; and James P. Martin, "Reading Race in Kleist's 'Die Verlobung in St. Domingo,'" *Monatshefte* 100, no. 1 (2008): 48–66.
5. Mary V. Dearborn, *Pocahontas's Daughters: Gender and Ethnicity in American Culture* (New York: Oxford University Press, 1986), 31–47. Of course, this paratextual framing is not specific to the German context of reception; many studies have pointed to the ambiguous black authorship of original English-language publications with black-authored narratives virtually walled in by prefaces and introductory notes. Take, for example, the publication of Frederick Douglass's first slave narrative in 1845, which was accompanied by an introduction by William Garrison as well as a letter by Wendell Philips, both white abolitionists.
6. Horst Dippel, *Germany and the American Revolution, 1770–1800: A Sociohistorical Investigation of Late Eighteenth-Century Political Thinking* (Chapel Hill: University of North Carolina Press, 1977), 6.
7. Ibid., 52. Christoph Daniel Ebeling in Hamburg was another important transatlantic mediator. However, whereas Ebeling's writings, among them *Erdbeschreibung und Geschichte von Amerika: Die Vereinigten Staaten von Nordamerika* (Hamburg, Germany: Christian Ernst Kollmann, 1793–1816), were received favorably in the United States, they garnered little attention in Germany at the time, as Ebeling did not hold a prominent academic position.
8. Dippel, *Germany and the American Revolution*, 46–47.
9. The quotations are taken from the English original, which appeared in a critical edition in 2001: Olaudah Equiano, *The Interesting Narrative of the Life of Olaudah Equiano, or Gustavus Vassa, the African, Written by Himself*, edited and with an introduction by Werner Sollors (New York: Norton, 2001), 177.
10. Ibid., 178.
11. Werner Sollors, "Introduction," in Equiano, *The Interesting Narrative of the Life of Olaudah Equiano*, xv.
12. Henry Louis Gates Jr., *The Signifying Monkey: A Theory of African American Literary Criticism* (New York: Oxford University Press, 1989), 153.
13. Volker Depkat, *Amerikabilder in politischen Diskursen: Deutsche Zeitschriften 1789–1830* (Stuttgart, Germany: Klett-Cotta, 1998), 370: "Die Art und Weise, in der über die Schwarzen in den [deutschen] Zeitschriften [dieser Zeit] gesprochen wurde, diente im deutschen Kontext vor allem dazu, sie dem Publikum als *Menschen* zu Bewusstsein zu bringen."
14. George Friedrich Benecke, "Preface," in *Olaudah Equiano's oder Gustav Wasa's, des Afrikaners merkwürdige Lebensgeschichte*, trans. George Friedrich Benecke (Göttingen, Germany: Johann Christian Dieterich, 1792), iv–v: "Drey Ausgaben in Einem Jahre und eine Uebersetzung können, däucht mir, immer eine Speculation rechtfertigen, wenn irgend jemand sich befugt finden sollte, eine solche Rechtfertigung zu fordern. Marktschreyerey wird es übrigens hoffentlich nicht seyn, wenn der Uebersetzer erklärt, daß er der unmaßgeblichen Meinung ist, es lasse sich aus einem Buche, in dem eine Menge Dinge vorkommen, von denen wir in Deutschland größten Theils keine anschauliche Ideen haben, wenigstens eben so viel lernen, als aus einer Liebes- und Heirathsgeschichte, deren Helden und Heldinnen man allenthalben in natura findet."
15. Peter Nusser, *Trivialliteratur* (Stuttgart, Germany: Metzler, 1991), 58.

16. Benecke, "Preface," v: "Nur bitte ich die Leser nicht zu vergessen, daß der Verfasser des Buches weiter nichts ist, als ein armer Neger, dessen Hand die größte Zeit seines Leben hindurch mit ganz anderen Dingen beschäftigt war, als mit der Feder."
17. Birgit Wägenbaur, "Ein vergessener Gründervater: Georg Friedrich Benecke und die Anfänge der Germanistik," *Euphorion* 94, no. 3 (2000): 337.
18. Peter Martin, *Schwarze Teufel, edle Mohren: Afrikaner in Geschichte und Bewußtsein der Deutschen* (Hamburg, Germany: Hamburger Edition, 1993), 13, 202.
19. A similar case is that of African American poet Phyllis Wheatley and her poetry. There are a number of English editions of Equiano's slave narrative that were published together with Wheatley's poems; none of these have appeared in a German translation. See Henry Louis Gates Jr., "Editor's Introduction: Writing 'Race' and the Difference It Makes," *Critical Inquiry* 12, no. 1 (Autumn 1985): 1–20.
20. Stuart Hall, "The West and the Rest: Discourse and Power," in *Race and Racializations: Essential Readings,* ed. Tania Das Gupta (Toronto: Canadian Scholars' Press, 2077), 56–60.
21. For a complete overview of Dieterich's publishing program and his career in the vicinity of the University of Göttingen, see Elisabeth Willnat, *Johann Christian Dieterich: Ein Verlagsbuchhändler in der Zeit der Aufklärung* (Frankfurt: Buchhändler-Vereinigung, 1993).
22. Rudolf Vierhaus (*Die Universität Göttingen und die Anfänge der modernen Geschichtswissenschaft*), Roland Ludwig (*Die Rezeption der Englischen Revolution im deutschen politischen Denken und in der deutschen Historiographie im 18. und 19. Jahrhundert*), and, most prominently, Hermann Wellenreuther (*Mutmaßungen über ein Defizit: Göttingens Geschichtswissenschaft und die angelsächsiche Welt*) have investigated the interest in the Anglophone world at the University of Göttingen from the perspective of one particular discipline; although their conclusions vary, all of them point to the singular circumstances—in terms of personal connections, scholarly and political networks, and an enormous number of scholarly publications in stock at the university library—that characterized Göttingen's specific situation with regard to the Atlantic world, which, so to speak, flanked the publication of Equiano's narrative.
23. John Ernest, *Resistance and Reformation in Nineteenth-Century African American Literature* (Jackson: University of Mississippi Press, 1995), 143.
24. Maria Diedrich, in *Love Across Color Lines* (New York: Hill and Wang, 1999), extensively reconstructed this friendship and long-standing love relationship.
25. Ibid., 130.
26. Ottilie Assing, "Vorwort," in Frederick Douglass, *Sclaverei und Freiheit,* ed. Ottilie Assing (Hamburg, Germany: Hoffmann & Campe, 1860), ix, my translation: "Wäre diese Lebensgeschichte ein Werk der Dichtung, eine künstlerische Schöpfung, so müßte man bedauern, daß sie nicht einige Jahre früher erschien, ehe das Interesse für solche Schilderungen durch die fast unzähligen Darstellungen des Sclavenlebens, welche seit dem Erscheinen des berühmten 'Uncle Tom' einen eigenen Zweig der Literatur ausmachen, fast erschöpft war; allein das vorliegende Werk ist keine solche Schöpfung, sondern eine wahre Geschichte, die Aneinanderreihung nackter, ungeschmückter, schrecklicher Tatsachen, welche, da es sich um eine Frage der Wirklichkeit mit allen ihren Consequenzen handelt, auf Diejenigen, welche die Wahrheit vertragen können, ungleich einschlagender, ergreifender und überzeugender wirken muß, als alle Werke der Dichtung."
27. Diedrich, *Love Across Color Lines,* 27.
28. Ibid., 145.
29. Assing, "Vorwort," xii–xiii, my translation: "Douglaß ist ein ziemlich heller Mulatte von ungewöhnlich großer, schlanker und kräftiger Gestalt. Seine Züge sind markiert, und eine stark gewölbte Stirn mit einem eigenthümlich tiefen Einschnitt an der Nasenwurzel, bogene Nase und schmale, schön geschnittene Lippen verrathen mehr von der weißen als von der schwarzen Abstammung. Das dichte, schon hie und da mit Grau gemischte Haar ist kraus

und aufstehend, doch nicht wollig. In seiner ganzen Erscheinung, welche von vergangenen Stürmen und Kämpfen erzählt, liegt der Ausdruck großer Energie und Willenskraft, die vor keinem Hinderniß zurückbebt, und vermöge deren allein es ihm in der That auch möglich war, den Verhältnissen zum Trotz sich zu seiner jetzigen Stellung emporzuarbeiten … Alles in ihm ist frisch, ächt, wahr und gut. Er besitzt ein ungewöhnliches Conversationstalent, versteht es, den Andern anzuregen und emporzuheben, und zeigt sich in der Unterhaltung heiter, belebt, geistreich und auf der Höhe der Bildung stehend. Von Leidenschaft für die Sache durchglüht, der er sein Leben gewidmet, ist er zu vielseitig begabt, um darum nicht auch jeden andern Gegenstand, der es verdient, mit Lebhaftigkeit zu ergreifen. Die verschiedenartigsten Dinge, große und kleine, allgemeine und persönliche wurden im Lauf der Unterhaltung berührt, und über alle traf ich Verständniß und Sympathie.—Douglaß' Frau ist ganz schwarz, und seine fünf Kinder tragen deshalb weit mehr vom Negertypus an sich, als er selbst."

30. Review in *Unterhaltungen am häuslichen Herd* 60 (1859): 771; my translation: "Die einfache, schmucklose Darstellung dieses wirklichen Sklavenlebens gibt ein nicht minder ergreifendes, durch jeden Wegfall romantischen Aufputzes, indess noch viel schärferes Bild des amerikanischen Sklaventums als dessen bisherige Schilderungen in Beecher-Stowe's *Onkel Tom's Hütte*."
31. Grace Edith MacLean, *"Uncle Tom's Cabin" in Germany*, Americana Germanica 10 (New York: Appleton, 1910), 79–80.
32. Leroy Woodson, *American Negro Slavery in the Works of Friedrich Strubberg, Friedrich Gerstäcker and Otto Ruppius* (Washington DC: Catholic University of America Press, 1949), 320.
33. Peter Brenner, *Reisen in die Neue Welt: Die Erfahrung Nordamerikas in deutschen Reise- und Auswanderungsberichten des 19. Jahrhunderts* (Tübingen, Germany: Niemeyer, 1991).
34. Recently, Eric Gardner attempted to piece together Webb's life: "'A Gentleman of Superior Cultivation and Refinement': Recovering the Biography of Frank J. Webb," *African American Review* 35, no. 2 (2001): 297–308.
35. Recent scholarship on Webb includes the introduction by Werner Sollors in *Frank J. Webb, Fiction, Essays, Poetry*, ed. Werner Sollors (New York: Toby, 2004), 1–13, and the essays by Rosemary Crockett and Richard Yarborough: Rosemary Crockett, "Frank J. Webb: The Shift to Color Discrimination," in *The Black Columbiad: Defining Moments in African American Literature and Culture*, ed. Werner Sollors and Maria Diedrich (Cambridge, MA: Harvard University Press, 1994), 112–22; and Richard Yarborough, "Strategies of Black Characterization in Uncle Tom's Cabin and the Early Afro-American Novel," in *New Essays on* Uncle Tom's Cabin, ed. Eric J. Sundquist (New York: Cambridge University Press, 1986), 45–84. See also Robert Reid-Pharr's introduction to Frank Webb's *The Garies and Their Friends*, ed. Robert Reid-Pharr (Baltimore: John Hopkins University Press, 1997), vii–xviii.
36. Crockett, "Frank J. Webb," 112.
37. Ibid.
38. Yarborough, "Strategies of Black Characterization," 78–79.
39. Reid-Pharr, "Introduction," xviii.
40. Robin Winks, "Introduction: Josiah Henson and Uncle Tom," in *Four Slave Narratives*, ed. Robin Winks (Reading, MA: Addison-Wesley, 1969), vii.
41. Ibid., xx.
42. Ibid.
43. Marie Schweikher, "Preface," in Josiah Henson, *Wirkliche Lebensgeschichte des Onkel Toms in Frau Beecher-Stowe's "Onkel Tom's Hütte,"* ed. and trans. Maria Schweikher (Bremen, Germany: Verlag des Tractathauses, 1878), 9.
44. Ibid.: "dem deutschen Leser nicht nur eine angenehme Lektüre für etliche Stunden verschaffen"; "ihm zu einem Segen werden."
45. Ibid., 5: "Evangelisierung der afrikanischen Stämme."

46. Belatedly, another German translation was published in 1990 by Insel, titled *Merkwürdige Lebensgeschichte des Sklaven Olaudah Equiano: von ihm selbst veröffentlicht im Jahre 1789;* the book is currently grouped in the Deutsche Bibliothek under the rubric of social sciences.
47. Next to a whole range of scholars, Clair Parfait recently attempted to explain Stowe's success in terms of the publishing history of the book. From the beginning, Parfait asserts, Stowe's publisher Jewett "hyped" the book as the spectacularly successful "story of the age" that was selling by the thousands. See Clair Parfait, *The Publishing History of* Uncle Tom's Cabin, *1852–2000* (Aldershot, UK: Ashgate, 2007), 47–48.
48. Hartmut Keil, "German Immigrants and African-Americans in Mid-Nineteenth Century America," in *Enemy Images in American History,* ed. Ragnhild Fiebig von Hase and Ursula Lehmkuhl (Providence, RI: Berghahn, 1997), 139.
49. Heike Paul, *Kulturkontakt und Racial Presences: Afro-Amerikaner und die deutsche Amerika-Literatur, 1815-1914* (Heidelberg: Winter UP, 2005), 252–53.
50. Leslie Fiedler, *The Inadvertent Epic: From* Uncle Tom's Cabin *to* Roots (New York: Simon & Schuster, 1979), 26.
51. Heike Paul, "Cultural Mobility between Boston and Berlin: How Germans Have Read and Reread Narratives of American Slavery," in *Cultural Mobility: A Manifesto,* ed. Stephen Greenblatt, Ines Županov, Reinhard Meyer-Kalkus, Heike Paul, Pál Nyíri, and Frederike Pannewick (Cambridge: Cambridge University Press, 2009), 122–91.

Chapter Seven

"On the Brain of the Negro"
Race, Abolitionism, and Friedrich Tiedemann's Scientific Discourse on the African Diaspora

Jeannette Eileen Jones

When the Royal Society of London published German scientist Friedrich Tiedemann's paper "On the Brain of the Negro, Compared with That of the European and Orang-Outang" on 9 June 1836, it did so knowing that the professor's findings were "at variance with the received opinions relative to the presumed inferiority of the Negro structure, both in the conformation and relative dimensions of the brain." Tiedemann, professor of anatomy and physiology at Heidelberg University and foreign member of the Royal Society, enjoyed a reputation as a renowned scientist and physician, known in European intellectual circles as "the great physiologist of Heidelberg." Challenging acknowledged experts on "the intellectual faculties of the Negro"—including his mentors, famed naturalists Georges Cuvier and Samuel Thomas von Sömmering—he set out to prove false the reigning scientific theory that Negro[1] brains resembled those of simians more than those of Europeans. Utilizing standard and recent craniological methodologies, Tiedemann concluded:

> As the facts which we have advanced plainly prove that there are no well-marked and essential differences between the brain Negro and European, we must conclude that no innate difference in the intellectual faculties can be admitted to exist between them. This has been denied by philosophers, naturalists, and travellers, who assert that the Ethiopian race is naturally inferior to the European in intellectual and moral powers. The data upon which such an opinion is based are either erroneous suppositions and

---

Notes from this chapter begin on page 149.

false deductions from anatomy and physiology, or superficial observations on the intellectual and moral faculties of the Negroes, made by partial or prejudiced travelers.[2]

As Stephen Jay Gould notes, Tiedemann's "stunning article" defied conventional scientific and popular knowledge about the intellectual status of people of (black) African descent at a time when most European race thinkers had rejected or abandoned the "egalitarian" and antiracist scientific perspectives articulated in the late eighteenth century, particularly in Germany.[3]

What makes Tiedemann's article read as a potential rupture in European (and Western) scientific racial thought is not only its conclusion, but its unabashedly political agenda. His decision to open his article alluding to the political relevancy of his work with the words "I take the liberty of presenting to the Royal Society a paper on a subject which appears to me to be of great importance in the natural history, anatomy, and physiology of Man; interesting in a political and legislative point of view"[4] suggests that Tiedemann understood that scientific studies on race were of acute political importance in transatlantic discourses, where ideas about republicanism and liberalism had circulated since the Enlightenment. Gould calls attention to the fact that Tiedemann wrote the article in English instead of German, when, like most of his German contemporaries, he had published his previous works in his native language or in Latin. He argues that Tiedemann did so not as a mere courtesy extended to his British audience, but to "honor and commemorate" Great Britain's passage of the Slave Trade Act of 1807.[5] Indeed, in the article Tiedemann applauded England's "noble and splendid act of national justice in abolishing the slave trade."[6] However, Tiedemann's mention of the legislative importance of his study in 1836 pointed to more recent British lawmaking and political debates—the passage of the Slavery Abolition Act of 1833, which freed all slaves in the empire on 1 August 1834, and created an apprenticeship system for free blacks in the West Indies.

In the last sentence of his article, Tiedemann noted: "Hayti and the colony of Sierra Leone can attest that free Negroes are capable of being governed by mild laws, and require neither whips nor chains to enforce submission to civil authority."[7] Tiedemann was most likely aware of the apprenticeship controversy that pitted former slaves and colonial planters against each other, the former demanding total freedom and the "customary privileges" allotted to them under slavery and the latter seeking to exact as much labor as possible from the newly freed population. The apprenticeship system was scheduled to end in 1840, but by July 1834, antiapprenticeship demonstrations had begun to take place on the islands. Abolitionists seized the opportunity to push for the total abolition of apprenticeship amid allegations and proof that masters treated their apprentices cruelly, often resorting to flogging them. Eventually, in 1838 a bill would be passed amending the slavery abolition act to regulate working hours, provide legal means for apprentices to extricate themselves from cruel masters, and eliminate whipping, among other reforms.⁸ Tiedemann must have been aware of the British anti-apprenticeship movement (led by the London Anti-Slavery Society) when writing his conclusion; thus, one can read it as an indictment of black apprenticeship and an attempt to convince members of the Royal Society that the system was not necessary to insure Negro compliance with the laws of British civil society.

Tiedemann's celebration of the abolition of the slave trade and allusion to the wrongheadedness of apprenticeship is not the only textual evidence of his antislavery sensibilities. Throughout the article, he used the rhetoric of moral suasion to dismiss slavery as a corruptive and impractical institution that could not be legitimated scientifically through fallacious arguments that Negroes were intellectually and morally inferior to whites. This suggests that Tiedemann had an audience broader than only the British in mind—namely, other slaveholding countries in the Western hemisphere, especially the United States, where antislavery activism had been on the rise since 1830. Understood in this context, his article reads as both a scientific treatise and abolitionist tract.

Tiedemann's "On the Brain of the Negro" must be inserted into the canon of transatlantic abolitionist literature in order to fully appreciate the ways in which continental Germans—not just German émigrés to the United States—contributed to the international campaign against slavery. According to David Brion Davis, the emergence of international abolitionism can be traced to the "heritage of religious, legal, and philosophical tensions associated with slavery"—namely, changing ideas in the West about the relationship between master and slave. Although the ancients reached some consensus about the legitimacy of "personal subordination" and bondage, by the time of the Enlightenment, philosophers, religious thinkers, and laymen increasingly questioned the legitimacy of slavery. At its core, slavery was an institution that denied one the ability to determine one's own destiny, and, thus, many regarded it as the grossest expression of illegitimate power relations between human beings. Yet, Davis cautions us not to read antislavery sentiment as a natural outcome of Enlightenment thought. Specifically referencing the Quakers' journey to an antislavery religious and political platform in the eighteenth century, Davis identifies four "developments in Western culture" that fostered a sustained and organized critique of the Atlantic slave system: (1) a "secular social philosophy" spearheaded by Montesquieu, who viewed slavery as incompatible with the human pursuit of happiness; (2) "the popularization of an ethic of benevolence" linked to British Protestantism, which rejected slavery as an impediment to "human progress"; (3) the evangelical belief in "instantaneous conversion and demonstrative sanctification," wherein the repudiation of slavery as a sin and a crime evinced one's own piety and rejection of "absolute power"; and (4) the rise of an eighteenth-century cult of primitivism that refashioned the Negro as "an innocent child of nature" who, although degraded in slavery, could enjoy the benefits of Western "civilization" once emancipated.⁹ Tiedemann's article rests at the intersection of these developments.

Although there is no evidence of evangelical sentiment in his prose, Tiedemann's vindication of Negro intellect drew upon secular notions of man's inalienable right to freedom, the view of the abolition of the slave trade as a "noble" act, and naturalists' reappraisals of continental Africans as "industrious" people of good "moral character."[10]

As scientific discourse, Tiedemann's article must be read as part of the German "egalitarian" tradition of theorizing race emerging in the late eighteenth century. Like his contemporaries, Tiedemann did not discard race as a biological fact. However, he discredited the idea that a single race possessed universal, innate characteristics that remained unchanged across time and space. Accordingly, his article, while asserting "Negro" as a valid racial category, makes distinctions among peoples that make up the black diaspora. To that end, Tiedemann argued that slavery and the slave trade led to the moral and intellectual degeneration of enslaved Negroes and otherwise "good" Africans engaged in slave trading. This contention lay at the crux of his scientifically based argument for Negro emancipation and black republicanism.

Exploring Tiedemann's intellectual biography reveals rather eclectic training with men who held different scientific interests and qualifications, as well as disparate views on the eighteenth century's "new" concept of "race." That Tiedemann's opinion on Negro "intellectual faculties" diverged so strongly from that of many of his pedagogues attests to the fluidity of racial thought—or what Sara Eigen and Mark Larrimore describe as the "rich and contradictory positions" held on race in the late eighteenth and early nineteenth centuries.[11] Tiedemann's defense of the Negro using comparative anatomy and craniological measurements conveys an egalitarian position on matters of intellectual and civic equality, yet a decisively Eurocentric disposition with regard to the aesthetics of the body. However, for him, whether or not Negroes were "handsome" proved irrelevant to his overall argument.

Ultimately, Tiedemann defended his position by using *both* scientific methodologies and historical "evidence" of Negro achievement. Based on the research of Blumenbach and Bishop Henri Grégoire, he fashioned a black diaspora comprised of Negroes who had "distinguished themselves" as military tacticians, politicians, clergymen, poets, musicians, physicians, philosophers, historians, mathematicians, and philologists. Interestingly, although Tiedemann was born in Kassel, Germany, in 1781, he made no mention of the *Kasseler Mohren*—Kassel's historic black population, which included "Moors" who appear in 1664 records and their descendants, as well as its then present black residents—African American Loyalist soldiers and their families who accompanied Hessian soldiers to Germany at the end of the Revolutionary War. This is more notable as several of the bodies dissected by German anatomists were Kasseler Moors. Tiedemann's black diaspora had little connection to his homeland, other than his mention of Anton Wilhelm Amo, an African philosopher born in Axim (in present-day

Ghana) who received his PhD in 1734 after studying at the universities of Halle and Jena.[12] Ultimately, Tiedemann's failure to mention the Kasselers of African descent betrays his conviction that any effective vindication of black intellectual equality required that he point out Negroes whose achievements could be appreciated by Europeans and white Americans. In a twist of irony, his celebration of the "intellectual powers of the Negroes" could not rely solely on the unknown, "ordinary" Africans and black people whose skulls he used to challenge the "erroneous" claims of his colleagues and mentors.

Friedrich Tiedemann and the "German Invention of Race"

As mentioned, Friedrich Tiedemann was born in Kassel, a thriving city in the landgraviate of Hesse-Kassel under the rule of Friedrich II (1760–85). During his tenure as landgrave, Friedrich II enacted several military reforms, which included the conscription of selected able-bodied men to serve in the army, to emphasize that land ownership, wealth, and private property were privileges reserved for those who demonstrated fealty to the landgraviate. The draft law of 1762 had far-reaching implications for nobles, farmers, and peasants alike. In 1776, Friedrich II signed a subsidy treaty with Great Britain that sent over nineteen thousand troops to the American colonies to fight in the Revolutionary War in exchange for over nineteen million Reichstaler. At the end of the war, the vast majority of "Hessians" (as they were called by the Revolutionaries) returned to Hesse-Kassel—along with at least thirty-one black soldiers and their families. On 29 February 1788, seven years after Tiedemann's birth, two "Moors," Wilhelm and Anne, were baptized in Kassel.[13]

In her groundbreaking study on race and sex in eighteenth-century science, Londa Schiebinger notes that Kassel had the highest black population in eighteenth-century Germany; however, the presence of "Moors" in the city dated back to 1664. In the 1780s, Frederick II established a "colony of Africans" at Wilhelmshöhe just outside of Kassel, which operated as an observatory of sorts, where scientists could study the "customs and anatomy" of the residents. As to the origins of the Blacks in Kassel, Maria Diedrich notes that those who came with the Hessians were descendant of Africans who had been taken to the Americas in the seventeenth and eighteenth centuries. They spoke a wide variety of European languages reflecting the colonial powers in the so-called New World.[14] Although Tiedemann was a child during the 1780s, it is probable, given his social station, that he encountered the "Moors" while walking in the city, attending church, or visiting the Wilhelmshöhe Berg Park prior to his departure for the University of Bamberg sometime in the late 1790s. According to several sources, Kassel's blacks died mostly from "consumption" (tuberculosis) and some committed suicide. Upon the deaths of the Wilhelmshöhe Africans, the colony's doctor sent their bodies to the Collegium Carolinum (opened in 1709) in Kassel, where anatomist Sömmering (Tiedemann's future mentor) dissected them, along with the body of a former black Loyalist soldier.[15]

Sömmering joined the Collegium faculty in 1788 as head of the anatomy theater. German and other European anatomists used the bodies of the Kassel blacks first dissected there to establish many of the accepted theories about sexual and racial difference in the eighteenth century.[16] These bodies would inform not only the works of Sömmering and his contemporaries, but also a generation of race thinkers who cited the conclusions he reached in *Über die körperliche Verschiedenheit des Mohren vom Europäer* (1784)[17] to argue for Negro inferiority. Although Sömmering wrote his influential book while at the University of Mainz, his ideas about race were part of a larger localized debate about the racial equality of blacks involving natural scientist Johann Friedrich Blumenbach and philosopher Christoph Meiners at the University of Göttingen, among others. For scholar John Zammito, the race controversy can be traced back to 1775, the year when Blumenbach presented his dissertation "On the Natural Variety of Mankind," Meiners released *Vermischte philosophische Schriften,* and Immanuel Kant published *Of the Different Human Races.* He argues that Meiners "might have been the precipitator" for both Blumenbach's and Kant's texts on race.[18] While the scope of this project precludes a close reading of all three texts, worthy of mention is the then rising theory that the races emerged from separate acts of creation. As Schiebinger notes, "polygenists, the worst of the racists ... taught that human races were immutable physical entities created separately at the beginning of time." This contradicted the findings of environmentalists who overwhelmingly embraced monogenesis—the idea that all humanity can be traced back to the biblical creation story of Adam and Eve. Thus, physical racial differences resulted from migration and adaptation to climatic conditions. All races were "potentially equal." Blumenbach was among those scientists who held that differences in physiognomy and bodily structure stemmed from environmental factors or human manipulation, and, thus, were not indicative of "innate inferiority." Kant also found monogenesis a more credible theory for the origins of humanity, while Meiners (and, incidentally, Georg Forster of the Collegium) supported polygenesis. Yet, Forster did not use his beliefs to justify racism.[19]

Before the major arguments put forth in Sömmering's study that Tiedemann repudiated are presented, it should be noted that Sömmering changed the title of the work in 1785, replacing *Mohren* with *Neger.* As Diedrich and other scholars have argued, this change in nomenclature reflected a shift in ideas about people of African descent during the eighteenth century in Germany. Essentially, Germans ceased to see blacks simply as exotica, symbols of "Oriental splendor" (*Mohren*), instead regarding them as subjects of scientific inquiry, medical specimens, and objects to be anatomized, whose very existence and "new" name *Neger* became discursive of an otherness rooted in bondage. Sömmering struggled with this change in terminology in the text, switching throughout between "*Neger*" (Negroes), "*Mohren*" (Moors), and "*Schwarze*" (blacks). For example, responding to critics of his original 1784 work, he stated in his introduction to the 1785 version: "I further reminded people that I talked about African *Neger,* and not about *schwarze Menschen* [black people] in general."[20] Here, Sömmering appeared to be making a distinction between the African "Negro" and people of African descent living in the Americas, although this statement leaves unclear his classification of the Kasseler blacks he anatomized.

In the preamble/introduction to the 1785 edition of his text, Sömmering wrote that during his residency in Hessen-Kassel, he "observed many Negroes living there, and ... was inspired to dissect several male and one female *Negerkörper* [Negro body]." On the last day of his trip, he was permitted by Dr. Baldinger, who was in charge of the African colony, "to examine a *Mohr,*" most likely an African American Loyalist soldier whose body some scholars claim was dissected at the Collegium.[21] Sömmering based his conclusion that "Negroes resemble simians more" than Europeans on those dissections, as well as on the illustrations of a "Mr. Range," which he characterized as "truthfully completed by referring to *Mohren* who are still alive." In lieu of his findings, Sömmering asked in the work, "do we have the right to treat them [*Neger*] with such coldness?" The "coldness" to which he referred included the enslavement of Africans in the Americas and "prejudices" shown Negroes in general. Defending himself against those who "misunderstood" the 1784 version of his text, Sömmering stated emphatically that he was "well aware of all the unfavorable consequences" that his study would have for "the treatment of these unfortunate people." Yet, he denied advocating the mistreatment of blacks, stating that no matter how much they resemble simians, "*Mohren* still remain human beings who are superior to any species (of simians)" and that "there are several among the *Schwarze* who are similar to their white brothers, and some even surpass them intellectually."[22]

Some influential German scientists immediately rushed to discredit Sömmering. Blumenbach and Georg Forster publically dismissed what they interpreted as Sömmering's proslavery stance and arguments about the inferiority of blacks. Some linked his conclusions to his tutelage under Dutch comparative anatomist Petrus Camper, whose study *Über den natürlichen Unterschied der Gesichtszüge* (1792) showed the European face as the epitome of physical beauty. Miriam Meijer notes in her study of Camper that, although Sömmering was his protégé, the latter's ideas about black inferiority should not be read as a logical result of this association. She argues that nineteenth-century misinterpretations of Camper's "facial angle thesis"—that the protrusion of the jaw determined man's proximity to apes—have led scholars to conclude that Camper helped establish racist anthropology, when, in fact, he saw the facial angle as "a means to prove that non-European racial characteristics were as natural as European ones," that "empirically ... all the races were equal."[23] However misused, Camper's facial angle methodology proved critical to Sömmering's study, which influenced a generation of race thinkers.

Tiedemann would not meet Sömmering until 1805, when he went to Paris to study with Georges Cuvier. Tiedemann had completed his secondary education in 1798 and begun his studies at Marburg. However, as was commonplace at the time for medical students, Tiedemann traveled across Europe to study with noted physicians at different universities. By 1805, both Cuvier and Sömmering were pioneers in the "new science" of comparative anatomy. Sömmering was so impressed with Tiedemann that he recommended him for a position at the University of Landshut in Bavaria. After a ten-year stint in Landshut, Tiedemann accepted a position at the University of Heidelberg, moving there in 1816. Viewing himself primarily as an anatomist, Tiedemann spent most of his time in Heidelberg working on the cerebral convolutions of the fetal brain, a field in which he distinguished himself.[24]

Tiedemann became a valued member of the medical faculty at the university, developing its anatomical collection and teaching a variety of courses in anatomy, zoology, and physiology. According to Arleen Tuchman, by "the early 1830s he had acquired a reputation as one of the best experimenters in Germany." However, by 1835 he began "withdrawing from university and scientific affairs." He ceased teaching his physiology and anatomy courses, allowing an adjunct professor, Theodor Bischoff, to teach them. In 1837, he requested an eighteen-month sabbatical.[25] Contrary to Tuchman's assertion, Tiedemann's publication of "On the Brain of the Negro" in 1836 is proof of his continued interest in scientific affairs, albeit through a political lens.

German Liberalism and Transatlantic Abolitionism

When reading Tiedemann's 1836 study, it becomes clear that his interest in the brain of the Negro and race science was no fleeting pastime. His conclusions were based on empirical research in museums, hospitals, and collections across northwestern Europe. His studies of skulls of the "Ethiopian Race" alone required him to travel to London, Edinburgh, Groningen (in the Netherlands), and Kassel. Only two of the forty-one Negro skulls were housed in the Heidelberg Anatomical Museum. Tiedemann claimed to have weighed all the skulls himself and listed all the places where "they are to be found, so as to enable any one to convince himself of the truth and correctness of" his research.[26] He also immersed himself in the race science literature published since the mid-1700s, as well as seventeenth-century studies on the anatomy of the brain published in French, German, English, and Latin. Whether Tiedemann could have completed this research in the year that he ceded his classes to Bischoff is debatable and perhaps irrelevant. The research conducted is so exhaustive that one has to wonder what accounted for Tiedemann's seemingly sudden interest in race science. Why did the eighteenth-century "race" studies of Sömmering and Camper (by no means outdated in 1836) and Cuvier's *Le Règne Animal* (1817) become so important to his scientific inquiries? Essentially, during the rise of transatlantic abolitionism in the early nineteenth century, Tiedemann became aware of how proslavery agitators used the works of his mentors and Camper to advance their cause. His own sense of liberalism moved him to discredit them.

Tiedemann was certainly aware of radical and liberal politics emerging in early nineteenth-century Germany, particularly as a resident of Heidelberg, a future center of liberal activity. As scholars such as Christopher Clark have noted, the German Confederation Act of 1815 left many social and political questions unanswered. The German constitutions ensured "'human rights' such as equality before the law, freedom of confession and of conscience and the security of property, but political rights, such as freedom of association and assembly or freedom of the press" eluded many Germans.[27] This disenchantment with the promises of confederation gave rise to the "liberals," a term that was in wide use by the early 1830s. Tiedemann appears to have shared some liberalist sentiments, for in 1829, he published a treatise denouncing the use of the sword in public executions as inhumane. Titled "Aufruf an die Humanität der Höheren Behörden der Gerechtigkeits-Pflege in Deutschland" (Appeal to the Humanity of the Higher Authorities for the Cultivation of Justice in Germany), the paper revealed his concerns about human rights, justice, and equity, including the treatment of prisoners.[28] Advocating for equal and humane treatment under the law was a trademark of liberals who saw themselves as "opponents of despotism and defenders of liberty." Purporting to "represent the people," liberal ranks included academics, the "commercial and educated bourgeoisie," noblemen, "the self-employed in trade, manufacture, and services," and some officials. While it is uncertain whether Tiedemann considered himself a "liberal," many of the University of Heidelberg's faculty assumed a liberal posture, reflecting the political climate of the state of Baden.[29] In this context, that Tiedemann would take up another liberal cause—abolitionism—is perhaps not surprising.

Most scholarship on German abolitionists focuses on émigrés to the United States, the majority of whom immigrated after the 1848 revolutions. These men and women reviled despotism and viewed slavery as one of its many forms. Hartmut Keil, Edmund Spevack, Maria I. Diedrich, Christoph Lohmann, and Lorie A. Vanchena explore Germans' engagement with abolitionism and the antislavery debate, mostly as immigrants residing in America.[30] Spevack notes that immigrant Karl Follen (later Charles Follen) anticipated the abolitionist posture embraced by the Forty-Eighters. Follen, "a radical German nationalist and left-wing republican" was a child of the German Enlightenment, who immigrated to the United States in 1824. By the mid-1830s, he had become a Unitarian and Garrisonian abolitionist who advocated political violence to achieve a truly revolutionary society. He viewed slavery as "illegal" and "un-American" and began delivering speeches on the antislavery circuit and publishing abolitionist essays.[31]

As a political refugee in America, Follen gave an antislavery speech in 1834, titled "Address to the People of the United States on the Subject of Slavery," that upset many proslavery apologists who saw his actions as hubristic. Given before the New England Anti-Slavery Society in Boston, the speech chastised slaveholding as antithetical to American values. Follen argued that "true republicanism does not exist in maintaining equality of rights among oppressors, but in honoring all men as equals in their natural and inalienable rights." The controversy surrounding Follen's talk led Harvard to dismiss him in 1835 as professor of German civilization, a position he had held since 1831.[32]

The years 1835–36 were tumultuous for abolitionists and antislavery activists. During this so-called mob year, proslavery forces increasingly targeted abolitionist gatherings. Antiabolitionist riots had broken out in 1834, but in 1835 antiabolitionist violence escalated. Garrison, who had influenced Follen tremendously, denounced the "reign of terror" engulfing the nation with acts that included the burning down of schools and of well-known abolitionists in effigy, the seizing of post offices to prevent the distribution of antislavery literature, the hosting of several antiabolitionists throughout the South, and the dragging of Garrison through the streets of Boston after a "mob" stormed a meeting of the Female Anti-Slavery Society. Antiabolitionist sentiment culminated in the 1836 "Gag Rule" passed by the House of Representatives, which forbade Congress to consider any antislavery petitions. These events unfolding in the United States circulated in international abolitionist circles. By the 1840s, several black abolitionists would flee to Europe, some of them to Germany, to spread the abolitionist message. One black activist, James W. C. Pennington, after being denied a divinity degree by Yale, was awarded an honorary doctorate by the University of Heidelberg in 1849 for his courageous stance against slavery.[33]

It seems likely that Tiedemann was aware of the antiabolitionist fervor sweeping America in 1836. Although he made no direct reference to the US antislavery debate, his footnotes indicate that he was certainly conscious of free African Americans who had "distinguished themselves" in a slaveholding society. For Tiedemann, the achievements of these blacks and others provided proof that Negroes excelled intellectually and exhibited "good natural capacity, good sense, wit, and penetration" when "not bodily and morally degraded by slavery and oppression."[34]

"Some Remarks on the Intellectual Faculties of the Negro"

Tiedemann's anatomizing of skulls from the "Ethiopian," "Caucasian," "Mongolian," "Malayan," and "American" races, as well as of the brains of several Negroes (including the infamous "Hottentot Venus") and Europeans, an orangutan, and a chimpanzee, yielded results that differed from those of the avowed experts. Tiedemann concluded that "there are no well-marked differences between the brain of the Negro and European, [therefore] we must conclude that no innate difference in the intellectual faculties can be admitted to exist between them." Instead, he argued that the supposed deficiencies in the "intellectual and moral faculties" of peoples of African descent resulted from "slavery and inhuman treatment" endured in the colonies and the corrupting influence of the slave trade on "the good character" of Africans living on the western coast of Africa.[35]

After over twenty pages devoted to comparative anatomy (see figures 7.1 and 7.2), wherein he critiqued the methodologies of other anatomists for not ascertaining the correlation between the "absolute size of the brain" and intellectual powers, Tiedemann reached five conclusions: (1) the brains of Europeans were not larger than those of Negroes; (2) the nerves of Negroes, when taking into consideration the size of the brain, were not thicker than Europeans, as Sömmering had argued to prove Africans' affinity to apes; (3) the spinal cord, medulla oblongata, cerebellum, and cerebrum of Negroes revealed no significant deviation from those of Europeans; (4) in "inward organization," the interior of Negro and European brains did not differ; and (5) the brain and nervous system of Negroes did not show more resemblance to simians than to those of Europeans. Nonetheless, Tiedemann conceded that "[i]t is true that many ugly and degenerate Negro tribes on the coast show some similarity in their outward form and inward structure to the Ape." Yet, Tiedemann held that some external and internal "similarities" between some Africans and apes, such as facial features, nose bones, humeri, foramen, etc., did not correlate to moral and intellectual development. Only homogeny in the brain—"the noblest part of the human body"—mattered.[36]

Tiedemann concluded his article by documenting the numerous effects of slavery and slave trading on Africans and Negroes in the "colonies" and noting the achievements of free, "distinguished" people of African descent. Tiedemann dismissed the opinions of eighteenth-century philosophers David Hume and Chistoph Meiners, who proclaimed the innate inferiority of Africans. Meiners's *Grundiss der Geschichte der Menschheit* (1785) made apparent his conviction that slavery was justified, as Africans proved to be biologically unfit for higher intellectual pursuits. Accusing Meiners and like-minded philosophers, naturalists, and travelers of only studying "unfortunate" Africans taken to the West Indies and "doomed" to "perpetual slavery and hard labour on the sugar plantations," Tiedemann lambasted thinkers and statesmen, including Thomas Jefferson, who argued that the "natural inferiority of the intellectual and moral faculties" of Negroes excused slavery. He reasoned that all of the negative traits associated with Africans—irrationality, viciousness, perversity, treachery, faithlessness, childishness,

I. Æthiopian Race.

	Names of the different Tribes.	Anatomical Collection.	Capacity of the cavum cranii.		
			oz.	dr.	gr.
1.	Eboes, or Ibos, Negro of Congo. Died at Sierra Leone	Anatomical Museum of Dr. Knox at Edinburgh	54	2	33
2.	Old Caffre	Camper's Anatomical Museum at Groningen	43	7	0
3.	Negro	St. Thomas's Hospital, London	42	6	30
4.	Eboes. Negro	Collection of Dr. Knox	42	2	37
5.	Negro	Guy's Hospital, London	42	0	23
6.	Negro	St. Thomas's Hospital	41	6	37
7.	Native of Madagascar	Phrenological Society, Edinburgh	40	5	30
8.	Negro	Soemmerring's Anatomical Museum	40	5	6
9.	Negro of Loango	Camper's Collection	40	0	20
10.	Negro	St. Thomas's Hospital	39	6	33
11.	Hottentot	Collection of Mr. South, London	39	6	21
12.	Negro of Guinea	Camper's Anatomical Museum	39	2	0
13.	Bosjes man	Mr. South's Collection	38	7	5
14.	Negro of North America	Anatomical Museum at Groningen	38	4	0
15.	Caffre	Mr. South's Collection	37	5	59
16.	Negro eleven years old	Groningen Anatomical Collection	37	5	0
17.	Negro	St. Bartholomew's Hospital, London	37	3	35
18.	Negro of Surinam	Anatomical Museum at Heidelberg	37	2	30
19.	Negro	St. Bartholomew's Hospital	37	2	11
20.	Negro	The same	37	1	22
21.	Negro	St. Thomas's Hospital	37	0	1
22.	Ashantee Negro	Hunterian Museum, London	36	5	32
23.	Bosjesman	Phrenological Society, Edinburgh	36	3	56
24.	Negro of Angola	Camper's Collection	36	4	20
25.	Negro	Guy's Hospital, London	36	1	32
26.	Negro	Heidelberg Anatomical Museum	35	7	0
27.	Negro	The same	35	6	40
28.	Native of Mozambique	Camper's Museum	35	4	0
29.	Negro of Guinea	The same	35	3	0
30.	Negro	The same	35	3	0
31.	Young Negro	The same	35	0	0
32.	Negro of Mozambique	Mr. South's Collection	34	6	0
33.	Negro of Curaçao	Groningen Anatomical Museum	34	4	0
34.	Negro of Cheribon	The same	33	3	0
35.	Bosjesman	Phrenological Society, Edinburgh	32	6	48
36.	Young Negro	Camper's Collection	32	0	0
37.	Young Negro of Madagascar	The same	32	0	0
38.	Negro	St. Bartholomew's Hospital	31	5	16
	B. Female Skulls.				
39.	Negress	Camper's Museum	31	4	0
40.	Old Hottentot woman	The same	31	0	0
41.	Negress	Guy's Hospital, London	24	7	39

By these Tables it is clear that the cavum cranii of Negro women is smaller than that of the men; consequently they have an absolutely smaller brain, like the European women.

MDCCCXXXVI.   3 T

Figure 7.1. Table listing the physical features of different African male skulls from Friedrich Tiedemann's 1836 paper, "On the Brain of the Negro."

and savagery—appeared only among those degraded by slavery and extended this reasoning to west Africans: he stated that their "original good character … has been corrupted and ruined by the horrors of the slave trade, since they have unfortunately become acquainted with Europeans. The introduction of brandy and other spirits, and the immorality, dissipation, cruelty, rapacity and fraud of the slave traders, have made the Negroes indolent, cunning, dissolute, and thiev-

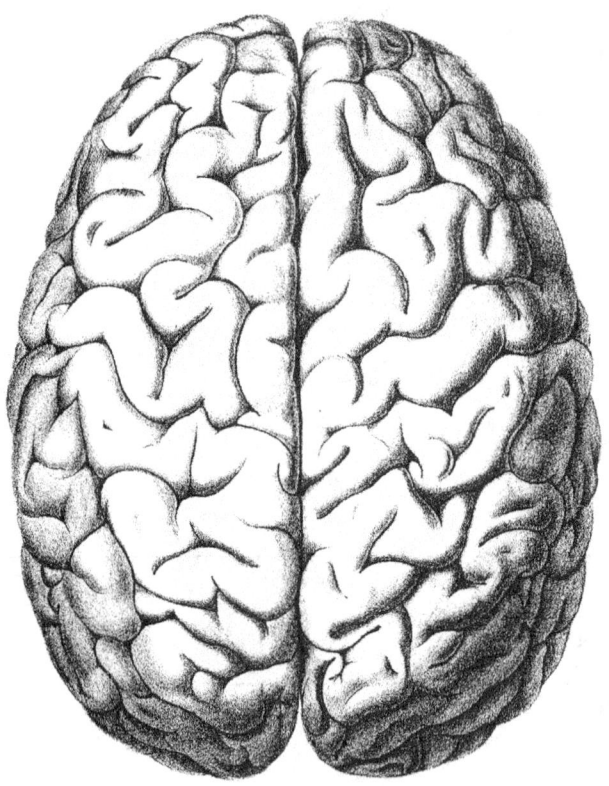

Figure 7.2. Anatomy plate of an African male brain used by Friedrich Tiedemann in "On the Brain of the Negro."

ish." In other words, as Tiedemann stated emphatically while noting that the abolition of the slave trade brought "industry" to the people of the coast, the slave trade was solely responsible for the degradation of the Africans. Ultimately, he reasoned, the "total abolition of the traffic of slaves" and the end of racial slavery in the Americas would return Negroes to their "original" character.[37]

In defending Negro intellect, Tiedemann constructed his own idea of the Negro as the "noble savage," describing people of African descent as good-natured, affectionate, happy, cheerful, witty, and sensible before coming into contact with violent Europeans. He referred to several "philanthropists," including Wilberforce and Ramsay, who collected anecdotes about the Negro's character and circulated them throughout England in the eighteenth century to sway public opinion in favor of abolition. If these testimonials were insufficient to convince Westerners of the nobility of emancipation, Tiedemann offered proof of Negroes who had "made a certain progress in the liberal arts and sciences ... and distinguished themselves by their talents in military tactics and politics." His list of achievers includes Anton Wilhelm Amo, Hannibal, Jean Baptiste Lislet Geoffroy, Thomas Fuller (aka the "Virginia Calculator"), Benjamin Banneker, Don Juan Latino, Ignatius Sancho, Olaudah Equiano (aka Gustavus Vassa), Othello of Baltimore, James Derham (sometimes Durham), Francis Williams, Phillis Wheatley, Toussaint Louverture, and the "sultans" of Africa, including Muhammad Bello, who succeeded Usaman dan Fodio as caliph of the Sokoto Caliphate. These individuals from western Africa, the United States, Russia, Germany, Spain, Jamaica, Haiti, France, and England demonstrated that Negroes were "capable of civilization." Moreover, Tiedemann argued that the mere existence of Haiti and Sierra Leone portended the future of Africans no longer under the threat of whips and chains.[38] Freedom would reverse the physical degeneration and moral degradation of the race.

Conclusion

In 1837, the *Concord Freeman,* the Democratic paper of Concord, Massachusetts, that supported abolitionism, cited Tiedemann's 1836 paper to counter proslavery advocates who claimed that blacks were biologically inferior to whites.[39] Eleven years later, the 1848 revolutions swept across Europe, addressing a continuum of political and social issues, from political corruption, absolutism, and monarchism to peasant struggles.[40] On 5 March 1848, German liberals gathered in Heidelberg "in order to discuss the most urgent measures for the Fatherland." Foremost on the agenda was to establish "the meeting of a national representation elected in all the German lands according to the number of the people" as soon as possible. The Declaration of Heidelberg led to the convening of the *Vorparlament* on 31 March at St. Paul's Church in Frankfurt to elect a new National Assembly. While

Tiedemann was not one of the fifty-one men in attendance at the Heidelberg meeting, he must have been aware of the spring revolution.[41]

Tiedemann never immigrated to the United States, as did Forty-Eighters and other Germans who supported abolitionism. Yet his findings on Negro intellect, made accessible to Americans through his Royal Society publication, remained relevant after his death in 1861. As late as 1863, the British anthropologist James Hunt, in his book *On the Negro's Place in Nature,* attested to the authority of Tiedemann's study among scientists. Yet he discredited Tiedemann's conclusions.[42] He wrote: "Tiedemann's researches, although very limited, have until recently been accepted as satisfactory." Hunt cited "recent" research by American scientists/physicians Samuel Morton and J. Aitken Meigs as the most "satisfactory" for disputing Tiedemann's claim that Negroes were not intellectually inferior to Europeans.[43] Morton, a professor of anatomy at the University of Pennsylvania, published *Crania Americana* in 1839, in which he classified the "races of Man," ranking the Negro as the lowest rung of humanity. Meigs, a member of the Academy of Natural Sciences of Philadelphia and a professor at the Philadelphia College of Medicine, came to a similar conclusion.[44] Hunt's text became very influential in American proslavery circles, and Tiedemann's article soon disappeared from antislavery memory.

Tiedemann's article appeared when scientists interested in race found themselves having to confront the issue of slavery, as any classification of Negroes inevitably influenced popular and political opinions on abolitionism. Many of the scientists engaged in the question of the intellectual and moral faculties of people of African descent during this period resided in slaveholding nations or European countries with slaveholding colonies in the Americas. Many of them felt compelled to defend slavery not only legally, based on liberal conceptions of private property, but also morally, as an institution best suited for debased and/or degenerated races. In contrast, Tiedemann appeared unencumbered by any allegiance to racial ideologies that supported slave trading and the slave economy in the Americas. Of course, by the time Hunt's book was published in 1863, several German scientists had continued to voice their dissent from Tiedemann's conclusions regarding racial difference and hierarchy. For example, zoologist and entomologist Hermann Burmeister supported several of Hunt's specious claims in his work—chief among them that Negroes could not stand "quite upright" due in part to the position of their toes, which bore "resemblance ... to those of the ape."[45]

For some scientists, the Northern victory in the US Civil War settled the question of the intellectual abilities of people of African descent. For others, the political ramifications of the ratification of the Thirteenth, Fourteenth, and Fifteenth Amendments only accentuated the need for science to continue to weigh in on the future of American citizenry and democracy. Nevertheless, scientific debate on racial politics (not race) in America seemed to have waned considerably in the Reconstruction years, coinciding with the ascent of anthropology and social Darwinism in American intellectual thought.[46]

The German Enlightenment and 1848 revolutions fostered an atmosphere of intellectual inquiry that allowed Friedrich Tiedemann and other liberal Germans to challenge accepted dogmas of racial hierarchy. However, by the end of the nineteenth century, when Germany joined the "scramble for Africa," many German scientists who embraced empire building endorsed scientific racism. German scientists would continue to play a seminal role in advancing discourses on race that impacted the African diaspora.

Notes

I would like to thank the German Historical Institute and the Heidelberg Center for American Studies, the former for allowing me to present this work in progress and the latter for supporting research for this chapter. Special thanks to my graduate student D. Elisabeth Maurer for her translation of the original document of the 1784 and 1785 versions of Samuel Thomas Sömmering's *Über die körperliche Verschiedenheit des Mohren vom Europäer*.

1. I use the term "Negro" in this chapter as it was used historically by scientists to denote a racial classification for people of African descent irrespective of national or colonial boundaries. Elsewhere, I use the terms blacks, Africans, West Indians, Afro-Caribbeans, African Americans, and people of African descent.
2. Frederick Tiedemann, "On the Brain of the Negro, Compared with That of the European and the Orang-Outang," *Philosophical Transactions of the Royal Society of London* 126 (1836): 497–527, 520.
3. Stephen Jay Gould, "The Great Physiologist of Heidelberg," *Natural History* 108, no. 6 (1999): 26; and Sara Eigen and Mark Larrimore, "Introduction: The German Invention of Race," in *The German Invention of Race,* ed. Sara Eigen and Mark Larrimore (Albany, NY: SUNY Press, 2006), 5.
4. Tiedemann, "On the Brain of the Negro," 497.
5. Gould, "The Great Physiologist of Heidelberg," 26.
6. Tiedemann, "On the Brain of the Negro," 526.
7. Ibid.
8. William A. Green, *British Slave Emancipation: The Sugar Colonies and the Great Experiment, 1830–1865* (Oxford: Oxford University Press, 1976), 129–32, 155–57; and Alex Tyrrell, "The 'Moral Radical Party' and the Anglo-Jamaican Campaign for the Abolition of the Negro Apprenticeship System," *English Historical Review* 99, no. 392 (1984): 482–83.
9. David Brion Davis, "What the Abolitionists Were Up Against," in *The Antislavery Debate: Capitalism and Abolitionism as a Problem in Historical Interpretation,* edited and with an introduction by Thomas Bender (Berkeley: University of California Press, 1992), 19–24.
10. Tiedemann, "On the Brain of the Negro," 520, 524–26.
11. Eigen and Larrimore, "Introduction," 2.
12. Tiedemann, "On the Brain of the Negro," 521–22; George Fenwick Jones, "The Black Hessians: Negroes Recruited by the Hessians in South Carolina and Other Colonies," *South Carolina Historical Magazine* 83, no. 4 (1982): 287–302; Maria I. Diedrich's chapter in this volume; and Paulin J. Hountondji, "An African Philosopher in Germany in the Eighteenth

Century: Anton-Wilhelm Amo," in *African Philosophy: Myth and Reality*, ed. Paulin J. Houtondji (Bloomington: Indiana University Press, 1983), 111, 116–18. According to Maria I. Diedrich, at least 150 black Loyalist soldiers, camp followers, and tambours relocated to Kassel. The bombing of Kassel during World War II destroyed many documents that could have provided us with a more accurate number of blacks who resided in Kassel after the Revolutionary War.

13. Charles W. Ingrao, *The Hessian Mercenary State: Ideas, Institutions, and Reform under Frederick II, 1760–1785* (Cambridge: Cambridge University Press, 1987), 139; Peter K. Taylor, "'Patrimonial' Bureaucracy and 'Rational' Policy in Eighteenth-Century Germany: The Case of Hessian Recruitment Reforms, 1762–93," *Central European History* 22, no. 1 (1989): 49–52; Jones, "Black Hessians," 302; and Maria Diedrich, this volume.
14. See Maria Diedrich's chapter in this volume.
15. University of Heidelberg, "Friedrich Tiedemann (1781–1861)," http://www.ub.uni-heidel berg.de/Englisch/helios/digi/anatomie/tiedemann.html (accessed 24 January 2013); Londa Schiebinger, "The Anatomy of Difference; Race and Sex in Eighteenth-Century Science," in "The Politics of Difference," special issue, *Eighteenth-Century Studies* 23, no. 4 (Summer 1990): 387–88; Diedrich, this volume; and Jones, "Black Hessians," 302.
16. Schiebinger, "The Anatomy of Difference," 388; Londa Schiebinger, *Nature's Body: Gender in the Making of Modern Science* (Boston: Beacon Press, 1993), 117–18, 146–47; Charles Ingrao, "'Barbarous Strangers': Hessian State and Society during the American Revolution," *American Historical Review* 87, no. 4 (1982): 971–72.
17. Samuel Thomas Sömmering, *Über die körperliche Verschiedenheit des Negers vom Europäer (1785)*, revised and edited by Sigrid Oehler-Klein (Stuttgart, Germany: Gustav Fischer Verlag, 1998). Translations by D. Elisabeth Maurer.
18. John H. Zammito, "Policing Polygeneticism in Germany, 1775: (Kames,) Kant, and Blumenbach," in Eigen and Larrimore, *The German Invention of Race*, 36–49.
19. Schiebinger, *Nature's Body*, 138; Zammito, "Policing Polygeneticism," 45–49.
20. Sömmering, *Über die körperliche Verschiedenheit des Negers vom Europäer*, 163.
21. Jones, "Black Hessians," n31.
22. Sömmering, *Über die körperliche Verschiedenheit des Negers vom Europäer*, 159–63.
23. Miriam Claude Meijer, *Race and Aesthetic in the Anthropology of Petrus Camper (1722–1789)*, Studies in the History of Ideas in the Low Countries Series (Amsterdam: Rodopi, 1999), 1–6; and Schiebinger, *Nature's Body*, 148–50.
24. Arleen Marcia Tuchman, *Science, Medicine, and the State in Germany: The Case of Baden, 1815–1871* (New York: Oxford University Press, 1993), 20–22; and Edwin Clarke and C.D. O'Malley, *The Human Brain and Spinal Cord: A Historical Study Illustrated by Writings from Antiquity to the Twentieth Century* (San Francisco: Norman Publishing, 1996), 395.
25. Arleen M. Tuchman, "From the Lecture to the Laboratory: The Institutionalization of Scientific Medicine at the University of Heidelberg," in *The Investigative Enterprise: Experimental Physiology in Nineteenth-Century Medicine*, ed. William Coleman and Frederic L. Holmes (Berkeley: University of California Press, 1988), 71–72.
26. Tiedemann, "On the Brain of the Negro," 504.
27. Christopher Clark, "Germany, 1815–1848: Restoration or Pre-March?" in *Nineteenth-Century Germany: Politics, Culture, and Society 1780–1918*, ed. John Breuilly (London: Arnold Press, 2001), 50.
28. See the University of Heidelberg's brief biography of Friedrich Tiedemann at http://www .ub.uni-heidelberg.de/Englisch/helios/digi/anatomie/tiedemann.html (accessed 24 January 2013). My translation of title.
29. Tuchman, *Science, Medicine, and the State in Germany*, 9, 20; and Clark, "Germany, 1815–1848," 43–52.

30. Edmund Spevack, "Charles Follen's View of Republicanism in Germany and the United States, 1815–1840," in *Republicanism and Liberalism in America and the German States, 1750–1850,* ed. Jürgen Heideking and James A. Henretta (Washington DC: The German Historical Institute; Cambridge: Cambridge University Press, 2002), 235–57; Maria I. Diedrich, *Love Across Color Lines: Ottilie Assing & Frederick Douglass* (New York: Hill & Wang, 1999); Christoph Lohmann, ed. and trans., *Radical Passion: Ottilie Assing's Reports from American and Letters to Frederick Douglass* (New York: Peter Lang, 1999); Gerhard Weiss, "The Americanization of Franz Lieber and the *Encyclopedia Americana,*" in Heideking and Henretta, *Republicanism and Liberalism,* 273–87; Lorie A. Vanchena, "From Domestic Farce to Abolitionist Satire: Reinhold Solger's Reframing of the Union (1860)," in Heideking and Henretta, *Republicanism and Liberalism,* 289–316; Harmut Keil, "Race and Ethnicity: Slavery and the German Radical Tradition," talk given in Madison, Wisconsin, sponsored by the Max Kade Institute for German-American Studies and the Center for the History of Print Culture, 3 February 1999; and Mischa Honeck, *We Are the Revolutionists: German-speaking Immigrants and American Abolitionists after 1848* (Athens: University of Georgia Press, 2011).
31. Jürgen Heideking and James A. Henretta, "Introduction," in Heideking and Henretta, *Republicanism and Liberalism,* 16; and Spevack, "Charles Follen," 253–57.
32. Charles Follen and Eliza Lee Cabot Follen, *The Works of Charles Follen with a Memoir of His Life in Five Volumes* (Boston: Hilliard, Gray, & Co., 1841), 196; and Leroy Hopkins, "Black Prussians: Germany and African American Education from James W.C. Pennington to Angela Davis," in *Crosscurrents: African Americans, Africa, and Germany in the Modern World,* ed. David McBride, Leroy Hopkins, and C. Aisha Blackshire-Belay (Columbia, SC: Camden House, 1998), 69.
33. Paul A. Gilje, *Rioting in America* (Bloomington: Indiana University Press), 81–82; Daniel Wrils, "'The Only Mode of Avoiding Everlasting Debate': The Overlooked Senate Gag Rule for Antislavery Petitions," *Journal of the Early Republic* 27, no. 1 (2007): 115–38; on Pennington, see Mischa Honeck's chapter in this volume.
34. Tiedemann, "On the Brain of the Negro," 524.
35. Ibid., 497, 500–4, 520–22.
36. Ibid., 519–20, 497–98.
37. Ibid., 521–22; and Thomas Strack, "Philosophical Anthropology on the Eve of Biological Determinism: Immanuel Kant and Georg Forster on the Moral Qualities and Biological Characteristics of the Human Race," *Central European History* 29, no. 3 (1996): 291.
38. Tiedemann, "On the Brain of the Negro," 524–26.
39. Len Gougeon, "Abolition, the Emersons, and 1837," *New England Quarterly* 54, no. 3 (1981): 356n20; and Richard S. Newman, *The Transformation of American Abolitionism: Fighting Slavery in the New Republic* (Chapel Hill: University of North Carolina Press, 2001), 163. Unlike Follen, Tiedemann lived in Europe during the 1848–1849 revolutions. His son Frederick—a contemporary of Ottilie Assing, who translated Frederick Douglass's slave narrative into German (see Heike Paul's chapter in this volume)—served as a colonel in the army during the revolution in Baden. See Carl Schurz, *The Reminiscences of Carl Schurz,* vol. 1, *1829–1852* (New York: McClure Company, 1907), http://www.trip.net/~bobwb/schurz/v1/index.html#chap7, (accessed 24 January 2013).
40. Charlotte L. Brancaforte, ed., *The German Forty-Eighters in America,* German Life and Civilization 1 (New York: Peter Lang, 1989).
41. "The Heidelberg Declaration," in *Dokumente zur deutschen Verfassungsgeschichte,* ed. E. K. Huber (Stuttgart, Germany: Kohlhammer, 1961), 1:264–65, translation available at http://www.keele.ac.uk/history/currentundergraduates/tltp/1848/DOCUMENT/A213_1.HTM, accessed February 7, 2013; and David Blackbourn, *The Long Nineteenth Century: A History of Germany, 1780–1918* (New York: Oxford University Press, 1998), 144–48.

42. Larry E. Tise, *Proslavery: A History of the Defense of Slavery in America, 1701–1840* (Athens: University of Georgia Press, 1990).
43. James Hunt, *On the Negro's Place in Nature* (London: Trübner, 1863), 11–13.
44. George Frederickson, *The Black Image in the White Mind: The Debate on Afro-American Character and Destiny, 1817–1914* (Indianapolis, IN: Wesleyan, 1987), 132.
45. Hunt, *On the Negro's Place in Nature,* 7, 9, 21.
46. Richard O. Curry, "The Abolitionists and Reconstruction: A Critical Appraisal," *Journal of Southern History* 34, no. 4 (1968): 532–34; Lee D. Baker, *From Savage to Negro: Anthropology and the Construction of Race, 1896–1954* (Berkeley: University of California Press, 1998); and Vernon J. Williams, *Rethinking Race: Franz Boas and His Contemporaries* (Lexington: University of Kentucky Press, 1996).

Chapter Eight

Liberating Sojourns?
African American Travelers in Mid-Nineteenth-Century Germany

Mischa Honeck

> England, France and Germany, the three great lights of modern civilization, are with us, and every American traveler learns to regret the existence of Slavery in his country.[1]
>
> Frederick Douglass, *"The Anti-Slavery Movement"*

Explorations of nineteenth-century transatlantic mobility have traditionally focused on the shiploads of impoverished and discontented Europeans departing for America in pursuit of new opportunities and a better life. Most of these people in transit left their country to escape grinding economic hardship; others to worship as they pleased; others because their political views clashed with those of the ruling elites. Whatever their reasons for shouldering the burdens of overseas travel, the immigrants from the Old World are located at the core of a master narrative that conceptualizes the early modern and modern Atlantic world as dominated by a westward current of settlers, slaves, goods, and ideas, as well as white Europeans exploring, conquering, and inhabiting presumably virgin lands. Such depictions, while ubiquitous, are misleading, because the Atlantic was never a one-way maritime highway. In the decades following Napoleon's defeat in 1815, Europe became a favored destination for a growing number of North American statesmen, entrepreneurs, intellectuals, and tourists, including a small but active group of black Americans.[2]

Prior to emancipation and beyond, the reality of chattel slavery and vicious practices of antiblack discrimination hampered African Americans' ability to partake fully and equally in the evolving democratic society. Yet these and other social and political impediments did not condemn America's black population to

---

Notes from this chapter begin on page 165.

passivity. Asserting their identities in the face of nearly overwhelming racial prejudice, African Americans established their own schools and churches, debated emigration, and joined the transatlantic struggle to abolish slavery. Between 1830 and 1860, a rising tide of black Americans set foot on Europe's shores, bent on mobilizing public opinion in the Old World against slavery and racial inequality in their home country. African Americans who crossed the Atlantic in that period often described their trips as liberating sojourns. The overall friendly reception and the absence of a strict color line in liberal European circles, they felt, contrasted markedly with America's institutionalized racism.[3]

While the transnational links connecting black activists to British and—to a lesser degree—French abolitionists have received some scholarly attention, African American crossings into mid-nineteenth-century Germany are still uncharted territory.[4] To what extent did the German states reinforce or deviate from what Werner Sollors referred to as the "European Dream," the African American myth of a continent untainted by racial prejudice?[5] How did black Americans fighting slaveholder aristocracy respond to a country where large swaths of land were under the heel of aristocrats of another type?

This chapter tackles these questions by illuminating and comparing the travel experiences of two African Americans, James W. C. Pennington and David F. Dorr. Apart from their shared racial heritage, the prominent clergyman Pennington and the otherwise obscure Dorr had little in common. A respected member of the international peace and abolitionist movements, the ex-slave Pennington toured the Old World as a free man and won the respect of several German intellectuals along the way. Dorr, on the other hand, entered the German states in the company of his white master and formally remained a slave until after his return from Europe. Despite these differences, however, this chapter will demonstrate that both men used European travel to enunciate a wide range of collective and personal agendas and were prone to view their German sojourns through the lens of their people's aspirations for freedom and belonging. For both, going abroad was an act of emancipation. On a more individual level, however, traveling also enabled Pennington and Dorr to chart their own distinct courses toward black empowerment, American citizenship, and human equality.

"Germany Stands High in Our Affections": James W.C. Pennington's Quest for Racial Uplift

In early December 1849, the scholar Friedrich Wilhelm Carové entered the chronicles of the University of Heidelberg with a landmark request. In a long and moving plea, Carové urged the theological faculty to confer the honorary doctorate of divinity upon an American minister whom he had met and come to appreciate earlier that year in Paris, James W.C. Pennington.

No ordinary candidate, Pennington was a renowned writer and orator, as well as a Presbyterian pastor and, more sensational still, a fugitive slave who could boast astounding intellectual accomplishments since his escape. Awarding the doctoral degree to this highly gifted black preacher, Carové emphasized, was one

Figure 8.1. James W. C. Pennington's honorary doctorate from the University of Heidelberg, 1849 (University of Heidelberg).

way for the faculty to underscore "the universal brotherhood of humanity" and atone "for the sins Europe ha[d] committed against natural and human rights." The faculty members concurred. Later that day, in a dignified ceremony, the degree "honor doctoris" was conferred upon "Jacob Guil Carol Pennington" (figure 8.1). It was the first time that an African American received this highest academic honor from a European university.[6]

Pennington's journey from slavery in Maryland to the halls of German academia opens a fascinating window to the world of transatlantic antislavery. Born Jim Pembroke, Pennington was an exceptionally intelligent young man and apprenticed by his master to a stonemason and then to a blacksmith. In 1828, after years of suffering under the slaveholder's lash, he made his bid for freedom. Abolitionists in Pennsylvania took the fugitive under their wings and gave him a formal education. Pennington learned quickly and rapaciously and soon outshone his mentors. In 1834, he relocated to New Haven, where he became the first black man to attend classes at Yale University. Completing his theological studies four years later, he was ordained a minister of the Presbyterian church. In the meantime, Pennington matured into a prolific writer, filling the columns of several antislavery periodicals and authoring a slave narrative as well as a comprehensive history of the African American people, which many have claimed was the first such work.[7]

Pennington's brand of abolitionism was profoundly evangelical. Like his white allies, he denounced slavery as a crime against God and called on slaveholders to abandon their sinful behavior.[8] Pennington insisted that blacks had a natural right to freedom, but he also argued staunchly against insurrection. He told free blacks that they had an obligation to seize any available opportunity to improve themselves morally and intellectually. Only "sound and thorough education among coloured men," he stressed, could effectively disrupt stereotypes of black inferiority. He rejected colonization because he believed that the surest way for blacks to gain equal rights was to demonstrate industry and patience in their country of birth. At the same time, he supported efforts to dispatch missionaries to Africa, the "heathen" land of his ancestors. His faith in the perfectibility of all humankind also made Pennington espouse other international reform initiatives of the day, most notably temperance and pacifism.[9]

Historians have sometimes addressed the religious, political, and cultural vectors that connected abolitionist ideas and activists across national and geographical boundaries, but only now are they beginning to scrutinize them in greater detail. Black bondage persisted in the French and British West Indies, Spanish America, and Brazil well into the nineteenth century, yet it was in the United States, a nation reared on the premise "that all men are created equal," where the inconsistencies between freedom and slavery seemed most glaring. By 1849, the year Pennington received his honorary doctorate from Heidelberg, emancipation had been decreed in Great Britain, France, Denmark, and Sweden. Not so in

Pennington's country of birth. The United States was more firmly enmeshed in the slave system than ever before, while the growing global demand for cotton led to a continual expansion of slave labor in the fields of Alabama, Louisiana, Mississippi, and adjacent regions.[10]

Convinced that abolition was not a local but a universal endeavor and part of a broader agenda of Christian self-advancement, Pennington enthusiastically accepted when he was invited to serve as a delegate to a series of international reform conventions in Brussels, London, Paris, and Frankfurt. The midcentury period witnessed the flowering of various democratic and revolutionary movements on both sides of the Atlantic, not a few of which were represented at these meetings. The emergence of this transnational web of reform was intricately bound up with the manifold historical processes that hastened the advent of modernity in the Atlantic world. Technological innovations, demographic growth, economic expansion, as well as free and forced migrations caused profound shifts in the Old and New Worlds and challenged traditional hierarchies and power structures. In the wake of the American and French Revolutions, ideas of liberty and equality called into question various forms of human subordination. Burgeoning civil societies and the popular uprisings of 1830 and 1848 emboldened reformers in Europe and North America, leading many to believe, optimistically and perhaps naïvely, that the scourges of tyranny, slavery, and in some cases even war could be eradicated once and for all. In this millenarian atmosphere, American abolitionists, English philanthropists, French socialists, and Italian and German revolutionists reached out to one another, nurturing a rich dialogue about the meaning of freedom, nationality, and humanity in an ever more intertwined Atlantic world.[11]

It was on one of these occasions, at the 1849 World Peace Congress in Paris, that Pennington befriended a German scholar and vice president of the congress, Friedrich Carové. This Paris congress marked the high point of the era's peace movement, which first gained ground in Europe as a consequence of the horrific casualties wrought by the Napoleonic Wars. Pacifism recruited devoted followers, particularly among Christian philanthropists from both sides of the Atlantic, most of whom cared equally about a plethora of other causes such as temperance, abolition, the boycott of slave goods, penal reform, and, less frequently, women's rights. The movement's idealistic approach to international relations found expression in a series of peace conferences that peaked in the founding of the short-lived League of Universal Brotherhood. League members of the more passionate sort, vowing to associate with "all persons, of whatever country, condition, or color" who joined their cause, pledged to renounce all wars and abstain from military service. Most other peace activists, however, threw their weight behind less radical demands and confined their efforts to promoting disarmament and the arbitration of international conflicts in a "congress of nations."[12]

More than seven hundred delegates from six countries convened in the French capital. Prominent attendees included the French poet Victor Hugo, the English free trader and archpacifist Richard Cobden, and the African American writer William Wells Brown. Carové, harassed and persecuted as a democratic demagogue in the aftermath of the Carlsbad Decrees of 1820, was moved by Pennington's remarks to the assembly that eloquently fused the black freedom struggle with the movement's promotion of universal peace. Slavery, the Presbyterian minister and former slave argued, was an act of war, the brutalization of one race by another, and therefore irreconcilable with the pacifist ideal. Setting himself up as the spokesman of an imagined global black community that was requesting inclusion in the body politic, Pennington urged the delegates to help his people assume an equal station in the "family of man"—not by force, but by acknowledging their entitlement to "wealth, education, character, and every thing that man holds dear."[13] Carové did not ask for details. He understood that helping the African American minister secure an honorary doctorate from a prestigious university such as Heidelberg would send out a powerful message against racial inequality. Both Heidelberg professor Karl Bernhard Hundeshagen and Pennington himself agreed. Bundeshagen remarked that Pennington hoped "[f]rom the granting of this petition for an impulse in favor of the blacks and the colored in general." Pennington himself claimed that he sought the degree not "on account of any personal merits" but as "an encouragement to the Sons of Ham" and "the Negro Race throughout the world, especially in America."[14]

His newly won accolades from Heidelberg fueled Pennington's resolve to attend the follow-up conference in Frankfurt and boosted his sympathies for a country he was yet to visit. By the time Pennington crossed the Rhine, segments of the liberal German intelligentsia had been pressing hard to incorporate antislavery legislation into the German Confederation's various statute books. A resolution in the 1848 National Assembly stating that "German soil tolerates no servitude" received rapturous applause but failed to garner enough votes to become part of the new basic rights catalogue. Earlier that year, no doubt stirred to action by the revolutionary whirlwinds that swept across continental Europe, Friedrich Carové, Hans von Gagern, Karl Theodor Welcker, and other humanitarian activists had authored the first all-German proclamation demanding the worldwide abolition of slavery. However, Germany's abolitionists would have to wait until 1857 for the Prussian legislature to give in to such requests by enacting a law that promised freedom to every black slave who wound up on Prussian territory.[15]

The 1850 Frankfurt Peace Congress, though not as well attended as the Paris meeting the year before, convened in the venerable Paulskirche, where two years earlier the country's first democratically elected parliamentarians had embarked on their ill-fated attempt to frame a constitution for a united German nation. The location's revolutionary mystique, the city's historic architecture, and the geniality of Frankfurt's citizens left a deep imprint on Pennington. Henry Highland Garnet, a member of the American delegation and another eminent black leader, remarked that he would "never ... forget the kindness" of his German hosts.[16] As in Paris, Pennington contributed actively to the convention's proceedings. He reunited with his friend Carové, socialized with European reformers, served on numerous committees, and presided over an antislavery meeting that denounced the pending Fugitive Slave Act in the United States. When he rose to bid his companions farewell, Pennington found words that depicted Germany as a nonracist and truly democratic society. As the conference minutes state:

> Rev. Dr. Pennington gloried to acknowledge that a better day was dawning upon America, upon Europe, upon the world—the intercourse of man with man, without respect to his nature, his language, his colour, his country, and his creed. He referred to an incident which had occurred at Frankfort [sic]: A little German boy came running up to him, attracted, no doubt, by his dark visage, but certainly not frightened at a black man. The little fellow threw his arms around his legs and smiled into his face. That was a recognition which he could never forget. It brought out his sympathies toward the German people, and it taught him the great truth that God had made of one flesh all mankind.[17]

Word of Pennington's success and polite treatment in German lands soon reached the antislavery community in the United States. The news of his honorary doctorate was widely and gleefully distributed in the abolitionist press. Theodore Parker, one of Boston's leading white radicals, praised Pennington's "great character" and "acknowledged learning," declaring that the black minister obtained his degree from a source "more honourable ... than that from which any clergyman in Massachusetts ha[d] received his." Another abolitionist used Pennington's reputation to disparage white supremacist talk that those born in slavery possessed "inferior powers and limited rights."[18] Pennington, too, continued to speak fondly of his trip to central Europe long after he had left Frankfurt. "Germany stands high in our affections," he confided to a British journalist in 1850, "not only on account of her literary fame, but because of the fidelity her sons ... have ever shown to the cause of human liberty."[19] When Pennington's friend and benefactor Carové passed away in 1852, the American and Foreign Anti-Slavery Society, an organization in which Pennington was active, organized a memorial service to venerate the Heidelberg scholar and his antislavery efforts.[20]

Black abolitionists like Pennington were quick to highlight the political significance of their European sojourns. Attacking slavery and racial discrimination from a cosmopolitan perspective, they found, made their arguments less local, more global, and thus more forceful. This rhetorical strategy allowed them to develop a powerful critique of American exceptionalism, to remind Americans of the enduring chasm between their enthusiasm for democracy and their practices of discrimination. In Pennington's abolitionist propaganda, Europe did not emerge as a place steeped in oppression and decadence but as a continent that forged ahead boldly on the path to emancipation and treated blacks more humanely than the slaveholding United States. White Americans, on the other hand, persistently barred people of a different hue from reaping the country's promise of unfettered freedom. Slavery, for abolitionists an ugly stain on the banner of America's national greatness, expanded westward, while the Fugitive Slave Act of 1850 terrorized free and enslaved blacks alike. Pennington was one prominent victim, as he lived under the constant threat of being reclaimed by his former master. It was not until 1852, after friends had bought his freedom, that the black minister could return safely to the United States. What he took with him was an elevated sense of recognition and a bolstered faith in the possibility of a multiracial republic.

"Spicy Towns in Germany": David F. Dorr's Claim to American Selfhood

Few records exist that shed light on the first three decades of David F. Dorr's life. A military roster from the Civil War states that Dorr was born a slave in 1828 in New Orleans.[21] His owner was Cornelius Fellowes, a wealthy lawyer who, as Dorr admitted, had raised him like a son. Intimate bonds between slave and master were generally frowned upon in the patriarchal culture of the American South, but Dorr's mixed background seemed to have facilitated an exception. Dorr labeled himself a "Quadroon," a contemporary term widely used to signify a person of one-quarter black ancestry. A Northern journalist found him light-skinned enough to "pass any where [sic] as a white man."[22] From 1851 to 1854, Dorr accompanied his master on a grand tour through Europe, northern Africa, and parts of the Near East, spurred by the promise that he would be manumitted when they returned to America. When Fellowes failed to keep his word, Dorr escaped from Louisiana to Ohio. In Cleveland, where Dorr took up permanent residence, he started compiling material out of a diary he had kept while traveling from America to the Orient and back. His goal was to publish an account of his journey to distant lands, which finally appeared in 1858.[23]

A Colored Man Round the World is a rare but insightful testimony of an American ex-slave narrating his experiences abroad while oscillating between two conflicting identities: both slave and traveler. It portrays the protagonist's encounter with various foreign peoples and describes his visit to major European and Middle Eastern cities: London, Paris, Frankfurt, Amsterdam, Venice, Athens, Constantinople, and Jerusalem. Though produced by a former slave, Dorr's text has little in common with other prominent slave narratives of the time. It is neither adorned with a preface attesting to the narrative's authenticity, then a conventional abolitionist strategy, nor does it contain heartrending descriptions of slave suffering or elaborate appeals to emancipation. Rather, Dorr created for himself the persona of the leisured American tourist, rejecting the role of the anguished fugitive recollecting his days in bondage. Significantly enough, the word "master" does not appear once in the text. When Dorr mentioned his former owner, he referred to him in an egalitarian, almost detached, manner as "Mr. Fellowes."[24]

Then again, Dorr's strategy of employing writing as a means of self-empowerment is apparent throughout the text. He already undermined prevalent assumptions of racial difference by marketing the book as travel literature, then a popular Anglo-American genre. From the very beginning, Dorr performed what Malini Schueller ventured to call "whiteface, a deliberate donning of whiteness that, unlike blackface, was not culturally sanctioned."[25] He moved with ease among Europeans and fellow American travelers and appropriated genteel habits and manners, displaying a level of erudition typically attributed to middle- and upper-class whites. In London, Dorr paused at the Great Exhibition of 1851, the first in a series of international fairs celebrating advancements in modern industrial technology, and saw Queen Victoria promenade through Hyde Park. Paris, where Dorr marveled at Notre Dame, the National Assembly, and other historic sites, found him entangled in conversations with noblemen from England, Italy, and Germany. Even in far-flung Constantinople, a cheerful Dorr enjoyed the privileges of white male travel. Absorbing the bustle and flurry of a slave market, he contemplated buying a woman for sexual pleasure, a radical yet highly problematic aspiration to imperial manhood by a person who endorsed its precepts, notwithstanding the fact that he used to be afflicted by it.[26]

And yet, despite his proclivity to speak with a white, middle-class voice, Dorr never lost sight of his black heritage. He took conspicuous pride in the part of his ancestry that in many parts of the nineteenth-century world had become synonymous with degradation and bondage. With impressive ease, he used the epithet "colored" in the title and dedicated the book to his beloved "slave mother." Abolitionist sentiments and pan-African ideas resonate in the dedication and preface, where the author lamented the cruel separation of slave families and traced black culture back to the accomplishments of the ancient Egyptians: "Ask Homer if their lips were not thick, their hair curly, their feet flat, and their skin black." Here, Dorr emulated better-known black intellectuals such as Frederick Douglass and James McCune Smith, who cultivated a brand of Egyptology that sought to invalidate the assertions of white ethnologists and phrenologists that African Americans were unfit for civilization.[27]

Following his preface, Dorr moved away from abolitionist polemic and began his whiteface performance to destabilize notions of racial hierarchy by resorting to genteel humor and irony. The narrator comments facetiously on most of the people he meets while unleashing his choicest vocabulary of sarcasm on fellow countrymen whose actions belie their presumptions of white supremacy. One Southerner chewing and spitting tobacco at a Paris dinner party annoyed Dorr and made him turn away in disgust "for fear he might claim nationality." At

London's Crystal Palace, Dorr ridiculed a South Carolinian whose proposition to bring his "haughty and sinewy negroes" to the fair sounded not only morally outrageous but raised doubts about his intelligence. Who, Dorr scoffed, could have guaranteed that his "property" would not grow feet and run away? Cornelius Fellowes, too, received his share of Dorr's scorn after Fellowes had been duped into handing out almost his entire travel savings to a band of Dutch beggars. Dorr no longer made it a secret that he despised almost everything about his master and mused that such people were not worthy of any man's deference.[28]

Race, nationality, class, and gentility also figure prominently in Dorr's literary recollection of his passage through the German territories. Entering Baden-Baden, then as today a romping place for the affluent and adventurous, was a true highlight for Dorr. In the world-famous casino, he was thrilled to rub elbows with aristocrats from all over Europe, listening with fascination to their tales of glamour and opulence. The kings of Bavaria and Prussia were famous guests; so was the Russian czar, who frequented Baden-Baden's gambling halls whenever his vacation schedule permitted it. Again, Dorr mingled with representatives of the Old World nobility and "all classes of society that like excitement—dukes, earls, marquises, barons, knights, valets, and even liveried coachmen, betting from 5 francs to 10,000 francs." Black bondage seemed an ocean apart from this "spiciest gambling place in Europe."[29] Admission and membership hinged on little more than civility, politeness, and gaming luck.

By contrast, the few Americans present were a bitter reminder that such color-blind socializing would surely have provoked a formidable uproar at home. Yet racial hierarchies as they existed in the Western hemisphere were turned upside down when two penniless American students approached Dorr deferentially, asking him whether he might help them acquire a loan from the Grand Duke of Baden. One of the students, Dorr smugly recalled, "was mighty polite when he met me ... and placed me under the truly painful necessity of being introduced to some person of note whom he had himself been a bore upon."[30]

Dorr, in the wake of such engagements, accumulated not just monetary but cultural capital as well. Although gambling in Baden-Baden amused him, he devoted far more energy to his reflections on local art, literature, and architecture. Continuing his journey northward, Dorr hiked up Heidelberg Castle, marveled at the giant wine cask, watched a student duel, cogitated on the remnants of the once proud Holy Roman Empire, traveled through "spicy towns," and paid homage to Goethe's genius at his birthplace in Frankfurt.[31] Politics, especially gestures of identification with European liberal reform and democratic nation building, seem strikingly absent in Dorr's travel narrative. But this does not mean that his writing was apolitical per se. In expressing his enchantment with romantic Germany's historical artifacts, a world replete with legends and couched in a mythical past, the narrator confidently partakes in a ritual of cultural and intellectual affirmation characteristic of nineteenth-century Anglo-American travel literature.

Writing with sophistication about foreign lands was seen as a white—predominantly male—elite prerogative marking a person's entrance into the sphere of *belles lettres* and his admittance to the polite and educated classes.[32] Dorr, well aware of this convention, appropriated the genre for his purposes. Aspirations to genteel refinement and claims to American selfhood are inextricably linked in the narrator's gaze. Rather than simply reinscribe the stereotype of the refined traveler, he demanded recognition for his hybrid self and suggested that every man, regardless of race, could ascend to the crests of civilization.

In that sense, Dorr's German sojourn is presented not so much as an escapist undertaking but instead serves to advance a radical redefinition of American individualism. Even as Dorr followed other African American travel writers in using Europe as a touchstone for criticizing slavery and racial segregation at home, he felt more comfortable reinventing himself as a cultured and internationally respected American gentleman. This stance permitted him to assess the slaveholding United States critically from the outside, not with words of anger and frustration, but with gentle irony, reminding his readers of America's unfulfilled promises. "Though a colored man," Dorr stated emphatically in his preface, "I hope to die believing that this federated government is destined to be the noblest fabric ever germinated in the brain of men or the tides of Time."[33] Thus, Dorr managed to embrace American exemplarism, the belief that the American republic could serve as a shining model of democratic self-rule, while at the same time broadening it to include voices drowned out by the country's white majority.

Journeys of Hope and Illusion

Traveling, the French sociologist Pierre Bourdieu contended in his famous theory of distinction, can trigger an enchanting experience with the unfamiliar and simultaneously spawn meaningful insights about one's place, geographical and social, in a wider world.[34] Had Pennington and Dorr lived to know the Frenchman, they might have echoed his point. Their pivotal experiences of encountering a continent without clear racial fault lines opened up avenues for personal development abroad but also testified to the need to remove all obstacles to self-advancement for people of color at home. Pennington and Dorr, while insisting on the urgency of emancipation, approached and interpreted black liberation from their own vantage points. Pennington held that agitation could further communal progress and a Christian recognition of universal humanity. Dorr found in literature a vehicle for self-assertion. In the quests of both African Americans, Germany functioned less as a specific geographical destination than as an inspiration for their visions of an egalitarian, nonracist society.

However, turning the "other" into a projection screen for and mirror image of one's hopes and aspirations can easily breed illusions—culturally constructed and ideologically biased stereotypes of that other. Measuring the societies of the Old World against the yardsticks of American slavery and racism produced an overly romanticized picture of nineteenth-century Germany, one that reprimanded the limitations of American equality while downplaying the inequalities of aristocratic Europe. Both Pennington and Dorr were remarkably silent on class inequities and political repression in post-Napoleonic German society. Even in the few passages where they alluded to such wrongs, they seemed incapable of divorcing them from the more closely and authentically felt reality of racial oppression. Too immersed in their own struggle for freedom, they had little to say on a European-wide crisis that had no immediate effect on their black selves. "Of all the German kingdoms the most despotic is Austria," Dorr noted, "but she hates slavery more than the 'freest government in the world.'"[35] Pennington, on the other hand, took his appreciation of Germany so far as to suggest that the German immigrants in America stood united "in their stern hatred for the system" that kept his people in bondage. When dreaming of Germany, black intellectuals like Pennington and Dorr were looking for ways to end their American nightmares, return to the aspirations of the Declaration of Independence, and realize its democratic ideals.[36]

Such ideologically fraught statements obscure the fact that German and German American opinions on slavery and race differed widely, not unlike those of other ethnic groups. In the course of the long nineteenth century, which Jürgen Osterhammel persuasively termed a "century of acceleration," the currents of the black and white Atlantic increasingly converged, but rarely with an equal outcome for those directly affected.[37] Few German Americans defended black bondage as a positive good. Yet although many objected to slavery's westward expansion, they found little fault with America's *herrenvolk* democracy, which derived the promise of equality for whites from the political exclusion of darker races. Only a handful of the political refugees of 1848 advocated abolition and civic equality regardless of skin color.[38] Racist views of blacks, too, were anything but absent from mid-nineteenth-century German public discourse. Leipzig editor Carl Berendt Lorck, who published a translation of Frederick Law Olmsted's account of German immigrant life on the Texan frontier, considered bondage the natural state for dark-skinned men. Clara von Gerstner, writing about her trip to the antebellum South, defended the institution's civilizing effects on benighted African slaves. And Johann Caspar Bluntschli, a Swiss professor who taught international law in Munich and Heidelberg, had no qualms vilifying people of African descent as "uncivilized savages" and "barbarians," thereby doing much to popularize notions of black inferiority.[39] Pennington's and Dorr's German sojourns underscore the political implications of antebellum African American travel, but they also invite us to weigh the potentials and pitfalls of intercultural encounters.

What, then, are the broader implications of their individual lives if we assess them through the lens of Paul Gilroy's black Atlantic? Gilroy famously connected his term with the desire of people of African descent "to transcend both the structures of the nation state" and the "restrictive bonds of ethnicity, national identification, and sometimes even 'race' itself." In their search for community, he argued, black intellectuals traveled and worked in a transnational frame, while maintaining only a superficial association with their country of origin, ready to renounce that association in favor of a global-coalitional politics in which antiracism and anti-imperialism would trump the confines of the local.[40]

After careful scrutiny, there are good reasons to challenge this interpretation. Dorr's and Pennington's transatlantic careers do not quite square with Gilroy's antinational paradigm. True, the intellectual culture in which Dorr and Pennington participated was decidedly transnational. Yet in their case, transnationalism was a tool rather than a conviction, not an end in itself, but the means toward developing a more inclusive idea of nationhood. Working with sympathetic Europeans in an era replete with the language of nationality and freedom helped black Americans to frame a cosmopolitan nationalism that interwove their quest for freedom without the confines of race, rank, or origin with their search for belonging.[41] Against the vision of a racially exclusive nation, they pitted an egalitarian concept of nationality, one that was grounded in civic instead of racial values. Just as white liberals saw early-nineteenth-century nationalism as intrinsically progressive and democratic, African American intellectuals used the nation as a vessel for their own aspirations for freedom and belonging. "I am American to the backbone," declared Pennington when he was in his prime, rebutting both advocates of colonization and African American activists propagating a loosely defined black globalism.[42] The kind of color-blind but rooted citizenship envisioned by Pennington and Dorr not only offered an escape from the Manichean dynamics of black and white, but also promised to give a homeless people a home.

Notes

1. Frederick Douglass, "The Anti-Slavery Movement: An Address Delivered in Rochester, March 19, 1855," in *The Frederick Douglass Papers: Speeches, Debates, and Interviews,* ed. John W. Blassingame (New Haven, CT: Yale University Press, 1982), 3:48–49.
2. On the rising significance of European travel for antebellum Americans, see William W. Stowe, *Going Abroad: European Travel in Nineteenth-Century American Culture* (Princeton, NJ: Princeton University Press, 1994); and Christopher Mulvey, *Transatlantic Manners: Social Patterns in Nineteenth-Century Anglo-American Travel Literature* (Cambridge: Cambridge University Press, 1990).
3. Richard M. Blackett, *Building an Antislavery Wall: Black Americans in the Atlantic Antislavery Movement, 1830–1860* (Baton Rouge: Louisiana State University Press, 1983); Alan J. Rice and Martin Crawford, eds., *Liberating Sojourn: Frederick Douglass & Transatlantic Reform* (Athens: University of Georgia Press, 1999); Jean Fagan Yellin, "Incidents Abroad: Harriet

Jacobs and the Transatlantic Movement," in *Women's Rights and Transatlantic Antislavery in the Era of Emancipation,* ed. Kathryn Kish Sklar and James Brewer Stewart (New Haven, CT: Yale University Press, 2007), 158–72; and Willi Coleman, "'Like Hot Lead to Pour on the Americans': Sarah Parker Redmond—From Salem, Mass., to the British Isles," in Sklar and Stewart, *Women's Rights and Transatlantic Antislavery,* 173–88.

4. Classic accounts of the Anglo-American antislavery network include Betty Fladeland, *Men and Brothers: Anglo-American Antislavery Cooperation* (Urbana: University of Illinois Press, 1972); Clare Taylor, ed., *British and American Abolitionists: An Episode in Transatlantic Understanding* (Edinburgh, UK: Edinburgh University Press, 1974); Blackett, *Building an Antislavery Wall;* and Seymour Drescher, "Servile Insurrection and John Brown's Body in Europe," in *His Soul Goes Marching On: Responses to John Brown and the Harper's Ferry Raid,* ed. Paul Finkelman (Charlottesville: University of Virginia Press, 1995), 253–95.

5. Werner Sollors, *Neither Black nor White Yet Both: Thematic Explorations of Interracial Literature* (New York: Oxford University Press, 1997), 339.

6. The University of Heidelberg holds a copy of the doctor of divinity certificate awarded to James W. C. Pennington. See also Herman E. Thomas, *James W. C. Pennington: African American Churchman and Abolitionist* (New York: Garland, 1995), 180–86; and Leroy Hopkins, "'Black Prussians': Germany and African American Education from James W. C. Pennington to Angela Davis," in *Crosscurrents: African Americans, Africa, and Germany in the Modern World,* ed. David McBride, Leroy Hopkins, and C. Aisha Blackshire-Belay (Columbia, SC: Camden, 1998), 67–70. The latest biography of Pennington is Christopher L. Webber, *American to the Backbone: The Life of James W.C. Pennington, the Fugitive Slave Who Became One of the First Black Abolitionists* (New York: Doubleday, 2011).

7. Compare to Thomas, *James W.C. Pennington;* James W.C. Pennington, *A Text Book on the History and Origins of the Colored People* (Hartford, CT: L. Skinner, 1841); and James W. C. Pennington, *The Fugitive Blacksmith; Or, Events in the History of James W.C. Pennington* (London: Charles Gilpin, 1849).

8. The religious roots of American abolitionism are examined in James Brewer Stewart, *Holy Warriors: The American Abolitionists and Slavery* (New York: Hill and Wang, 1996); Steven Mintz, *Moralists and Modernizers: America's Pre-Civil War Reformers* (Baltimore: Johns Hopkins University Press, 1995); and John R. McKivigan and Mitchell Snay, eds., *Religion and the Antebellum Debate over Slavery* (Athens: University of Georgia Press, 1997).

9. Pennington, *The Fugitive Blacksmith,* 56; Thomas, *James W.C. Pennington,* 68–75, 88.

10. America's entanglement and place in the Atlantic slave system are masterfully discussed in the works of David Brion Davis, most notably in *Problem of Slavery in Western Culture* (New York: Oxford University Press, 1988) and *Inhuman Bondage: The Rise and Fall of Slavery in the New World* (New York: Oxford University Press, 2006). On the rising global significance of cotton in the nineteenth-century world economy, see Sven Beckert, "Emancipation and Empire: Reconstructing the Worldwide Web of Cotton Production in the Age of the American Civil War," *American Historical Review* 109 (2004): 1405–38.

11. See Robert E. Palmer's landmark study, *The Age of the Democratic Revolution: A Political History of Europe and America, 1760–1800,* 2 vols. (Princeton, NJ: Princeton University Press, 1959, 1964). In many ways, the period this chapter is concerned with is more deserving of Palmer's title than the period to which it was originally applied. Ira Berlin underscored the nineteenth-century paradox that expanding ideas about human equality stood in utter contrast to increasing social inequalities in his "Comments on Jürgen Osterhammel's 'In Search of a Nineteenth Century,'" *Bulletin of the German Historical Institute, Washington DC* 32 (2003): 32.

12. On the history of these international peace conventions in the 1840s and 1850s, see W. H. van der Linden, *The International Peace Movement, 1815–1875* (Amsterdam: Tilleul, 1987); David Nicholls, "Richard Cobden and the International Peace Congress Movement, 1848–1853,"

Journal of British Studies 30 (1991): 351–76; and Sandi E. Cooper, *Patriotic Pacifism, Waging War on War in Europe, 1815–1914* (New York: Oxford University Press, 1991), 13–60. From an American perspective, see W. Caleb McDaniel, "Our Country Is the World: Radical American Abolitionists Abroad" (PhD diss., Johns Hopkins University, 2006).

13. *Report of the Proceedings of the Second General Peace Congress, held in Paris, on the 22nd, 23rd and 24th of August, 1849,* 83–86. On Friedrich Wilhelm Carové, see Wilhelm von Faber, "Friedrich Wilhelm Carové 1789–1852: Ein Beitrag zum deutschen Liberalismus im Vormärz" (PhD diss., University of Munich, 1954); and Hartmut Schmidt, "'Kein Deutscher darf einen Sclaven halten'—Jacob Grimm und Friedrich Wilhelm Carové," in *Bedeutungen und Ideen in Sprachen und Texten,* ed. Werner Neumann and Bärbel Techtmeier (Berlin: Akademie-Verlag, 1987), 189.

14. Thomas, *James W.C. Pennington,* 181; Pennington to the *British Banner,* 4 January 1850, in *The Black Abolitionist Papers,* vol. 1, ed. C. Peter Ripley and Roy E. Finkenbine (Chapel Hill: University of North Carolina Press, 1991), 241.

15. See Schmidt, "'Kein Deutscher darf einen Sclaven halten,'" 183–92. A copy of the *Aufruf zur Bildung eines deutschen Nationalvereins für Abschaffung der Sklaverei* was sent to the secretary of the French Abolitionist Society; Seymour Drescher, "British Way, French Way: Opinion Building and Revolution in the Second French Slave Emancipation," *American Historical Review* 96 (1991): 729–30. The main driving force behind Prussia's antislavery law of 1857 was by all accounts the naturalist and explorer Alexander von Humboldt, who was an outspoken critic of black bondage. See also Philip S. Foner, *Alexander von Humboldt on Slavery in the United States* (Berlin: Deutsche Bibliothek, 1981), 30–58.

16. *Report of the Proceedings of the Third General Peace Congress,* 66.

17. *Report of the Proceedings of the Third General Peace Congress,* 67. Another detailed account of the Frankfurt meeting was published in *The Boston Daily Atlas,* 7 October 1850.

18. Theodore Parker, *The New Crime Against Humanity: A Sermon Preached at the Music Hall, on Sunday, June 4, 1854* (Boston: Mussey, 1854), 8; Wilson Armistead, ed., *Five Hundred Thousand Strokes for Freedom: A Series of Antislavery Tracts* (London: W. & E. Cash, 1853), 353; and *The Thirteenth Annual Report of the American and Foreign Anti-Slavery Society, Presented at New York, May 11, 1853* (New York: Lewis J. Bates, 1853), 190.

19. Pennington to the *British Banner,* 4 January 1850.

20. Parker, *The New Crime Against Humanity,* 8; Armistead, *Five Hundred Thousand Strokes for Freedom,* 353; and *The Thirteenth Annual Report of the American and Foreign Anti-Slavery Society,* 190.

21. Dorr apparently fought on the side of the Union during the Civil War; see the *Official Roster of the Soldiers of the State of Ohio in the War of the Rebellion, 1861–1866* (Cincinnati: Baldwin, 1886), 2:234.

22. "A Colored Man Round the World," *Cleveland Plain Dealer,* 20 September 1858.

23. For some basic data concerning Dorr's life, I rely on the introduction by Malini Johar Schueller in David F. Dorr, *A Colored Man Round the World,* ed. Malini J. Schueller (Ann Arbor: University of Michigan Press, 1999), xi–xv.

24. Dorr, *A Colored Man Round the World,* 61–70.

25. Schueller, "Introduction," xxvii.

26. Dorr, *A Colored Man Round the World,* 19–25, 31–41, 120–24.

27. Ibid., 11. See also Schueller, *U.S. Orientalisms: Race, Nation, and Gender in Literature, 1790–1890* (Ann Arbor: University of Michigan Press, 1998), 80–107. On antebellum Americans' fascination with Egypt, see Eddie S. Glaude, *Exodus! Religion, Race, and Nation in Early Nineteenth-Century Black America* (Chicago: University of Chicago Press, 2000); and Scott Drafton, *Egypt Land: Race and Nineteenth-Century American Egyptomania* (Durham, NC: Duke University Press, 2003).

28. Dorr, *A Colored Man Round the World*, 20, 40, 67–69.
29. Ibid., 50.
30. Ibid., 50–52.
31. Ibid., 53.
32. See Stowe, *Going Abroad*, 13.
33. Dorr, *A Colored Man Round the World*, 11.
34. Pierre Bourdieu, *Distinction: A Social Critique of the Judgement of Taste*, trans. Richard Nice (Cambridge, MA: Harvard University Press, 1984).
35. Dorr, *A Colored Man Round the World*, 162.
36. Pennington to the *British Banner*, 4 January 1850.
37. Jürgen Osterhammel, *Die Verwandlung der Welt: Eine Geschichte des 19. Jahrhunderts* (Munich: C.H. Beck, 2009), 126.
38. On the German American Forty-Eighters and antislavery, see Bruce Levine, *The Spirit of 1848: German Immigrants, Labor Conflict, and the Coming of the Civil War* (Urbana: University of Illinois Press, 1992), 151–209; Hartmut Keil, "German Immigrants and African Americans in Mid-Nineteenth Century America," in *Enemy Images in American History*, ed. Ursula Lemkuhl and Ragenhild Fiebig-von Hase (Providence, RI: Berghahn Books, 1997), 137–57; Martin Öfele, *German-Speaking Officers in the United States Colored Troops, 1863–1867* (Gainesville: University of Florida Press, 2004), 1–37; and Mischa Honeck, *We Are the Revolutionists: German-Speaking Immigrants and American Abolitionists after 1848* (Athens: University of Georgia Press, 2011). The term "*herrenvolk* democracy," which is usually applied to mark democratic regimes in which citizenship is restricted to the dominant ethnic group, was coined by Pierre van den Berghe in *Race and Racism: A Comparative Perspective* (New York: Wiley, 1967), 18.
39. Frederick Law Olmsted, *Wanderungen durch Texas und im mexikanischen Grenzlande*, ed. and trans. C.B. Lorck (Leipzig, Germany: Lorck, 1857), xii–xvi; Clara von Gerstner, *Beschreibung einer Reise durch die Vereinigten Staaten von Nordamerika in den Jahren 1838 bis 1840* (Leipzig, Germany: Hinrichs, 1842), 325–28; and Johann Caspar Bluntschli, *Das moderne Kriegsrecht der civilisierten Staaten* (Nördlingen, Germany: C.H. Beck, 1874), 89.
40. Paul Gilroy, *The Black Atlantic: Modernity and Double Consciousness* (London: Verso, 1993), 4, 19.
41. Useful accounts of the historical roots of Euro-American cosmopolitanism are Michael Scrivener, *The Cosmopolitan Ideal in the Age of Revolution and Reaction, 1776–1832* (London: Scribner, 2007); Allison Games, *The Web of Empire: English Cosmopolitans in an Age of Expansion, 1560–1660* (New York: Oxford, 2008); and Bruce Robbins, "Actually Existing Cosmopolitanism," in *Cosmopolitics: Thinking and Feeling Beyond the Nation*, ed. Pheng Cheah, Bruce Robbins, and Social Text Collective (Minneapolis: University of Minnesota Press, 1997). On American abolitionism and cosmopolitan thought, see an unpublished paper by Caleb McDaniel, "'Our Country Is the World': American Abolitionists, Louis Kossuth, and Philanthropic Revolutions," presented at the Annual Meeting of the OAH, 25 March 2004.
42. Webber, *American to the Backbone*, 189.

Chapter Nine

GLOBAL PROLETARIANS, UNCLE TOMS, AND NATIVE SAVAGES
Popular German Race Science in the Emancipation Era

Bradley Naranch

Introduction

When it came to matters of race, slavery, and freedom, Friedrich Ratzel wrote in an 1869 article that appeared in the popular scientific journal *Globus* that most of his fellow Germans were easily led astray.[1] Decades of abolitionist activism and the recent events of the American Civil War had convinced many observers of the immorality of human bondage. Ratzel (1844–1904), who received his doctorate in zoology the previous year and was working as a freelance journalist, was concerned that large sectors of the reading public lacked the basic awareness of new scientific theories concerning race, climate, and culture needed to form educated opinions about such complicated matters.[2] "Should slavery be abolished altogether or can it be maintained in principle and scientifically legitimated?" he wrote. "These were the questions that were discussed on the beer bench and around the tea table, in our pure white Central European homeland, where an actual Negro is a rare attraction, without any sign of true enlightenment concerning such matters."[3]

For Ratzel, overexposure to philanthropic critiques of American slavery prevented Germans from an objective appraisal of the cultural limitations of nonwhite races. He criticized the "dominant trend" to adopt liberal "slogans" regarding human nature and the applicability of universal "principles" like free trade, equality, and love for humanity (*Menschenliebe*).[4] To grant freedom to a culturally undeveloped or primitive population was like placing a "tropical plant

---

Notes from this chapter begin on page 182.

in a Nordic field of ice," like a "corrosive poison." "With words like 'freedom,'" he concluded, "one hopes to bring about miracles and does not realize how divergent conditions make such a general scheme for humanity unworkable. To repeat ourselves: true love of humanity must first be informed by an understanding of human nature before it can be used to help others, and not run the risk of offering stones, not sustenance, to those in need."[5]

Ratzel's acerbic remarks may have been allusions to German critics of American slavery, such as Friedrich Kapp and Ottilie Assing, who played active expatriate roles in German liberal print culture and supported the abolitionist movement.[6] His concerns, however, were distinctly global in scope. In the Dutch East Indies, colonial systems of forced labor suited to the developmental stage of the local populations created the basis for economic growth and social stability. Growing criticism in the Netherlands of the "cultivation system" of compulsory labor used in the East Indies had generated a reform movement espousing the principles of human equality and freedom of trade.[7] Introducing systems of free labor into the colonies would result in the decline of the plantation economies and return the populations to their "natural" state of "indolence" and "despotism."[8] By offering a scientific defense for regimes of compulsory labor for "colored" workers in tropical plantation economies, Ratzel challenged efforts by humanitarian activists to portray Africans and other enslaved populations in a sympathetic moral and political light. He dismissed their views as well intentioned but naïve, out of step with new theories of race that emphasized the permanent condition of human inequality.[9]

Like *Globus* editor Karl Andree (1808–75), Ratzel was part of what British historian Catherine Hall has described as a generational shift in attitudes toward the African diaspora between the 1830s and the late 1860s, one in which "a structure of feeling dominated by the familial trope and a paternalist rhetoric had been displaced by a harsher racial vocabulary of fixed differences."[10] *Globus* provided a forum for challenging German views on slavery and race generated by the widespread popularity of Harriet Beecher Stowe's best-selling novel *Uncle Tom's Cabin*.[11] Reading *Uncle Tom's Cabin* or slave narratives written by African Americans like Frederick Douglass, Heike Paul has compellingly argued, enabled Germans to identify points of contact and symbolic affinity between the lives of German migrants to America as well as domestic servants and lower-class laborers at home.[12] According to Paul, such spaces for interracial solidarity on the basis of shared experiences of discrimination, displacement, and onerous working conditions had disappeared by the 1870s. Literary representations of African Americans and German Americans began to emphasize inherent disparities between white German migrants and emancipated blacks. Paul links this hardening of racial categories to the failure of Reconstruction as well as the rise of colonial activism in imperial Germany. Germans "became white" and entertained their own fantasies of colonial rule in Africa, while African Americans were "Africanized" and rendered more savage, indolent, and threatening.[13] "The symbolic closeness at midcentury transformed itself into an asymmetrical divide that made the emancipation discourse of African Americans appear irreconcilable with discourses of German emancipation and, indeed, of dominance."[14]

Close reading of Andree's writings confirms the discursive shift in German representations of the black diaspora away from paternalistic icons like "Uncle Tom" toward those emphasizing the indelible indigenous roots of a "savage" black identity. As Andree's writings reveal, however, such shifts took place earlier than the 1870s and did so within a global as much as a German-American context. Also at issue for Andree and Ratzel was the nature of labor and wage relations in postemancipation, capitalist societies.[15] How, in the absence of slavery, could black workers be compelled to work? The later interest among German officials in Togo in adapting sharecropping techniques from the American South, as Andrew Zimmerman has described, was prefigured in earlier debates prompted by the gradual abolition of slavery in the Americas and the European colonies in the nineteenth century. The discursive construction of a dark-skinned race of Atlantic world peasants capable of producing tropical commodities and export crops for metropolitan consumption, such as cotton, tobacco, coffee, or cocoa, revealed

Map 9.1. Friedrich Ratzel, map of the spread of "colored races" in the United States, c. 1870.

how global economic changes enabled new intellectual and cultural ideas about black identity to form.[16]

German perceptions of African Americans in the United States were also shaped by a growing interest in the influx of Chinese migrants in the American West following the 1849 gold rush and the changing conditions of life for Native Americans. Comparing the character, migration, and work habits of the "colored races" added an additional layer of complexity to German popular scientific writings. In a major, two-volume cultural and physical geography of the United States published in 1880, Ratzel devoted as much attention to the condition of Native Americans as he did to that of African Americans.[17] He appended a short section on Chinese migration to a larger chapter on black slavery and emancipation and included a full-page map depicting the "distribution of the colored races" (Chinese, Indian, and Negro) in the United States (see Map 9.1).[18] German readers of middle-class journals like *Globus,* this chapter will show, were exposed to a range of contrasting images of a black diaspora that was at once modern and primitive, localized and global, American and African. The ambivalence over how best to describe persons of African descent, as "Negroes," "natives," or "coloreds," frustrated efforts at anthropological categorization as either a "civilized" or "natural" people and complicated later political debates over the legal status and rights of African subjects in the colonies. Modern science, Andree promised, would clarify such issues by using race as a lens to make sense of a rapidly changing world of highly mobile labor forces. In place of the idealistic claims of "pseudo-philanthropy," modern race science offered to edify German readers about the wider world beyond the boundaries of central Europe. The resulting categories and conclusions did not result in greater clarity, but only brought about added confusion.

Globalization Narratives in German Print Culture

Karl Andree was born on 20 October 1808 in Braunschweig.[19] His lifelong interests in ethnography, global commerce, geography, and journalism stemmed from his early contact with Alexander von Humboldt (1769–1859) and Carl Ritter (1779–1859), who established the first academic chair in geography at the University of Berlin. Andree had also studied at the universities of Jena and Tübingen before embarking on a journalistic career that took him to Cologne, Frankfurt, Leipzig, and Bremen. An outspoken liberal nationalist, Andree frequently ran into conflicts with local authorities. It was only after the 1848 revolution that he eventually settled in Dresden in 1854, where he continued his writing and editing careers. In 1859, he published a two-volume compilation of essays, *Geographische Wanderungen,* which contained a number of highly critical discussions of the abolitionist movement and US efforts at resettling freed slaves in Liberia.[20] In 1862, he began publishing an illustrated magazine devoted to world travel, popular science, commerce, and technology, *Globus,* which he continued to oversee until his death in 1873.[21]

Andree crafted a detailed vision in his writings of a globalizing world in which Germany was caught up in complex webs of commercial transactions, networks of communication, and systems of transport. In the 1861 edition of his *Geographie des Welthandels* (Geography of World Trade), which he dedicated to the Bremen senator Arnold Duckwitz, Andree described the global array of consumer items concentrated in his Dresden study, marveling at the economic networks that could deposit such a diversity of goods in a single location: a mahogany writing table from Honduras, an English carpet with wool delivered from the La Plata or New South Wales, tea from China or Assam, coffee from Java, sugar from Brazil or Cuba. Around him were newspapers from Hong Kong, Hamburg, Valparaiso, New York, St. Louis, and Adelaide. A visiting friend entered the room wearing a fur coat that he assumed to be from the forests of Siberia and purchased at a Leipzig trade fair. On second thought, he identified its provenance as originating in Ojibwa territory north of Winnipeg and imported to Germany by the Hudson Bay Company. "Whether we enter the homes of the rich or the poor," he observed, "we encounter objects from entirely different parts of the world. Trade has given us the opportunity to unite them, and this fact accounts for the importance of the geographical element in world commerce."[22]

At other times, Andree reversed the commodity flows, imagining German toys and musical instruments in the hands of Pacific Islanders, brought halfway across the globe by Bremen whaling ships that stopped to resupply in Hawai'i.[23] While the United States received extensive coverage, Andree consistently embedded it within larger economic networks that extended beyond the continent. He commented favorably on Chinese migration to California and provided up-to-date accounts of the newly opened steamship and railroad lines in the Pacific and Central America. An outspoken critic of the abolitionist movement, Andree ran numerous stories on the state of race relations in the years of Reconstruction.[24] The Atlantic world held a particularly important place in his description of world trade, but this included reports on the west African palm oil trade, one in which Hamburg merchants were very active, or on American resettlement of freed slaves in Liberia.[25] Andree's unrestrained optimism in the powers of science, technology, and commerce was sustained by a capacious understanding of Germanic racism that grouped together America, Britain, and Germany as part of a Teutonic brotherhood destined to conquer the world and create new democratic states wherever they took up permanent residence. It was similar to the discourses of Anglo-Saxonism that American and British writers relied upon as an explanatory force propelling imperial conquest and settlement.[26]

Andree's early career also coincided with the German-language publication in 1852 of *Uncle Tom's Cabin,* and the reception of Stowe's novel shaped his racial rhetoric. In an article on west Africa bearing the telling title "In Uncle Tom's Ancestral Home," Andree expressed concern that antislavery activists had spread false viewpoints about human equality.[27] He described the novel as "immoral through and through" and Stowe herself as "puritanical" and "blindly fanatical."[28] He highlighted failed attempts by American missionary societies to improve living conditions in Liberia by dispatching freed slaves to the west African coast. Such mixed-race elites, he suggested, themselves became slave owners of indigenous laborers, were dependent on American food exports of meat and canned goods for their survival, and did little to create an independent foundation for the "black republic" that white philanthropists envisioned.[29] "Will Mrs. Stowe perhaps not write a Negro novel that takes place in Liberia," he wrote, "one that depicts the nigger aristocracy in their dark kingdom and oppression of the natives that they have flogged?"[30] Whites and blacks had never lived together in conditions of social equality. "Black Africa" was "unhistoric" and existed in a "vegetative" state. Its inhabitants practiced forms of human sacrifice, slavery, polygamy, fetishism, "snake cults," and other forms of occult magic.[31] Without strict oversight, Africans in the Caribbean would collapse into a state of civilizational decay, as was the case in Haiti. Africans in the diaspora were destined to passive service, even in the "most favorable circumstances," as "proletarian" laborers in tropical markets around the world.[32]

Andree continued to express negative views of African emancipation and cultural capacity in the first of three volumes of his major work, *Geographie des Welthandels* (1861).[33] The following year, he began publication of *Globus* and continued to serve as its editor and lead writer until his death in 1875.[34] The goal of *Globus,* as described in the forward to the first volume, was to present to a general audience a total picture of the latest trends in geography and ethnography as well as a chronicle of trends in world travel and commerce.[35] Aboriginal protection societies had spread false viewpoints about the nature of the human world that did not take into account the newest findings of anthropology and ethnology. Universal principles that failed to consider the racial differences among the world's population, or that did not grasp the impact of the environment upon the level of social development in a particular region, prevented the general public from coming to correct judgments about historical and political developments: the great human families of the world have very different cultural values; one cannot measure all of them with the same standard measurement or get by with general postulates. In the end, one must concede that there are higher- and lower-ranking races, primitive tribes with very different capabilities and immanent instincts, which the process of civilization cannot overcome.[36]

Race, Labor, and Social Darwinism

Over the course of the 1860s, Andree succeeded in developing *Globus* into an influential media platform for promoting new developments in science and technology (see figure 9.1). It complimented the extensive coverage given to overseas affairs in other liberal magazines, such as Ernst Keil's *Die Gartenlaube,* Oscar Peschel's *Das Ausland,* August Petermann's *Mitteilungen aus Justus Perthes' geographischer Anstalt,* and Otto Ule's *Die Natur.*[37] Race relations were a critical component of Andree's new magazine, and many of his personal contributions were devoted to applying anthropological theories of racial difference to the analysis of political and social trends inside and outside of Europe. The debates in the United States over the legal status of free and enslaved African Americans provided ample opportunities for Andree to discuss the issues of labor, cultural assimilation, and interracial marriage that were the core questions of what he termed the "race problem" in North and South America.[38] "The relationship of dark-skinned, mixed-blood people to civilization and culture is of enormous importance," he wrote in 1863, "and simplistic styles of speech about 'human equality' explain absolutely nothing and do not bring us any further along. We must grasp the problem more deeply; we must let facts and experiences, not the empty phrases of pseudo-philanthropy, influence our judgments."[39]

Globus provided a forum for early social Darwinian theorists, whose ideas about race, culture, and history were subjects of considerable controversy, to disseminate their views to a wider German audience.[40] Because Andree was heavily dependent on foreign source material for many of his articles, the magazine also introduced readers to English, French, and American authors, who relied upon notions of racial hierarchy, evolutionary anthropology, and cultural degeneracy. Many of Andree's articles, such as an 1866 piece highly critical of English historian Henry Thomas Buckle, author of the *History of Civilization in England,* and the philosopher John Stuart Mill, actively intervened on the side of the new sciences of cultural geography, anthropology, and *Völkerpsychologie* in order to question the utility of universal conceptions of individual liberty.[41] Andree also applauded the creation in 1863 of the London Anthropological Society, founded in part to counter the political power of British antislavery and aboriginal rights groups.[42] In his view, new scientific research had proven the basic falseness of humanist principles of equality, and he frequently interspersed the languages of science and politics in articles that criticized the idealistic assumptions of liberal activists: "Nature has organized humanity hierarchically, not democratically, and—to use the expression—not in an egalitarian fashion … The principle of equality cannot stand up to the notion of racial stratification. It is one of those inane ideas that have no foundation but hot air; it is not in the least 'liberal,' but quite simply absurd."[43]

Globus routinely ran excerpts from German- and English-language newspapers that described the contentious debates over the legal rights to marriage, voting, and education that African Americans should receive.[44] Andree's magazine functioned as a central European outpost for post-Reconstruction reactionary discourses of racial antagonism to enter the German public sphere. "We could fill

Figure 9.1. Otto Ule, cover illustration from 1862 depicting exotic jungle wildlife and a savage-looking man/beast in a tree (upper right).

entire numbers of *Globus* with the most piquant reports about the Negro question and the Negro plague," he wrote. "The fanatical wing of the ultra-radical abolitionists has put the craziest notions in the heads of the blacks, like the promises of 'rebel' property and their white wives. One tells them that coloreds are much better than the whites, whose blood must be enriched with black additions."[45] While Andree noted that European economic development in tropical regions of the world would have been impossible without forced labor and believed that Africans were well suited to their roles as the "proletarians" of the global economy, he also felt it inevitable that the violence and destructiveness of slavery had angered the "more noble spirits residing in the hearts of well-meaning people" and inspired the "crusade" against the slave trade that gave rise to the "philanthropist." In seeking to emancipate slaves from their conditions of bondage and human degradation, however, such individuals failed to appreciate the need for Africans transplanted from their homelands to be compelled to work, lest they return to a state of indolence and savagery in the absence of European oversight.[46]

Similarly, Andree questioned whether freed blacks living in the United States should ever be granted the same full legal rights as white residents, even in Northern states that had abolished slavery prior to the Civil War. Noting the extent to which segregationist attitudes pervaded both the North and the South, he wrote of a "unique social phenomenon" affecting American society: "we see two nations, a white one and a colored, which come of age in the same political sphere but which nonetheless live on an unequal basis with each other."[47] Regardless of where they traveled, blacks were treated as "pariahs" and members of a "foreign nation" living in the midst of a white world, one in which allegations of black ancestry and mixed bloodlines could lead to court cases to prove the falseness or verity of such accusations.[48]

Slavery was not only an issue affecting the United States, since the manual labor of African Americans and other global "proletarians" was critical to the growth of the consumer economy at home. Because European demand for tropical products like sugar, cotton, coffee, tea, and cocoa remained high and would continue to rise in the future, the global economy needed new sources of labor to replenish the ranks of the recently freed or soon to be freed African slaves.[49] The importation of low-wage laborers from British India and China signaled the start of a new era of long-distance labor migration that would sustain high levels of tropical commodity production despite the decline of the slave economy. The first "coolie ship" from China to deposit its human cargo in North America delivered "the flakes of snow that precede the avalanche, and this East Asian avalanche will cover over the black population and drive them under, or at least make the services of East Asian workers essential."[50]

Andree could not resist mentioning that at the time when abolitionist sentiment in America and the British West Indies was beginning to have a political and cultural impact, British military forces were waging war in China to open up that market to imports of opium. Growing British influence in China following the establishment of Hong Kong had accelerated the flow of Chinese laborers to destinations in South America, California, the Caribbean, Australia, and the Dutch East Indies. Since they came from a *Kulturvolk,* Andree argued, such workers were more valuable and reliable than Native Americans, Pacific Islanders, Africans, and mixed-race populations who were unsuited to "higher purposes."[51] The increased circulation of Asian laborers in the global economy would help to resolve the "massive ethnic crisis" that European contact with the indigenous populations in America and the Pacific had first brought about and that the piecemeal dismantlement of the Africa slave trade had exacerbated. "Now is the time for those 300-million yellow-gold East Asians to become cosmopolitical. Until now, their powers were tied down and restricted to a limited area. Now they will be released and travel overseas in search of work everywhere they can find it."[52]

An east Asian "exodus" would be a boon to the world economy, particularly to the development of trans-Pacific commerce between China, Japan, and the western coastlines of North and South America. Andree noted the increased use of Japanese workers on American-run sugar and coffee plantations in Hawai'i and the growth of the Chinese labor force in California.[53] As replacements for the "passive" and indolent Polynesian islanders, the more industrious and "energetic Asians" would vastly improve the speed and efficiency of tropical commodity production. He compared the trans-Pacific flow of emigrants from China with the transatlantic migration of European workers to Brazil, Argentina, and North America, which the new steam and rail networks circling the globe had made possible.[54]

The reliance on African laborers and indigenous populations for the production of foodstuffs and tropical goods for European consumption would be greatly lessened by the opening up of China to the world's labor markets, Andree assured his readers. The deployment of new technologies to transport more resilient, industrious workers from Asia, who had been selected on the basis of their purported cultural and racial attributes, would alleviate the negative effects of European global expansion on those indigenous populations that had perished as a result of contact with foreign cultures. The demographic upheavals of the transatlantic slave trade and the European settlement of Australia, New Zealand, and the Americas had fundamentally transformed the global landscape by destroying indigenous populations and replacing them with millions of new colonists. The arrival of the "white, civilized man" sealed the "death sentence for those less resilient human types, the savages and half-savages of the world" in a process that was "tragic" and a "melancholy drama," but that was an unavoidable effect of the modern economy:[55] the most primitive of the world's populations, like the aboriginal peoples of Australia, New Zealand, and Tasmania, were destined for extinction.[56]

For Andree, race was an essential scientific instrument for studying the ongoing expansion of European influence overseas. He focused on how colonialism had altered the global distribution of the world's population through the establishment of long-distance networks of labor, trade, and commercial production. The economic changes brought on by the technological advances of the mid-nineteenth century, Andree argued, were of such significance for the relationship between the world's major populations that earlier forms of knowledge, particularly those derived from religion and humanistic studies of antiquity, were inadequate to understanding the present: "The world has become wider, the peoples of the world have moved closer together. There are no more isolated regions, and the world's traffic has become cosmopolitical. … Today, one looks at humankind completely differently than before."[57]

To explain variations within Europe, Andree also relied heavily on notions of cultural and racial mixing that reflected his understandings of the impact of the Middle East, Asia, and northern Africa on European history. The "savage, dark, and bigoted" aspects of the Spanish character, he suggested, were due to the influence of the "Moorish element" and Spain's geographic proximity to Africa.[58] In southern Italy, the "fetishism" of Catholics who venerated saints' monuments and practiced "colorful, sumptuous rituals" was not much more developed than the religious rites of the African "Negro."[59] Outside of the United States, *Globus* reported on the status of mixed-race populations in a variety of colonial settings.[60] The world was portrayed as being in motion, characterized by changing racial configurations and cultural influences. Racial mixing was a secondary effect of the process of European global expansion. This perspective was forcefully articulated in Andree's discussions of the rise of what he variously referred to as "half-breeds," "*Mischlinge*," "mulattoes," "mestizos," or "Ladinos" in Central America.[61] The Dutch-speaking "Malaysians" of the Cape Colony, *Globus* reported, resembled "Spanish and French Basques" in appearance, with "a slender figure, strong body shape, and pleasant facial features."[62]

Using ideas of racial character, Andree even sought to reinterpret the major events of European history in terms of the intellectual and moral differences between various European "essences," "elements," "types," and "characters."[63] The Germanic qualities of rationality, independence, physical toughness, sobriety, and asceticism, he maintained, were opposed to "Gallic," "Latin," or "Celto-Romantic" affection for authoritarian rule, obedience, superstition, emotionality, playfulness, and spectacle. In order to describe the "characters" of the great military, political, religious, artistic, and intellectual men of European history, Andree made similar use of racial, cultural, and ethnic terminology. Raphael was an "Italian type," while Michelangelo was influenced by his "Gothic blood." Voltaire's sense of humor, phraseology, and superficiality made him an example of a "Celt of Gallic descent." Oliver Cromwell was a typical "Anglo-Saxon," Napoleon a "Greco-Italian Frenchman," and George Washington was "Germanic." William

Shakespeare was from an amalgamated "Celto-Teutonic race, commonly called the Anglo-Saxon" that harmonized the "fiery passion" of the Celtic peoples with the "warmth of Germanic affection and love."[64]

The Political Economy of the Global Color Line

In drawing readers' attention to the circulation of foreign laborers, the expansion of the European colonial empire, and the processes of cultural assimilation in overseas locations, *Globus* made questions of racial identity a critical component for the understanding of the dynamics of modern history.[65] A proper recognition of the role played by racial differences inside and outside of Europe, Andree held, was essential for promoting economic growth and maintaining social cohesion. By intervening forcefully in transnational debates over race, slavery, and free labor, scientific popularizers helped to disseminate a new wave of images of the black diaspora during a time of German liberal resurgence, national unification, and informal imperial expansion.[66] They cast doubt on abolitionist claims and created a method for using race to understand changes in the world economy that had clear implications for Germany's later experiments in colonial development.[67] Given the fact that Germany was not a slave-holding society and possessed no colonial empire of its own at the time, it is striking to note the intensity with which such topics were discussed in the German press at the midcentury, and—if Ratzel is to be believed—among ordinary men and women in beer halls and afternoon tearooms.[68]

At the same time, these dialogues also suggest a degree of resistance among sectors of the German public to scientific justifications of slavery and plantation labor regimes. Ratzel too showed signs of uncertainty about the best methods for increasing the economic productivity of black workers. During his American travels, he expressed negative opinions about the ability of former slaves to participate in political life in the United States and regarded them as easily manipulated pawns of white elected officials.[69] In the 1880 edition of his geographical and cultural history of the United States, however, he wrote of the successes of the sharecropping system in increasing the level of cotton exports beyond prewar levels. When forced to provide for themselves in the wage labor economy, African American freedmen achieved impressive levels of growth. In surveying the conditions in the American South after the end of Reconstruction, Ratzel concluded that the end of slavery had not led to an economic collapse. He still regarded Africans as inferior to whites as manual laborers, but he admitted that African Americans were no longer "men of the tropics who live like children in nature and do not work."[70] Ratzel's scientific prejudices prevented him from regarding African Americans as intellectual equals, but his softened attitude toward their potential for useful work in the global commodities market created a space for negotiation with individuals, like Booker T. Washington, who were associated with the Tuskegee Institute.[71]

In the early 1870s, Ratzel toured not only the United States but also Cuba and Mexico. These experiences influenced his views about territorial expansion and population growth, which he would later develop into systematic theoretical form.[72] Jens-Uwe Guettel has shown that Ratzel judged the availability of new land and natural resources in the American West to be essential for the future growth and prosperity of the United States. He was critical of settler violence against Native Americans but believed that more industrious peoples were destined to make better use of the continent.[73] Ratzel also developed an interest in the impact of Chinese migration in the West and criticized efforts by California officials to restrict the settlement of such potentially skilled wage labor.[74] So taken was he with the Chinese communities he encountered that he made them the central focus of his research upon returning to Germany. His 1876 monograph *Chinese Migration* was a historical investigation of Chinese continental expansion, overseas colonization, the "coolie trade," and diasporic community building that represented east Asian society as a dynamic center of civilization and commerce.[75] Six years later, safely established as a professor in Munich, Ratzel would synthesize his findings as "human geography" (*Anthropogeographie*), which applied the principles of earth science to the study of history.[76] In the 1870s, his global vision was still one dominated by migratory peoples in motion, not of expanding states and empires. By the mid-1880s, on the eve of German colonialism in Africa and the Pacific, Ratzel's views were again in flux, and he became a vocal supporter of the colonial movement. His later views on overseas migration and *Lebensraum*, however, were built upon his earlier encounters in America and writings on slavery, migration, and black emancipation.

Conclusion

The latest wave of scholarship on German colonialism has generated new interest in Germany's long history of connections with both Africa and the black diaspora, but it seldom takes into account the impact of transatlantic factors in shaping German attitudes toward race.[77] Afro-German history also has focused primarily on contact with persons of African descent during the late nineteenth and twentieth centuries.[78] While of vital importance, this research fails to capture the full spectrum of competing images of black identity that circulated in nineteenth-century Germany. As a result of midcentury debates over slavery, race, and free labor, popular scientific writers like Andree and Ratzel saturated the public sphere with a wide array of stories about the changing makeup of the world's populations resulting from globalization. These stories affected German perceptions of race decades before the onset of formal colonization in Africa and the

Pacific.[79] A better understanding of the transatlantic debates over race, slavery, and African American identity puts the history of German colonialism within a global context, one in which questions of Native American genocide and east Asian labor migration are equally relevant. Exploring these fascinating connections is an essential task in recasting the existing narratives of modern German as well as modern world history.

Notes

1. F. R. [Friedrich Ratzel], "Weisse und Farbige im Indischen Archipelagus," *Globus: Illustrierte Zeitschrift für Länder- und Völkerkunde* 16 (1869): 375–78.
2. On Ratzel's early journalistic experiences and relationship with *Globus*, see Günther Buttmann, *Friedrich Ratzel: Leben und Werk eines deutschen Geographen 1844–1904* (Stuttgart, Germany: Wissenschaftliche Verlagsgesellschaft, 1977), 30–33.
3. Ratzel, "Weisse und Farbige," 375. All translations by Bradley Naranch unless otherwise indicated.
4. Much of the current scholarship on nineteenth-century German views of slavery focuses on the role of German emigrants and political exiles (Forty-Eighters) in the United States. See Mischa Honeck, *We Are the Revolutionists: German-Speaking Immigrants and American Abolitionists after 1848* (Athens: University of Georgia Press, 2011); Harmut Keil, "Das Verhältnis deutscher Immigranten zu Sklaverei und Abolition in der Mitte des 19. Jahrhunderts," in *Migration und Erinnerung: Reflexionen über Wanderunserfahrungen in Europa und Nordamerika*, ed. Christiane Harzig (Göttingen, Germany: Vandenhoeck & Ruprecht, 2006), 105–22; and Harmut Keil, "German Immigrants and African Americans in Mid-Nineteenth Century America," in *Enemy Images in American History*, ed. Ragnild Fiebig-von Hase and Ursula Lehmkult (Providence, RI: Berghahn Books, 1997), 137–57.
5. Ratzel, "Weisse und Farbige," 377–78.
6. Heike Paul, *Kulturkontakt und Racial Presences: Afro-Amerikaner und die deutsche Amerika-Literatur, 1815–1914* (Heidelberg, Germany: Winter, 2005), esp. 97–108, 156–65; and also her contribution in this volume. The role of 1848-era German immigrants in the political debates over slavery in the midwestern states of Kansas and Nebraska is covered by Bruce Levine, *The Spirit of 1848: German Immigrants, Labor Conflict, and the Coming of the Civil War* (Urbana: University of Illinois Press, 1992), 149–212. For a case study from the American South, see Jeff Strickland, "Ethnicity and Race in the Urban South: German Immigrants and African Americans in Charleston, South Carolina, during Reconstruction" (PhD diss., Florida State University, 2003).
7. Public criticism in the Netherlands of colonial labor practices in the East Indies was prompted in part by the publication of Eduard Douwes Dekker's novel *Max Havelaar* in 1860, under the pseudonym Multatuli: *Max Havelaar: Or the Coffee Auctions of the Dutch Trading Company*, trans. Roy Edwards (New York: Penguin Books, 1987). See also the analysis provided by Ann-Marie Feenberg, "Max Havelaar: An Anti-Imperialist Novel," *MLN* 112, no. 5 (1997): 817–35.
8. Ratzel, "Weisse und Farbige," 378.
9. Alfred Kelley, *The Descent of Darwin: The Popularization of Darwinism in Germany, 1860–1914* (Chapel Hill: University of North Carolina Press, 1981).

10. Catherine Hall, *Civilising Subjects: Metropole and Colony in the English Imagination 1830–1867* (Chicago: University of Chicago Press, 2002), 440.
11. Heike Paul, "Schwarze Sklaven, weisse Sklaven: The German Reception of Harriet Beecher-Stowe's *Uncle Tom's Cabin*," in *Amerikanische Populärkultur in Deutschland: Case Studies in Cultural Transfer Past and Present*, ed. Katja Kanzler and Heike Paul (Leipzig, Germany: Leipziger Universitätsverlag, 2002), 21–39.
12. Paul, *Kulturkontakt*, 127–85. See also Heike Paul's contribution in this volume.
13. Paul, *Kulturkontakt*, 229–78, 315–16.
14. Ibid., 277.
15. Geoff Eley, "Historicizing the Global, Politicizing Capital: Giving the Present a Name," *History Workshop Journal* 63 (2007): 164–66.
16. Andrew Zimmerman, *Alabama in Africa: Booker T. Washington, the German Empire, and the Globalization of the New South* (Princeton, NJ: Princeton University Press, 2010); Sven Beckert, "Von Tuskegee nach Togo: Das Problem der Freiheit im Reich der Baumwolle," *Geschichte und Gesellschaft* 31 (2005): 505–45; see also Kendahl Radcliffe's contribution in this volume.
17. Friedrich Ratzel, *Die Vereinigten Staaten von Nord-Amerika*, vol. 2, *Culturgeographie unter besonderer Berücksichtigung der wirhschaftlichen Verhältnisse* (Munich: R. Oldenbourg, 1880), 107–60. On German literary representations of Native Americans, see H. Glenn Penny, "Elusive Authenticity: The Quest for the Authentic Indian in German Public Culture," *Comparative Studies in Society and History* 48, no. 4 (2006): 798–818; Colin G. Calloway, Gerd Gemunden, and Susanne Zantop, eds., *Germans and Indians: Fantasies, Projections, Encounters* (Lincoln: University of Nebraska Press, 2002); and Jeffrey Sammons, *Ideology, Mimesis, Fantasy: Charles Sealsfield, Friedrich Gerstäcker, Karl May, and Other German Novelists of America* (Chapel Hill: University of North Carolina Press, 1998).
18. Ratzel, *Die Vereinigten Staaten*, 195–218.
19. Richard Andree, "Karl Andree," in *Karl Andree's Geographie des Welthandels*, ed. Franz Heiderich and Robert Sieger (Frankfurt: Heinrich Keller, 1910), 1:3–11.
20. Karl Andree, *Geographische Wanderungen*, 2 vols. (Dresden, Germany: Rudolf Kuntze, 1859).
21. Woodruff D. Smith, *Politics and the Sciences of Culture in Germany, 1840–1920* (New York: Oxford University Press, 1991), 91–94.
22. Karl Andree, *Die Geographie des Welthandels*, 2nd ed. (Stuttgart, Germany: Julius Maier, 1877), 1.
23. Karl Andree, "Das Erwachen der Südsee," in K. Andree, *Geographische Wanderungen*, 2:318–20.
24. Karl Andree, "Die Neger und Weissen in Nordamerika," *Globus* 1 (1862): 287; K. Andree, "Anzeichen des Rassenkampfes in Nordamerika," *Globus* 9 (1866): 153–56.
25. K. Andree, *Geographie des Welthandels*, 461–78; and Karl Andree, "Die afrikanische Republik Liberia und die Farbigen in den Vereinigten Staaten von Nordamerika," in K. Andree, *Geographische Wanderungen*, 2:350–75.
26. Duncan Bell, *The Idea of Greater Britain* (Cambridge: Cambridge University Press, 2008); and Reginald Horsman, *Race and Manifest Destiny: The Origins of Racial Anglo-Saxonism* (Cambridge, MA: Harvard University Press, 1981).
27. Karl Andree, "In Onkel Toms Urheimat," in K. Andree, *Geographische Wanderungen*, 2: 376–404.
28. Ibid., 404.
29. K. Andree, "Die afrikanische Republik Liberia," 2:350–75.
30. Ibid., 367.
31. K. Andree, "In Onkel Toms Urheimat," 382-403.
32. K. Andree, "Die afrikanische Republik Liberia," 356.
33. Karl Andree, *Geographie des Welthandels mit geschichtlichen Erläuterungen*, 3 vols. (Stuttgart, Germany: Julius Maier, 1861–77).

34. R. Andree, "Karl Andree," 10.
35. Karl Andree, "Introduction," *Globus* 1 (1862): iii–iv.
36. Ibid., iv.
37. Andreas Daum, *Wissenschaftspopularisierung im 19. Jahrhundert: Bürgerliche Kultur, naturwissenschaftliche Bildung, und die deutsche Öffentlichkeit 1848–1914*, 2nd ed. (Munich: Oldenburg, 2000); and Kirsten Belgum, *Popularizing the Nation: Audience, Representation, and the Production of Identity in* Die Gartenlaube (Lincoln: University of Nebraska Press, 1998).
38. K. Andree, "Die Neger und Weissen in Nordamerika," 287; K. Andree, "Anzeichen des Rassenkampfes in Nordamerika," 153–56.
39. K. Andree, "Die Neger in Central-Amerika," *Globus* 3 (1863): 94.
40. Daum, *Wissenschaftspopularisierung,* 65–84, 300–7; Woodruff D. Smith, *Politics and the Sciences of Culture in Germany, 1840–1920* (New York: Oxford University Press, 1991), 91–94.
41. K. Andree, "Die Wichtigkeit des Rassenelements in der Geschichte: Gegen Heinrich Thomas Buckle's *Geschichte der Civilisation*," *Globus* 9 (1866): 135–39. For similar disputes in 1860s Britain, see Catherine Hall, "Competing Masculinities: Thomas Carlyle, John Stuart Mill, and the Case of Governor Eyre," in *White, Male, and Middle Class: Explorations in Feminism and History* (Cambridge: Cambridge University Press, 1992), 255-93; and Felix Driver, *Geography Militant: Cultures of Exploration and Empire* (Oxford: Blackwell, 2001), 96–100.
42. K. Andree, "Anthropologische Beiträge I," *Globus* 10 (1866): 57. For background on the London Anthropological Society, see J.W. Burrow, "Evolution and Anthropology in the 1860s: The Anthropological Society of London, 1863–71," *Victorian Studies* 7 (1963): 137–54; Ronald Rainger, "Race, Politics, and Science: The Anthropological Society of London," *Victorian Studies* (1978): 51–70; and George W. Stocking Jr., *Victorian Anthropology* (New York: Free Press, 1987).
43. K. Andree, "Die Veränderungen in der gegenseitigen Stellung der Menschenrassen und die wirtschaftlichen Verhältnisse," *Globus* 14 (1868), 19; see also K. Andree, "Raceneigenthümlichkeiten und Charakteranlagen," *Globus* 11 (1867): 19–21.
44. K. Andree, "Anzeichen des Rassenkampfes in Nordamerika," 153–56.
45. Ibid., 154.
46. K. Andree, "Die Veränderungen," 18.
47. K. Andree, "Die afrikanische Republik Liberia," 370.
48. Ibid., 371–74.
49. Karl Andree, "Umwandlungen im Weltverkehr der Neuzeit: Colonialwaaren, Colonialarbeiter, Sklaverei," *Deutsche Vierteljahreschrift* 73 (January 1856).
50. K. Andree, "Die Veränderungen," 18.
51. On the distinctions between *Culturvolk* and *Naturvolk* in German anthropological discourse, see Andrew Zimmermann, *Anthropology and Antihumanism in Imperial Germany* (Chicago: University of Chicago Press, 2001), 38, 213–16.
52. K. Andree, "Die Veränderungen," 21.
53. K. Andree, "Die ostasiatische Auswanderung," *Globus* 14 (1868): 87–89.
54. Ibid., 88.
55. K. Andree, "Anthropologische Beiträge II," *Globus* 10 (1866): 143.
56. K. Andree, "Das Erwachen der Südsee," 2:318–20.
57. K. Andree, "Die Veränderungen," 17.
58. K. Andree, "Die Wichtigkeit des Rassenelements," 138.
59. K. Andree, "Die drei grossen Völkergruppen," *Globus* 12 (1867): 77.
60. K. Andree, "Die 'Malaien' der Kapstadt," *Globus* 3 (1863): 126; and K. Andree, "Ethnologische Beiträge I," *Globus* 3 (1863): 280–82.
61. Karl Andree, "Ein Blick auf Central-Amerika," in K. Andree, *Geographische Wanderungen,* 2:88–120.

62. K. Andree, "Die 'Malaien' der Kapstadt," 126.
63. K. Andree, "Die Wichtigkeit des Rassenelements," 138; and K. Andree, "Raceneigenthümlichkeiten," 20.
64. K. Andree, "Raceneigenthümlichkeiten," 20–21.
65. K. Andree, "Ethnologische Beiträge I," 280; and Karl Andree, "Prologue," in K. Andree, *Geographische Wanderungen*, 1:ii.
66. Matthew P. Fitzpatrick, *Liberal Imperialism in Germany: Expansionism and Nationalism 1848–1884* (New York: Berghahn Books, 2008).
67. Sebastian Conrad, *Globalisierung und Nation im deutschen Kaiserreich* (Munich: C.H. Beck, 2006).
68. Such interest supports the arguments of Susanne Zantop about the significance of colonial fantasy in nineteenth-century Germany. See Zantop, *Colonial Fantasies: Conquest, Family, and the Nation in Precolonial Germany, 1770–1870* (Durham, NC: Duke University Press, 1997).
69. Paul, *Kulturkontakt*, 239; and Ratzel, *Die Vereinigten Staaten von Nord-Amerika*, 205–6.
70. Ratzel, *Die Vereinigten Staaten von Nord-Amerika*, 2:211.
71. Paul, *Kulturkontakt*, 298–99; and Andrew Zimmerman, "A German Alabama in Africa: The Tuskegee Expedition to German Togo and the Transnational Origins of West African Cotton Growers," *American Historical Review* 110, no. 5 (2005): 1362–98. See also Radcliffe's contribution in this volume.
72. Friedrich Ratzel, *Städte- und Kulturbilder aus Nordamerika*, 2 vols. (Leipzig, Germany: Brockhaus, 1876); Mark Bassin, "Friedrich Ratzel's Travels in the United States: A Study in the Genesis of his Anthropogeography," *History of Geography Newsletter* 4 (1984): 115–34; and Woodruff D. Smith, "Friedrich Ratzel and the Origins of Lebensraum," *German Studies Review* 3 (1980): 58.
73. Jens-Uwe Guettel, "Reading America, Studying Empire: German Perceptions of Indians, Slavery, and the American West, 1789–1900" (PhD diss., Yale University, 2007), 242–49.
74. Friedrich Ratzel, "Die Entwicklung des Westens der Vereinigten Staaten," *Globus* 36, 237–38; Friedrich Ratzel, "Über Californien (1876)," in *Kleine Schriften*, vol. 2, ed. Hans Helmolt (Munich: R. Oldenbourg, 1906), 1–18; and Friedrich Ratzel, "Ostasien und die Vereinigten Staaten," in Helmolt, *Kleine Schriften*, 291–93.
75. Friedrich Ratzel, *Die chinesische Auswanderung* (Breslau, Poland: F. U. Kern, 1876).
76. Friedrich Ratzel, *Anthropogeographie: oder Grundzüge der Anwendung der Erdkunde auf die Geschichte* (Stuttgart, Germany: J. Engelhorn, 1882–1891).
77. Patricia Mazón and Reinhild Steingröver, eds., *Not So Plain as Black and White: Afro-German Culture and History, 1890–2000* (Rochester, NY: University of Rochester Press, 2005); Marianne Klein-Arendt and Reinhard Klein-Arendt, eds., *AfrikanerInnen in Deutschland und Schwarze Deutsche: Geschichte und Gegenwart* (Münster, Germany: LIT, 2004); Marianne Bechhaus-Gerst, ed., *Die (koloniale) Begegnung: AfrikanerInnen in Deutschland 1880–1945, Deutsche in Afrika 1880–1918* (New York: Lang, 2003); Michael Peraudin and Jürgen Zimmerer, eds., *German Colonialism and National Identity* (London: Routledge, 2010); Eric Ames, Marcia Klotz, and Lora Wildenthal, eds., *Germany's Colonial Pasts* (Lincoln: University of Nebraska Press, 2005); Alexander Honold and Klaus R. Sherpe, eds., *Mit Deutschland um die Welt: Eine Kulturgeschichte des Fremden in der Kolonialzeit* (Stuttgart, Germany: J. B. Metzler, 2004); Birthe Kundrus, ed., *Phantasiereiche: Zur Kulturgeschichte des Deutschen Kolonialismus* (New York: Campus, 2003); and Sara Friedrichsmeyer, Sara Lennox, and Susanne Zantop, eds., *The Imperialist Imagination: German Colonialism and Its Legacy* (Ann Arbor: University of Michigan Press, 1998).
78. Raffel Scheck, *Hitler's African Victims: The German Army Massacres of Black French Soliders in 1940* (New York: Cambridge University Press, 2006); Heide Fehrenbach, *Race after Hitler: Black Occupation Children in Postwar Germany and America* (Princeton, NJ: Princeton Uni-

versity Press, 2005); Tina M. Campt, *Other Germans: Black Germans and the Politics of Race, Gender, and Memory in the Third Reich* (Ann Arbor: University of Michigan Press, 2004); Clarence Lusane, *Hitler's Black Victims: The Historical Experiences of Afro-Germans, European Blacks, Africans, and African Americans in the Nazi Era* (New York: Routledge, 2003); Fatima El-Tayeb, *Schwarze Deutsche: Der Diskurs um "Rasse" und nationale Identität, 1890–1933* (Frankfurt: Campus, 2001); and May Opitz, Katharine Oguntoye, and Dagmar Schultz, eds., *Showing Our Colors: Afro-German Women Speak Out,* trans. Anne V. Adams (Amherst: University of Massachusetts Press, 1992).
79. George Steinmetz, *The Devil's Handwriting: Precoloniality and the German Colonial States in Qingdao, Samoa, and Southwest Africa* (Chicago: University of Chicago Press, 2007).

Chapter Ten

WE SHALL MAKE FARMERS OF THEM YET
Tuskegee's Uplift Ideology in German Togoland

Kendahl L. Radcliffe

In 1900, a group of nine individuals made up of Tuskegee Institute students, staff, and graduates were invited by the Kolonial Wirtschaftliches Komitee to develop cotton plantations in the German colony of Togo.[1] Tuskegee Institute's participation in this colonial venture occurred at a time when European and American imperial power seemed unchallengeable to those who suffered under its weight. Yet, despite the constraints of the systems of American segregation and European colonialism, the Tuskegee personnel sought to promote pan-African solidarity and development through the cotton-growing project.

The historical transatlantic triangle of the Tuskegee Institute, German Togo, and Germany is important in three ways (see map 10.1). First, it brings into sharp relief African and African American attempts to become self-sufficient within the newly established economic and racial order of the Atlantic world. Both the oppressive systems of Jim Crow in the United States and racialist colonial policies imposed in Africa required that people of African descent utilize a backdoor approach in entering this new global system. I argue that the concept of the local and the global already existed within the African American identity. By 1900, almost a half a century removed from slavery, black people on both sides of the Atlantic could nurture that inner connection with diaspora on their own terms. In the context of the local/global, my dissertation, "The Tuskegee-Togo Cotton Scheme, 1900–1909" (1998), was the first in-depth study to chronologically reconstruct these historic events as they unfolded and to explore the theme of "racial uplift" as a pan-Africanist response to turn-of-the-century globalization. Andrew Zimmerman has since engaged with these themes in his own work,

---

Notes from this chapter begin on page 208.

188 | *Kendahl L. Radcliffe*

Map 10.1. Map of German Togoland (Source: Albert F. Calvert, *Togoland* [London: T.W. Laurie ltd., 1918], Plate I).

privileging the more contemporary term "transnational" and also providing a valuable, comprehensive look at German colonial labor policy from a Marxist perspective.

However, the recent discourse on the scheme tends to deemphasize the idea of racial uplift, a core value shared throughout the diaspora at the time, and focuses on German colonial observations, void of intimacy with African American interpretations of what actually transpired in Togo. My intent here is to re-center this core value I explored earlier but in greater detail with respect to the different methods and perspectives of the men instructed to implement "uplift" on the ground: James Nathan Calloway, the leader of the expedition; John Winfrey Robinson, the last to remain in Togo; and Booker T. Washington, the Tuskegee Institute founder and leader.

Racial uplift was about smoothing the treacherous path toward full enfranchisement via economic, political, and social institution building from within. Opinions varied concerning which collective approach should be pursued. In the classic academic sense, uplift is often perceived as a black, middle-class, trickle-down undertaking in its aim to improve the spiritual, intellectual, and material needs of black folks. However, the uplift agenda relied less on the dictates of the black middle class and white acceptance, and more on the collective support and approval of the overwhelmingly poor black masses. Some argued for an aggressive approach; others argued for a more cautious, measured one. Men like Washington worked hard to garner such collective support by emphasizing an aggressive economic approach along with a tempered political agenda to be administered in small doses to a hostile white America.

Uplift is often portrayed as an "ethnocentric" folly of the African American imagination. According to Zimmerman:

> The collaboration of Tuskegee Institute with the German government of Togo brought together two dimensions of African cotton growing, which reflected two dimensions of colonization of Africa: on the one hand, an emancipatory, if misguided and ethnocentric, effort to improve the conditions of blacks on both sides of the Atlantic; and, on the other hand an anti-emancipatory effort to establish black cotton farming in Africa that would enrich white economic elites in Europe as much as it did their counterparts in the United States.[2]

Far from a folly, it was a necessary tool of the struggle. Zimmerman's description of Tuskegean involvement in German colonial designs as complicit indicates that his view does not take into account the complex nature of the private and public agenda of people of African descent under the relentless violence of the yoke of segregation and colonialism.[3]

Equally problematic in this perspective is how it posits "ethnocentrism" as a pathway to African American "colonial" designs. In the early twentieth century,

African Americans and Africans found themselves constantly negotiating these segregated and colonial spaces in an attempt to undermine them. This assertion of agency is crucial to understanding the African American mind-set and intent at that time. It was about creating possibilities to restore black people to the best of their abilities under such dire circumstances. Engaging the Germans was a tactical strategy, not a blind pursuit or mimicry of the German agenda. These young men were part of a privileged few (one generation removed from slavery) with an overwhelming understanding of the responsibility and significance of what it meant to "return home." What we find in this narrative is the desire to connect with and understand a part of themselves that the Germans would not necessarily relate to, nor come to know. We also find the perennial conflict between public and private, local and global. To paraphrase Marx, through the dialectic of reason we find the truth. These men were in search of their own truth however flawed, and this should not be dismissed as folly nor as a case of two sides of the same "colonial" coin. Africans and African Americans were a subjugated people and the Germans were a colonial power.[4]

Second, the historic triangle emphasizes some of the practical and problematic issues on an institutional level. The Tuskegee effort in Togo challenges many assumptions held about German colonial economic policies and, by implication, highlights the extent to which the "Tuskegee Model" captured the imagination of European officials and influenced colonial policy. However, with regard to this saga, it is important to emphasize that "a major Black-American institution engaged directly with a world power—Germany—without intervention of the U.S. government or a philanthropic institution."[5] For it was the Tuskegean approach that had caught the attention of the Germans, who were also developing a philosophy of utilizing scientific agriculture to solve their own dependence on foreign agricultural products. Conversely, from the Tuskegee perspective—and this needs to be stressed—the endeavor in Togo was a reflection of the institution's overall concern with the economic development of Africa and Africans under colonialism in spite of it. Indeed, the transference of the "Tuskegee model" of agricultural education (even with its flaws) would contribute to transforming the farming practices of the Togolese and the African landscape.[6]

Finally, the Tuskegee/Germany/Togoland triangle sheds light on Booker T. Washington's habit of making sure that African American concerns with regard to Africa rode on the coattails of American interests, perhaps to a fault. Sometimes, the administration's interests were not clearly defined, but Washington still sought to affect policy and diplomacy as it related to Africa and often succeeded. Writing to the editor of the *Colored American,* he noted that sections of Africa not under the direct control of a European country could nevertheless be within a "sphere of influence" such as that of the United States. "If we are to go to Africa and be under the control of another government," he argued, "I would prefer to take our chances in the sphere of influence of the United States."[7]

Washington was not overtly opposed to colonialism, but he opposed colonial policy that displaced people of African descent completely from their land. Whether this ideology could be reconciled with the purpose of a colonial economy based on conscripted labor is debatable. Many Germans had a racialist, highly paternalistic perception of "Negroes," yet credited African Americans with valuable skills and abilities. As one contemporary observer put it: "It is often thought that the Negro of North America, completely entrusted with cotton cultivation, are more suitable for the education of their Black African brothers in this regard than Europeans."[8] This was a perception a man like Booker T. Washington could exploit on a level that worked to his advantage to wield his influence on even the most ardent racist. These dynamics had a profound impact on the future of colonial discourse on Africa and the role that Europeans saw African Americans playing in their colonial grand designs. At the same time, it was a tactic in which Washington was a prominent actor, a fact that did not go unnoticed by his critics.[9]

Washington's 1895 "Cotton Exposition" speech, in which he encouraged black America to "cast down your buckets where you are,"[10] was an attempt to bring a halt to the exodus of African Americans from the South and to oppose the ongoing discussions of African American emigration to Africa. As far as Washington was concerned, at that time most black colonization schemes were endorsed by agencies of imperialism. Yet, by the close of the century, his writings manifest his decision to take a more cautious approach: to wait and see about the role blacks could play in the imperial order.[11] For instance, in his 1899 letter to the editor of the *Colored American,* he wrote:

> Henry M. Stanley the explorer ... tells me that he knows no place in Africa where we of the United States might go to advantage, but I want to be more specific. Let us see how Africa has been divided and then decide whether there is a place left for us.[12]

However, the future economic ramifications of the Togo project for Tuskegee and its reputation were too great to ignore. At the same time, he denied that this effort conflicted with his long-held opposition to emigration schemes: "This is not in any sense an emigration scheme, as all these person[s] were hired to work at salary by the Colonial Society."[13]

The Kolonial Wirtschaftliches Komitee, Cotton, and the Pacification of the "Natives"

The established, primary supplier of raw cotton to Germany, England, and France in the late nineteenth century was the United States. Between 1897 and 1902, it produced about 75 percent of the world's cotton. During the same period, 75 to

85 percent of England's cotton imports came from America. In Germany, where textile manufacturing was the second-largest industry, 70 to 82 percent of the cotton came from US producers.[14]

Europe had long faced periodic crises in cotton supply. In the early part of the nineteenth century, the Napoleonic Wars had for a time created shortages of raw cotton. A second and more damaging crisis was the Civil War and the effect of the Union blockade of 1861–65 on the export of raw cotton. It caused a temporary collapse in the textile manufacturing industry in Europe, a situation creating widespread unemployment, destitution, and even starvation. The third crisis emerged gradually in the last quarter of the nineteenth century. In that period, American textile manufacturing expanded and, in the process, consumed more and more of the American cotton crop. By the beginning of the twentieth century, the cotton shortage for textile manufacturers outside the United States had become acute.[15]

On 18 June 1896, Karl Supf, a German businessman, die-hard colonialist, and ardent supporter of cotton cultivation in Africa, met with eleven other businessmen to discuss the formation of a cotton council that would actively pursue and encourage colonial development of the product. They called themselves the "Committee for the Importation of Products from the German Colonies." Their goals were "the winning of the German industry and commerce over to using and distributing the products of German colonies together with the furthering of the economic development of our colonies." In 1897, they renamed themselves the Kolonial Wirtschaftliches Komitee (Colonial Economic Committee, hereafter the KWK).[16]

The KWK was a joint-stock institution combining private firms with close governmental ties that could support extensive research programs in the field of colonial agriculture as it related to cotton. It sought to combine "practical knowledge with scientific results."[17] The KWK was divided into nine departments that investigated improved farming techniques and the implements used in farming, and conducted experiments in cotton agriculture—all with the aim of "protecting" the textile industry. The KWK also applied pressure on the government to improve colonial infrastructures, calling for it to build roads and railways in its overseas possessions.[18] Because of the urgency to produce cotton, the KWK ceased its research in the German South Pacific colonies in 1902 and instead focused its efforts solely on Africa and, more specifically, on Togo. It produced an official publication, *Der Tropenpflanzer*, which not only described the technical details of various agricultural experiments, but also functioned as a tool of colonial propaganda to be utilized in Germany.[19] The publication's main goal was to use "scientific agriculture" to find a more efficient way to exploit cotton. Neither France nor Britain had an equivalent interest group like the KWK for their African colonies in either the private or public sector until some years later.[20]

The hostile nature of the relationship between German colonial officials and Africans in Togo in the 1890s created a situation in which the Germans were forced to pay a fair price for cash crops grown by peasants in order to get any portion of a viable crop for export to Germany. Yet German firms grew increasingly unwilling to pay such a price, and the crop had to be introduced by military force in some areas, with German officials dictating the farming methods to be employed. Soldiers from the nearest military station then bought up the harvest at a price authorities fixed in faraway Bremen.[21]

The colonies represented a potential end to German dependence on American-grown agricultural products. The key to making it work was the "pacification" of the "natives" and, as Supf put it, "making the Natives economically dependent on us." He added that "[o]nly the economic dependence of the people will actually make us masters of our colonies." One way to encourage Africans to grow cotton was through a head tax payable in cotton. "The contribution of tax to the protecting power is for the native an almost natural thing," Supf argued, as it was equivalent to paying tribute to the chief. In his view, cotton would form the "cornerstone" of the cultural development of the colonies. He envisioned giving gins to villagers throughout Togoland.[22] In essence, Africans would own the gins and other implements of farming, but neither the land on which they worked nor the cotton they produced. This would be in direct conflict with Washington's Tuskegee agenda.

The Tuskegee Model and Scientific Agriculture

The concepts of industrial education and engaging in scientific agriculture were already strong currents of thought in Europe. Europeans were intent on developing scientific agriculture, and Germany, for its part, spent a great deal of time and money developing industrial education and scientific agriculture to improve its own industries and farming productivity during the second half of the nineteenth century. The growth of industrial education was directly related to the growth of industry in Europe and the United States. Industry growth required new skills and improvements in worker knowledge.

This attitude spilled over into agriculture as it became increasingly tied to industrialization, mechanization, and the sciences. The everyday farmer and his farm were no longer seen as efficient or employing a structured methodology or system. Rather, "[a]n understanding of geology, meteorology, botany, horticulture, zoology, biology, and entomology were all important to the 'system,'"[23] that is, the system of scientific agriculture. In colonial Togo, the German concern was to teach Africans to grow cotton in a "rational" and "scientific way" with the hope of securing a cheaper supply of cotton and ending Germany's dependence on American-grown cotton.[24]

It was Tuskegee's use of scientific agriculture as a way to improve independent farm productivity that caught the attention of the Germans, who also utilized this approach in their attempt to end their dependence on foreign-grown agricultural products. Aware of Tuskegee's reputation, the KWK sought Booker T. Washington's assistance. From their perspective, the possibility of ending the United States' near monopoly of cotton production required, and in fact depended on, the cooperation and skills of the Tuskegee experts.[25]

Washington himself equated black self-sufficiency with black land ownership and the development of resources through ownership. Part of Washington's dream was to increase this ownership for African Americans by 25 percent in the belief that such progress would enable them to achieve economic and political independence. In Africa, he was interested in stemming the tide of further European encroachment on African lands by supporting endeavors that did not destroy independent peasant production. In a letter to one KWK official, Washington wrote with regard to the expedition:

> I should very much hope that your Company will not make the same mistake that has been made in the South among our people, that is, [to] teach them to raise nothing but cotton. I find that they make much better progress financially and otherwise where they are taught to raise something to eat at the same time they are raising cotton.[26]

The expedition offered Tuskegee men an opportunity to do work in Togo that would allow the Tuskegee model to thrive in Africa. Given the practical tone of his message and the Tuskegee model of development, Washington obviously treated his students as the leaders of the race. They were to be the vehicles through which his vision of black self-sufficiency would spread:

> I want students who are going out from Tuskegee, to have it firmly fixed in your minds that wherever you go, however small the piece of land you occupy, you have got to get the most out of the soil, or somebody else will crowd you out. The same is true in regard to labor, commercial business and education. If we do not develop the talents in these respects to the very highest degree, somebody else, some other nation will crowd in upon us and we shall not be able to hold our own.[27]

The Tuskegee uplift model appealed to Africans and African Americans through its emphasis on independent black schools and black economic development. Europeans in Africa as well as whites in the United States saw it, of course, in a different light; namely, as a way to ensure a skilled and semiskilled black labor source. At least in the beginning, the KWK agreed to—or conveyed that it would—support independent peasant production in Togo (hence Booker T. Washington's sanctioning of the project). For the KWK, Tuskegee provided the perfect foundation on which to carry out its agenda of developing cotton throughout Germany's African colonies. For Washington, the expedition presented an economic and technical challenge that Africans and African Americans could strategically surmount to ensure their own survival in the face of colonial expansion and racial segregation.[28]

The First Expedition and James Nathan Calloway

Baron Beno von Herman auf Wain, Duke of Württemburg and a representative of the German Embassy in Washington DC, was given the task of finding a cotton expert for the Komitee's planned expedition. Under the auspices of the KWK, Baron Beno sent a series of letters to Booker T. Washington to negotiate the terms on which this scheme was to be developed. In his initial letter to Washington of 3 September 1900, the baron referred to a conversation the two men had had in Rosalind, Massachusetts, in August in which Washington had proposed that Tuskegee provide some sort of agricultural/technical assistance to the German colony of Togo. [29]

Württemburg was a region of Germany with a thriving textile industry. The Royal Bureau of Commerce and Trade in Stuttgart had invested large sums in the linen districts of Alba and the handkerchief industries of Westheim, both of which had suffered from Irish competition.[30] As the Duke of Württemberg, Baron Beno was very familiar with the importance of the connection between industrial education and the textile industries. The Royal Bureau of Commerce and Trade was responsible for monitoring all the industrial schools in Württemburg and also served as the "institution which collects all sorts of information, data, etc. in regard to the needs of the schools and makes proposals concerning the establishment of new ones."[31] Baron Beno's close association with industrial schools probably inspired him to meet with Washington in August of 1900 to discuss the possibility of Tuskegean assistance.[32]

In his letter of 3 September, Beno presented an aggressive itinerary for such an expedition that covered every specific detail, from a set date of departure to the specifics in the contract. He requested two cotton planters and one mechanic to teach Africans in Togo "how to plant and harvest cotton in a rational and scientific way" with minimal incentives: each man's salary was to be one hundred dollars a month or less if the company "gave them 50 percent of the cotton harvested the first year for their personal benefit so as to induce them to plant and raise as much and as good a cotton as possible." These incentives were so low that Washington at first had difficulty gathering support from the Tuskegee Executive Committee. The individual contract was to last for one year, or more if the KWK determined that the desired results had been met. The agreement could, however, be rescinded in case of disciplinary problems, whereupon the individual in question could be sent back at his own expense.[33]

Discipline was clearly an issue for Beno and the KWK. Beno questioned whether these young men possessed the necessary qualities to exercise authority over the "natives" working for them. Furthermore, he wondered if they had the "necessary respect towards the German government official, who of course would try to help them as best they could in their work." In effect, Beno indirectly requested a chaperone, hinting that he wanted "a man of highest education, who would help them in organizing the whole work and who would do the scientific work of examining the soils, keeping the books, paying out the accounts, etc."[34]

In his reply to Beno, Washington acknowledged the KWK's concern over the necessity of having a "mature" individual accompanying the men and expressed his excitement about the prospect of forty-year-old James Nathan Calloway serving as the chaperone and project organizer.[35] A graduate of the Fisk University class of 1890 and inspired by Booker T. Washington's commencement speech at Fisk that year, he had joined Tuskegee to teach mathematics from 1893 to 1897. By 1897, he was asked to manage the experimental Marshall Farm at the institute and remained at Tuskegee as an agricultural instructor until his retirement in 1930. What made Calloway especially qualified for the job was his fluency in German. Calloway volunteered and was given a twelve-month leave of absence from Tuskegee and agreed to the salary of two hundred dollars per month to be paid by the KWK, effective the day of departure.[36]

Washington had also chosen three of his best graduates to go to Togo as a first contingent on 21 November 1900: Shepherd Lincoln Harris, John Winfrey Robinson, and Allen Lynn Burks (see figure 10.1).

Washington assured Beno that these young men would "treat the German officials with the necessary respect," and that they were "kindly disposed, respectful gentlemen," who, he believed, would also "secure the respect and confidence of the natives."[37] The rhetoric Washington employed in this case is a prime example of his ability to assuage the fears of whites, concerned with "Negro's" who may "forget their place."[38] In May 1902, Calloway brought with him the second contingent of Tuskegeans: William Drake of Lafayette, Alabama, a junior at Tuskegee; Hiram Dozier Simpson, also a junior, of Hamilton, Georgia, and his wife; Walter Bryant of Jacksonville, Florida; and Horace Greely Griffin of Giddings, Texas.[39] This contingent faced immediate tragedy. The surf the day of their arrival on 3 May 1902 "was bad," as Calloway described it, "but not the worst." Fifty yards from the Lome shore, the small boat carrying them to shore from their ship was crushed under the weight of a heavy wave. Horace Griffin, Walter Bryant, and Simpson's wife were dragged from the sea, Calloway wrote to Booker T. Washington, "more dead than alive." A few months later, the deployed Tuskegeans also lost Shepherd Lincoln Harris to blackwater fever. This would not be the last tragedy to befall the Tuskegeans during their tenure in German Togo.[40]

We Shall Make Farmers of Them Yet | 197

Figure 10.1. Members of the first expedition to German Togoland, left to right: Shepherd Lincoln Harris, John Winfrey Robinson, James Nathan Calloway, and Allen Lynn Burks (Source: Library of Congress).

The Cultivation of Cotton in Togo

As part of the KWK's goal of promoting experimental farms throughout the colony, all of the surviving young men were given their own farms to manage by the summer of 1902. Calloway no longer supervised Harris (before his death), Burks, Robinson, or the two new additions, Griffin and Bryant, directly or daily, yet Calloway did make sure that each farm ran smoothly. Allen Lynn Burks was responsible for managing an experimental farm in Lome that was initially very promising, prompting the KWK to give him four more farms: Akeppe, Tove, Agua, and Davie. Griffin and Bryant were each given a farm in Assahoun. Cotton collection in the colony became just as—if not more—important as identifying suitable cotton-growing locations for the KWK and the Tuskegeans. Tove Plantation was the KWK's prime cotton collection station because of its proximity to the interior cotton-growing areas and its easy access to the coast. The Tuskegeans established other cotton collection stations in Klein Popo, Kpeme, Ho, Kete Kratchi, Kpandu, and Yendi, all of which produced abundant amounts of cotton grown locally by Africans. Over the course of that year, 1902, these stations were equipped with gins and bale presses imported from the United States.

The Tuskegeans were also charged with making recommendations concerning cotton ginning and baling in some of the more remote districts, such as Sansanne Mangu and the Sokode-Bassari region. The goal of these stations was to limit the distance farmers would have to travel to make a profit. It was also hoped that this would encourage more Africans to plant cotton and sell it to the Germans. The planned Lome-Palime railroad and other lines to the interior of the country were to facilitate the entire process. Robinson proved the most scientifically oriented of the Tuskegeans. Already in the first four months of 1902, he took advantage of his travels to expand the scientific side of the project. He visited Agotime and Gbele Dayi and traveled along Lake Togo all the way to Adangwe, a cotton-producing region, closely observing the native cotton grown in those areas. From these analyses, Robinson identified what he thought were the four best cotton varieties the country had to offer, extensively detailing and classifying the types of cotton that came through the stations, noting the length of the fibers and their color, content, and origin.[41]

Although Calloway's budget remained five thousand marks per month for all expenditures, including salary, the KWK requested that he dismiss some of his laborers to reduce the costs of the experimental farms. This would allow more time and money to be spent on seed distribution to the missions, merchants, and KWK cotton stations and on sending "messengers around to all the chiefs [to let it be known] that you will buy any quantities of cotton they may produce." The KWK also told Calloway to spend as much as necessary, emphasizing that more money could be sent if needed to "purchase all the cotton in the colony." The

KWK instructed Calloway to go to the African cotton growers if they refused to come to Tove, using wagons and oxen to bring cotton back to the station.⁴²

Yet to be determined was the degree and level to which Africans were to be integrated into the colony's cotton economy. It had already been established that they were to be the producers, but incentives had to be created and examples needed to be set. Setting examples was part of the original plan of having African Americans as model cotton farmers scattered throughout the colony. However, as 1902 progressed, it became quite evident that Calloway and Robinson, the predominant characters in this uplift saga, had common and divergent concerns about the project's feasibility. To Robinson's dismay, the new regime's emphasis on collecting rather than planting cotton became even more prominent. Robinson felt that a twofold approach was best for motivating Africans to participate. For one thing, they should receive tested, disease-free seeds proven to produce "an abundant and healthy staple." Second, the government should pay a fair price for the cotton they produced.⁴³ A major problem the KWK had to confront was a countrywide rumor that Africans receiving seeds from the distribution center would not receive any money for their cotton.

Although this remained a rumor, it nonetheless made the situation somewhat difficult. Robinson, as the middleman, understood that adequate representation was needed in order to instill trust: "The people here believe that whatever a white or a foreigner undertakes he does for his own advantage at the natives' expense. We must try to disprove this view, at least as far as cotton is concerned." Robinson suggested that the KWK enter into a contractual agreement with farmers to plant cotton on their farms and in their yam fields. For each hectare a farmer agreed to plant in cotton, he would be advanced a sum that could be used for clearing the land. Once the farmer had cleared the land and planted the seeds as instructed, then "a few more marks would be given, and so on until the harvest." He proposed that these types of contractual arrangements be made with chiefs and people from notable families in the beginning. In so doing, Robinson took account of the fact that such people had the best access to land and labor and a position most strongly tied to the German governing system.⁴⁴ Yet, he was proposing a system of negotiation rather than force. He was also supporting independent production. Robinson also recommended that additional experimental farms managed by Africans be established along the coast.

Since the inception of the expedition, the KWK had envisioned settling African Americans in Togo as model farmers for their African subjects. After Drake, Simpson, and Harris had died, the KWK grew eager to secure replacements. As word of these young men's deaths spread, the task of finding graduates or students to go became difficult, if not impossible. One thing is for certain—the Tuskegee Executive Committee was not receptive to the project, and there was a "lack of sympathy with the enterprise." This sentiment seemed to have "communicated itself to the young men at the school," exacerbating the problem. The KWK's new contract also failed to excite the Executive Committee because it lacked any economic incentive.[45] By July, a desperate Washington wrote his treasurer Warren Logan, "I wish you would make another effort to find two good men. I very much fear that the success of the movement will be crippled if we do not send men, and I think that even at considerable cost and extra time we ought to find them."[46] In the end, he was unsuccessful, rendering the progress of the scheme totally dependent on the men already there.

The information Robinson sent to the KWK and his final report on his work make it quite clear that he was not in favor of settling more African American farmers in Togo; rather, he had tremendous faith in Africans as cotton farmers. Noting the KWK's concern with expenses, he made it plain that pursuing African American settlement would cost a great deal of money. Moreover, Robinson apparently saw his own role in the endeavor as setting a good example:

> The men who come here from America or Europe should represent ideas ... and should see that people here execute them. He should do nothing a native clerk or head-man can do as well. It is poor economy to pay an American 200 marks a month to oversee a squall of laborers when a native clerk will do the same work about as well for 50 marks.[47]

In 1902–3 Calloway, on the other hand, was still holding on to the idea of African American settlers working in Togo among "native" Africans. Although he was aware that the tragic deaths of the Tuskegeans deployed earlier to Togo would make securing such men difficult, he strongly advocated continued recruitment of African Americans in a 1903 letter to the Germans:

> I hope the experiment this year will give us a good idea whether the settlement of more Americans as cotton farmers is advantageous and desirable. In this respect, not to be forgotten is the profit that comes when the natives learn from the Americans about the wants, namely in clothing and tools, that have eluded them so far. They are becoming thereby, on the one hand better consumers than before and must at the same time, work more to supply themselves with these objects. For these reasons I consider desirable the settlement of a limited number of Americans, even if this requires a subsidy for years to come.[48]

Success and failure weighed heavily on Calloway's conscience. While Robinson became more self-assured, Calloway began to second-guess his own uplift intentions. This internal conflict registered in his private letters to his wife, who was eager for him to return to the United States:

> Why should you think I am wrong to come here and help Africa? Are we not sacrificing our own pleasure to do this work[?] Why should God be displeased because I receive a little pay that the children may be educated? The reason you cannot pray without hesitations [is] because you want me home and yet you want me to help in

bringing civilization to Africa. Now be patient and trust God and you shall have both. I don't feel I am called or needed here for many more months. … My coming here may make travelers out of all our children. They will always wish to come to Africa but this will be true of others who know our work here.[49]

Utilizing his public voice with the Germans, Robinson, however, had the ability to manipulate the Germans' impressions of the situation by soberly presenting both worst- and best-case scenarios as alternatives. He held nothing back. Yet one cannot help but feel that he was unintentionally upstaging Calloway, the leader of Tuskegee's Togo expedition and his superior, in his analysis. Where Calloway was hesitant because his own motives were more in line with the sense of racial uplift, Robinson was direct and used the carrot-and-stick approach to draw the Germans in:

If we want to throw in the towel now we would thereby demonstrate shameful resoluteness. I am for following a rational plan in a logical manner. The colony is now undergoing its trade period, and since the basis of trade is usually immediate profit, we should naturally ask ourselves whether the business pays for itself. I answer the question negatively for neither today nor tomorrow nor in the [near] future will a profit be obtained. Those who actually care about the development of the country, however, look far into the future and foresee the moment when the colony really can produce riches, they will recognize that it is good business to boldly thrive further until a firm foundation or the certainty of obtaining good results has been achieved.[50]

In an attempt to counter Calloway's African American settler stance, Robinson concluded: "If the population in its present state of civilization is considered it must be said that there is no occupation for which they are more suitable than cotton cultivation, and that no others could take their place." Robinson, in effect, was negotiating the terms of "uplift," placing Africans (not African Americans) in the center of this endeavor. Imbued with a sense of purpose, Robinson wrote to Washington:

In one of the lectures which you wrote me some time ago you advised me to "labor earnestly, quietly and soberly, discharging my duty in the way that would make me one of the most influential persons in the community." Being faithful in small things is one of the fundamental principles of Tuskegee and is what I am able to do without even striving. It has become natural for me to be faithful, it matters not how small or insignificant the service, I find myself possessing much influence in the work in which I am now engaged.[51]

Toward the end of 1902, Calloway, it appears, no longer fully embraced the idea of using American settlers. Some of his convictions arose out of his perception of how poorly some Tuskegeans seemed to adjust to the African setting, expecting "to live too high and find things [as] convenient as in the US," and who were "discouraged" when things did not turn out that way. Instead, he argued that "[i]t may be best to use native men farmers, [and] clerk[s] and dash the people 5 pfennigs each place to build [a] house and clear five hectares of land."[52] Five pfennigs paid to Africans was a paltry sum compared to the two hundred dollars Calloway received every month. How could the Germans not take both men's advice?[53]

By the beginning of 1903, there was little incentive for either the KWK or the Tuskegeans to continue as they had for the previous two years. Bryant's and Griffin's cotton crops were so unsuccessful that no commission could be made. Robinson and Burks fared slightly better on their Tove plantations, earning a commission of 5 percent each off of nineteen thousand pounds of unginned cotton.[54] In December, Burks left for a three-month vacation to Europe. However, the KWK decided that Burks was not to return to Togo for another year and that no more American cotton farmers were to be sent, for Calloway had little regard for him and referred to him as "poor stuff" in a letter to his wife.[55]

Instead, the Germans gave up all attempts to plant cotton under this scheme and asked the Tuskegeans to direct their attention to the collection, transport, and ginning of cotton in Togo.[56] Calloway returned to the United States in February of 1903. Griffin and his wife chose to stay on and remained there until 1905. Robinson, however, continued to work until his mysterious drowning death in 1909, but not before creating one of his greatest legacies in German Togo: the Cotton (later Agricultural) School in Nuatja, based on the Tuskegee experimental station model.[57]

John Winfrey Robinson and His Cotton School in Nuatja

Although experimental stations existed in various agricultural schools throughout the United States, the Tuskegee program's success was dependent on the reciprocal relationship Tuskegee had formed with Macon County's black residents. Washington had envisioned a well-rounded holistic approach to rural development. The experimental station program reflected the ideal that the town of Tuskegee, Alabama, would become a model community of black economic development through land ownership and efficient land use, with Tuskegee students playing a crucial role in this model community. With an emphasis on service to the community, the curriculum at the basic level provided instruction in civics, economics, and gardening. A two-year program in agriculture was required for those whose goal was to cultivate a farm of between thirty and forty acres. A four-year program provided instruction for those who would manage large-scale farms or serve as demonstrators in the rural extension programs.[58] Tuskegee Institute's most famous faculty member was the great botanist and inventor George Washington Carver. His emphasis on crop diversification became even more pertinent for Southern farmers during the boll weevil epidemic, which had disastrous consequences for large parts of the cotton crop in the early twentieth century. Carver instructed all of the men who went to Togo, and his influence was evident in Robinson's curriculum.

Drawing inspiration from his alma mater, Robinson made sure that the uplift philosophy of independent farming was firmly rooted in the Cotton School's curriculum. Students in Nuatja were later to serve as "model farmers" in their own communities. The goal was to give each graduate cattle, plows, and harnesses. By 1907, the KWK changed the name of the school from Cotton School to "Agricultural School in Nuatja." That same year, the school had increased enrollment to about one hundred students and some twenty to thirty short-term contract workers, assigned to construction, field labor, transport, and various jobs as needed. Students were enrolled for a period of three years and were exempted from paying taxes during their tenure. Although they gained practical knowledge, they also had an opportunity to manage their own small farms. Students learned how to properly clear land in the first year and how to break oxen and use the plow in the second, when they also received one hectare of land. In the third year, then, students spent most of their time working on their own farms. More importantly, they could keep any profit they made. In addition to planting and harvesting cotton, they also grew food crops such as yams, corn, and peas, thereby incorporating a diversification of crops reflective of African and African American (and especially George Washington Carver's) agricultural techniques. In addition, students at Nuatja took one hour of classes in German each day. The government aimed to produce a bilingual German/Ewe instructional book on agriculture that was "to be gotten out by a Tuskegee graduate"—presumably Robinson.[59] Finally, a small stipend was awarded to students to spark interest in attending the school.

Like his mentor Washington, Robinson had long workdays: he oversaw the daily operation of the school and instructed several classes. His typical day began at 5:30 in the morning and ended at 5:30 in the evening, though he often worked well into the night. He spent them teaching students how to properly harness animals, plow fields, and plant cotton and corn. He was also responsible for construction, as he explained: "I have to superintend and plan all of our primitive buildings of which some are brick, some plank, and some mud covered with grass." Moreover, he oversaw the "buying of cotton" and the hiring of "laborers to take these bales to the coast." On top of these duties as instructor and overseer, he still continued his role as chief scientist, making "experiments for use of commercial fertilizers to improve methods of farming."[60]

In January 1907, there was an agricultural exhibition at Palime under Robinson's charge. Alongside signaling the opening of the Lome-Palime railway line, which followed the route Calloway had suggested, it enabled Europeans and Africans who had never visited the interior to catch a glimpse of the fruits of the colonial agriculture of the previous seven years. The exhibition was designed to promote investment in colonial enterprises and stimulate Togolese interest in modern cultivation techniques.[61] The Atakpame district played host and provided accommodations for the some two hundred European visitors and the estimated fifteen thousand Africans expected to attend.[62] Enthusiasm in advance of the exhibition was high not just among the Europeans, but also among the Togolese, with about thirty-five hundred exhibits being sent to Palime, though many of them had to be rejected for lack of space and time. The exhibition lasted for two days, during which time Africans and Europeans were transported to and from the coast for free on the railroad.[63]

Robinson's contributions to the exhibit, for which he earned an honorary award, were not limited just to cotton and its varieties, but included displays of the actual science of growing cotton, as well as of producing other agricultural commodities, in consequence of George Washington Carver's emphasis on diversification. One observer highlighted this diversity in a report on the exhibition:

> An instructive collection about cotton-parasites, [and] plans and writings on cotton agriculture in general, complemented this special exhibition which also included students of the cotton school of the Colonial Economic Committee in Nuatja; the most excellent products of agriculture, such as peanuts, maize, rice, and butter, and ceramics; and tools manufactured by students. Worth mentioning here also are the peanut creepers pressed into bales which serve as excellent fodder in Nuatja. The draught cattle exhibited by the school in Nuatja were of the best quality and prove that one can breed excellent live-stock here. We also saw the same cattle at work during plowing and sowing on the second day of the exhibition where they proved well trained indeed.[64]

Robinson's stressful but fruitful career in Togo unfortunately ended too soon. In August 1909, he wrote that he expected to remain in Togo for two more years and then return to the United States. He was "conscious of growing weaker" and, although he tried to "save" himself, he saw "no other way but to spend and be spent," adding, "[m]y whole desire is to accomplish something."[65] Indeed, Robinson, the last remaining Tuskegean, was fulfilling his duty to open a ginning station in northern Togo when he drowned during his journey on the Mono River later that very month.[66]

The Demise of German Cotton-Growing Efforts in Togo

Between 1905 and 1907, Atakpame, the district in which Robinson's school resided, was the most successful cotton production district in the entire colony, largely through his efforts. Not only were the Togolese producing larger amounts of cotton, but it was also cotton of exceptional quality. However, after Robinson's death, a major change took place. The KWK agreed to hand the school's operation over to the colonial government. The government, for its part, agreed to "keep the matter of cultivation as its first purpose," and to "consult the committee from time to time on the subject." The KWK also handed over all of its ginning stations to various merchants, concession companies, and the government.[67] Within a short period, these new owners proved to be incapable of maintaining the momentum established by the KWK and the Tuskegeans. Their involvement marked the beginning of the demise of modern cotton cultivation in German Togoland.

By 1910, the KWK exerted very little influence over the development of cotton growing, and enthusiasm began to wane on all levels. The Bremen Cotton Exchange was not pleased with the quality of cotton coming from Togo. One representative emphasized the poor quality compared to the colony's initial harvest, concluding that "somewhere in Togo," radical mistakes were being made in the "selection or distribution of seed-corn or in the treatment of the harvest."[68] At that time, German colonialists continued to harbor the same range of viewpoints and vested interests they had displayed at the beginning of the century. Many chose to blame the independent farmers for the poor quality rather than the gin mills. Most plantation advocates saw "native culture" or reliance on independent cultivation as overrated and looked to Tanganyika's plantation mode—in which Africans were forced to grow cotton—as the ideal. Independent farming, they argued, was a system that accommodated Africans, not German industry: "Our colonies have to orient their agricultures according to the needs of the mother country, and not, as the governor believes, according to what is most convenient to the Negro."[69] Plantation owners largely agreed that the government needed to pressure the Togolese in order to meet their stated goal. Such "forced labor," they supposed, was a necessary evil for labor-intensive crops like cotton. Most of the colonies were engaged in the violent suppression of revolts arising from exactly such pressure, and Togo was no exception. This climate contributed to the unraveling of the Germans' foray into cotton growing after 1910. Other factors were poor seed selection, competition with neighboring colonies, poor price incentives (that would support the independent producer), and a failure to really understand the benefits of traditional farming practices. The solid infrastructure (railways, roads) they had built, the new farming methods they applied, and the sound distribution system they had developed, believed to be the magic formula, were simply not enough. A degree of failure via a combination of all of these elements helped to turn German "scientific colonialism" upside down.

Booker T. Washington on German Colonial Policy

While 1910 was a disastrous year for the Germans' cotton enterprise in Togo, it was also the year Booker T. Washington made his grand tour of Europe to study the conditions of the working-class poor and to promote his ideas on industrial education. On this tour of Europe, he gave a series of interviews and speeches that not only enraged his critics, but also alienated him from a number of his supporters, both black and white. Although scheduling changes prevented him from delivering his formulaic speech in Berlin, the text, modified to address Germany's involvement in cotton cultivation in Togo, nevertheless appeared in *Der Tropenpflanzer*. His comments seem to sanction European colonial policy, as well as diminish the cruelty of slavery, Jim Crowism, and lynching, and promote the idea of racially inherent traits in black people. The reaction that this speech engendered among other black leaders in the United States was so strong that its most controversial elements bear repeating in full here:

> I wanted to begin by thanking the German people for the interest it takes in the Negro in the German-African Colonies. With great attention have I been following the politics and plans of the official German circles vis-a-vis the native of Africa. Their work proceeds in a healthy, cumulative way.
>
> They do not seek to oppress the African people but rather to help them become more useful for themselves and for the German people. Their example of the treatment of Negroes can be a model for other nations as well.
>
> Nothing should keep Africa from becoming a great country of cotton producers. By his nature, the Negro is a cotton farmer, and if carefully guided, encouraged, supported and protected, he can become an equally good cotton farmer in Africa as he already is in the United States of North America. I repeat … Tuskegee Institute is always happy to help you realize your farsighted plans in this respect.[70]

Other black leaders in the United States who opposed this view were more than displeased. In October 1910, W. E. B. Du Bois composed and published "An Open Letter to the People of Great Britain and Europe," signed by twenty-two prominent African Americans, to clarify the seemingly benign picture Washington had painted of black life in the United States,[71] and to emphasize the difference between Washington's views on this matter and those of most African Americans. It also aimed to place Washington, very publicly, in check:[72]

> We vehemently contradict the assumption that the American Negroes allot themselves among a minority, that they should submit to oppression and excuse the wrongs that are done to them. At times helplessness may force us into subjugation, but the voice of protest of 10 million Americans will continue to assault the ears of their fellow citizens as long as America remains unjust.[73]

While Washington attempted to reconcile in his own mind the idea of black economic mobility as the key to solving the problem of white intolerance in the United States, Du Bois here pointed out the blatant contradictions between Washington's accommodationist rhetoric and the lived reality of most African Americans in the United States, particularly in the South.

The differences in attitude between the two men are very evident in the observations of one German, Moritz Schanz, who visited Tuskegee in 1907. While in the United States to attend the International Cotton Congress held in Atlanta in October of that year,[74] Schanz included a meeting with Washington in his itinerary. For white Americans, and for Europeans to an even larger extent, Washington was the spokesperson for the black race, as well as the broker between black and white. Unfortunately, in straddling the race fence, the leader of the Tuskegee Institute often became the victim of his own rhetoric. "Blacks," he told Shanz, "must make the best of a given circumstance, overcome the prejudices through development of our own natural talents; be correct yourself, and the world will behave correctly towards you."[75] This comment reveals a fatal flaw in Washington's "uplift-accommodationist" rhetoric: although behind closed doors Washington was skillful at placing pressure on powerful white elites for change, his public persona seemed to place no public demand on whites, so that many of his critics perceived him as one-dimensional.[76]

Conclusion

Calloway's correspondence to Germany and the United States illustrates the substantial difference between his and Washington's interpretation of the Tuskegeans' role in Africa. In his early letters, Calloway describes the new farms to be set up throughout the colony as "settlements" and the African Americans who would be placed in charge of them as "colonists":[77] terms Washington was loath to use. This is significant because the experiment's longevity certainly depended on the Tuskegeans' view of themselves in relation to the success of the project, as well as their commitment to it. "Settlements" imply the need for long-term goals. Calloway's new attitude transmitted itself to the other men, who all extended their contracts for another eight to twelve months in that first year. Their goal was to "reflect credit upon our race and America and above all to our dear old Al' [alma mater]."

However, at least at the early stage of the experiment, the Tuskegeans paid no attention to traditional African farming methods. For example, with their male-centric view, they disregarded the participation of women and children. The goal was to "change the work of men … wagons must take the burden of carrying loads and the men left to make the plantations. Now the cotton is made by women and children with country hoes." Unfortunately, the plow, not the hoe, was to be the tool of choice. Plowing subjected the thin topsoil layer to rapid leaching of nutrients by hard tropical rains and encouraged fast erosion. Consequently, the apparent success of the harvests of 1904, 1905, and 1907 on the experimental farm gave way to absolute disappointment by 1910. Yet the Germans and Tuskegeans, with little knowledge of tropical agriculture and soils, placed the blame elsewhere. "Natives," wrote Calloway "must be taught to produce more cotton on the same surface with the same labor."[78] The farming techniques they introduced to the Togolese were traditions rooted in the Deep South. While intercropping was an Africanism practiced on both sides of the Atlantic, many other techniques were not, particularly the use of the plow (an American/European tool), and women tending both cash and subsistence crops (west African). The Tuskegeans had little understanding of this gendered dynamic.

Despite the crop failures and inappropriate farming practices, the Togolese themselves did manage to benefit from the experiment from an "uplift" perspective—most of all on their own terms. They increased demand and created alternative markets, as well as competitive pricing. They adopted the modern farming practices that worked from the Tuskegeans and discarded what did not, like the use of the plow. This use of the plow not only depleted the soil rapidly over time, but also depended on the use of draft animals not suited to the tropical climate. Moreover, the Togolese benefited from Germans' need for tropical products from Togo, such as palm products, cocoa, coffee, rubber, corn, and coconuts. Many of these required little effort for the Togolese to grow or collect, and all of them held a competitive advantage over cotton. Since the German colonial government had little money to invest in the colony and lacked the manpower to oversee plantation management, it had no choice but to rely on independent producers. When the Germans applied too much pressure, various forms of resistance often ensued.

Thus, while the scheme may have failed to provide what the Germans were hoping for—an independent source of cotton—it gave the Togolese new opportunities to attempt to manipulate the system to their own advantage. For the Tuskegeans, it failed to inspire further African American "gentlemen" farmer settlements. However, the Tuskegeans strengthened the selling power of the Togolese and indigenous cotton and textile markets via the distribution of improved seeds, as well as education in the latest agricultural and ginning techniques. Through Calloway and, in particular, through Robinson, many Togolese gained access to a new range of methods to better cope with the Tuskegee presence, and even to benefit on their own terms from it in not so limited ways. This, in turn, undermined the German agenda of transforming the "native" into a loyal subject.[79]

Notes

1. This chapter is dedicated to the memory of the late Bud Calloway, who generously gave me unlimited access to his family papers many years ago so that this history could be known. It was a rare privilege for which I will forever be grateful. This chapter reiterates and draws explicitly from the major themes I addressed in my dissertation, "The Tuskegee-Togo Cotton Scheme: 1900–1909" (PhD diss., University of California, Los Angeles, 1998). My research guided and

informed works that followed, some more than others. For example, see Sven Beckert, "From Tuskegee to Togo: The Problem of Freedom in the Empire of Cotton," *Journal of American History* 92, no. 2 (2005): 498–526. Beckert comes to some similar conclusions.
2. Andrew Zimmerman, *Alabama in Africa: Booker T. Washington, the German Empire and The Globalization of the New South* (Princeton, NJ: Princeton University Press, 2010), 13. Zimmerman offers a Marxist class analysis and psychoanalytic perspective to explain what he sees as the complicit intentions of the Tuskegeans. See also Andrew Zimmerman, "A German Alabama in Africa: The Tuskegee Expedition to German Togo and the Transnational Origins of West African Cotton Growers," *American Historical Review* 110, no. 5 (2005): 1362.
3. According to Zimmerman, "the Tuskegee cotton expedition to Togo brought together German and American models and ideologies of race and free agricultural labor. It brought together the long American history of slavery and emancipation, Jim Crow, sharecropping, and the promises of a New South, with the long German history of the colonization of Eastern Europe, the partition of Poland, the end of serfdom, the migrations of Germans and Poles, and the promise of an expert state that used social science to control and develop its territory and population" (*Alabama in Africa,* 1). First, I argue that it also brought together the long history of African American scientific innovation and uplift ideology. Black folk were not simply reacting to the above-mentioned historical legacies; they were also innovating and creating a worldview about Africa separate and apart from a European or Euro-American perspective. Second, with regard to the European turning points, the German nation did not exist until the late nineteenth century. To be sure, Poland was partitioned into three almost equal parts among Prussia, Austria, and Russia; however, Poland was not colonized per se, as it was conquered by enemies who shared similar cultural origins, a common Euro-Christian heritage (Zimmerman, *Alabama in Africa,* 238–39). They were also a European people who were not viewed as subhuman by their conquerors, as were Africans farmers and African American sharecroppers.
4. Booker T. Washington's negotiated dance with "white elites" is often portrayed as "selling out." However, Washington's implementation and articulation of the white elite agenda were complex and far from one-dimensional. A well-articulated assessment of Washington as a man who ingeniously undermined racism as best he could given the circumstances and time can be found in Raymond W. Smock's *Booker T. Washington: Black Leadership in the Age of Jim Crow* (Chicago: Ivan R. Dee Press, 2009).
5. Radcliffe, "The Tuskegee-Togo Cotton Scheme," 3.
6. Ibid.
7. "BTW to the Editor of the Washington, D.C. *Colored American,*" 20 July 1899, in Louis R. Harlan, ed., *Booker T. Washington Papers* (hereafter *BTW Papers*) (Urbana: University of Illinois Press, 1976), 3:164–65.
8. KWK, "Bericht über englische Baumwoll Kulturversuche," in *Deutch-Kolonial Baumwoll Unternehmungen, 1902–1903* (Berlin: KWK, 1903), 67.
9. Radcliffe, "The Tuskegee-Togo Cotton Scheme," 169–72.
10. Booker T. Washington, "Atlanta Compromise Address," in Harlan, *BTW Papers,* vol. 1 (Urbana: University of Illinois Press, 1972), 73–76.
11. This was certainly the case with regard to the Liberian crises in which Washington was to play a key role between 1908 and 1911. It was Washington who brought Britain, France, and Germany's imperialist ambitions for the republic founded by ex-slaves to the attention of the Roosevelt and Taft administrations and insisted on US intervention in the matter.
12. "BTW to the Editor of the Washington, D.C. *Colored American,*" 164–65. During his visit to London in 1899, Washington met the explorer Henry M. Stanley, who shared his views on European imperialism in Africa with him. In his letter, Washington details his doubts about African Americans settling in Africa. One of the *Colored American* editors (according to Bud Calloway) was Thomas J. Calloway, brother to James Nathan Calloway, leader of the Tuskegee

expedition to Togo. Thomas J. Calloway was also the organizer of the Negro Exhibit at the Paris Exposition in 1900, and asked his friend Du Bois to act as the official representative. Thomas J. Calloway acquired the position after asking Washington to appeal to then President McKinley to provide funds for the exhibit.

13. See the introduction to James N. Calloway, "Tuskegee Cotton Planter in Africa," *Outlook*, 29 March 1902.
14. Prof. Dr. Helferrich, *Die Baumwollfrage: Ein weltwirtschaftliches Problem* (Berlin: E.S. Mittler & Sohn, 1904), 13. See also Radcliffe, "The Tuskegee-Togo Cotton Scheme," 26.
15. US Department of Commerce and Labor, *Consular Reports* (Washington: GPO, 1903), 43, in which one French official is quoted as saying: "The market is dominated by one fact which directly menaces the consumers and manufacturers of the old world. It is the development of American manufactured goods. Heretofore, American cotton needed us as much as we needed it, but now American spindles are using what we need. After some years looms are multiplied sufficiently there to absorb all the twelve or fifteen million bales harvested in the U.S. Europe would for the most part be compelled to close her mills." See also Radcliffe, "The Tuskegee-Togo Cotton Scheme," 13–14.
16. Richard V. Pierard, "A Case Study of German Economic Imperialism: The Colonial Economic Committee," *Scandanavian Economic History Review* 16 (1968): 155–67.
17. Peter Duignan and L. H. Gann, *The Rulers of German Africa, 1884–1914* (Palo Alto, CA: Stanford University Press, 1977), 30.
18. Arthur J. Knoll, *Togo under Imperial Germany, 1884–1914* (Palo Alto, CA: Hoover Institution Press, 1988), 144.
19. Peter H. Duignan and L. H. Gann, *The Economics of Colonialism* (Cambridge: Cambridge University Press, 1975), 242.
20. In 1903, the French and the Belgians each founded their own Association Cottonièré. The British Cotton Growers Association followed in 1904. All of these organizations were modeled on the KWK; see also Radcliffe, "The Tuskegee-Togo Cotton Scheme," 27.
21. Stocker, *Booker T. Washington,* 180.
22. Karl Supf, "Introduction," in *Deutsche Kolonial-Baumwolle: Berichte 1900* (Berlin: Deutsche Kolonialgesellschaft, 1900), 8.
23. Alan I. Marcus, *Agricultural Science and the Quest for Legitimacy: Farmers Agricultural Colleges and Experiment Stations 1870–1890* (Ames: Iowa State University Press, 1985), 18; see also Radcliffe, "The Tuskegee-Togo Cotton Scheme," 28.
24. Radcliffe, "The Tuskegee-Togo Cotton Scheme," 12.
25. Ibid., 37.
26. Harlan, *BTW Papers* (Urbana: University of Illinois Press, 1977), 5:640; see also Radcliffe, "The Tuskegee-Togo Cotton Scheme," 38.
27. "A Sunday Evening Talk," 2 December 1905, in Harlan, *BTW Papers* (Urbana: University of Illinois Press, 1979), 8:469.
28. Radcliffe, "The Tuskegee-Togo Cotton Scheme," 38.
29. Ibid., 32.
30. US Department of Commerce and Labor, *Consular Reports,* 17.
31. Ibid., 17.
32. Radcliffe, "The Tuskegee-Togo Cotton Scheme," 33.
33. Radcliffe, "The Tuskegee-Togo Cotton Scheme," 36.
34. Harlan, *BTW Papers,* 5:633–35. See also Radcliffe, "The Tuskegee-Togo Cotton Scheme," 34.
35. "To Beno von Herman auf Wain," 20 September 1900, *BTW Papers,* 5:639–40.
36. Ibid., 640.
37. Ibid., 641.
38. Calloway quoting Washington in "Tuskegee Cotton Planters in Africa," *Outlook,* 29 March 1902, 772; see also James N. Calloway, "Cotton Raising in Togoland," *Southern Workman* 31 (1902).

39. "From James Nathan Calloway," 17 March 1902, in Harlan, *BTW Papers* (Urbana: University of Illinois Press, 1977), 6:418.
40. Radcliffe, "The Tuskegee-Togo Cotton Scheme," 91–95.
41. Ibid., 103–4.
42. James N.Calloway, "KWK to JNC," 10 July 1902, Calloway Papers (Woodland Hills, California); see also Radcliffe, "The Tuskegee-Togo Cotton Scheme," 109.
43. John W. Robinson, "Sonderbericht der Versuchsstation Tove," in *Deutsch-Koloniale Baumwoll-Unternehmungen* (Berlin: KWK, 1903), 28-29; see also Radcliffe, "The Tuskegee-Togo Cotton Scheme," 113–14.
44. Robinson, "Versuchsstation Tove," 29; see also Radcliffe, "The Tuskegee-Togo Cotton Scheme," 114–15.
45. Among the economic disadvantages, the new contract stated that the Tuskegeans would have to pay for the return passage to the United States. Service was to be for the period of five years at forty marks, the equivalent of nine dollars a month. All other KWK monies would go toward paying for labor, building materials, and equipment. As Scott noted, "this is absolutely no inducement at all since even the land remains the property of the Kolonial Komitee. Whatever cotton is harvested must be sold to the Komitee, but it is perhaps easy to determine that there will be no great amount of this considering all things." "From Emmett J. Scott," 24 June 1902, in Harlan, *BTW Papers,* 6:488–89.
46. "BTW to Warren Logan," 14 July 1902, Booker T. Washington Archives, Tuskegee, box no. 3.
47. John W. Robinson, "Monthly Report to KWK," 15 January 1902, Calloway Papers, (Woodland Hills, CA); see also Radcliffe, "The Tuskegee-Togo Cotton Scheme," 115.
48. James N. Calloway, "Inspection der Baumwollfarmen und Baumwollmärkte in Togo," *Deutsch-Koloniale Baumwoll-Unternehmungen* (Berlin: KWK, 1903), 35.
49. James N. Calloway, "JNC to Wife," 2 November 1902, Calloway Papers, (Woodland Hills, CA); see also Radcliffe, "The Tuskegee-Togo Cotton Scheme," 116–18.
50. Robinson, "Versuchsstation Tove," 28.
51. John W. Robinson, "Cotton Farming in Africa," in Booker T. Washington, *Working with the Hands* (New York: Doubleday, 1904), 198.
52. James N. Calloway., "JNC to KWK," 5 September 1902, Calloway Papers (Woodland Hills, CA).
53. Radcliffe, "The Tuskegee-Togo Cotton Scheme," 119–20.
54. James N. Calloway, "KWK to JNC," 25 August 1902, Calloway Papers (Woodland Hills, CA).
55. James N. Calloway, "JNC to KWK," 21 January 1903, Calloway Papers (Woodland Hills, CA).
56. Ibid.
57. Today, Nuatja is the town of Notsé. It is also a historically important town in Ewe history. Nuatja was founded in the seventeenth century. By 1720, it had become the dispersal point for perhaps thousands of Ewe who secretly fled Nuatja in order to escape the cruelty of its ruler, King Agakoli. Each of the three town clans fled in a different direction, establishing the towns of Ho in the west, Lome in the south, and Agouévé and Bagida in the northwest. See Samuel Decalo, *Historical Dictionary of Togo* (Metuchen, NJ: Scarecrow Press, 1976), 123. See also Sandra F. Greene, "Notse Narratives: History and Memory in West Africa," *South Atlantic Quarterly* 101 (2002): 1015–42.
58. For an extensive discussion of the Tuskegee Extension Program and curriculum, see Leedell W. Neyland, *Historically Black Land-Grant Institutions and the Development of Home Economics, 1890–1990* (Tallahassee: Florida A&M University Foundation, 1990), esp. chap. 7, "Cooperative Extension Service in 1890 Institutions," 147–89.
59. Radcliffe, "The Tuskegee-Togo Cotton Scheme," 129–41; see also Karl Supf, *Deutsch-Koloniale Baumwoll-Unternehmungen* (Berlin, 1907), 9:15–18; and "Tuskegee Graduates in Africa,"

Southern Letter, April 1907. By 1910, the government was still discussing the publication of such a book. It is uncertain if the book was actually produced, and, if so, if it was based on the work Robinson started. To gain insight into the Tuskegee perspective with regard to progressive farming techniques advocated by George Washington Carver, see Mark Hersey, "Hints and Suggestions to Farmers: George Washington Carver and Rural Conservation in the South," *Environment History* 11 (2006): 239–68.

60. "Tuskegee Graduates in Africa," *Southern Letter*, April 1907.
61. Early in the school's history, during the 1904 international conference in Vienna, the KWK organized a panel to discuss the results of the school. Like the KWK, both the British Cotton Growers' Association (BCGA) and the Association Cotonnière, of France, supported the idea of independent African cotton cultivation and observed the Togo experiment with much interest: Supf, *Deutsch-Koloniale Baumwoll-Unternehmungen*, 8:10.
62. S. Soskind, "Die Ausstellung zu Palime," *Der Tropenpflanzer* 11 (1907): 159–60.
63. Of course, Europeans and Africans were to travel separately: the train for Togolese visitors left at 6:00 a.m. and the train for European visitors left at 8:40 a.m.
64. Soskind, "Die Ausstellung zu Palime," 160.
65. John W. Robinson, "At Work in West Africa," *Southern Letter*, August 1909. This is a rather sad and haunting letter, given its timing shortly before his death.
66. Moritz Schanz, "Eine ungehaltene Rede von Booker Washington in Berlin," *Der Tropenflanzer* 13 (1910): 641–45.
67. Supf, *Deutsch-Koloniale Baumwoll-Unternehmungen*, 10:14–16.
68. "Verhandlungen der Baumwoll-Kommission des Kolonial Wirtschaftlichen Komittees E.V. DKG," Berlin: DKG, November 21, 1910, 17.
69. Radcliffe, "The Tuskegee-Togo Cotton Scheme," 158–59; see also Erik Grimmer-Solem, "The Professors Africa: Economists, the Elections of 1907 and the Legitimation of German Imperialism," *German History* 25 (2007): 313–47.
70. Schanz, "Eine ungehaltene Rede von Booker Washington in Berlin," 624–43.
71. See "An Open Letter to the People of Great Britain and Europe," in Harlan, *BTW Papers* (Urbana: University of Illinois Press, 1981), 10:422–25. It is very telling that this letter appeals to the people of Great Britain and not to the British government.
72. Radcliffe, "The Tuskegee-Togo Cotton Scheme," 170–71.
73. Moritz Schanz, "Die Negerfrage in Nordamerika," *Der Tropenpflanzer* 8 (1910): 583.
74. Moritz Schanz, "Nergerziehung in Nordamerika und Booker T. Washington," *Der Tropenpflanzer* 7 (1908): 221.
75. Schanz, "Die Negerfrage in Nordamerika," *Der Tropenpflanzer* 8 (1910): 582.
76. See Du Bois's quotation in the text, and also Robert J. Norrell, *Up From History: The Life of Booker T. Washington* (Cambridge, MA: Harvard University Press, 2009). Norrell's book sheds light on Washington's little-known (even to his critics) efforts to destroy disenfranchisement.
77. James N.Calloway, "JNC to KWK," 10 June 1902, Calloway Papers (Woodland Hills, CA). For a full discussion, see Radcliffe, "The Tuskegee-Togo Cotton Scheme," 170–72.
78. One of the main goals of the KWK was to introduce the plow to the average Togolese farmer. But the plow, while historically important in improving the productivity of European farming, was an inappropriate tool of progress for west Africans. Unlike Africans, colonial agriculturalists were unaware of the potential destructiveness of turning shallow west African soils with the plow. While an abundant and quick harvest could be acquired this way at first, the success was always short-lived. "From Shepherd Lincoln Harris," 15 May 1901, in Harlan, *BTW Papers*, 6:110–11.
79. See Radcliffe, "The Tuskegee-Togo Cotton Scheme," 123–24.

Chapter Eleven

EDUCATION AND MIGRATION
Cameroonian Schoolchildren and Apprentices in Germany, 1884–1914

Robbie Aitken

In the Holthausen cemetery in Mülheim on the Ruhr in northern Westphalia, one particular gravestone attracts attention for being somewhat unusual (see figure 11.1). The words on the headstone read: "Rest in peace. Here lies Prince Equalla Deido, born 27 April 1876 in Douala, Cameroon, died 1 May 1891 in Holthausen."[1] This grave, one of the few visible reminders of Germany's colonial past, is testimony to an increasing presence of African colonial subjects in Germany at the turn of the twentieth century.

Equalla Deido was one of several thousand men and women of African descent from various regions of sub-Saharan Africa and from farther afield such as Haiti and the United States who were present in Germany in the period between high colonialism and the outbreak of World War I. Indeed, the development of a permanent, small, but visible black population in

Figure 11.1. Grave of Prince Equalla Deido in Mülheim, Germany (Source: Robbie Aitken).

Notes from this chapter begin on page 227.

Germany was primarily an unforeseen consequence of German colonialism and Germany's emergence as a maritime power. In particular, there was an almost constant migration of colonial subjects from Germany's newly acquired African protectorates, Togo, German East Africa, and, to a lesser extent, Namibia. Numerically dominating this African colonial population, however, were young men from Germany's protectorate of Cameroon, principally from the influential coastal town of Douala.

Cameroonian migrants reached Germany by various means. Personal servants accompanied colonial officials, missionaries, or private individuals on home leave, while others participated in ethnological exhibitions. A handful of Cameroonians taught as language instructors at the Hamburg Colonial Institute or at the Berlin Seminar for Oriental Languages. An uncertain number of others arrived at German ports, often as members of the increasingly international workforce in the German merchant fleet or as stowaways or adventurers. In general, however, the initial impetus for travel came from the requests of elite families in Cameroon, especially the Duala, that their children be schooled or trained in Europe. Between 1885 and 1914, over sixty youngsters, including Equalla Deido, are known to have left the German protectorate for Germany with this purpose in mind, and it is this group of educational migrants that forms the focal point of this chapter.[2] Although there is a growing literature on the African presence in Germany, it tends to focus either on individual biographies or on the Weimar and National Socialist periods.[3] In comparison, far less research has been devoted to the imperial period, the formative period in the creation of a permanent African community in Germany, during which educational migrants were among the first colonial subjects to arrive in Germany; they formed one of the most prominent and visible African groups. Their presence was commented upon in colonial newspapers and their experiences were frequently covered by the local press in the towns in which they lived. At the same time, the European missions, colonial authorities, and the German Foreign Office debated the advantages of training Africans in Germany. This chapter concentrates on the type of schooling and/or apprenticeships the migrants undertook, the role of the colonial authorities in organizing and controlling educational visits, and the problems of reacculturation returning migrants faced. In doing so, it grants us insight into migrants' variable experiences as well as their reception in Germany. Furthermore, it demonstrates the influence that the presence of these migrants had upon future German policy regarding migration from the protectorates.

Equalla Deido, or Songue Epee Ekwalla Eyoum Ebelle, to give him his full Duala name, was the eldest son of Epee Ekwalla Deido (also known as Jim Ekwalla or King Deido), the traditional leader of the Deido quarter of Douala, and Njowe Kwane, one of his seven wives. By the onset of German colonial rule over Cameroon, the Duala were socially and politically organized into several key groupings, the two foremost being the Bell and Akwa lineages. The Deido group was originally a faction of the Akwa lineage. As their leader, Epee Ekwalla Deido was an influential figure and one of the signatories of the 1884 Treaty of Protection, which helped establish German control over Cameroon. Like a number of Duala notables, he played an important role in sponsoring local education by making land available to the German administration or the European missions in order for schools to be set up. Thus, in 1889 he granted the administration land in Deido on the condition that it construct its second school there and that it provide a European teacher.[4] At the beginning of 1890, twenty-five selected local youngsters, including Equalla, received four hours of daily instruction from the German teacher, Friedrich Flad, in basic reading, writing, and arithmetic skills, as well as singing.[5] Like Equalla, the majority of youngsters who were to leave for Germany had already attended either mission or government schools, and many had already been confronted with at least some basic German.

In addition, the Duala in their role as coastal middlemen had been quick to seize upon the opportunities opened up by the access to education that they hoped would benefit them in their relations with European traders and European governments.[6] Due to the efforts of the British Baptist Missionary Society, which had entered Cameroon around the middle of the nineteenth century, many Duala were literate long before the Germans arrived.[7] Furthermore, there was a tradition among some elite Duala families of sending their sons to Europe to be educated as a means of heightening their own prestige and increasing their political influence.[8] This was part of a larger nineteenth-century tradition of elite families along the west African coast that their sons be trained in Europe and in particular in Britain.[9] In Cameroon, this practice became increasingly common under German colonial rule. Elite Duala families themselves took the initiative in sending their children to Germany. As early as 1885, two influential figures within Duala society, the Bell paramount Ndumbe Lobe Bell and the Akwa government translator David Meetom (Mwange Ngondo), had first approached the governor of Cameroon, Freiherr Julius von Soden, to request that their sons be educated in Germany.[10] Epee Ekwalla Deido similarly believed in the benefits of a European experience for his children. In the spring of 1885, a younger son, Ebobse, was one of the first Duala to arrive in Germany, where he spent several weeks in Berlin under the care of German consul Eduard Schmidt.[11]

Schoolchildren

The initial response from both the colonial authorities in Berlin and the colonial administration in Douala to the idea of selected Cameroonian youngsters undertaking schooling or an apprenticeship in Germany was positive.[12] Governor Soden declared himself willing to support limited migration for educational purposes in the hope of binding prominent families to the colonial system, as well as out of a desire to create a skilled indigenous labor force that could be integrated into the colonial economy and the lower levels of the administration.[13] The administration thus acted as a mediator between the elite families and the educational institutions or German firms in Germany. Importantly, this involved little or no expense on its part. Instead, it was the parents of migrants who financed their children's education. In 1885, the administration estimated that this would cost parents around 2,000 marks a year. In reality, during the first decade of Cameroonian migration the actual sum was closer to 1,000 marks.[14] Included in this amount were the costs of schooling, clothing, food, and accommodation. This was a huge sum given that in 1885 the average German worker earned a yearly wage of just over 580 marks.[15] In view of the high costs, it is not surprising that it was almost exclusively children of Duala leaders, notables, or wealthy traders who were educated in Germany. Alongside Equalla, this group included Ludwig Mpundu Akwa, the future anticolonial activist and son of Akwa paramount Dika Akwa, and the future Bell paramount and anticolonial martyr Rudolf Duala Manga Bell, as well as three of his brothers and, later, his first son. Occasionally, domestic servants from lesser circumstances who accompanied returning members of the colonial administration or private individuals to Germany were also educated or trained at their master's expense.

The schooling that Cameroonian youngsters received was to some extent dependent upon their age on arrival in Germany, the institution that they attended, and the denominational background of the school. In Mülheim, for example, Equalla likely attended the local Victoria School, an evangelical elementary school (see figure 11.2 of Equalla in his uniform). The Cameroonian pupils received the same instruction as their German counterparts, typically covering a wide range of subjects, including German language skills, math, and a foreign language. In addition, some also received private tutoring at home. In general, throughout the entire colonial period these educational migrants received positive school reports in Germany,

Figure 11.2. Portrait of Prince Equalla Deido (Source: Unknown).

which frequently praised their ability, diligence, and behavior during lessons.[16] Yet, in spite of the progress they made they had little or no access to higher education and were sent back to Cameroon once their secondary education was complete.

Apprentices

A further two dozen or more Cameroonian youngsters left Cameroon to be trained as apprentices in Germany. Alongside the practical skills they were taught, they also received a basic education and were provided with private tutoring in the German language. Typically, apprentices were trained in trades geared toward their future participation in the development of the protectorate. These included construction skills such as carpentry, joinery, masonry, and metalworking, as well as crafts like tailoring, cooking, and shoemaking. A contract drafted between the colonial administration and the Corporation for Reinforced Concrete in Berlin gives an insight into the contractual obligations placed upon firms training Africans.[17] The company, which pioneered the use of new building techniques in Germany, had been responsible for work on several administration buildings in Douala, including the hospital. Their representative in Cameroon selected the young Duala M'bende Epo to undertake a three-year apprenticeship in Berlin. According to the contract of June 1892, the company was to meet all costs of his training, including accommodation and clothing. Furthermore, it was to finance elementary education in reading, writing, and math for Epo, who had already been receiving such lessons in Douala. For its part, the administration committed to paying for the travel costs to and from Germany, while then Governor Zimmerer agreed to pay for two suits and other clothes for Epo's outward journey out of private funds. Finally, the contract stipulated that Epo had to follow his teacher's orders and that, should he show signs of "immoral behavior" such as laziness or recalcitrance, the company would be entitled to send him back to Cameroon.

The Corporation for Reinforced Concrete was not the only German firm present in the protectorate to actively look to recruit indigenous apprentices to instruct in Germany. The construction and architectural company F. H. Schmidt funded the training of eight African youngsters at its Altona branch between 1887 and 1895. There were two underlying reasons these firms were prepared to make this investment. First, in contrast to German Southwest Africa, there was never any question of Cameroon becoming a settler colony for European migrants, primarily because of its tropical climate. As a consequence, few skilled European craftsmen migrated to the protectorate. A decade after the onset of German colonial rule, the *Deutsches Kolonialblatt*, the official mouthpiece of the colonial authorities, put the entire European population of Cameroon at 215 in its report for the period from August 1892 to July 1893.[18] Out of this number, there were only four carpenters, three machinists, and one metalworker. In light of debates over the ability of Europeans to acclimatize and work in tropical regions, European firms sought to develop a skilled indigenous workforce, which, crucially, could also be paid far lower wages. Secondly, until firms set up their own workshops in the protectorate, local youngsters would have to be trained outside of Cameroon.

Life in Germany

African colonial migrants, both schoolchildren and apprentices, were not granted German citizenship. Instead, they occupied an inferior, ill-defined legal position as subjects of a German protectorate (*Schutzgebietsangehöriger*). At times this was variously described by additional terms such as "person under German protection" (*Deutscher Schutzgenosse*) or simply as "native" (*Eingeborener*). Their presence in Germany was deemed desirable only as long as it suited the purposes of the colonial project. Even before they left for Europe, limits were imposed upon their period of stay, and the colonial authorities sought to regulate their freedom of movement and exposure to German society. This determined that, in general, educational migrants lived sheltered lives in Germany. The Cameroonian administration, in particular, stressed the need for strict supervision to be exercised during migrants' stays. This was deemed increasingly necessary after the Duala apprentice Alfred Bell (Belle Ndumbe), nephew of Ndumbe Lobe Bell, and one of the first Cameroonians to arrive in Germany in 1887, had expressed apparent sympathy for the social democratic workers' movement.[19] The colonial authorities, both in Germany and in the overseas territories, feared that socialism might gain a foothold in the colonies among the indigenous populations. They believed that the spread of concepts such as freedom, equality, and civil rights would undermine the rigid social and political structure of the colonies, which was based upon a principle of inequality and biased in favor of the colonizers.

Alfred had been involved in passing on letters of protest in which the brutality and unfairness of German rule was condemned from his family in Douala to leading government figures.[20] He himself questioned Germany's right to exercise authority over Cameroon in an interview with the London newspaper *The Pall Mall Gazette*. A copy of a later reproduction of the letter in a South Africa–based, English-language newspaper[21] was brought to the attention of the German authorities. As a consequence, he was eventually sent home before completing his apprenticeship. On account of the difficulties encountered with Alfred, plans to send gifted students at the administration's schools in Douala to Germany for a further year of training as teachers, clerks, or translators were dropped.[22] Nonetheless, the Cameroonian administration did not abandon its involvement in educating Africans in the metropole, but instead resolved to exercise even more control over migrants' visits. This demonstrated the continued importance it placed on the venture, while at the same time signaling the start of a growing concern as to the longer-term benefits and prospects of educating Africans in Germany.

On their nineteen-day voyage to Germany, young Duala migrants were usually in the care of a supervising European, a returning civil servant, colonial businessman, or missionary. Although it was not unknown for youngsters to be sent to Germany in pairs, young Cameroonians tended to live in relative isolation from other Africans in Germany. The youngsters, primarily members of Cameroon's social and political elite, frequently lived in distinctly middle-class or lower-middle-class environments. As the Cameroon administration requested, they were placed under the care of a watchful host family or institution, often in smaller German towns, where it was believed greater control could be exercised over their movements and experiences. Often, schoolteachers or similar authority figures acted as hosts, keeping the colonial authorities updated on the behavior and progress of their charges. Thus, in Mülheim Equalla stayed with the headmaster of the school he attended, Heinrich de Jong, and his wife Anna.

The available documents unfortunately allow only a fleeting insight into migrants' experiences and their reception in Germany. Local newspapers frequently ran stories about their stay, covering events such as their arrival, baptism, or departure. Such coverage reflected genuine local interest in the lives of migrants, whose very presence provided a visible link to the overseas empire for small communities otherwise largely untouched by the German colonial project. Many of them had likely never encountered men and women of African heritage before. Equally, this coverage suggests an underlying patronizing fascination with young Africans' ability to adapt to their new environment, as well as with their supposed "otherness." The public scrutiny youngsters faced could be unsettling. For example, local papers in Aalen even printed summaries of Duala Manga's and Tube Meetom's school reports.[23] This greatly upset Duala Manga, whose results were less favorable than Tube Meetom's.

Overall, migrants' experiences of Germany were highly variable and were greatly dependent on their situational context. In Aalen, efforts were made to make Duala Manga and Tube Meetom feel welcome; they were greeted by the town's brass band upon arrival. According to a former schoolmate, the two were popular among their fellow pupils: "Their friendship was greatly sought after, because both were physically very agile, good runners and swimmers. Rudolf [Duala Manga] possessed immense physical strength; nothing could easily happen to anyone who was his friend."[24] In contrast, Alfons Demba and Richard Lukenje were subjected to verbal abuse from local schoolchildren in Görlitz; their ability to resist this provocation was praised in a school report.[25] Alfred Bell was likewise aware of and upset by comments his presence attracted on the streets of

Berlin and remarked that it was "coarse and unmanly to laugh at a person or to insult him because his skin happens to be dark."[26] Undoubtedly, this exposure to discrimination and prejudice was something all Cameroonian migrants faced.

While Alfons Demba and Richard Lukenje developed a strong relationship with their host mother, who financed their education and helped to find the pair an apprenticeship, others, like Mpundu Akwa, experienced difficulties with their hosts' heavy-handed control and eventually changed families.[27] In at least one case, the Cameroonian administration struggled to find a host for African youngsters, demonstrating that not all communities were open to the prospect of providing a new home for colonial migrants. In 1888, it was unable to find a master in Paderborn willing to take on Josef Timba and Mbanga Akwa, who had traveled to Germany with Mpundu Akwa.[28] Instead, the youngsters were sent to be trained at the Catholic Arch Abbey St. Ottilien in Türkenfeld, near Munich.[29]

Throughout the entire colonial period, emphasis was often placed on the provision of moral and religious guidance for educational migrants. Within colonial discourse, the perceived moral and cultural inferiority of the colonized Africans was a prominent theme. This fed into notions of the civilizing nature of colonialism and a belief in the need to morally "raise" the indigenous populations to the level of the European. It also served to justify colonial brutality. In Germany, a large number of African migrants received confirmation or were baptized, often apparently at the request of the youngsters themselves. Such ceremonies were popular events. The congregation attending the baptismal ceremony for Mbanga Akwa at St. Ottilien in 1889 was so large that it had to be moved from the institution's own chapel to the larger, nearby church.[30] Among those in attendance was Ludwig Windthorst, head of the Catholic German Center Party, who had become Mbanga Akwa's godfather and after whom he was now to be named.[31] A report of the event was even sent to Pope Leo XIII in Rome, and Mbanga Akwa also received a letter of congratulations from his cousin Mpundu Akwa, who was later baptized. This illustrates the interest Germany's Catholic elite showed in the welfare and religious upbringing of African youngsters, both in Germany and in the protectorates.[32] It must also be seen in the context of Catholic and Center Party efforts to gain government permission to establish Catholic missions in the overseas territories.

Adapting to the climate in Germany and frequent, related bouts of ill health were also typically part of migrants' experience. Progress reports sent to the colonial authorities usually made reference to their health. Migrants were particularly susceptible to respiratory diseases like tuberculosis and pneumonia, which continued to affect the German public at large in spite of improvements in public health. Out of four Duala youngsters who had arrived to train with F. H. Schmidt in Altona in 1892, one died of pneumonia within a year, and two others returned home early at their own request following prolonged bouts of ill health.[33] At least half a dozen Cameroonians are known to have died from respiratory diseases in imperial Germany, with a further three dying of unknown causes. Among this number is Equalla, who died within six months of having arrived in Mülheim. While in Mülheim it has been suggested that he died of pneumonia, oral history in Deido tells the story of him dying in a duel defending his honor, after having been subjected to discriminatory remarks.[34] For Cameroonian parents, who entrusted their children to the care of the colonial administration or European firms, the news of a child's death in far-off Germany was devastating. Equalla's grief-stricken father is said to have grown a beard as a sign of mourning after his son's death and to have later visited Equalla's grave in Mülheim.[35] A local newspaper report supports this, telling of a visit paid to the Holthausen cemetery by members of the 1902 Duala delegation to Germany, which traveled to Europe to protest against colonial abuses.[36]

Returning Migrants and Travel Restrictions

Upon completing their education or training, African migrants were expected to return to Cameroon and put their skills to work. The German colonial administration in Cameroon often arranged employment opportunities for them. Josef Timba, who had trained as a shoe maker, was provided with materials and equipment on credit in order to construct a shoe making workshop. To help him meet his payments, a position as a clerk was also arranged for him.[37] African clerks with German language and translating skills were constantly sought after, and several returning migrants took positions either working at lower levels within the administration or at European firms. This also enabled the administration to keep these returnees under observation. After their homecoming, migrants often faced reacculturation issues. The twelve-year-old Ndumbe Elokan is unlikely to have been the only Cameroonian to encounter communication problems. After three years in Wiesbaden, he arrived back in Douala no longer able to speak his native language.[38] Greater problems, however, resulted from difficulties in reintegrating into the rigid, hierarchical social structure of colonial society.

Young Cameroonians whose progress at school or in apprenticeships had been praised by teachers, masters, and host parents in Germany often found that the authorities and European employers in Cameroon dismissed their skills and experience. For example, an administrative report assessing Tube Meetom's skills after six years in Germany claimed that he had learned little more than the German language and that his cooking abilities were inferior to those of any unskilled Togolese youngster.[39] As a consequence, he was to be retrained as a clerk. Similarly, after an initial positive report on their progress, Governor Seitz wrote that Alfons Demba and Richard Lukenje were not as capable as Duala who had been trained in workshops in Cameroon and that they were falling into bad habits such as laziness.⁴⁰ Seitz concluded that this illustrated how slight an impression a period of European education or training left on Africans. At the root of such comments was a change in the Cameroonian administration's attitude toward educational migration. As workshops for training young Africans were established in Cameroon, training them in Europe grew less necessary. This coincided with criticism of returning migrants' behavior and attitude from within the administration and sections of Cameroon's European population. Derogatory descriptors such as "trouser-wearing Negro" (*Hosen-Nigger*) emerged in colonial discourse to mock Africans who, in their (imperfect) mimicry of European manners and customs, were seen to be challenging notions of the essential difference between Europeans and non-Europeans that was so central to colonial rule.

For example, the *National Zeitung* reproduced the scathing comments from 1898 on returnees of Heinrich Vieter, an apostolic Prefect and member of the Catholic Pallottine mission to Cameroon:

> Here in Cameroon one finds a large number of natives [*Neger*] who were in Germany for educational purposes. On the whole, one must say that this has brought no happiness to those educated, or better "spoiled," there. The results are largely discontent with their situation [and] demands that will not be satisfied. They were treated in Germany as something special, even as princes.⁴¹

The last remark likely refers to the audiences with members of Germany's royal families and ruling elite that a handful of Cameroonians, like Alfred Bell, were granted during the first years of migration.⁴² This was to the chagrin of the colonial administration, who believed that such visits instilled migrants with a false sense of importance.⁴³ Returning migrants were frequently considered to be "spoiled," "arrogant," or "lazy," and a disruptive influence upon fellow Africans. Thus, the Protestant Basel Mission student Dinne Dumbe, who had trained as a cook in Württemberg, was accused of causing unrest in the mission school in Douala. Disparaged as being "half Europeanized," he failed to come back for the new school year, much to the missionaries' relief.⁴⁴ Richard Lukenje was so unhappy in Cameroon that he asked to be allowed to return to Germany, which his former host mother in Görlitz fully supported. The Cameroonian governor, however, refused to grant him his wish. The authorities used such disappointment and discontent among returning migrants to justify action taken against them as well as to criticize African education in Germany. Yet, it merely masked problems that migrants must have experienced in once again being subjected to the strict racial hierarchy of the colonial arena, with frequent abuses of power by the colonizers and the constant humiliations this entailed.⁴⁵ In addition to being more aware of the exploitation that they were subjected to, they were likely also frustrated that their hopes of finding better employment as a result of their European education remained unrealized.

Increasingly, the benefits of African education in Europe were brought into question by the administration in Cameroon. This was part of a larger debate taking place in both Germany and the protectorates concerning the presence of African colonial subjects in Europe. The colonial authorities' educational policies were failing to produce the loyal, docile subjects that they had hoped for. Instead, migrants like Alfred Bell were even actively engaging with German anticolonialists. Additionally, several Cameroonians had run up considerable debts in Germany that the administration feared it would have to cover.[46] The administration was also considerably concerned about attempts by Reverend Hughes at the Colwyn Bay, African Training Institute in Wales to recruit Cameroonian youngsters to be trained for future British colonial projects.[47] The administration was disappointed with the results of its educational policy, but it was loath to allow a colonial rival to potentially benefit from training German colonial subjects.

In response, it restricted Cameroonians' ability to leave the territory,[48] issuing a first travel ban in December 1893, three months after the German governor of the Marshall Islands had introduced similar legislation in the South Seas protectorate.[49] Under the new legislation, Cameroonians who wanted to leave now required the governor's permission; they had to fill out an application form and pay a ten-mark fee, regardless of the outcome. Severe penalties awaited those breaking the new restrictions; the migrants themselves, members of their family, or persons who encouraged them to leave faced a potential thousand-mark fine or imprisonment. This legislation was part of a general withdrawal of administrative support for the migration of Cameroonians to Europe for educational purposes or otherwise. By 1900, several of Germany's other overseas protectorates had implemented similar travel restrictions, and the Colonial Department was routinely turning down requests from German firms to train Africans in Germany.[50]

Mission-Sponsored Migration

From 1894 onward, the introduction of travel barriers resulted in steadily decreasing migration from the Cameroonian protectorate. Nonetheless, from the aftermath of the travel restrictions to the outbreak of World War I, elite Duala families and a handful of other prominent Cameroonian families remained insistent on sending their children to Europe. They now turned to the European missions to train or educate their children in Germany, or they sought to use their connections to European firms or individuals to help organize a stay abroad. The various missions were the driving force behind the development of an education system in Cameroon, which missionaries believed would improve their success in spreading their message and gaining converts.[51] In addition, their success depended on positive relations with the local indigenous elite. It is therefore not surprising that several wealthy and influential notables approached them about educating their children in Germany. The missions themselves, however, were divided over the issue of allowing Africans to travel to Europe.

As early as 1888, the largest European mission in Cameroon, the Protestant Basel Mission, warned its missionaries not to return to Europe with African youngsters and turned down several requests from Cameroonian notables keen on their children studying in Germany.[52] In general, it shared the administration's discriminatory viewpoint that exposure to German society had a corruptive influence on Africans. An 1892 report on the training of African youngsters in Europe, produced by the Basel missionary Heinrich Bohner for the German administration in Cameroon, exemplified this.[53] With reference to F.H. Schmidt's recent recruitment of four apprentices to be sent to Altona, Bohner questioned the chances of this strategy being successful and instead described two equally disadvantageous outcomes. In the first scenario, the youngsters would be pampered and would return to Cameroon with unrealistic demands, leading to feelings of neglect and unhappiness. Alternatively, they would come into contact with the ideas of social democracy, which would render them entirely useless for the development of the protectorate. Bohner instead pointed to the Baslers' established practice of training Africans in Africa as a potential blueprint. The report met with the agreement of Governor Zimmerer, who expressed hope that Schmidt's apprentices would be the last to leave for Germany.[54]

Nonetheless, in 1909 the Baslers agreed to make an exception in the case of Noah Sosiga, at the request of Sosiga's father Fon Nyonga II, arranging for him to be schooled in the small town of Spöck in southern Germany. The mission saw no alternative but to acquiesce because Sosiga's father was the traditional leader of Bali in the western grasslands of Cameroon and his support was deemed vital to the mission's success in the region.[55] While Sosiga's father hoped that his son would spend at least ten years in Germany, the youngster returned to Cameroon less than a year later, partly because the mission was unable to find a suitable family to take care of Sosiga.[56] This all too brief episode ended the Baslers' willingness to sponsor African education in Germany and was seen as confirmation of their belief that African migration to Europe was disadvantageous.

In contrast, after initial skepticism, Eduard Scheve, a central figure in establishing the German Baptist Mission in Cameroon, advocated the benefits of educating Africans in Europe. Between 1893 and 1909, at least eight Cameroonian youngsters from Douala and Victoria (now Limbé) were sent to live with Scheve and his family in the Moabit district of Berlin. There they were treated and brought up like Scheve's own children, with whom they shared a room.[57] The colonial authorities approved of this arrangement because they viewed Scheve as a trusted educator, capable of supervising the youngsters' stay. The Cameroonians under Scheve's care appear to have developed a strong relationship with him; one colleague spoke of the "veneration" they showed the pastor.[58] Among his charges were the cousins Bertha Ebumbu Mbenge and Esther Sike Bilé, two of only a handful of Cameroonian women to spend a prolonged period in Germany. The youngsters were educated in local schools and were trained to later assist with teaching in the mission's schools in Cameroon.

The Catholic Pallottine Mission also sponsored the education and apprenticeships of around a dozen Cameroonians in the small town of Limburg an der Lahn in Hessen, where the mission was based. As yet, little more than the names of these individuals has been recovered from the paltry documentary evidence presently available. Here again, it was anticipated that the youngsters would work for the mission upon their return to Cameroon. While a number of Cameroonians who received a mission education in Germany did indeed dedicate their lives to the spread of Christianity in Cameroon, several others broke all ties with the missions once back in Africa.[59]

In spite of the 1893 measures and the even harsher restrictions imposed in 1910, Cameroonians continued to successfully reach Germany, with or without official permission, and sometimes to be educated there, in part due to the help of the missions. As a result, around three dozen youngsters arrived in Germany for educational purposes after the imposition of the initial travel ban. This represented a relative decrease in numbers, but it is striking that several of these later migrants received administrative permission to leave the protectorate even though the colonial authorities had ended their support for the metropolitan education of Africans. Among this number was Otto Equalla, another of Equalla Deido's brothers, who accompanied his father as part of the Duala delegation of 1902 and was left in Scheve's care in Berlin when his father returned to Cameroon.[60] Unusually, the German authorities appear to have paid for Otto's education. From the scant sources available, it is unclear why this should have been the case. Indeed, there is far less available information in general about these later educational migrants. This is likely because the colonial authorities appear to have no longer played any role in facilitating their migration and, consequently, they no longer received regular updates about migrants' progress.

Conclusion

The onset of World War I, rather than travel restrictions imposed by the administration, brought an end to virtually all Cameroonian migration to Germany.[61] Between 1884 and 1914, education had been a key factor in stimulating this migration, with Cameroonian, primarily Duala, elites actively initiating it. Educational migrants' experiences in Germany were largely shaped by their status as colonial subjects and by the policies of the Cameroonian administration, which sought to restrict and control their exposure to German society. Once it became apparent to the colonial authorities that they were unable to fully supervise and control migrants' experiences, they came to view the presence of colonial subjects in Germany as counterproductive and withdrew their support. This meant that an ever-decreasing number of migrants left for Germany. The majority of educational migrants appear to have returned to Cameroon before the outbreak of war, where their reintegration into colonial society was often difficult. Hopes of taking up skilled positions within the colony economy often remained unfulfilled. Instead, returning migrants were frequently frustrated by the lack of opportunities available to them as well as by the discrimination they faced as a result of the strict racial segregation of colonial society. In turn, the authorities interpreted this as evidence of their arrogance or degeneration and used it as an argument for travel restrictions.

A small number of migrants, particularly those arriving in the immediate prewar period, remained in Germany on a longer-term basis either out of choice or necessity. They became part of an increasingly visible and networked African community. There they had to overcome numerous obstacles in order to carve out an existence for themselves, ranging from social isolation and discrimination to the question of their status in the postwar period. Others, like Equalla, died in Germany. It is unclear who paid for Equalla's gravestone, but his body was at first buried in a simple grave and reburied months later in a hereditary plot paid for by the de Jong family.[62] It was not entirely unknown for local communities to erect memorials or hold services for young Africans who had died during their stay in Germany. Thus, an elaborate funeral attended by over four hundred people was held for the Togolese Eque Soloman James Garber in Berlin in 1892, while in 1903 German friends of the young Duala apprentice bookbinder Daniel Njo Disom, who died in Hersfeld, Hessen, arranged for a gravestone to commemorate his life.[63] While Disom's grave has long since disappeared, Equalla's provides an important reminder of the migration of Africans to Germany during the imperial period. His transnational story is remembered not only in the form of his grave in Mülheim, but also by a window in the church of Bonamadourou in Deido (see figure 11.3).

Figure 11.3. The window in the church at Bonamadourou that is said to depict Equalla and his sister (Source: Robbie Aitken).

The church, an extension of an earlier chapel, was officially opened by the Protestant Basel Mission in 1912 and the window, which depicts Jesus with two Cameroonian children, was donated with funds raised by Swiss children in September 1911. According to oral tradition in Deido, the children are said to represent Equalla and his younger sister Endale Epeye Ekwalla.[64]

Notes

1. When the gravestone was restored in 1989, the date of death was incorrectly carved as being 1901; Equalla died in 1891. I am grateful to Ngando Mackay in Deido, Douala, for telling me the story of Equalla and allowing me access to his research. Pastor Sonnenberger in Holthausen also provided me with material. See Dietrich Sonnenberger, "Der Prinz von Holthausen hat wieder Familie—neue Erkenntnisse rund um ein 'rätselhaftes Grab,'" *Nachrichten der evangelischen Kirchengemeinde Holthausen,* April–May 2005, 10–11. See also Stefanie Michels, "Mülheim an der Ruhr: Der kleine schwarze Prinz. Das Grab von Moses Equalla Deido," in *Kolonialismus hierzulande: Eine Spurensuche in Deutschland,* ed. Ulrich van der Heyden and Joachim Zeller (Erfurt, Germany: Sutton Verlag, 2008), 417–21.
2. This chapter is based on a larger project on the lives of Cameroonian migrants and their children in Germany, 1884–1960, supported by a grant from the UK Arts and Humanities Research Council (grant number 112228). On the basis of this research, the names and biographical information of over seven hundred Africans have been recovered: over a third of these originally came from Cameroon.
3. See, in particular, Katharina Oguntoye, *Eine Afro-Deutsche Geschichte: Zur Lebenssituation von Afrikanern in Deutschland von 1884 bis 1950* (Berlin: Hoho Verlag, 1997); Peter Martin and Christine Alonzo, eds., *Zwischen Charleston und Stechschritt: Schwarze im Nationalsozialismus* (Hamburg, Germany: Dölling und Galitz Verlag, 2004); Tina Campt, *Other Germans: Black Germans and the Politics of Race, Gender and Memory in the Third Reich* (Ann Arbor: University of Michigan Press, 2004); Tobias Nagl, *Die unheimliche Maschine: Rasse und Repräsentation im Weimarer Kino* (Munich: Text und Kritik, 2009); and Ulrich van der Heyden, ed., *Unbekannte Biographien* (Berlin: Kai Homilius, 2008).
4. Contract between the Governor and the Headman Epea Kwala [sic] from Bonebela, 29 September 1889, Bundesarchiv Berlin (hereafter BArch) R1001 4073, 95.
5. Report on the Condition of the School in Bonabela-Deido, 1 September 1890, BArch R1001 4073, 144–45.
6. Concerning the Duala as "middlemen," see Ralph Austen and Jonathan Derrick, *Middlemen of the Cameroon Rivers: The Duala and Their Hinterland, c. 1600–c. 1960* (Cambridge: Cambridge University Press, 1999), 1–4.
7. Concerning the British Baptist Missionary Society in Cameroon, see Jean-Paul Messina and Jaap van Slageren, *Histoire du christianisme au Cameroun: Des origins à nos jours* (Paris: Éditions Karthala, 2005), 27–36; and Samuel Johnson, *Schwarze Missionare—Weiße Missionare! Beiträge westlicher Missionsgesellschaften und einheimischer Pioniere zur Entstehung der Baptistengemeinde in Kamerun (1841–1949)* (Kassel, Germany: Onken Verlag, 2004).
8. Jean-Pierre Félix Eyoum, Stefanie Michels, and Joachim Zeller, "Bonamanga: Eine Kosmopolitische Familiengeschichte," *Mont Cameroun,* no. 2 (2005): 14.
9. David Killingray, "Africans in the United Kingdom: An Introduction," in *Africans in Britain,* ed. David Killingray (Ilford, UK: Frank Cass, 1994), 7–9.

10. Governor Soden to Prince von Bismarck, 8 August 1885, BArch R1001 4297, 3–5.
11. See "Konsul Schmidt aus Kamerun," *Teltower Kreisblatt,* 21 April 1885, 3, and in the section "Steglitz," *Teltower Kreisblatt,* 4 July 1885, 4. Here Deido is falsely referred to as Bobb, son of King Dido.
12. Ministry of Intellectual, Educational and Medical Affairs to Bismarck, 3 October 1885, BArch R1001 4297, 8–10.
13. Soden to Bismarck, 8 August 1885, BArch R1001 4297, 3–5.
14. The parents of Mpundu Akwa and Tube Meetom paid 1,000 marks in 1889 and 1895, respectively. In Meetom's case, the Foreign Office paid half the costs. It is unclear whether they took over all payments after Meetom's father was executed as a rebel. Vandenesch, Government and School Advisor, to Royal Governmental President, Pilgrim, 8 August 1889, BArch R1001 5571, 27; and Dean Knapp to the Basel Mission, 23 January 1895, Mission 21 Basel (hereafter, Mission 21), Q-3-4, Mixed correspondence A-M, 1891–96.
15. Figure from Gerd Hohorst, Jürgen Kocka, and Gerd Ritter, *Sozialgeschichtliches Arbeitsbuch II* (Munich: C.H. Beck, 1978), 107.
16. There are a number of examples in the files BArch R1001 5571–76.
17. Governor Zimmerer, Contract Concerning the Education of M'bende Epo from Akwadorf, 25 June 1892, BArch R1001 5571, 134–35.
18. "Report on the State and Development of the Protectorate of Cameroon, 1 August 1892 to 31 July 1893," *Beilage zu Nr. 20 des "Deutschen Kolonialblattes"* (hereafter *DKB*) 4 (1893): 1.
19. On Bell, see Wolfgang Mehnert, "Schulpolitik im Dienste der Kolonialherrschaft des deutschen Imperialismus" (PhD diss., Karl Marx Universität, 1965), 125–34.
20. Alfred Bell to Joseph Bell, 31 October 1888, BArch R1001 4297, 88–89.
21. *The Pall Mall Gazette,* "An African Prince on German West Africa," 16 April 1890, 1. Reprinted in *The African Times,* 1 May 1890, 68; in BArch R1001 5571, 70.
22. See von Soden to von Bismarck, 30 June 1888, BArch R1001 4071, 99–102; Foreign Minister von Bismarck to von Soden, 23 January 1889, BArch R1001 4072, 12–16; and Mehnert, "Schulpolitik," 126.
23. Schoolteacher Oesterle to the Colonial Department of the Foreign Office (hereafter AAKA), 1 April 1894, BArch R1001 5572, 99–100.
24. All translations are my own unless otherwise stated. Hermann Stützel, quoted in Henning Petershagen, "Afro-Aristokrat in Aalen ausgebildet," *Südwest Presse,* 31 May 1997, in Stadtarchiv Ulm. See also Eyoum, Michels, and Zeller, "Bonamanga," 16.
25. Report, Realschule-Director Baron, 20 November 1893, BArch R1001 5572, 65–66.
26. *The Pall Mall Gazette,* "An African Prince on German West Africa."
27. On Demba and Lukenje's relationship to their host mother, see Elisa von Joeden-Forgey, "Nobody's People: Colonial Subjects, Race Power, and the German State, 1884–1945, " (PhD diss., University of Pennsylvania, 2004), 352–69. On Mpundu, see Soden to Bismarck, 7 November 1889, BArch R1001 4298, 92.
28. Vandenesch to Pilgrim, 2 August 1889, BArch R1001 5571, 29–30.
29. "Die Taufe dreier Neger in St. Ottilien," in *Missionsblätter St. Ottilien* 1 (1888–1889): 586–91. Two further African youngsters were at St. Ottilien, the Liberian Leo Dagwe and the Sudanese Hassi.
30. Ibid, 590.
31. Ibid.
32. Windthorst was not the only influential Catholic to act as godfather to young African migrants. Karl Graf Drechsel zu Deuffstetten was the godfather of another child at St. Ottilien, the Sudanese Hassi, while Graf von Brühl was the godfather of the Duala Franz Peter Mundi ma Lobe. Notice, *Norddeutsche Zeitung,* 30 October 1890, BArch R1001 5571, 98; and Baptismal record, Mundi ma Lobe, Diözesanarchiv Limburg, Lim k 17, 1893, Nr. 131—Geburt.

33. F. H. Schmidt to AAKA, 8 April 1893, BArch R1001 5572, 26; F. H. Schmidt to AAKA, 10 February 1894, BArch R1001 5572, 79; and Joki Dikonge to Schmidt, 24 June 1894, BArch R1001 5572, 135.
34. Interview Ngando Mackay, Douala, March 2006; Sonnenberger, "Der Prinz von Holthausen hat wieder Familie."
35. Interview Mackay.
36. *Mülheimer Zeitung,* 12 September 1902. I am grateful to Peter Schick in Mülheim for sending me this information. See also Michels, "Mülheim an der Ruhr," 420.
37. "Ein eingeborener Neger als Kanzlist und Schuhmachermeister in Kamerun," *DKB* 3 (1892): 23.
38. Soden to Chancellor Caprivi, 9 July 1890, BArch R1001 4299, 8–9.
39. Puttkamer to AAKA, 24 December 1897, BArch R1001 5574, 147–48.
40. Seitz to Chancellor, Hohenlohe-Schillingsfürst, 1 August 1896, BArch R1001 5573, 165.
41. *National Zeitung,* 25 August 1898, in BArch R1001 5575, 13.
42. Alfred Bell apparently met Bismarck. See *The Pall Mall Gazette,* "An African Prince on German West Africa." Samson Dido met Crown Prince Friedrich Wilhelm, later Friedrich III, while four Cameroonian sailors met Emperor Wilhelm I. Soden to Bismarck, 7 December 1886, BArch R1001 4297, 64–66.
43. Ibid. See also Report of the Teacher Christaller, included in Soden to Bismarck, 27 October 1888, BArch R1001 4297, 45–51.
44. Brother Mader, Yearly Report of the Middle School in Bethel 1892, 2 February 1893, Mission 21, E-2, 5 1892, Nr. 137.
45. See Joeden-Forgey, "Nobody's People," 338.
46. For examples, see Alfred Bell: Soden to Bismarck, 7 November 1889, BArch R1001 4297, 90–93; Rudolf Duala Manga Bell: Governor Puttkamer to Imperial Chancellor, Hohnelohe-Schillingsfürst, 8 December 1896, BArch R1001 5574, 24.
47. See "Auswanderung Eingeborener aus Kamerun," *DKB* 5 (1894): 111–12. Two sons of the Baptist preacher Josua Dibundu were sent to be educated in Wales before the travel restrictions were put in place. The administration believed that ten more youngsters were preparing to leave for Wales and that Hughes was looking for fifty youngsters in all. For more on the Institute, see Ivor Wynne Jones, "Africans in Wales: The Story of the Congo Institute," in *A Tolerant Nation: Exploring Ethnic Diversity in Wales,* ed. Charlotte Williams, Neil Evans, and Paul O'Leary (Cardiff: University of Wales Press, 2003), 77–92.
48. The travel restrictions were also introduced to prevent potential indigenous workers from leaving the colony. Adolf Rüger, "Die Enstehung und Lage der Arbeiterklasse unter dem deutschen Kolonialregime in Kamerun (1895–1905)," in *Kamerun unter deutscher Kolonialherschaft,* vol. 1, ed. Helmuth Stoecker (Berlin: Rütten und Loening, 1960), 206.
49. Decree concerning the Emigration of Natives from the Imperial Protectorate, 11 December 1893, *DKB* 5 (1894): 105.
50. Travel restrictions were introduced in German East Africa in 1896, Togo in 1899, and, in 1899, the governor of German Southwest Africa argued that a previous law of 1891 could be used to prevent Africans from leaving the territory. Further legislation was introduced preventing colonial subjects from being brought to Germany for display purposes. The files BArch R1001 5575–77 contain several negative responses to requests for African apprentices or employees.
51. On mission education in Cameroon, see Kenneth Orosz, *Religious Conflict and the Evolution of Language Policy in German and French Cameroon, 1885–1939* (New York: Peter Lang, 2008).
52. Committee Protocol § 406, 8 April 1888, Mission 21. Also, Committee Protocol § 4, 3 January 1896, Mission 21.
53. Bohner to Zimmerer, May 1892 (exact date unknown), BArch R1001 5571, 141–48.

54. Zimmerer to Bohner, 18 May 1892, Mission 21, E-2, 5, 42.
55. Committee Protocol § 735, 5 July 1909, Mission 21.
56. Committee Protocol § 879, 1 September 1909, Mission 21.
57. Scheve names five Cameroonian children who, at various times, lived with him. Eduard Scheve, *Die Mission der deutschen Baptisten in Kamerun (West-Afrika) (von 1884 bis 1901)* (Cassel, Germany: Verlag der Missions-Gesellschaft der deutschen Baptisten, 1901). At least three others, Alexander Douala Manga Bell, Richard Manga Bell, and Otto Equalla, stayed with him later.
58. Jürgen Günther, "Mission im kolonialen Kontext. Beiträge zur Geschichte der Mission der deutschen Baptisten in Kamerun 1891 bis 1914" (unpublished master's thesis, University of Hamburg, 1985), 66.
59. Richard Edube Mbene served the Baptist mission until his death: Alfred Scheve, "Richard Edube Mbene," *Unsere Heidenmission* 1 (1907): 36–37; Joseph Ayisi, brought by the Pallottine Mission to Germany, played an important role in spreading Catholicism in Cameroon: Philippe Laburthe-Tolra, *Vers la Lumière? Ou le Désir d'Ariel. A propos des Beti du Cameroun Sociologie de la conversion* (Paris: Karthala, 1999), 251; Peter Munguli, trained by the Pallottine Mission in Limburg, left the religious life once back in Douala: Heinrich Vieter and Jean Criaud, *Les premiers pas de l'Eglise au Cameroun: Chronique de la mission catholique 1890–1912* (Yaoundé, Cameroon: Publications du Centenaire, 1989), 60.
60. Alfred Scheve, "Vier Generationen," *Unsere Heidenmission,* no. 2 (1902): 12–14; Notice, 23 July 1904, BArch R1001 5577, 35.
61. In the immediate postwar period, a handful of Cameroonians arrived in Germany, while several other youngsters left the newly French-controlled mandate territory of Cameroon to be educated in France.
62. Information from Peter Schick.
63. On Garber, "Where the Black Man is Brother," *New York Times,* 4 March 1892, 5. On Disom, *Fröhliche Weihnacht wünscht allen lieben deutschen Sonntagsschülern der Vorstand der Missionsgesellschaft der deutschen Baptisten Steglitz bei Berlin* (Cassel, 1908), in Onckenarchiv des Bundes Evang.-Freikirchlicher Gemeinden in Deutschland, Berlin.
64. Interview Mackay. My thanks to Ngando Mackay for showing me the church in Bonamadourou. It is unclear whether the two children depicted in the window were originally intended to represent Equalla and his sister. A report on the opening of the church mentions the window, but not any link to Equalla. S. Ebding, "Kirchweih in Bonebela in Kamerun," *Evangelische Heidenbote,* no. 7 (1912): 52.

Afterword

AFRICANS IN EUROPE
New Perspectives

Dirk Hoerder

The novelty of multifaceted research on Africans—on their presence in Europe, in "black studies" once skin color becomes a marker, and on Africans in German-speaking central Europe, in particular—permits scholars to follow their own inclinations, to be exploratory, and perhaps to speculate. This liberal climate has fostered the development of new perspectives and a spatial analysis of networks of African mobility—whether forced or free. However, even under such auspicious conditions, scholars are bound by unspoken assumptions that they have been socialized to hold from infancy and that are reinforced by disguised undertones in prevailing discourses and conceptualizations. One of these is that men and women who achieved status and material wealth in Europe had native roots there and were, perhaps, part of a larger European civilization. In other words, they were white.

In this afterword, I will briefly connect reflections on Africans in German-speaking societies to those in other European societies to emphasize once again that Africans have been present in Europe for centuries; I will outline three approaches that might help scholars change perspectives on Africans in Europe; and I will discuss, again briefly, transatlantic and trans-European networks of African mobility. The data on "others" in Europe and their societies of origin, which have always been available but have been selectively overlooked for centuries, indicate a story different from the whiteness-centered one. When the Portuguese voyaged from their Iberian civilization to Benin in west Africa in the early 1480s, they found the city to be "the powerful capital of a considerable empire" with ramparts and entry gates, a large palace, and wide streets. Comparing the capital to cities in the Netherlands, a Dutch visitor regarded it as more spacious.

Notes from this chapter begin on page 240.

In its market, raw iron, finished utensils, and the artwork of iron masters were sold.[1] White historians, in an uncivilized imposition, obliterated Western awareness and memory of these accomplishments to spread the story of a continent inhabited by peoples incapable of self-directed agency but useful as slaves. Only in the 1930s did European artists and ethnologists rediscover the artwork and, even later, the complexity of African cultures, while historians continued to produce racialized ideologies for another half-century.

In the last few decades, however, historians of the German-speaking regions have finally emerged from their nationalist boxes and reminded themselves of the breadth of the Hohenstaufen Empire: it stretched from Sicily to Lower Saxony and was not an empire merely "of the German nation" but, in the thirteenth century, centered on Palermo, where the court of Frederick II included Arab North Africans, sub-Saharan Africans, and Mediterraneanized Normans. If historians of Germany or other particular states, as well as historians of continents and of slave labor, would open their eyes to religious symbols or combine the history of states with Europe-wide religiousness, black saints and the black Virgin would come into focus. The religious history of Europe as a whole and the German regions in particular abounded with highly visible African elements that later generations expunged from their national historiographies. For example, Maurice, an African and a military officer of the Roman Empire, was sanctified, and cathedrals in northern Germany from Münster to Magdeburg have been dedicated to him for centuries.[2] The veneration of black Virgins, probably originating in Africans' respect for fertility, seems to have spread from Africa via the Iberian Peninsula as far as the Polish-cultured regions. It may also have incorporated traditions of the cult of the Egyptian goddess Isis that had already been adapted in the Ottoman Empire's many-cultured and multireligious practices.[3]

Similarly, if we shift gears from political and religious to economic history, the Copenhagen slave-trading companies in the Danish and northern German regions,[4] especially that of the Schimmelmann family, as well as the activities of the Fugger and Welser families in the south, come into view. In Augsburg and elsewhere in Europe during his travels, Albrecht Dürer depicted men and women of African origin, including one respectful portrait of 1508 that may represent an Augsburg merchant or merchant clerk.[5] From the North Sea coastal ports, German rulers invested in the slave trade and captains sent African boys to their families from tiny ports on the island of Sylt via Emden to Middelburg in the Netherlands.

Other examples from this volume, from the southwest and the center of the German regions, add important new facets to this entwining of German and European with African history. In the mid-sixteenth century, Vicente Lusitano, born to a white father and a black mother in Portugal around 1522, pursued a career as a composer and music theorist that spanned both his mother's African and his father's European backgrounds, southern and northern Europe

(Rome, Venice, and Stuttgart), and Catholicism and Protestantism. Europe's musicologists, however, dissociated him from his mixed origin, regarding him as white—indeed, he had to be in view of their assumptions.[6] Toward the end of the eighteenth century, Hessian troops, sent against their will—almost like slaves—to fight on the British side during the American War for Independence, returned to Kassel with at least 150 African Americans, including soldiers and their families.[7] Slaves from the Danish Caribbean, who had been brought as servants to Copenhagen but were then liberated and baptized, migrated to Hamburg and married local women.[8] From medieval to early modern history, from the post-1871 imperial outreach of the German empire to the Federal Republic, German regions and cities were connected to the Africas and Americas. Across the centuries, men and women of African origin showed agency and achieved status and respect.

Once historians change both their starting point in place and time and their frames of reference, the interaction of Africa and Europe reemerges in view and analysis. Europe has never been merely white. Nor have those "of African origin" been black only. There are many shades of white and black along a continuum of pigmentation, as well as many fusions of cultural practices and intellectual achievements from different parts of the entwined African-Asian-European-American world. This short, reflective chapter will address some of the assumptions that obliterate historical memory. Slaves have been said to lack agency, but is it not the historians and the general public, enslaved by assumptions, frames of reference, and grids of meaning, who have lacked the agency to free themselves from such bondage?

A first reframing of perspectives concerns the starting point of Africans in Europe. Traditional scholarship has taken Portugal's transportation and humiliation of the first black Africans as slaves in the mid-1440s as the point of departure. From there, the accepted narrative, supported by data, if only by a selection of them, expanded in place and time to enslaved dark-skinned people in Spain, then in England and in France, sometimes also in the Netherlands, and almost never in Denmark. Yet historians could choose other starting points from the available data. Even if they remained within the "slavery" paradigm, they could incorporate the Netherlands and Denmark (which owned what Europeans called the Virgin Islands), which would indicate an African presence across southern, western, and northern Europe, including the German regions and, perhaps, Sweden. Historians could also expand their perspective to include Mediterranean slavery, which differed from the later chattel slavery in the Atlantic world, and the sexual power men in a household felt they had over enslaved servant women of African origin. The laws in some city-states legitimized the offspring born to bound women and free men. Another option would be for historians to turn to the Ottoman Empire, with its different forms of bound servants, bound statesmen, and bound women as marriage partners for the elites. Such men and women came from Egypt, Nubia, and east Africa, as well as from the Circassian region in the borderlands between Europe and Asia. The trading connections across the Black Sea and northward along the rivers to Russia's capital would bring eastern Europe into the sphere of analysis—Hannibal (1696–1781), the Russian military commander and great-grandfather of Alexander Pushkin, had his origins in Africa.

A second reframing of questions and approaches would turn from time and place to status hierarchies in medieval and early modern Europe. It would not fix its gaze on "slavery" and equate the term with chattel slavery as developed in the Atlantic world's plantation regime, which was capitalized and organized in Europe, but would look at contexts of bound relationships in various European societies. At the top, vassalage bound a middle level of lords and nobles to the crowned head of a society; at the bottom, serfdom bound peasants to the lords of the land. In England, for example, starting in the mid-fourteenth century, agricultural, common, and artisan laborers were bound to masters for a year. They could change masters or mistresses only at one specified date in late fall. Entire societies were structured by a hierarchy of estates, in which each and every group had an assigned place and status and usually expressed its social position by means of visible and codified signs—most often dress. Children inherited and were bound to their fathers' positions. Migrants of African origin, whether free or enslaved, became a part of this social ensemble. Some took up positions as individuals in a court environment or joined the merchant "class," to use a more modern term, and like everyone else, they were bound to their position in society.

For centuries, the young of all social levels in these societies were destined for prearranged marital partnerships. Nobles and urban patricians married off daughters and sons according to the economic and territorial interests of the family, and peasant families attempted to consolidate landholdings. The young were bound to the decisions of their parents and to family strategies. The modern concepts of individual "freedom" and choice were not part of societal practices. Within such a scheme, "court moor" appears to be a "social slot" in the hierarchy, and Iberian slaves form a social substratum among bound urban laborers and peasants. Since skin color was not yet clearly dichotomized into white and black, nor necessarily worth mentioning, black-white interactions are often difficult for historians to trace. When Africans in Europe married locally or had children out of wedlock, their children were not characterized as "moors," "Africans," or "blacks" in baptismal records or other documents. Skin color was a visible but not a defining characteristic of human beings.

At the top end of the social scale, in courtly culture, Africans were viewed as "exotic." This term denoted something expensive, unique, and worth transporting and giving a special visibility.[9] Exquisite Chinese porcelain, cloth from India, white ivory from Africa—all received their place in collections of "curiosities." Such *Kuriositätenkabinette* reflected an interest in the extraordinary, the different. The presence of exotic persons indicated a court's openness, awareness of the wider world, and willingness to inquire. In terms of power and cultural hierarchies, such presence was meant to demonstrate the respective noble family's or dynasty's prosperity and far-reaching connections. Only later, in the nineteenth-century frame of mind, did Orientalism—to follow Edward Saïd's conceptualization[10]—turn a regard for difference driven by curiosity into a gaze that labeled. The "other" came to be cordoned off in relation to a (narrow) view of self, and European intellectuals arrogated to themselves the power to define and to impose such categories on the rest of the world.

All across Europe, scholars, in their inquiry into unknown worlds and peoples, placed in-migrating or transported Africans—whether from northern, central, or western Africa, from Egypt or the sub-Saharan east—into their societies' contexts of bondage and color coding, and labeled them religious "heathens." But a number of factors did reshape the image of Africans and others in general, including interstate and interimperial power struggles, the expansion of colonization and trade beyond Europe, warfare and competition between the Catholic Habsburg Empire and the Muslim Ottoman Empire, and the small but heavily armed Portuguese state's appetite for Africa and its gold and human beings, commodified over time.

When, in 1444, the first sizable shipment of enslaved Africans arrived in the port of Lagos in Portugal's Algarve in southwestern Europe, they were treated in an extremely dehumanizing manner. Consequently, one might hypothesize that, though intimate relations were still legal and ubiquitous, the inhumanity of chattel slavery was already present at this time.[11] Yet this perspective oversimplifies the matter: economic, political, and societal frames were more complex than that. In the economic sphere, Portugal's Crown was in the process of redefining intercommunity relations. Trade protocols had traditionally permitted unarmed merchants to voyage and trade between dynastic societies in Europe and across the Mediterranean to Africa. To remain competitive, these merchants needed to keep transaction costs low, so they relied on negotiations with rulers whose territory they entered and on established customs of exchange ("protocols") with local merchants and trading partners of other cultures, skin colors, or states. Outside their state of birth, they were "foreigners" in modern parlance, but in the thinking of the times they were connectors to long-distance trade and goods not available locally. As a functional necessity, they were allocated a slot in the social structure and hierarchy of a society. For internal economic reasons, the Portuguese Crown decided to end the "culture of negotiation" and to combine mercantile outreach and state power by arming merchant vessels and asserting its merchant-military superiority over suppliers, competitors, and partners elsewhere. While it could not impose this change from peaceful trade to conquest on the mighty neighboring Castilian lands or the English competitors on the seas, it could impose it southward onto African peoples and, then, eastward onto peoples around the Indian Ocean. The Portuguese captain-commander Vasco da Gama inflicted cruelty on Muslim pilgrims of high social rank to terrorize the trading communities in southern India's ports. The increasing violence against Africans—by all slave-trading states, the west African coastal supplier states included—was part of this new self- and worldview that accompanied European powers' penetrations into regions inhabited by peoples of other customs and colors. Simultaneously, the Church—and its secular dynastic supporters—otherized non-Christians and, over time, expelled Jews and Muslims from Iberia and other parts of Europe. At the juncture of the late medieval and early modern periods, Europe's mercantile, religious, and political elites, in an unholy alliance, redefined the relations between human beings, to the lasting detriment of non-Europeans across the world.

In southeastern Europe, the expansion of the Ottoman Empire along its western frontier into lands its Habsburg competitors considered their own precipitated a pan-European reaction. This advance of Muslims, who abolished feudalism in the Balkan societies that they acquired and liberated, posed both an economic and a religious threat to the prevailing European order. Thus, clerical intellectuals and Habsburg diplomats began to label the Ottoman Empire's many-cultured armies and its complex interethnic and interreligious imperial structures "bloodthirsty Turks," "infidels," or "heathens." The imperial-religious wars this conflict prompted brought another group of free migrants or prisoners of war to Christian Europe: Ottoman subjects originally of Muslim faith. Consequently, in addition to Africans, "former Turks"—which implied a conversion from Islamic to Christian faith—entered the picture. While the label may have suggested a shaded skin color, it certainly did indicate different dress in the codes of the times. The limited research on this group and the lack of skin color references in the documentation leave it unclear whether "former Turks" were of Asian, eastern Mediterranean, or African origin. In any case, Africans and former Turks fit into "slots" of their own in European societies, which had been divided into orders and estates at the beginning of the early modern period. These slots were distinct and separate from the slave status and its accompanying imagery of Europe's developing plantation belt overseas, with its forced and commodified nonwhite human labor.

A third reframing entails taking a closer look at the meanings of both "black" and "African" in European languages and how they changed over time. While the meaning of the term "African" has been fairly constant, the meaning of "black" has shifted considerably over time. "African" seems clear: the armed expeditions of the Portuguese brought people from west Africa to Europe. Bondage—outlined above as regards European practices—did exist in many African societies as a rights-in-person slavery in concept and practice, although it differed from later Euro-American concepts of chattel slavery. Such bondage could and did involve the trading of bound persons. Regarding labor, women were valued over men and were therefore traded off less often. This type of bound existence could be and was transformed by manipulative African rulers and traders to supply the Portuguese with captive subjects or captives from neighboring, less well-armed societies.

In terms of labeling by color, "black" is far more complex. Kate Lowe points to the disastrous consequences of a mistranslation of the Bible—the Queen of Sheba was said to be "black *but* beautiful" instead of "black *and* beautiful."[12] In both biblical and other usages, "black" carried multiple connotations. Since no general negative association was as yet fixed, a variety of usages were common. The devil, usually characterized as a black angel rather than a white one, was also called "luci-fer," the bringer of light. Dutch burghers as depicted by the Flemish school of painters were dressed in black as were many orders of nuns and friars—here, the color certainly had no negative connotation. "White as snow" and "black as ebony"—like the juxtaposition of ivory and ebony—referred to beauty. This is evident in the practice of cabinetmakers—many of them migrants from German regions—in the Saint Antoine suburb of Paris to work ebony and other woods into furniture for the city's bourgeoisie and the court, as well as in the fact that some shops in the suburb used heads of blacks as ensigns. From China and Japan, Europe's traders imported black lacquer work, an expensive luxury of exquisite beauty. Some European artists acquired their skills as lacquerers by imitating Asian styles.[13] Given this historical association of the color "black" with beauty, it clearly required effort and intent to make the negative association dominant.

In all historical junctions, the significations of black or Mediterranean "brownness" were multiple. At the times of the trans-Mediterranean wars over possession of the Iberian Peninsula and the Crusades in the eastern Mediterranean, the chroniclers, usually paid by the Church, sounded fairly perplexed in their comments on the attractiveness of "dark" women to the Christian (i.e., lighter-skinned) soldiers. The English painter Benjamin West (1738–1820), in his *Christ Blessing Little Children* (1781), depicted Christ, the children, and the women—presumably their mothers—as white, and the men in the background—presumably the fathers—as of "brown" or "dark" or "eastern Mediterranean" complexion. Imaginations or depictions of skin color were not necessarily consistent. Turning from imagined to actual skin color and its representations, it can be noted that Alpine peasants working in high altitudes and exposed to ultraviolet sunlight never appeared to be "white"-skinned in naturalist paintings, and the racializing ideologies of the late nineteenth and early twentieth century described Italians as "olive" or "swarthy" and eastern Europeans as "dark."[14] Skin color in its many shades was valued differently at different times. The black-white dichotomy is a simplification that obscures the complexities of complexion. The idealized "white" may, in other contexts, appear to be pale and connote lifelessness or lack of vigor, as in "pale-faced."

In sum, examining the implicit grids of meaning within which Africans in Europe have traditionally been placed and reframing them with empirical data—

that is, as we have suggested here, by critiquing the starting point of "slavery in Portugal," placing the views of Africans within trans-European power hierarchies and practices of bondage, and assessing period-sensitive meanings of "black"—permits a more differentiated analysis. Reintroducing Africans into European history after their symbolic annihilation by white nationalist historians, these new frameworks counter the tendency of some recent scholars to view all blacks as exploited victims and thus deprive them of agency. Such views project nineteenth-century practices of chattel slavery and US historians' pre-1960s views of African Americans back onto thirteenth- to eighteenth-century European societies. Images were developed over centuries and had multiple meanings that changed over time. Interactions were codified, questioned, and recodified. Dichotomies—black-white, European-African, or free-slave—force complex interactions and perceptions into narrow categories devoid of real meaning.

Given the comparatively small number of Africans in Europe, it is not surprising that Africans might be seen as individuals in a particular place without connection to the larger world, as a few dark-skinned persons with little or no societal impact. This is especially true for the German-speaking regions, where there were no Atlantic ports and participation in Europe's imperial power struggles and colonizing outreach came relatively late. Nonetheless, we need to ask how Africans got to their many locations in Europe and whether they could move or had to stay put. Close empirical examination reveals two long-distance networks: one transatlantic, the other intra-European. In the mid-fifteenth century, a coastal north and south Atlantic shipping trade replaced the trans-Mediterranean exchanges that had brought the first Africans to Europe. From Iberia, these connections quickly expanded to England and France, to the Netherlands and Denmark. German shipowners and captains from the North Sea ports inserted themselves into these routes, carried slaves, and occasionally brought Africans considered special to the port towns: boys—rarely girls—to be raised in their families, or young men and sometimes women to provide or sell to, or bestow upon, courts and merchant families. These individuals were "special" but not necessarily otherized. In fact, their skin color provided a glimpse of the larger world rather than being a marker of inferiority. In the trade with the plantation belt, these same networks and perhaps even the same ships and captains also provided chattel slaves, giving them over to exploitative, brutal, and life-threatening working conditions. In the nineteenth century, a few Americans of African origin came to Europe; one couple, for example, served at the Russian court in Saint Petersburg. Not all Africans remained in Europe—the black scholar in Halle and later at Dutch universities, Anton Wilhelm Amo, felt that the European academic world discriminated against him and departed.[15]

Within Europe, Africans at the courts moved (or were moved) within aristocratic networks of connectivity and migration. Since information is scarce, we do not know whether those in bourgeois families or serving as clerks in merchant houses could and did move. The German-speaking (rather than German) nobility was part of a trans-European aristocracy connected to the courts of London and Moscow. African court servants, when asking to be baptized, could suggest godparents and named members of European royalty. Other Africans, less visible as members of the lower orders, were able to marry local women and raise children with them. Little or no notice was taken of anything "visibly" different. This makes it difficult for today's historians to reinsert Africans into European history. What all this points to is that the nineteenth-century black-white dichotomy has no basis in the empirical data and is no more than a nineteenth-century racist phenomenon.

The positions Africans took in European hierarchies and the European views about them before the emergence of national cultures in the early nineteenth century were highly differentiated. Once these national cultures emerged and particular views of African otherness and inferiority came to dominate, dissenting voices and conflicting opinions over the meaning of blackness persisted. Jeannette Eileen Jones's and Bradley Naranch's chapters ably demonstrate such voices in German public discourse. Also, black people themselves, born either in or outside Europe, made increasing use of the modern transportation and communication revolutions to tell their stories, to talk back, and to disprove white assertions that people of African origin were genetically ordained for little more than slavery or servitude.[16] And yet, demands to include darker-skinned human beings in emerging national communities were by and large muffled by voices proclaiming that blood and race, rather than political convictions, constituted the impermeable boundaries of citizenship. Future research will have to determine the extent to which such fault lines differed from society to society, and how German black-white binaries can be integrated into larger European and global developments, both through comparative and transnational modes of analysis. This volume has laid the foundation and mapped the field, but more work is required to grasp the dynamics of multinational encounters, transregional networks, and ethnic and racial stereotyping across the centuries in the German-speaking parts of Europe and beyond more fully.

Yet this much can be said with certainty: the Age of Revolutions, liberating as it was in many respects, proved to be a watershed in the way peoples related to one another. The rise of "the people," allegedly unified in national cultures, excluded all others—not only Africans. However, while ascriptive racializations mushroomed in the nineteenth century, so did movements for self-liberation. Enslaved and free Africans seized the revolutionary (and Enlightenment) concept of human rights to express their political demands in terms Europeans could understand. Although Europeans realized that enslaved Africans had liberated themselves and formed societies of their own in the Americas almost from the introduction of slavery, they failed to understand it as a fundamental human right and instead labeled it "running away." Challenged by the revolutionary thought and struggles of black people, in particular by the self-liberation of the enslaved Africans in Haiti, Europeans had to justify the slave regime anew. In the modern period, the terms of reference thus became different. So did the means of power to suppress free thought and self-determination in the colonized regions of Africa.

Notes

1. Basil Davidson, *The African Slave Trade*, rev. ed. (Oxford: Oxford University Press, 2004), 232–33; and Dirk Hoerder, *Cultures in Contact: World Migrations in the Second Millennium* (Durham, NC: Duke University Press, 2002), 143–44.
2. See the chapter by Paul H. D. Kaplan in this volume.
3. Marie France Boyer, *The Cult of the Virgin: Offerings, Ornaments and Festivals*, trans. from the French by Jane Brenton (London: Thames & Hudson, 2000).
4. Christian Degn, *Die Schimmelmanns im atlantischen Dreieckshandel: Gewinn und Gewissen* (Neumünster, Germany: Wachholtz, 1974).
5. Art historians are debating the identity of the person portrayed. Katharina Oguntoye, May Opitz, and Dagmar Schultz, eds., *Farbe bekennen: Afro-deutsche Frauen auf den Spuren ihrer Geschichte*, rev. ed. (Frankfurt: Fischer, 1992), provide the "merchant clerk" reference.
6. See the chapter by Kate Lowe in this volume.
7. See the chapter by Maria I. Diedrich in this volume.
8. Dirk Hoerder, "Historical Dimensions of Many-Cultured Societies in Europe: The Case of Hamburg, Germany," in *Socio-Cultural Problems in the Metropolis: Comparative Analyses*, ed. Dirk Hoerder and Rainer-Olaf Schultze (Hagen, Germany: ISL, 2000), 121–39. See also the contribution histories by Eckart Kleßmann, *Aus Ländern in Hamburg—Ausländer in Hamburg* (Hamburg, Germany: Der Ausländerbeauftragte des Senats der Freien und Hansestadt Hamburg, 1993); and Frank Kürschner-Pelkmann, *Fremde bauen eine Stadt* (Hamburg, Germany: Der Ausländerbeauftragte des Senats der Freien und Hansestadt Hamburg, 1993).
9. See the chapter by Anne Kuhlmann in this volume.
10. Edward W. Saïd, *Orientalism* (New York: Pantheon, 1978).
11. The landing scene is described in Kate Lowe, "Introduction: The Black African Presence in Renaissance Europe," in *Black Africans in Renaissance Europe*, ed. T. F. Earle and Kate Lowe (Cambridge: Cambridge University Press, 2005), 1–14.
12. See the chapter by Kate Lowe in this volume.
13. The painter Edward Bird (1772–1819), a member of the British Royal Academy of Arts, was apprenticed as a "japanning" painter. In eighteenth-century japanning, black varnish was applied to furniture to imitate "Oriental" lacquer.
14. Donna Gabaccia, "The 'Yellow Peril' and the 'Chinese of Europe': Global Perspectives on Race and Labor, 1815–1930," in *Migration, Migration History, History: Old Paradigms and New Perspectives*, ed. Jan Lucassen and Leo Lucassen (Bern, Switzerland: Peter Lang, 1997), 177–96.
15. Allison Blakely, "(Re)Evaluating Blackness: Kant, Blumenbach, and the Limits of Enlightenment Universalism" (paper presented at the conference "Black Diaspora and Germany Across the Centuries," German Historical Institute, Washington DC, 19 March 2009).
16. See the chapters by Mischa Honeck and Kendahl L. Radcliffe in this volume, in particular.

Selected Bibliography

Ayim, May, Katharina Oguntoye, and Dagmar Schultz, eds. *Showing Our Colors: Afro-German Women Speak Out.* Amherst: University of Massachusetts Press, 1992.

Baker, Lee D. *From Savage to Negro: Anthropology and the Construction of Race, 1896–1954.* Berkeley: University of California Press, 1998.

Barbosa, Alves. *Vicentivs Lvsitanvs: Ein portugiesischer Komponist und Musiktheoretiker des 16. Jahrhunderts.* Lisbon: Estado da Cultura, 1977.

Baurmeister, Carl Leopold. *Revolution in America: Confidential Letters and Journals 1776–1784 of Adjutant General Major Baurmeister of the Hessian Forces,* ed. and trans. Bernard A. Uhlendorf. New Brunswick, NJ: Rutgers University Press, 1957.

Beckert, Sven. "From Tuskegee to Togo: The Problem of Freedom in the Empire of Cotton." *Journal of American History* 92, no. 2 (2005): 498–526.

Bitterli, Urs. *Die Entdeckung des schwarzen Afrikaners: Versuch einer Geistesgeschichte der europäisch-afrikanischen Beziehungen an der Guineaküste im 17. und 18. Jahrhundert.* Zurich: Atlantis, 1970.

Blackshire-Belay, Carol, ed. *The African-German Experience: Critical Essays.* Westport, CT: Praeger, 1996.

Blakely, Allison. "Problems in Studying the Role of Blacks in Europe." *Perspectives: American Historical Association Newsletter* 35, no. 5 (May–June 1997): 1–14.

Böhm, Uwe Peter. "Farbige in Hessischen Diensten." *Zeitschrift für Heereskunde* 47 (1983): 81–84.

Boogaart, Ernst van den. "De Brys' Africa." In *Inszenierte Welten—Staging New Worlds: Die west- und ostindischen Reisen der Verleger de Bry, 1590–1630. De Brys' Illustrated Travel Reports, 1590–1630,* ed. Susanna Burghartz, 95–155. Basel, Switzerland: Schwabe, 2004.

Brentjes, Burchard, and Anton Wilhelm Amo. *Der schwarze Philosoph in Halle.* Leipzig, Germany: Koehler & Amelang, 1976.

Campt, Tina. *Other Germans: Black Germans and the Politics of Race, Gender, and Memory in the Third Reich.* Ann Arbor: University of Michigan Press, 2004.

Chin, Rita, Heide Fehrenbach, Geoff Eley, and Atina Grossmann, eds. *After the Nazi Racial State: Difference and Democracy in Germany and Europe.* Ann Arbor: University of Michigan Press, 2009.

Ciarlo, David. *Advertising Empire: Race and Visual Culture in Imperial Germany.* Cambridge, MA: Harvard University Press, 2011.

Collenberg, Weygo Comte Rudt de. "Haus- und Hofmohren des 18. Jahrhunderts in Europa." In *Gesinde im 18. Jahrhundert,* ed. Gotthardt Frühsorge, Rainer Gruenter, and Beatrix Freifrau Wolff Metternich, 265–80. Hamburg, Germany: Meiner, 1995.

Debrunner, Hans Werner. *Presence and Prestige: Africans in Europe: A History of Africans in Europe before 1918.* Basel, Switzerland: Basler Afrika Bibliographien, 1979.

Degn, Christian. *Die Schimmelmanns im atlantischen Dreieckshandel: Gewinn und Gewissen.* Neumünster, Germany: Wachholtz, 1974.

Devisse, Jean. *The Image of the Black in Western Art.* Part 2: *From the Early Christian Era to the "Age of Discovery."* Vol. 1: *From the Demonic Threat to the Incarnation of Sainthood.* Cambridge, MA: Harvard University Press, 1979.

Diedrich, Maria. *Love across Color Lines: Ottilie Assing and Frederick Douglass.* New York: Hill & Wang, 1999.

Diedrich, Maria, and Jürgen Heinrichs, eds. *From Black to Schwarz: Cultural Crossovers between African America and Germany.* Berlin: LIT, 2010.

Dorr, David F. *A Colored Man Round the World,* ed. Malini J. Schueller. Ann Arbor: University of Michigan Press, 1999.

Dorsch, Hauke. *Afrikanische Diaspora und Black Atlantic: Einführung in Geschichte und aktuelle Diskussion.* Münster, Germany: LIT, 2000.

Duignan, Peter, and Lewis H. Gann. *The Rulers of German Africa, 1884–1914.* Palo Alto, CA: Stanford University Press, 1977.

Earle, Tom F., and Kate J.P. Lowe, eds. *Black Africans in Renaissance Europe.* Cambridge: Cambridge University Press, 2005.

Edwards, Brent Hayes. "The Uses of Diaspora." *Social Text* 66 (2001): 45–73.

Eggers, Maureen Maisha, Grada Kilomba, Peggy Piesche, and Susan Arndt, eds. *Mythen, Masken und Subjekte: Kritische Weissseinsforschung in Deutschland.* Münster, Germany: Unrast, 2005.

Eickelmann, Renate, ed. *Der Mohrenkopfpokal von Christoph Jamnitzer* (exh. cat.). Munich: Bayerisches Nationalmuseum, 2002.

Eigen, Sara, and Mark Joseph Larrimore, eds. *The German Invention of Race.* New York: SUNY Press, 2006.

El-Tayeb, Fatima. *Schwarze Deutsche: Der Diskurs um "Rasse" und nationale Identität 1890–1933.* Frankfurt: Campus Fachbuch, 2001.

Ember, Melvin, Carol R. Ember, and Ian Skoggard, eds. *Encyclopedia of Diasporas, Immigrant and Refugee Cultures around the World.* Vol. 1: *Overviews and Topics.* New York: Springer, 2004.

Eyoum, Jean-Pierre Félix, Stefanie Michels, and Joachim Zeller. "Bonamanga. Eine kosmopolitische Familiengeschichte." *Mont Cameroun,* no. 2 (2005): 11–48.

Fehrenbach, Heide. *Race after Hitler: Black Occupation Children in Postwar Germany and America.* Princeton, NJ: Princeton University Press, 2005.

Firla, Monika. "Afrikanische Pauker und Trompeter am württembergischen Herzogshof im 17. und 18. Jahrhundert." *Musik in Baden-Württemberg* 3 (1996): 11–41.

———. "Das Ballet 'Atlas Oder Die vier Theil der Welt' (Durlach, 1681): Ein seltenes Libretto in der Württembergischen Landesbibliothek Stuttgart." *Musik in Baden-Württemberg* 4 (1997): 133–48.

———. "'Hof-' und andere 'Mohren' als früheste Schicht des Eintreffens von Afrikanern in Deutschland." In *Neue Heimat Deutschland. Aspekte der Zuwanderung, Akkulturation und emotionalen Bindung,* ed. Hartmut Heller, 157–76. Erlangen, Germany: Universitätsbund Erlangen-Nürnberg, 2002.

———. "Quellen des Landeskirchlichen Archivs Stuttgart zur Erforschung der Afrikanischen Diaspora des 18. Jahrhunderts in Württemberg." *Blätter für württembergische Kirchengeschichte* 99 (1999): 90–112.

———, ed. *Exotisch-höfisch-bürgerlich: Afrikaner in Württemberg vom 15. bis 19. Jahrhundert: Katalog zur Ausstellung des Hauptstaatsarchivs Stuttgart.* Stuttgart, Germany: Hauptstaatsarchiv Stuttgart, 2001.

Fitzpatrick, Matthew P. *Liberal Imperialism in Germany: Expansionism and Nationalism 1848–1884.* New York: Berghahn Books, 2008.

Friedrichsmeyer, Sara L., Sara Lennox, and Susanne M. Zantop, eds. *The Imperialist Imagination: German Colonialism and Its Legacy.* Ann Arbor: University of Michigan Press, 1998.

Gilman, Sander. *On Blackness without Blacks: Essays on the Image of the Black in Germany.* Boston: G.K. Hall, 1982.

Gilroy, Paul. *The Black Atlantic: Modernity and Double Consciousness.* London: Harvard University Press, 1993.

Gnammankou, Dieudonné. "African Diaspora in Europe." In *Encyclopedia of Diasporas: Immigrant and Refugee Cultures around the World.* Vol. 1: *Overviews and Topics,* ed. Melvin Ember, Carol R. Ember, and Ian Skoggard, 15–24. New York: Kluwer Academic/Plenum Publishers, 2004.

Greene, Larry, and Anke Ortlepp, eds. *African Americans and Germany: Two Centuries of Exchange.* Jackson: University Press of Mississippi, 2011.

Grimm, Reinhold, ed. *Blacks and German Culture: Essays.* Monatshefte Occasional Papers 4. Madison: University of Wisconsin Press, 1986.

Guettel, Jens-Uwe. "Reading America, Studying Empire: German Perceptions of Indians, Slavery, and the American West, 1789–1900." PhD diss., Yale University, 2007.

Günther, Jürgen. "Mission im kolonialen Kontext: Beiträge zur Geschichte der Mission der deutschen Baptisten in Kamerun 1891 bis 1914." Unpublished master's thesis, University of Hamburg, 1985.

Häberlein, Mark. "'Mohren,' ständische Gesellschaft und atlantische Welt: Minderheiten und Kulturkontakte in der Frühen Neuzeit." In *AtlanticUnderstandings: Essays on European and American History in Honor of Hermann Wellenreuther,* ed. Claudia Schnurmann and Hartmut Lehmann, 77–102. Hamburg, Germany: LIT, 2006.

Hein, Jørgen. "Der Mohrenkopfpokal von Christoph Jamnitzer—Provenienz, Deutung und Kontext." *Münchner Jahrbuch der bildenden Kunst,* 3rd ser., 53 (2002): 163–74.

Helas, Philine. "Schwarz unter Weißen: Zur Repräsentation von Afrikanern in der italienischen Kunst des 15. Jahrhunderts." In *Fremde in der Stadt: Ordnungen, Repräsentationen und soziale Praktiken (13.–15. Jahrhundert),* ed. Peter Bell, Dirk Suckow, and Gerhard Wolf, 301–31. Frankfurt: Peter Lang, 2010.

Heyden, Ulrich van der, ed. *Unbekannte Biographien.* Berlin: Kai Hoilius, 2008.

Hine, Darlene Clark, Tricia Danielle Keaton, and Stephen Small, eds. *Black Europe and the African Diaspora.* Urbana: University of Illinois Press, 2009.

Hoerder, Dirk. *Cultures in Contact: World Migrations in the Second Millennium.* Durham, NC: Duke University Press, 2002.

———. "Europe's Many Worlds and Their Global Interconnections: Migration Movements in Historical Perspective." In *Enlarging European Memory: Migration Movements in Historical Perspectives,* ed. Mareike König and Rainer Ohliger, 21–32. Ostfildern, Germany: Jan Thorbecke, 2006.

Höhn, Maria, and Martin Klimke. *A Breath of Freedom: The Civil Rights Struggle, African American GIs, and Germany.* New York: Palgrave Macmillan, 2010.

Honeck, Mischa. *We Are the Revolutionists: German-Speaking Immigrants and American Abolitionists after 1848.* Athens: University of Georgia Press, 2011.

Horsman, Reginald. *Race and Manifest Destiny: The Origins of Racial Anglo-Saxonism.* Cambridge, MA: Harvard University Press, 1981.

Hund, Wulf D., Christian Koller, and Moshe Zimmermann, eds. *Racisms Made in Germany.* Vienna: LIT, 2011.

Jensen, Jürgen, ed. *Afrikaner in Europa—Eine Bibliographie. Africans in Europe—A Bibliography. Africains en Europe—Une Bibliographie.* Münster, Germany: LIT, 2002.

Joeden-Forgey, Elisa von. "Nobody's People: Colonial Subjects, Race Power, and the German State, 1884–1945." PhD diss., University of Pennsylvania, 2004.

Johnson, Samuel. *Schwarze Missionare—Weiße Missionare! Beiträge westlicher Missionsgesellschaften und einheimischer Pioniere zur Entstehung der Baptistengemeinde in Kamerun (1841–1949).* Kassel, Germany: Onken Verlag, 2004.

Jones, Adam. "Introduction." In *Brandenburg Sources for West African History, 1680–1700,* ed. Adam Jones, 6–16. Studien zur Kulturkunde 77. Wiesbaden, Germany: Franz Steiner, 1985.

Jones, George F. "The Black Hessians: Negroes Recruited by the Hessians in South Carolina and Other Colonies." *South Carolina Historical Magazine* 83 (1982): 287–302.

Kaplan, Paul H.D. "Black Africans in Hohenstaufen Iconography." *Gesta* 26, no. 1 (1987): 29–36.

———. "Introduction to the New Edition." In *The Image of the Black in Western Art,* vol. 2, new ed., ed. Henry Louis Gates Jr. and David Bindman, 1–30. Cambridge, MA: Belknap Press of Harvard University Press, 2010.

———. *The Rise of the Black Magus in Western Art.* Ann Arbor: UMI Research Press, 1985.

———. "Titian's Laura Dianti and the Origins of the Motif of the Black Page in Portraiture." Part 1: "The Vogue for Black Servants in Renaissance Italy." *Antichità Viva* 21, no. 1 (1982): 11–18.

———. "Titian's Laura Dianti and the Origins of the Motif of the Black Page in Portraiture." Part 2: "From Laura Dianti's Page to Othello and Van Dyck." *Antichità Viva* 21, no. 4 (1982): 10–18.

———. "Caspar Van Senden, Sir Thomas Sherley and the 'Blackamoor' Project." *Historical Research* 81 (2008): 366–71.

Keil, Hartmut. "German Immigrants and African Americans in Mid-Nineteenth Century America." In *Enemy Images in American History,* ed. Ragnhild Fiebig-von Hase and Ursula Lehmkuhl, 137–57. Providence, RI: Berghahn Books, 1997.

Kellenbenz, Hermann. "Deutsche Plantagenbesitzer und Kaufleute in Surinam vom Ende des 18. bis zur Mitte des 19. Jahrhunderts." *Jahrbuch für Geschichte Lateinamerikas* 3 (1966): 141–63.

Kelley, Alfred. *The Descent of Darwin: The Popularization of Darwinism in Germany, 1860–1914.* Chapel Hill: University of North Carolina Press, 1981.

Kiel, Rainer-Maria. "Das christgläubige Mohrenland oder Was Caspar von Lilien über Äthiopien predigte." *Archiv für Geschichte von Oberfranken* 65 (1985): 379–94.

———. *Zwischen Integration und Sensation: Afrikaner im Bayreuth des 17. bis 19. Jahrhunderts.* Unpublished manuscript, Bayreuth, 1998.

Kittel, Ingeborg. "Mohren als Hofbediente und Soldaten im Herzogtum Braunschweig-Wolfenbüttel." *Braunschweigisches Jahrbuch* 46 (1965): 78–103.

Knoll, Arthur J. *Togo under Imperial Germany, 1884–1914.* Palo Alto, CA: Hoover Institution Press, 1988.

Küppers-Braun, Ute. "Kammermohren: Ignatius Fortuna am Essener Hof und andere farbige

Hofdiener." *Das Münster am Hellweg: Mitteilungsblatt des Vereins für die Erhaltung des Essener Münsters* 54 (2001): 17–50.
Langbehn, Volker, ed. *German Colonialism, Visual Culture, and Modern Memory.* London: Routledge, 2010.
Langbehn, Volker, and Mohammad Salama, eds. *German Colonialism: Race, the Holocaust, and Postwar Germany.* New York: Columbia University Press, 2011.
Lind, Vera. "Privileged Dependency on the Edge of the Atlantic World: Africans and Germans in the Eighteenth Century." In *Interpreting Colonialism,* ed. Byron R. Wells and Philip Stewart, 369–91. Oxford: Voltaire Foundation, 2004.
Lohmann, Christoph, ed. and trans. *Radical Passion: Ottilie Assing's Reports from America and Letters to Frederick Douglass.* New York: Peter Lang, 1999.
Lowe, Kate J.P. "Black Africans' Religious and Cultural Assimilation to, or Appropriation of, Catholicism in Italy, 1470–1520." *Renaissance and Reformation/Renaissance et Réforme* 31, no. 2 (2008): 67–86.
———. "The Lives of African Slaves and People of African Descent in Europe during the Renaissance." In *Revealing the African Presence in Renaissance Europe* (exh. cat.), ed. Joaneath Spicer. Baltimore: Walters Art Museum, 2012.
———. "La place des Africains sub-sahariens dans l'histoire européenne, 1400–1600." In *Les Africains et leurs descendants en Europe avant le XXe siècle,* ed. Dieudonné Gnammankou and Yao Modzinou, 71–82. Toulouse, France: La Maison de l'Afrique à Toulouse, 2008.
Lüden, Catharina. *Sklavenfahrt mit Seeleuten aus Schleswig-Holstein, Hamburg und Lübeck im 18. Jahrhundert.* Heide, Germany: Westholsteinsche Verlagsanstalt Boyen, 1983.
Lusane, Clarence. *Hitler's Black Victims: The Historical Experiences of Afro-Germans, European Blacks, Africans, and African Americans in the Nazi Era.* New York: Routledge, 2003.
Mangold, Sabine. *Eine "weltbürgerliche Wissenschaft": Die deutsche Orientalistik im 19. Jahrhundert.* Stuttgart, Germany: Steiner, 2004.
Marchand, Suzanne L. *German Orientalism in the Age of Empire: Religion, Race, and Scholarship.* New York: Cambridge University Press, 2009.
Martin, Peter. *Schwarze Teufel, edle Mohren: Afrikaner in Geschichte und Bewusstsein der Deutschen.* Hamburg, Germany: Hamburger Edition, 2001.
———. "Un souffle venu de loin: Les 'Maures' Noirs au service des princes allemands de l'époque baroque." In *Les Africains et leurs descendants en Europe avant le XXe siècle,* ed. Gnammankou and Modzinou, 111–26.
Martin, Peter, and Christine Alonzo. *Zwischen Charleston und Stechschritt: Schwarze im Nationalsozialismus.* Hamburg, Germany: Dölling & Gallitz, 2004.
Mayer, Ruth. *Diaspora: Eine kritische Begriffsbestimmung.* Cultural Studies 14. Bielefeld, Germany: Transkript, 2005.
Mazón, Patricia, and Reinhild Steingröver, eds. *Not so Plain as Black and White: Afro-German Culture and History, 1890–2000.* Rochester, NY: University of Rochester, 2005.
McBride, David, Leroy Hopkins, and Carol Blackshire-Belay, eds. *Crosscurrents: African Americans, Africa, and Germany in the Modern World.* Columbia, SC: Camden House, 1998.
McDaniel, W. Caleb. "Our Country Is the World: Radical American Abolitionists Abroad." PhD diss., Johns Hopkins University, 2006.
Meer, Sarah. *Uncle Tom Mania: Slavery, Minstrelsy, and Transatlantic Culture in the 1850s.* Athens: University of Georgia Press, 2005.

Mellinkoff, Ruth. *Outcasts: Signs of Otherness in Northern European Art of the Late Middle Ages*. 2 vols. Berkeley: University of California Press, 1993.
Michels, Stefanie. "Mülheim an der Ruhr: Der kleine schwarze Prinz: Das Grab von Moses Equalla Deido." In *Kolonialismus hierzulande. Eine Spurensuche in Deutschland*, ed. Ulrich van der Heyden and Joachim Zeller, 417–21. Erfurt, Germany: Sutton Verlag, 2008.
Michels, Stefanie. *Schwarze deutsche Kolonialsoldaten: Mehrdeutige Repräsentationsräume und früher Kosmopolitismus in Afrika*. Bielefeld, Germany: Transkript, 2009.
Nagl, Tobias. *Die unheimliche Maschine: Rasse und Repräsentation im Weimarer Kino*. Munich: Text und Kritik, 2009.
Oguntoye, Katharina. *Eine Afro-Deutsche Geschichte: Zur Lebenssituation von Afrikanern in Deutschland von 1884 bis 1950*. Berlin: Hoho Verlag, 1997.
Oldendorp, Christian Georg Andreas. *History of the Evangelical Brethren on the Caribbean Islands of St. Thomas, St. Croix, and St. John*, ed. Johann Jakob Bossart, Engl. ed. trans. Arnold R. Highfield and ed. Vladimir Barac. Ann Arbor, MI: Karoma, 1987.
Orosz, Kenneth. *Religious Conflict and the Evolution of Language Policy in German and French Cameroon, 1885–1939*. New York: Peter Lang, 2008.
Paul, Heike. *Kulturkontakt und Racial Presences: Afro-Amerikaner und die deutsche Amerika-Literatur, 1815–1914*. Heidelberg, Germany: Winter, 2005.
———. "Schwarze Sklaven, weisse Sklaven: The German Reception of Harriet Beecher-Stowe's *Uncle Tom's Cabin*." In *Amerikanische Populärkultur in Deutschland: Case Studies in Cultural Transfer Past and Present*, ed. Katja Kanzler and Heike Paul, 21–39. Leipzig, Germany: Leipziger Universitätsverlag, 2002.
Petrat, Gerhardt. "Zwerge, Riesen, Mohren." In *Höfe und Residenzen im spätmittelalterlichen Reich*. Vol. 2: *Bilder und Begriffe*, part 1: *Begriffe*, ed. Werner Paravicini, 69–74. Ostfildern, Germany: Jan Thorbecke, 2005.
Pieken, Gorch, and Cornelia Kruse. *Preußisches Liebesglück—Eine deutsche Familie aus Afrika*. Berlin: Propyläen, 2007.
Pierard, Richard V. "A Case Study of German Economic Imperialism: The Colonial Economic Committee." *Scandanavian Economic History Review* 16 (1968): 155–67.
Poikane-Daumke, Aija. *African Diasporas: Afro-German Literature in the Context of the African American Experience*. Berlin: LIT, 2006.
Polaschegg, Andrea. *Der andere Orientalismus: Regeln deutsch-morgenländischer Imagination im 19. Jahrhundert*. Berlin: Walter de Gruyter, 2004.
Radcliffe, Kendahl. "The Tuskegee-Togo Cotton Scheme: 1900 to 1909." PhD diss., University of California, Los Angeles, 1998.
Raphael-Hernandez, Heike, ed. *Blackening Europe: The African American Presence*. New York: Routledge, 2004.
Rischmann, Martin. "Mohren als Spielleute und Musiker in der preussischen Armee." *Zeitschrift für Heeres- und Uniformkunde* 91–93 (1936): 82–84.
Roeck, Bernd. *Außenseiter, Randgruppen, Minderheiten: Fremde im Deutschland der frühen Neuzeit*. Göttingen, Germany: Vandenhoeck & Ruprecht, 1993.
Rosenhaft, Eve, and Robbie Aitken, eds. *Africa in Europe: Studies in Transnational Practice in the Long Twentieth Century*. Liverpool: Liverpool University Press, 2013.
Sadji, Uta. "'Unverbesserlich ausschweifende' oder 'brauchbare Subjekte'? Mohren als 'befreite' Sklaven im Deutschland des 18. Jahrhunderts." *Komparatistische Hefte* 2 (1980): 42–52.
Sammons, Jeffrey. *Ideology, Mimesis, Fantasy: Charles Sealsfield, Friedrich Gerstäcker, Karl May, and Other German Novelists of America*. Chapel Hill: University of North Carolina Press, 1998.

Schäfer, Wolfram. "Von 'Kammermohren,' 'Mohren'-Tambouren und 'Ost-Indianern." *Hessische Blätter für Volks- und Kulturforschung* 23 (1988): 35–79.

Schreuder, Esther. "'Blacks' in Court Culture in the Period 1300–1900: Propaganda and Consolation." In *Black Is Beautiful: Rubens to Dumas,* ed. Esther Schreuder and Elmer Kolfin, 20–31. Zwolle, Netherlands: De Nieuwe Kerk, 2008.

"Schwarze Militärmusiker und Spielleute." *Deutscher Soldaten-Kalender* 7 (1959): 177–80.

Sensbach, Jon F. *Rebecca's Revival: Creating Black Christianity in the Atlantic World.* Cambridge, MA: Harvard University Press, 2005.

Smith, Woodruff D. *Politics and the Sciences of Culture in Germany, 1840–1920.* New York: Oxford University Press, 1991.

Sollors, Werner. *Neither Black Nor White Yet Both: Thematic Explorations of Interracial Literature.* New York: Oxford University Press, 1997.

Sollors, Werner, and Maria Diedrich, eds. *The Black Columbiad: Defining Moments in African American Literature and Culture.* Cambridge, MA: Harvard University Press, 1994.

Stevenson, Robert. "The First Black Published Composer." *Inter-American Music Review* 5 (1982): 79–103.

Stowe, William W. *Going Abroad: European Travel in Nineteenth-Century American Culture.* Princeton, NJ: Princeton University Press, 1994.

Suckale-Redlefsen, Gude. *Mauritius: Der heilige Mohr/The Black Saint Maurice.* Houston: Menil Foundation, 1987.

Tautz, Birgit. *Colors 1800, 1900, 2000: Signs of Ethnic Difference.* Amsterdam: Rodopi, 2004.

Thomas, Dominic. *Black France: Colonialism, Immigration, and Transnationalism.* Bloomington: Indiana University Press, 2006.

Thomas, Herman E. *James W. C. Pennington: African American Churchman and Abolitionist.* New York: Garland, 1995.

Tiedemann, Frederick. "On the Brain of the Negro, Compared with That of the European and the Ourang-Outang [Abstract]." *Abstracts of the Papers Printed in the Philosophical Transactions of the Royal Society of London* 3 (1830–1837): 398–99.

Tuchman, Arleen M. "From the Lecture to the Laboratory: The Institutionalization of Scientific Medicine at the University of Heidelberg." In *The Investigative Enterprise: Experimental Physiology in Nineteenth-Century Medicine,* ed. William Coleman and Frederic L. Holmes, 65–99. Berkeley: University of California Press, 1988.

Tustin, Joseph P. "Introduction." In Johann Ewald, *Diary of the American War: A Hessian Journal: Captain Johann Ewald, Field Jäger Corps,* ed. and trans. Joseph P. Tustin, xix–xxxi. New Haven, NC: Yale University Press, 1979.

Uhlendorf, Bernhard A., ed. and trans. *The Siege of Charleston, with an Account of the Province of South Carolina: Diaries and Letters of Hessian Officers.* Cranbury, NJ: Scholar's Bookshelf, 2007.

Vaughan, Virginia Mason. *Performing Blackness on English Stages, 1500–1800.* Cambridge: Cambridge University Press, 2005.

Wagener-Fimpel, Silke. "Mohren in Schaumburg-Lippe im 18. Jahrhundert." In *Schaumburg und die Welt: Zu Schaumburgs auswärtigen Beziehungen in der Geschichte,* ed. Hubert Höing, 124–25. Bielefeld, Germany: Verlag für Regionalgeschichte, 2002.

Webber, Christopher L. *American to the Backbone: The Life of James W. C. Pennington, The Fugitive Slave Who Became One of the First Black Abolitionists.* New York: Doubleday, 2011.

Weber, Klaus. *Deutsche Kaufleute im Atlantikhandel 1680–1830: Unternehmen und Familien in Hamburg, Cádiz und Bordeaux.* Munich: Beck, 2004.

Weindl, Andreas. "Die Brandenburger im 'Atlantischen System' 1650–1720." *Arbeitspapiere zur Lateinamerikaforschung* 2, no. 3 (2001).
Wright, Michelle M., and Tina Campt, eds. "Reading the Black German Experience." Special issue, *Callaloo: A Journal of African Diaspora Arts and Letters* 26, no. 2 (2003).
Zantop, Susanne. *Colonial Fantasies: Conquest, Family, and Nation in Precolonial Germany, 1770–1870.* Durham, NC: Duke University Press, 1997.
Zeleza, Paul Tiyambe. "Rewriting the African Diaspora: Beyond the Black Atlantic." *African Affairs* 104 (2005): 35–68.
Zimmerman, Andrew. *Alabama in Africa: Booker T. Washington, the German Empire, and the Globalization of the New South.* Princeton, NJ: Princeton University Press, 2010.
———. *Anthropology and Antihumanism in Imperial Germany.* Chicago: University of Chicago Press, 2001.
———. "A German Alabama in Africa: The Tuskegee Expedition to German Togo and the Transnational Origins of West African Cotton Growers." *American Historical Review* 110, no. 5 (2005): 1362–98.

Contributors

Robbie Aitken is a reader in history at Sheffield Hallam University, UK. He is the co-author of *Black Germany: The Making and Unmaking of a Diaspora Community, 1884–1960* (Cambridge University Press, 2013), the co-editor of *Africa in Europe: Studies in Transnational Practice in the Long Twentieth Century* (Liverpool University Press, 2013), and the author of *Exclusion and Inclusion: Gradiations of Whiteness and Socio-Economic Engineering in German Southwest Africa, 1884–1914* (Bern: Lang, 2007).

Maria I. Diedrich is professor emeritus of American studies at the University of Münster, Germany. Her published books include *Cornelia James Cannon and the Future American Race* (Amherst: University of Massachusetts Press, 2011); *Love Across Color Lines: Ottilie Assiing and Frederick Douglass* (New York: Hill and Wang, 1999); *The Black Columbiad: Defining Moments in African American Literature and Culture,* coedited with Werner Sollors (Cambridge, MA: Harvard University Press, 1994); *From Black to Schwarz: Cultural Crossovers between African America and Germany,* coedited with Jürgen Heinrichs (East Lansing: Michigan State University Press, 2011). Her current research focuses on the fate of African Americans who joined the Hessians during the American Revolution and accompanied the returning Hessian troops to Germany.

Dirk Hoerder taught global history of migrations and North American social history at Arizona State University and the University of Bremen. He also taught at York University, Toronto, Duke University, University of Toronto, and Université de Paris 8-Saint Denis. He has published *Creating Societies: Immigrant Lives in Canada* (Montreal: McGill-Queen's University Press, 1999); *Cultures in Contact: World Migrations in the Second Millennium* (Durham, NC: Duke University Press, 2002), his "Revising the Mono-Cultural Nation-State Paradigm: An Introduction to Transcultural Perspectives" introduces the anthology *The Historical Practice of Diversity: Transcultural Interactions from the Early Modern Mediterranean to the Postcolonial World* (New York: Berghahn Books, 2003), and *What is Migration History?,* coedited with Christiane Harzig and Donna Gabaccia (Cambridge, UK: Polity, 2009).

Mischa Honeck is a research fellow at the German Historical Institute in Washington, D.C. He is the author of *We Are the Revolutionists, German-Speaking Immigrants and American Abolitionists after 1848* (Athens: University of Georgia Press, 2011). His main research areas are the histories of race, ethnicity, gender, and youth in the United States and the transatlantic world.

Jeannette Eileen Jones is associate professor of history and ethnic studies at the University of Nebraska–Lincoln. She is a historian of the United States, with expertise in American cultural and intellectual history, transnational history, and African American Studies. Her research explores the role of race in shaping American cultural and intellectual discourse and production, focusing on the ways in which "race" as a popular and scientific category operated as a potent signifier of difference—cultural, biological, social, and political—in late nineteenth and early twentieth century America. She is the author of *In Search of Brightest Africa: Reimagining the Dark Continent in American Culture, 1884–1936* (Athens: University of Georgia Press, 2010). She is currently working on her next book project, *America in Africa: U.S. Empire, Race, and the African Question, 1847–1919* and a digital project *"To Enter Africa from America: U.S. Empire, Race, and the African Question, 1847–1919."*

Paul H. D. Kaplan is professor of art history in the school of humanities, Purchase College, State University of New York. He is the author of *The Rise of the Black Magus in Western Art* (Ann Arbor: UMI Research Press, 1985) and a major contributor to several volumes of the new edition of *The Image of the Black in Western Art* (Cambridge, MA: Harvard University Press, 2010–2012). He has been a fellow at the Hutchins Center for African and African American Research at Harvard University, and has been a consultant and contributor to NYU's Acton "Blackamoors" project at the Villa La Pietra, Florence.

Martin Klimke is associate dean of humanities and associate professor of history at New York University Abu Dhabi, and a former research fellow at the German Historical Institute, Washington, D.C. He is the author of *The Other Alliance: Global Protest and Student Unrest in West Germany and the U.S., 1962–1972* (Princeton, NJ: Princeton University Press, 2010) and coauthor of *A Breath of Freedom: The Civil Rights Struggle, African-American GIs, and Germany* (New York: Palgrave Macmillan, 2010). He is also the coeditor of the publication series Protest, Culture and Society (Berghahn Books) and several collected volumes on various aspects of transatlantic and transnational history.

Anne Kuhlmann is a research fellow for Russian history at the Cultural Foundation of the German Federal States in Berlin. In 2010, she received the Sponsorship Award of the Society for Historical Migration Research (Bonn, Germany) for her PhD dissertation on black people in seventeenth- and eighteenth-century Germany. Her research areas are migration history and Eastern European and German transnational history.

Kate Lowe is professor of Renaissance history and culture at Queen Mary, University of London. She coedited *Black Africans in Renaissance Europe* (Cambridge University Press, 2005) with T. F. Earle, and *The Global City: On the Streets of Renaissance Lisbon* (London: Paul Holberton Press, 2015) with Annemarie Jordan Gschwend.

Bradley Naranch is visiting assistant professor of history at the University of Montana. He received his PhD from Johns Hopkins University in 2007. He is a specialist in the history of nineteenth-century Germany and is working on a book-length manuscript that revises conventional histories of German national unification by incorporating largely forgotten stories of overseas expansion and empire building from the 1830s to the early twentieth century.

Heike Paul is professor of North American cultural and literary studies at the Friedrich Alexander University Erlangen-Nuremberg, Germany, and also chairs the DFG-funded doctoral program "Presence and Tacit Knowledge". She is on the board of directors of the Bavarian America Academy and currently is the vice president of the German Association for American Studies. Her publications include *Cultural Contact and Racial Presences: African Americans and the German Literature, 1815–1914* (Heidelberg: Universitatsverlag Winter, 2005), and *The Myths That Made America: An Introduction to American Studies* (Bielefeld: Transcript-Verlag, 2014).

Rashid-S. Pegah is a cultural historian. He worked as a research assistant on projects organized by the Bach-Archiv Leipzig (sponsored by the Alfried Krupp von Bohlen und Halbach Foundation), by the Bavarian Academy of Sciences, Munich, and by the Foundation Prussian Palaces and Gardens Berlin-Brandenburg, Potsdam. Between 1993 and 2003, he collaborated on diverse broadcasts by the editorial department for early music of the former radio station, Sender Freies Berlin.

Kendahl L. Radcliffe is full professor of history at El Camino College, Compton Center and a lecturer of African American studies at the University of California, Los Angeles. Her past and present research focuses on the reconciliation, negotiation, and in many instances, rejection of European, economic, and cultural paradigms at the turn of the last century by people of African descent. She is contributor and coeditor of the book, *Anywhere but Here: Black Intellectuals, the Atlantic World and Beyond* (Jackson: University Press of Mississippi, 2013).

INDEX

A

abolitionism, 115, 116, 118, 134–52, 156, 166, 168
Adangwe, 198
Africa, 1, 3, 5–9, 11–17, 21–25, 28, 30, 31, 38, 39, 41, 43, 47, 51, 54, 58, 63, 66–68, 74, 77, 78, 83, 85–88, 93, 95, 104, 107, 109, 117, 119, 120, 125, 127, 129, 135, 138, 144, 147, 149, 156, 160, 161, 166, 170, 172–74, 177–79, 181, 183, 185, 186, 187, 189–92, 194, 199–201, 203, 206, 210, 212, 213, 215, 217–19, 223, 224, 228, 229, 231–36, 240
African Americans, 6, 11–13, 15–16, 94, 95, 109, 110, 115–33, 137, 140, 143, 149, 151, 153–68, 170, 172, 175, 177, 180, 182, 186, 187, 189, 190, 194, 195, 199, 201, 203, 206, 209, 233
Africans, 3, 8–11, 15, 21–37, 38, 39, 42, 43, 48–56, 57–63, 69, 71–73, 74–91, 95, 96, 98, 129, 130, 137, 138, 140, 144, 146–49, 170, 174, 177, 178, 180, 186, 190, 191, 193, 195, 198–205, 209, 212, 214, 217, 219–29, 231–40
Agotime, 198
agua, 198
Ahrensburg, 64
Akeppe, 198
Akwa, Ludwig Mpundu, 216
Akwa, Mbanga, 220
Alabama, 15, 157, 183, 185, 196, 202, 209
Alba, 195

Alentejo, 51
Alexandria, Chaterine of (St.), 30
Afonso, 45, 51, 219, 220, 221. *See also* Mbemba, Nzinga
Afonso V (King), 30, 52
Alps, the, 34, 75
Altona, 217, 220, 224
Alzire, 62, 71
Amage (Queen of Sarmatia), 83–85, 87, 90
America, 3, 5, 6–17, 31, 43, 64, 85, 87, 88, 92–111, 115–33, 136, 138, 140, 142, 143, 147, 148, 152, 153, 154, 156–68, 169–75, 177–85, 187, 189–93, 194, 198, 200–202, 204, 206–10, 211, 213, 233, 236, 238, 239
American and Foreign Anti-Slavery Society, 159, 167
American Civil War, 12, 166, 169
American Revolution, 10, 59, 92–94, 98, 99, 109–11, 116, 117, 130, 137, 138, 150, 157
Amo, Anton Wilhelm, 62, 65, 66, 68, 72, 137, 147, 150, 238,
Amsterdam, 36, 41, 160
Andree, Karl, 12, 170, 172, 183–85
Annunciate Mary, 23
Ansbach, 76, 79, 89
Antwerp, 23
Apulia, 21, 74
Aragon, Constanze of, 74
Ascheberg, 62
Asia, 3, 5, 9, 17, 85–88, 177–79, 181, 182, 184, 233, 234, 236, 237
Asia Minor, 3
Assahoun, 198

Assing, Ottilie, 121, 123, 125, 128, 131, 151, 170
Atakpame district, 204
Athens, 160
Atlanta, 207, 209
Aurich, 60, 70
Austria, 62, 70, 164, 209
Austria, Margaret of, 28, 29, 36

B
Baptistry of St. John, 22
Baden, Jacobäa of, 30, 33, 36
Baden-Baden, 162
Badin, Adolph Couschi, 62
Baldung, Hans, 22, 26
Bali, 224
Barkas, Hannibal, 86, 88
Baumeister, Carl Leopold von, 94, 110
Bavaria, 30, 75, 89, 141, 162
Bavaria, William V of, 51
Bayreuth, 60, 61, 70, 76–81, 83, 86, 87, 89, 90
Bayreuth, Margrave of, 60, 62, 76–78, 90
Beecher Stowe, Harriet, 121, 124–26, 128, 129, 170, 183
Beham, Barthel, 30–32, 36, 37
Belacâne, 8
Bell, Alfred, 218, 219, 222, 223, 228, 229. *See also* Ndumbe, Belle
Bell, Ndumbe Lobe, 215, 218
Bell, Rudolf Duala Manga, 216, 229
Benecke, George Friedrich, 131
Berbice, 65
Berleburg, 63, 65
Berlin, 1, 14, 18, 34, 70, 75–78, 85, 87, 90, 129, 133, 172, 206, 212, 215, 217, 220, 224–27, 229, 230
Berlin Seminar for Oriental Languages, 214
Bilé, Esther Sike, 225
Bismarck, Otto von, 1, 228, 229
Blackamoor, 49, 55
Blanco, Pero, 52. *See also* White, Peter
Blumenbach, Johann Friedrich, 139
Bluntschli, Johann Caspar, 164, 168
Bohemia, 29, 30, 36, 52
Bohemia, Zedena of, 29
Bohner, Heinrich, 224
Bordeaux, 7, 17
Boston, 9, 23, 116, 133, 143, 159
Bourdieu, Pierre, 163, 168

Braga, 30
Brandenburg, 17, 22, 70, 75–79, 87, 90
  Albrecht of, 27, 32, 36
  Brandenburg African Company, 7, 17
  Elizabeth of, 27
Brandenburg-Culmbach, Georg Albrecht of, 78
  Georg Friedrich Sr. of, 76
  Georg Wilhelm of, 80, 81
Brandenburg-Culmbach-Bayreuth, Christian Ernst of, 77, 89
Braunschweig-Lüneburg, Erich of, 26, 76
Brazil, 50, 156, 173, 178
Bremem Cotton Exchange, 205
Bremen, 35, 116, 127, 172, 173, 193
Bremerlehe, 100
Brentel, David, 53
Breu, Jörg the Younger, 50, 56
Britain, 16, 71, 109, 111, 115, 129, 135, 138, 156, 173, 183, 184, 192, 206, 209, 212, 215, 227
British Baptist Missionary Society, 215, 227
British India, 177
British West Indies, 156, 177
Brixen, 22
Brown, William Wells, 124, 158
Bruges, 40, 41
Brunswick, 65, 66, 76, 85, 87, 110
Brunswick and Lüneburg, Rudolph August of, 66
Brunswick-Lüneburg-Celle, Dukes of, 76
Brunswick-Lüneburg-Hanover, 76, 87
Brunswick-Lüneburg-Hanover, Sophie Dorothé von, 85
Brunswick-Lüneburg-Wolfenbüttel, Dukes of, 76
Brussels, 39, 157
Bry, Johann Theodor de, 83, 90
Bryant, Walter of Jacksonville, 196, 198, 202
Bückeburg, 62
Burks, Allen Lynn, 196–198
Byzantine Empire, 3

C
Cadiz, 7, 17
Calenberg, 9, 21–37
  Elizabeth of, 32
  Erich I of, 26, 32
California, 130, 173, 178, 181

Calloway, James Nathan, 189, 195–97, 209, 211
Cameroon, 13, 213–230
Canada, 94, 109, 120, 126
Canossa, 74
Cape of Good Hope, 83
Caribbean, 3, 5, 7, 12, 18, 94, 102, 110, 149, 174, 178, 233
Carlsbad Decrees, 158
Carolinas, 94, 101
Carové, Friedrich Wilhelm, 154, 155, 157–159, 167
Carpenter, Benjamin 100
Carver, George Washington, 202–204, 212,
Cassel, 25, 63, 108, 110, 230
Castile, Juana of, 39
Catalonia, 28
Catherine (St.), 23, 26, 30
Catholic Arch Abbey St. Ottilien, Türkenfeld, 220
Catholic German Center Party, 220
Catholic Pallottine mission, 222, 225
Catholicism, 37, 55, 230, 233,
Charles V, 28, 39–41, 54
Charleston, 15, 105, 110, 182
China, 173, 177, 178, 237
Christoph, Eberhard, 60
Cleveland, 160
Clinton, Henry, 49
Cobden, Richard, 158, 166
Collegium Carolinum, 103, 139
Cologne, 21, 34, 172
Colonial Economic Committee, 192, 204, 210
Colwyn Bay, 223
Commani, Carl of, 62, 65, 71
Committee for the Importation of Products from the German Colonies, 192
Congo, 45, 63, 83, 229
Connecticut, 94
Constantinople, 160, 161
"coolie trade," 181
Copenhagen, 60, 78, 232, 233
Coridon, Ferdinand Christian, 62, 65
Cornwallis (Lord), 102, 106, 107
Corporation of Reinforced Concrete, Berlin, 217
Corradi, Giulio Cesare, 83
Cotton (later Agricultural) School, Nuatja, 202–204, 211

Cuba, 173, 181
Cuvier, Georges, 134, 141, 142
Cyriacus (St.), 23
Czech lands, 22

D

Danube, 53
Danzig, 44
Davie, 198
Dean, Trevor, 45, 55
Debrunner, Hans-Werner, 4, 5, 16, 18, 38, 55, 57, 68–70, 72, 88, 129
Deido, 213–216, 221, 225–28
  King, 214. *See also* Deido, Epee Ekwalla
  Epee Ekwalla, 214, 215
  Equalla (Prince), 213, 214, 216, 225, 227
  Otto Equalla, 225, 230
Demba, Alfons, 219–21
Denmark, 60, 78, 117, 156, 233, 238
Denmark and Norway, Christian VI of, 60
Disom, Daniel Njo, 226
Doerstling, Emil, 1
Dolenta, Maria Viktoria, 63
Dominicus, George, 62, 71
Dorr, David F., 12, 154, 160–65, 167, 168
Douala, 213–15, 217, 218, 221, 222, 224, 229, 230
Douglass, Frederick, 11, 116, 120, 123, 128, 130, 131, 151, 153, 161, 165, 170
Draper's Company, 39
Dresden, 60, 75, 77, 78, 90, 117, 172, 173, 183
Du Bois, W.E.B., 129
Du Puys, Remy, 40, 41
Dumbe, Dinne, 222
Dunmore (Lord), 99
Dürer, Albrecht, 23, 34, 35, 232
Düsseldorf, 87
Dutch East Indies, 170, 178

E

East Frisia, 60, 70
  Christine Charlotte of, 61
Elbing/Elblag, 42
Elias, Norbert, 59, 69, 70
Elokan, Ndumbe, 221
England, 36, 39, 48, 49, 62, 69, 72, 76, 102, 110, 117, 120, 129, 135, 147, 153, 161, 175, 191, 192, 233, 234, 238

Epo, Duala M'bende, 217
Equalla, Jim, 214. *See also* Deido, Epee Ekwalla
Equiano, Olaudah, 11, 116, 127, 130, 133, 147
Erdmuth Sophia (princess), 77, 78, 89
Ermland, 42, 44
Ernst, Albrecht, 61
Ernst, Anna Elisabeth, 92
Ernst, Christian, 61, 76–78, 80, 89, 90, 130
Eschenbach, Wolfram von, 8
Essen, 62, 69
Este, Isabella de, 28, 35, 69
Ethiopia, 22, 39, 44, 63, 134, 141, 143
Europe, 3–18, 22, 23, 25, 28, 29, 31, 34–39, 42, 44, 45, 48–60, 63, 66–78, 82, 83, 85–89, 93–96, 98, 102, 104–106, 108, 115, 117, 119, 121, 129, 134, 135, 138–41, 143, 144, 146–51, 153, 154, 156–167, 169, 171, 172, 175, 177–80, 186, 187, 189–94, 200, 202–10, 212, 214, 215, 217–24, 231–40
Evora, 30
Ewald, Johann, 94, 101, 102, 109, 110

F

Fabri, Philemon, 79
Fellowes, Cornelius, 160, 162
Ferber, Maurice, 42, 44
Fernandes, Jorge, 50
Ferrara, Duchess of, 30
Fidis (St.), 31–33, 36
Firla, Monika, 56, 62, 69, 71, 89, 90
Fisk University, 196
Flad, Friedrich, 215
Flemish Grimani Breviary, 28
Florence, 35, 47, 55, 87
Follen, Karl, 142
Fon Nyonga II, 224
Fortuna, Ignatius, 62, 69, 71
Forty-Eighters, 128, 142, 148, 151, 168, 182
France, 16, 28, 36, 147, 153, 156, 191, 192, 209, 212, 230, 233, 238
Frankfurt, 127, 147, 157–60, 162, 167, 172
Frankfurt Peace Congress, 158
Frederick III, 36, 51
Frederick Wilhelm I, 85
Frederick William "the Great", 75
French Revolution, 157
Freundt, Achacy, 44
Friedrich August I, 78

G

Gabon, 83
Gagern, Hans von, 158
Gajarek, Sigmund Martin, 81
Garber, Eque Soloman James, 226, 230
Garnet, Henry Highland, 158f.
Gbele Dayi, 198
Genoa, 87
Georgia, 94, 101, 196
German East Africa, 214, 229
German Foreign Office, 214
German Historical Museum, 1
German South Pacific colonies, 192
German Togoland, 12, 187–212
Germantown, 101
Germany, 1, 3–18, 21–23, 25, 28, 31, 35–39, 42–49, 51–58, 60, 62–65, 69–72, 74–78, 80, 81, 83, 89, 91, 93–96, 98–100, 107–109, 115–33, 134–43, 147–51, 153, 154, 156–164, 166, 168, 169–75, 180–86, 187, 189–96, 198–212, 213–30, 231–33, 237–40
Gerstner, Clara von, 164, 168
Ghana, 64, 138
Giddings, 196
Gloucester, 106
Goethe, Johann Wolfgang von, 119, 162
Gold Coast, 83
Goldofsky, Johann Daniel, 65, 72
Gomes, Fernão, 45, 55
Görlitz, 219, 222
Gottlieb, Christian, 62, 71
Goudstikker Collection, 25, 35
Great Britain, 109, 135, 138, 156, 206, 212
Gregor Maurus (St.), 21, 25
Griffin, Horace Greely (of Giddings, Texas), 196
Guild of Trumpeters and Drummers, 61
Guinea, 49, 72
Guinea, Gregorio de, 49

H

Haiti, 147, 174, 213, 240
Haitian Revolution, 95

Halle, 9, 22, 25–27, 33, 36, 72, 73, 117, 120, 138, 238
Hamburg, 17, 18, 83, 121, 130, 173, 233, 240
Hamburg Colonial Institute, 214
Hamilton, Georgia, 196
Hanibal, Abram, 62
Hanover, 62, 75, 76, 85, 87
Hanseatic, 42, 44, 48, 49, 53, 240
Harris, Shepherd Lincoln, 196, 197, 212
Hautgerva, 95
Hawkins, John, 45, 55
Heidelberg, 12, 134, 141–43, 147–151, 154–56, 158, 159, 162, 164, 166
Heister, Leopold von, 101
Helgoland, 1
Henrique, 45. *See also* Ne-Kinu, Ndoadidiki
Henson, Josiah, 11, 116, 125–28, 132
Herder, 95, 129, 130
Herman auf Wain, Beno von, 195, 210
Hersfeld, Hessen, 226
Hesse, 10, 93, 94, 96, 99, 101–103, 107–109, 138, 140, 225, 226
Hessen, Landgrave of, 49
Hessian State Archive, 96, 98
Hessians, 4, 9, 10, 19, 93–100, 102–105, 107, 109, 138, 149, 150
Ho, 198, 211
Hodges, Graham R., 94, 109, 110
Hohenstaufen, Frederick II of, 21, 34, 74
Holland, 65
Holthausen, 213, 221, 227, 229
Holy Land, 8, 30
Holy Roman Empire of the German Nation, 7, 58
House of Brunswick-Lüneburg, 76, 87
House of Medici, 87
Hughes (Reverend), 223, 229
Hugo, Victor, 158
Humboldt, Alexander von, 167, 172
Hundeshagen, Karl Berhard, 158
Hungary, 62

I
Iberia, 9, 10, 49, 53, 56, 231, 232, 234, 236–38
imperialism, 185, 191, 209, 210, 212, 228
International Cotton Congress, Atlanta, 207
Israel, Johann, 83

Italy, 3, 9, 23, 28, 36, 37, 53, 55, 56, 161, 179

J
Jacksonville, 196,
Jaeger Corps, 101, 103,
Jamnitzer, Christoph, 47, 55
Jerusalem, 160
Johann Georg II, 78, 89
Johann Georg IV, 78
Johann Gerorg III, 78
Jong, Anna de, 219, 226
Jong, Heinrich de, 219, 226
Jungkenn-Müntzer, Friedrich Christian von, 99

K
Kant, Immanuel, 11, 18, 139, 151
Kapp, Friedrich, 170
Kete Kratchi, 198
Kiel, Rainer-Maria, 70, 78, 89
King, Boston, 107, 111
Kingdom, 83, 164, 174
Kipping, Johann Wolfgang, 81–83
Kittel, Ingeborg, 16, 62, 69, 72
Klein Popo, 198
Klosterneuburg, 22, 34
Kniesteedt, von, 79
Knyphausen, Wilhelm von, 101, 107, 110
Kolonial Wirtschaftliches Komitee (KWK), 187, 191, 192
Konstanz, 39, 54
Köster, Georg C., 99
Kpandu, 198
Kpeme, 198
Kraków, 36, 44
Küppers-Braun, Ute, 62, 69, 71
Kwane, Njowe, 214

L
Laelius (Caius Laelius), 81, 82
Lafayette, William Drake of, 196
Laickner, Susanna Clara, 61, 78
Lambert, Henrik, 48
Lankmann of Falkenstein, Nicolaus, 51
Lauingen, 53
League of Universal Brotherhood, 157
Lee, Henry, 103

Leipzig, 35, 66, 116, 124, 127, 164, 172, 173
Lencastre, Afonso de, 51
Leo XIII (Pope), 220
Liberia, 172–74, 183, 184, 209, 228
Limbé, 224. *See also* Victoria
Limburg an der Lahn, 225
Lincoln, Earl of, 49
Lisbon, 49, 51, 52, 70
Logan, Warren, 200, 211
Lohenstein, Daniel Casper von, 81–83
Lome, 196, 198, 203, 211
London, 39, 46, 53, 70, 89, 95, 111, 116, 124, 134, 141, 149, 157, 160–62, 209, 218, 239
London Anthropological Society, 175, 184
London Anti-Slavery Society, 136
Long Island, 100
Lorck, Carl Berendt, 164, 168
Louisiana, 157, 160
Low Countries, 28, 29, 41, 150
Lower Saxony, 25, 232
Lübeck, 18, 49
Lucera, 21, 74, 75
Lukenje, Richard, 219–22, 228
Lüneburg, 25, 26, 35, 66, 76, 85, 87
Lusitano, Vicente, 51, 232

M
Macon County, 202
Magdeburg, 9, 21, 22, 25, 26, 34, 35, 232
Magdeburg, Ernst von, 9, 25–27
Mair, Paulus Hector, 50, 56
Mantua, 28
Maran, François, 79, 80
Marburg, 96, 98, 109, 110, 141
Marshall Farm, 196
Marshall Islands, 223
Marx, Karl, 190
Marxism, 59, 189, 209
Maryland, 16, 156
Masinissa (Numidian king), 80–83, 85, 86
Massachusetts, 147, 159, 195
Master of the Goslar Sibyls, 23, 24, 26, 27
Maurice (St.), 9, 21–28, 30, 31, 34–36, 42–44, 52, 54, 69, 232
Mauvillon, Jakob von, 103
Maximilian (Emperor), 26, 28, 49f.
Mbemba, Nzinga, 45. *See also* Alfons
Mbenge, Bertha Ebumbu, 225

Mecklenburg, 65, 66
Mediterranean, 3, 25, 62, 76, 232, 233, 235–38
Meetom, David, 215. *See also* Ngondo, Mwange
Meetom, Tube, 219, 221, 228
Meiners, Christoph, 139, 144
Melfi, 74
Messina, 74
Middle East, 3, 12, 30, 37, 160, 179
migrants, migration, 3, 7, 9, 13, 17, 69, 88, 107, 139, 157, 170, 172, 173, 177, 178, 181, 182, 209, 213–30, 234, 236–38, 240
Mill, John Stuart, 175, 184
Mina, Gomes da, 45
Mississippi, 157
mixed-race population, 92, 174, 178, 179
Moabit district, 224
Mohr, Christian Ferdinand, 60
Mohr, Rudolph, 66–68, 72
Monastery of S. Zeno, 21
Moravian Church, 64
More, Christophe le, 29
Morus, Johannes, 75
Moses, Moritz, 92
Moses, Wilhelm, 92
Mostaert, Jan, 29, 36, 41
Mozambique, 83
Mülheim on the Ruhr, 213
Munich, 50, 75, 164, 181, 220
Münster, 25, 69, 232
Munster, Hans von, 49
Münzer, Hieronymus, 52, 56
Murhardsche Library, 96, 97
Mustapha, 62, 71

N
Namibia, 214
Napoleon Bonaparte, 153, 157, 164, 179, 192
National Assembly, 147, 158, 161
Native Americans, 172, 178, 181, 183
Ndumbe, Belle, 218. *See also* Bell, Alfred
Near East, 160
Ne-Kinu, Ndoadidiki, 45. *See also* Henrique
Neukirch, Benjamin, 85
New Haven, 156
New Jersey, 94
New Orleans, 126, 160

New York, 94, 98, 100, 102, 103, 107, 110, 116, 121, 123, 173
Newark, 103
Nicholas (St.), 22, 23
Norfolk, 106
North Carolina, 106
Norway, 60, 78
Nova Scotia, 94, 102, 109, 110
Nuatja, 202–204, 211
Nuremberg, 23, 36, 45, 47, 49, 52, 76

O

Oettingen, 61
Oettingen-Oettingen, Albrecht Ernst II of, 61
Ohio, 160, 167
Olmsted, Frederick Law, 164, 168
opera, 10, 77, 80–83, 85–88
Orient, 1, 7, 8, 18, 64, 98, 99, 139, 160, 167, 198, 205, 214, 235, 240
Orlamünde, Georg Jhener von, 23, 25, 26,
Österreichische Nationalbibliothek, 40, 41
Ottoman Empire, 9, 77, 232, 233, 235, 236

P

Paderborn, 220
Painter, Nell Irving, 96
Palime, 198, 203, 204, 212
Paris, 93, 141, 154, 157–61, 167, 210, 237
Parker, Theodore, 159, 167
Parzival, 8
Pennington, James W.C., 12, 143, 151, 154–60, 163–68
Pennsylvania, 101, 148, 156
Peter (St.), 23
Peter, August Wilhelm, 65, 72
Philadelphia, 95, 98, 99, 109, 124, 148
Philip II, 49
Philippine (Landgravine), 99
Plön, 62
Poděbrady, George, 29
Poland, 42, 44, 78, 209
Poland, Augustus II of, 78
Polaroli, Carlo Francesco, 83
Pomerania, 22
Pompadour, Madam de, 8
Portsmouth, 106
Portugal, 9, 29, 36, 49, 51–53, 55, 56, 117, 232, 233, 235, 238
Portugal, Afonso V of, 52

Portugal, João II of, 52
Portugal, Leonor of, 51
Protestant Basel Mission, 222, 224, 227
Protten, Christianus Jakob, 64
Protten, Rebecca (widowed Freundlich), 64
Prussia, 1, 2, 4, 42, 44, 59, 64, 65, 75–77, 85–88, 151, 158, 162, 166, 167, 209
Prussia, Frederick I of, 85

R

racism, 12, 14, 18, 57, 100, 108, 122, 124, 125, 127, 139, 140, 149, 154, 164, 168, 173, 191, 209, 239
Ratzel, Friedrich, 12, 169–72, 180–83, 185
reconstruction, 127, 149, 152, 170, 173, 180, 182
Reich, Anna, 46
revolutions of 1848/1849, 142, 147, 149, 172
Rhode Island, 94
Richmond, 106
Rijksmuseum, 36, 41
Ripa, Caesar, 86, 91
Ritter, Carl, 172
Robinson, John Winfrey, 189, 196, 197, 202
Roeck, Bernd, 62, 71
Roman Empire, 42, 61, 63, 75, 87, 162, 232
Rome, 51, 82, 86, 88, 220, 233
Rosalind (Massachusetts), 195
Rotes Grenadierbataillon, 64
Royal Bureau of Commerce and Trade, 195
Royal Society of London, 134, 149
Rozmital, Joanna of, 29
Rozmital, Leo of, 29, 30, 36, 52

S

Sabac el Cher, August Albrecht, 1
Sabac el Cher, Gustav, 1, 2, 14
Sabadon, Johannes, 92, 95
Sabadon, Marie Elisabeth (née Ernst), 92
Sadji, Uta, 62, 71
Saïd, Edward, 7, 18, 235
Salerno, 74
Salzburg, 75
Sansanne Mangu, 198
Santiago de Compostella, 29, 30
Santo Domingo, 7, 129

Sarmatia, Ulderico of (King), 84
Saxe-Weißenfels, 80, 81
Saxony, 22, 75, 77
    Catherine of, 9, 26–29, 35
    Henry the Pious von (Duke), 26
    Prince Elector of, 35, 60
Schäfer, Wolfram, 16, 62, 69, 96, 109
Schanz, Moritz, 207, 212
Schascko, 52. *See also* Schaseck
Schaseck, 36, 52. *See also* Schascko
Schaumburg-Lippe, Wilhelm of, 62
Scheve, Alfred, 224, 230
Schimmelmann, Heinrich Carl, 64, 232
Schleswig and Holstein, Duchies of, 7
Schmidt, Eduard, 215
Schmidt, F.H., 217, 220, 224, 229
Schulthaiss, Christoph, 39, 54
Scipio Africanus (Publius Cornelius Scipio Africanus), 81, 82
Seabrook Island, 104
Senden, Caspar van, 49, 55
Setúbal, 50
Seville, 7
Seville, Duke of, 52
Shanz, 207
Sheba, Queen of, 22, 28–31, 237
Sicily, 3, 74, 232
Sierra Leone project, 102
Sigismund I, 44
Silesia, 81, 85
Simmons Island, 104
Simpson, Hiram Dozier, 196, 199
slave narrative, 116–18, 120–22, 125, 129–32, 151, 156, 160, 170
slave trade, 7, 9, 17, 45, 47, 60, 62, 64, 94, 95, 117, 118, 135–37, 144, 146, 147, 177, 178, 232, 240
Smith, James McCune, 161
Social Darwinism, 149, 174
Soden, Julius von (Freiherr), 215, 228, 229
Sokode-Bassari region, 198
Soliman, Angelo, 62, 71
Sömmerring, Samuel Thomas von, 95
Songue Epee Ekwalla Eyoum Ebelle, 214. *See also* Deido Equalla
Sophonisbe, 81, 82. *See also* Sophonobia
Sophonobia, 81. *See also* Sophonisbe
South Carolina, 104, 105, 109, 110, 149, 182
South Seas protectorate, 223

South Tyrol, 22
Spain, 3, 36, 49, 50, 52, 117, 147, 179, 233
Spanish America, 156
Spöck, 224
Sprengel, Matthias Christian, 117, 118
Stanley, Henry M., 191, 209
statesmen, 144, 153, 233
Stein, Carl vom, 78
Stockholm, 48, 55
Stuttgart, 51, 56, 60, 62, 65, 71, 75, 90, 116, 127, 195, 233
Sub-Saharan Africa, 41, 48, 49, 51–53, 213, 232
Suckale-Redlefsen, Gude, 25, 34–36, 54, 69
Supf, Karl, 192, 210, 211
Suriname, 62, 65
Sweden, 48, 156, 233
Switzerland, 42
Syphax (King of Masaeisylians), 81, 82, 90, 91

T
Tambour July/Juley, 95
Tambour London, 95
Tambour Wilhelm, 95
Tetzel, Gabriel, 52
Texan frontier, 164
Theban Legion, 22, 42, 43, 52
Tiedemann, Friedrich, 12, 134–39, 141–51
Timba, Josef, 220, 221
Togo, 6, 14, 171, 183, 185, 187, 189, 190, 191–96, 198–206, 208–12, 214, 221, 226, 229
Togoland, 12, 187, 188, 190, 193, 197, 205, 210
Tomicki, Peter, 44
Tove, 198, 199, 202, 211
Treasure, Geoffrey, 75, 88
Truth, Sojourner, 96, 109, 110
Tucher, Anton II, 46
Tunisia, 74
Türkenfeld, 220
Tuskegeans, 13, 189, 190, 195, 196, 198, 200–202, 204, 205, 207–209, 211
Tuskegee Executive Committee, 195, 199
Tuskegee Institute, 12, 181, 187, 189, 202, 206, 207
Tuskegee, Alabama, 202
Tyrol, Ferdinand II of, 49

U

Underground Railroad, 126
Ungenad, Christoffero, 52
University of Heidelberg, 141–43, 150, 154, 155, 166
University of Naples, 74
University of Siena, 44
Upper Nile, 42

V

Venice, 29, 51, 53, 83, 87, 160, 233
Verdun, Nicholas of, 22
Verona, 21, 34
Vicentino, Nicola, 51
Victoria (Queen), 161
Victoria, 224. *See also* Limbé
Victoria and Albert Museum, 46, 55
Victoria School, 216
Vienna, 34, 40, 41, 50, 62, 70, 75, 98, 212
Vieter, Heinrich, 222, 230
Virginia, 94, 99, 101, 102, 106, 117, 147

W

Wales, 223, 229
Wallraff, Günter, 14
Warmia, 42
Washington DC, 71, 195, 240
Washington, Booker T., 13, 15, 181, 183, 189–91, 194–96, 205, 209–12
Webb, Frank, 11, 116, 123–25, 128, 132
Weihenmayer, Anton, 53
Weimar, 75, 214, 227
Weißenfels, 80, 81
Welcker, Karl Theodor, 158
Welfs, the, 26
West Africa, 6, 7, 17, 30, 51, 146, 173, 174, 185, 208, 209, 211, 212, 215, 228, 229, 231, 236
West Indies, 7, 64, 117, 135, 144, 156, 177
Westheim, 195
Westphalia, 25, 213
Wettin, Ernst von, 22
White, Peter, 52. *See also* Blanco, Pero
Wiesbaden, 70, 221
Wilhelm II (German Emperor), 1
Wilhelm IX (Landgrave), 10, 92
Windthorst, Ludwig, 220, 228
Wittgenstein-Berleburg, Count of, 65
Wolfenbüttel, 16, 58, 65, 66, 68, 69, 76, 90
Wolff, Christian, 68
World Peace Congress, 157
Württemberg, 49, 56, 60, 69, 71, 75, 80, 89, 90, 195, 222
    Christoph of, 51

Y

Yale University, 143, 156
Yendi, 198
Yorktown, 102, 106, 107

Z

Zanzamanc, 8
Zanzibar, 1

www.ingramcontent.com/pod-product-compliance
Lightning Source LLC
Chambersburg PA
CBHW072148100526
44589CB00015B/2139